EXPERIENCED
COGNITION

EXPERIENCED COGNITION

Richard A. Carlson
The Pennsylvania State University

LEA LAWRENCE ERLBAUM ASSOCIATES, PUBLISHERS
1997   Mahwah, New Jersey   London

Lawrence Erlbaum Associates, Inc., Publishers
10 Industrial Avenue
Mahwah, New Jersey 07430

Library of Congress Cataloging-in-Publication Data

Carlson, Richard A. (Richard Alan)
    Experienced cognition / Richard A. Carlson.
        p.   cm.
    Includes bibliographical references and index.
    ISBN 0-8058-1732-8 (alk. paper). — ISBN 0-8058-1733-6 (pbk. :
alk. paper).
    1. Consciousness. 2. Cognition. 3. Cognitive psychology.
I. Title
BF311.C2775 1997
153—dc21   97-17199
                                                               CIP

Books published by Lawrence Erlbaum Associates are printed on acid-free paper,
and their bindings are chosen for strength and durability.

Printed in the United States of America
10 9 8 7 6 5 4 3 2 1

Contents

PART III: CONSCIOUSNESS AND SKILLED COGNITIVE ACTIVITY

PART IV: IMPLICATIONS

     A Perspective on the Cognitive Unconscious   289

 15 Toward a Cognitive Psychology of Persons   309

     References   319

     Author Index   345

     Subject Index   353

Preface

Consciousness is a difficult topic. It is often avoided by cognitive scientists, especially those with a commitment to "hard," experimental laboratory research on cognition. Yet each of us is conscious, and there is no more fundamental topic for cognitive theory. This book is about consciousness and cognitive skill—cognition as we experience it and as we become experienced. In this book, I describe a theoretical framework, *experienced cognition*, for understanding cognition at the level of the conscious mental states that make up our stream of awareness. The central idea of this framework is the cospecification hypothesis: that an experiencing self and experienced objects are simultaneously specified in the information available to perception and from memory. The major theme of my argument is that this hypothesis allows us to describe consciousness in a way that is consistent with the critical assumptions of current cognitive theory. A great deal of available empirical and theoretical research on cognition contributes to our understanding of consciousness, and the experienced cognition framework is founded on that research.

My goal is to develop a theory of consciousness that works from the point of view of experimental cognitive psychology. In contrast to many writers, I believe that a scientific understanding of consciousness is desirable and possible, and can enrich both our cognitive theories and our understanding of ourselves as persons. My primary audience is cognitive psychologists, but I believe that this book will be of interest to scholars in the other cognitive sciences and related disciplines who are interested in consciousness and cognition.

The book is divided into four parts. Part I (chapters 1–3) introduces the basic ideas of the experienced cognition framework and places them in the context of the contemporary computational approach to cognition and of empirical research on cognitive skill. In Part II (chapters 4–7), I develop the theoretical bases of the framework in greater detail, to show the continuities among perceptual-motor, symbolic, and emotional awareness and their relations to the nonconscious information processes that support them. Part III (chapters 8–13) is concerned with applying the experienced cognition framework to a number of central topics in cognitive theory, including working memory, problem solving, reasoning, and cognitive skill. Part IV (chapters 14–15) is concerned with some implications of the experienced cognition framework, offering perspectives on the current debate about the cognitive unconscious and on the prospects for person-level cognitive theory.

Long as this book is, there are many topics crucial to our ultimate understanding of consciousness that are covered only in passing or not at all. Among these topics are the social aspects of consciousness, ranging from the self experienced as a social entity to social influences on development; domains of cognitive processing such as language production, auditory perception and awareness, reading, dreams, creativity, and imagination; the acquisition and organization of conceptual knowledge; and, of course, the burgeoning field of cognitive neuroscience and brain function. Some readers will undoubtedly feel that no book can contribute to our understanding of consciousness, absent one or more of these topics; others will want to add to this list. I believe, however, that experienced cognition is a promising starting point for developing a deep, scientific understanding of consciousness.

Questions about consciousness and learning drew me to psychology, and my first term paper for a psychology course was about learning without awareness. I think it would be fair to say that consciousness was not a fashionable topic among experimental psychologists when I started graduate school in 1979, although the beginnings of today's widespread interest in the topic were apparent. As a graduate student, I had the great good fortune to work with Don Dulany at the University of Illinois. Don's elegant theoretical work on propositional control in learning paradigms attracted me to Illinois and still stands as a model of insight and theoretical rigor in the analysis of consciousness and cognitive processes. In 1979, Don encouraged me to pursue my interests in consciousness, predicting that "in a decade," work on consciousness would be in the mainstream of cognitive psychology! Don's influence on my thinking and career can hardly be overstated. Although my ideas, and especially my emphases, have diverged from his in a variety of ways, we continue to occupy nearby locations in theoretical space. I am very grateful for his role in my scientific career.

ACKNOWLEDGMENTS

Many people helped make this book possible. First were the students in my consciousness seminars. The book began as a series of seminar lectures I delivered during spring semester 1992, and took its penultimate form during my fall 1995 seminar as I finished chapters for just-in-time delivery to my students. Both groups offered innumerable helpful comments and questions. Connie Moore has my deep gratitude for transcribing the tapes of the 1992 seminar. My colleagues Davida Charney and Mark Detweiler participated in that first seminar and provided much helpful discussion (and, yes, I will get back to those questions later!). In addition to participating in that seminar, Lynn Liben helped in many ways: As head of the Psychology Department at Penn State, she has provided support for this project in both tangible and intangible ways; as a colleague and friend, she has helped me to appreciate the importance of (among other things) developmental and spatial issues for understanding consciousness. The members of the cognitive area faculty at Penn State during the development of this project served as a sounding board for many of these ideas: Martha Burton, Mark Detweiler, Judy Kroll, Jim Martin, Kevin Murnane, and David Rosenbaum all contributed in ways they may not realize. Several graduate students working in my lab during this time collaborated in pursuing the empirical studies: Melanie Cary, David Lundy, Jackie Shin, Myeong-Ho Sohn, and Jay Wenger have all played critical roles in this research program. Other colleagues at Penn State and elsewhere who have been especially helpful and influential include Jim Farr, Gordon Logan, Mel Mark, and especially Walt Schneider (who heard many of these ideas when they were much less than half-baked!). The Psychology Department and College of Liberal Arts at Penn State have provided a very supportive environment for this work, including a critical sabbatical semester in 1994.

I would also like to thank Judi Amsel for her encouragement and support of this project, and for her efforts to make it happen. Laura Novick, Jonathan Schooler, and several anonymous individuals who reviewed the manuscript for Lawrence Erlbaum Associates made many helpful suggestions that have greatly improved the book.

A project like this of course requires support from friends and family, and I have been fortunate to have had more than my share. My deepest thanks go to my wife, Lori Forlizzi, who has experienced cognition right along with me, reading everything here multiple times. Without her, this project would not have been possible.

—*Richard A. Carlson*

I

EXPERIENCED COGNITION: CONSCIOUSNESS AND COGNITIVE SKILL

1

Experienced Cognition and the Cospecification Hypothesis

No one really knows what consciousness is, what it does, or what function it serves.
—Johnson-Laird, 1983, p. 448

What should cause some fear, actually, is the idea of selfless cognition.
—Damasio, 1994, p. 100

INTRODUCTION

Consciousness and learning are central topics for psychology. Questions about how we experience and adapt to our environments—including the inner environment of the body and the social environments comprising other persons and artifacts—set the research agendas for a wide range of disciplines in the cognitive sciences. My purpose in writing this book is to describe a framework for thinking about consciousness and learning. The basis for this framework is what I call the *cospecification hypothesis* of consciousness, a hypothesis that is part of a cognitive, informational theory of what consciousness is and what it does. My hope is that this framework points the way toward understanding consciousness in a range of cognitive phenomena and toward developing a cognitive psychology that encompasses a scientific understanding of first-person perspectives, a cognitive psychology of persons.

I call this framework *experienced cognition* because that label captures the central themes I develop. First, I believe that successful cognitive theory must begin with, and account for, cognition as experienced by the individual. Consciousness is central to both the phenomena and explanations that make up the domain of cognitive theory. Second, I believe that understanding consciousness and cognition depends on understanding the changes that occur as we become experienced—as we learn and acquire cognitive skills. The ways in which we can be aware and the consequences of that awareness for our activities depend on our skills and change as we acquire increasing skill. In particular, studying the acquisition and performance of cognitive skills can provide insight into our conscious control of our activity. Finally, we experience our cognition as embodied and as situated in a variety of environments. Experienced cognition must therefore be understood in light of an ecological approach to psychology, an approach that emphasizes that persons are organisms acting in and on environments.

My intention is not to review the huge literature on consciousness (although that is a worthy goal, attempted with some success by Davies & Humphreys, 1993, and by Farthing, 1992). Instead I develop the experienced cognition framework on its own terms, borrowing from or comparing with other approaches as it seems useful. My perspective is that of an experimental cognitive psychologist. Cognitive psychology has generally been distinguished from the other cognitive sciences in part by its use of a level of description that is psychological in the traditional sense of corresponding to contents that are or could be part of conscious mental states. I agree with Natsoulas (1992, p. 364) that very often "consciousness is what psychologists actually examine" (Carlson, 1992). Some authors (e.g., Dennett, 1991) regard adopting this level of analysis as a mistake or temporary expedient. My opinion, which of course informs everything written in this book, is quite different. I believe that description of mental processes at the level of conscious mental states, and therefore theorizing at the level of lawful relations among such states, has a privileged status in the development of psychological theory. In my view, no psychological theory that fails to recognize consciousness as central to human cognition can claim to be comprehensive or correct.

Consciousness in Psychology and Cognitive Science

Cognitive scientists have made a great deal of progress in understanding many traditional issues concerning mental activity, but cognitive science has also received its share of criticism (e.g., Dreyfus, 1992; Harré & Gillett, 1994). In my view, the most important criticism of current cognitive science is that it lacks a compelling theory of consciousness and, thus, a means of linking persons and their experience to cognitive theory. Although some (e.g., Dennett, 1987) have argued that successful cognitive theories must be conceived at a subpersonal level, I believe that a cognitive theory that accommodates rather than explains away the existence of conscious, experiencing selves is both possible and desirable, a theme I return to in the final chapter.

The last decade or so has seen an enormous upswell of cognitive science literature on consciousness, by psychologists (e.g., Dulany, 1991; Umiltà & Moscovitch, 1994), philosophers (e.g., Dennett, 1991; Searle, 1992), linguists (e.g., Jackendoff, 1987), neuroscientists (e.g., Edelman, 1989) and neuropsychologists (e.g., Shallice, 1988), computer scientists (e.g., Minsky, 1986), and even physicists (e.g., Penrose, 1989). It has been some time now since consciousness was taboo in mainstream psychological journals although many psychologists still feel uneasy with the term *consciousness* (Natsoulas, 1992; Umiltà & Moscovitch, 1994). The scientific and philosophical literature on consciousness has grown to the point that it is impossible for any one scholar to read all that is written on the topic.

Despite all the energy and ink recently devoted to the topic of consciousness—and intending no slight to the thoughtful work of many researchers—I think it is fair to say that we do not have a plausible general theory of consciousness. In part, this is because there is not general agreement on either what is to be explained (automaticity? qualia?) or on what would constitute an explanation. Perhaps the most popular contemporary approach is to attempt to explain consciousness in biological or quasi-biological terms, to answer the question, "How could a brain—or a computer-simulated neural network—generate consciousness?" However, even a cursory review of the literature demonstrates the wide variety of current approaches.

The term *consciousness* itself has many senses (Natsoulas, 1983). Later in this chapter, I propose a specific hypothesis about consciousness that implies a particular view about the core concept of consciousness. It may be useful to offer at this point a preliminary sketch of that core concept as I see it. I am most concerned with that sense of consciousness that might be labeled *primary awareness*—the fundamental, unreflective experience of an individual experiencing and acting in an environment. Central to consciousness in this sense is the notion of subjectivity, of an experiencing self with a point of view. This is the sense of consciousness that has, in my opinion, been discussed least adequately by cognitive scientists and their precursors; as Searle (1992) noted, "It would be difficult to exaggerate the disastrous effects that the failure to come to terms with the subjectivity of consciousness has had on the philosophical and psychological work of the past half century" (p. 95). Understanding consciousness in this sense depends critically on the concept of self as agent, the idea of conscious control of mental and physical activity. *Agency* is the experience of oneself as an originator or controller of activity, and is central to understanding conscious experience.

Most discussions of consciousness or control in cognitive science are characterized by one of two stances—the implicit agent stance or the absent agent stance. In the *implicit agent* stance, the mind is characterized as a system controlled by an implicit agent sometimes referred to as the executive or just the subject, as in "the subject uses working memory (or semantic memory, or any other proposed cognitive system) to accomplish the task." This stance acknowledges subjectivity but fails to explain it or to really integrate it into theory. In the *absent agent* stance, the focus is entirely on information about the presumed objects of thought and control and agency are not discussed at all. The subject of sentences describing mental events becomes the brain, or the cognitive system, rather than the person whose mental events they are. I have more to say about how cognitive scientists have treated (or failed to treat) the subjectivity of consciousness in the next chapter.

Let me finish these introductory comments by emphasizing two additional points: First, consciousness is not a thing but a systemic, dynamic property or aspect of persons—typically engaged in purposive activity in an information-rich environment—and their mental states. Second, consciousness is not a special or extraordinary occurrence, but in fact is an utterly mundane aspect of human experience.

Consciousness and Cognitive Causality

Consciousness plays a central role in the causality of cognitive processes by serving to control mental and physical activity. This is of course not the only reason we value our conscious experience, but I believe that it is the key to understanding experienced cognition.

One of the major limitations of current accounts of consciousness is the failure to describe conscious states in terms of variables that link those states with theoretical descriptions of cognitive activity (an important exception is Dulany's work, e.g., 1991). Consciousness is thus described in intuitive terms, and a great deal of research effort has been spent in trying to show that some presumed process is unconscious and dissociable from conscious cognition (for a review, see Greenwald, 1992). Indeed, relatively casual claims that something is unconscious are much more frequent in the literature than are detailed analyses of any aspect of conscious thought. And, as with other proposed distinctions such as implicit and explicit memory, conscious and unconscious processes are often seen as activities of separate, dissociable systems. In contrast to this nonanalytic stance and the separate systems assumption (Dulany, 1991), I argue that describing the structure of consciousness in informational terms can provide variables for theoretical descriptions of cognitive activity (see Table 1.1).

At the core of my account of consciousness is that to be conscious is literally to have a point of view, which provides a here-and-now referent

TABLE 1.1
An Experienced Cognition Glossary

Writing about consciousness is often characterized by obscure terminology, as authors try to avoid common but imprecise or theoretically loaded terms. This brief glossary is intended to orient readers to the jargon that I have found unavoidable, and to clarify the sense in which I intend some terms that are familiar from other contexts.

Agency. Agency is the experience of oneself as an originator or controller of activity.

Conditions of satisfaction. Conditions of satisfaction are the circumstances or states of affairs that must exist if a mental state is to be satisfied—for example, if a belief is to be true, a perception veridical, or a wish fulfilled.

Content. The content of an individual's mental state is that aspect of the state that has meaning or carries information, from the point of view of that individual. Roughly speaking, the contents of mental states are the answers to questions such as, "what are you thinking?" "what do you see?" or, "what are you trying to do?"

Cospecification. Cospecification is a property of an informational array, such that the array simultaneously specifies an experiencing self and experienced objects.

Declarative knowledge. Declarative knowledge is knowledge that is used by being consulted, for example by representation in private speech. Declarative knowledge contrasts with procedural knowledge (see later this table).

Dispositional. A state or content is dispositional when not currently instantiated; as such, it lacks intentional structure and is causally functional only as an enabling condition for a potential instantiated state.

Egolocation. Egolocation is any process that distinguishes self-specific and object-specific aspects of an informational array. More generally, egolocative processes are those that either establish such a distinction or take it as information.

Epiphenomenon. An epiphenomenon is a side effect that results from a process but has no further causal influence or effects.

Information. This term can be defined most neutrally as "that commodity capable of yielding knowledge" (Dretske, 1981, p. 44). Commonly used in cognitive science as a loose category term, alternative core ideas include symbolic representation and representation by resemblance. Here, I rely on Gibson's (1961, 1966) specificity definition of information: Any pattern or state of affairs that is specific to another state of affairs carries information about it.

Informational array. An informational array is a pattern or arrangement of information characterized by systematic relations of adjacency that support processes of traversal. An example is the array of information carried by light reaching the eyes, characterized by spatial adjacency relations that support scanning.

Intentionality. Commonly used by philosophers of mind to designate the property of mental states, that they are about, directed at, or refer to something other than themselves. Here, the phrase *intentional structure* is used to refer to the analysis of a conscious mental state in terms of variables describing the state's mode and content. This term is distinct from, but unfortunately confusable with, *intention* in the sense of an instantiated goal or purpose.

Instantiated. To instantiate something is to make it concretely actual at a specific time. For example, a belief is instantiated when its content is actually considered in a mental state with the psychological mode *believe*; at other times, what we describe as beliefs are dispositional (see earlier definition).

Mode. A psychological mode is the attitude or perspective from which a content is considered; examples include *believe, perceive,* and *intend.* In terms of the cospecification hypothesis, mode refers to the manner in which the self is specified in a particular mental state (e.g., as believing, perceiving, or intending).

(Continued)

7

TABLE 1.1
(Continued)

Object. The situation or state of affairs that a mental content is about or directed toward. In the case of perception, this may be an object in the ordinary sense; more generally, the objects of mental states can include (for example) desired but nonexistent states of affairs, prior mental states, and so on.

Procedural knowledge. Procedural knowledge is knowledge that can be used or instantiated only by enacting or performing it. This contrasts with declarative knowledge (see earlier definition).

Representation. A representation is a physical pattern that carries information about a state of affairs and that can be manipulated as a surrogate for that state of affairs (e.g., Palmer & Kimchi, 1986). Theorists' representations of mental processes are often confused with mental representations supposed to be manipulated by the experiencing individual.

Self. The self as used here refers to the experiencing individual, the "I" who is the subject of conscious experience. This sense of self is foundational for, but more limited than, broader conceptions that include reflection or self-consciousness, self-knowledge, and so on.

Subjectivity. Subjectivity refers to the personal or private nature of conscious experience, the observation that one's point of view is private and unique.

Symbol. As standardly used in cognitive science, a symbol is a representational unit that can be assigned content or meaning, and that participates in mental activity on the basis of its syntactic relations with other symbols.

---

for the spatial and temporal organization of cognitive activity. The central idea or intuition here is that the conscious, experiencing self functions as an agent in the cognitive control of activity. Understanding how that can be amounts to understanding cognition in terms that make essential reference to a first-person perspective.

THREE THEMES FOR UNDERSTANDING EXPERIENCED COGNITION

In my view, consciousness, learning, and an ecological perspective on cognition are inextricably linked. These topics thus serve as organizing themes for understanding experienced cognition. In this section, I describe the background and motivation for each of these themes.

Consciousness as Primary Awareness and Subjectivity

Consciousness in the sense of primary awareness is the critical starting point for theory because it is this sense that points to the experiencing self involved in controlling the flow of mental events. At one level of description, cognition can be described as a sequence of conscious mental states. Despite James' (1890) much-cited description of the "stream of consciousness," contemporary cognitive scientists have made relatively little explicit effort to understand cognition as a sequence of conscious, experienced mental states. The term *mental state* is meant to abstract from an individual's stream of experience and activity those units that in common sense we refer to as having a thought or seeing an object, units at a temporal scale from roughly a few tenths of a second to a few seconds. Each mental state may be described as the experience of some content from some point of view, a characterization elaborated in chapters 4 through 6. I assume that experienced cognition can be described at least approximately as a continuous series of such states, and in later chapters, I elaborate this assumption.

Many of the processes that properly concern cognitive scientists can, however, be appropriately described as cognitive but not conscious. Consider, for example, the process by which written language evokes comprehension. Some computational process must mediate this process (for no one would claim that such a process involves only the direct pickup of information), and that computational process must involve knowledge (for no one would argue that the ability to read particular words is innate). And although we do not (I believe!) read while we are unconscious, the relation between our visual awareness of the written word and our semantic awareness of its meaning calls for an explanation in terms other than a sequence of conscious mental states. To many cognitive scientists, such examples imply that consciousness is merely the tip of the iceberg of cognitive processing (e.g., Farthing, 1992) or even entirely epiphenomenal (e.g., Harnad, 1982; Jackendoff, 1987; Thagard, 1986)—in either case, it seems clear to many that these considerations imply a "cognitive unconscious" (Schachter, 1987) in many ways compatible with the personal unconscious postulated by Freud (Erdelyi, 1985). But understanding what such claims entail requires a theory of consciousness that has not yet been presented. Throughout this book, I use the term *nonconscious* to refer to informational (i.e., knowledge-bearing, thus cognitive) processes that cannot be understood on the model of conscious mental processes. I reserve the term *unconscious* for theoretical proposals that—like Freud's—assume that some mental states are like conscious ones (for example, having content or intentional structure; see chapters 4–5), but are not experienced in the sense that conscious states are. This usage is at odds with some current proposals (e.g., Marcel, 1983), but marks a distinction that I believe is important for understanding the implications of particular theoretical claims. Alternatively, it seems appropriate to describe persons as unconscious when they are deeply asleep or comatose (although dreaming might be an interesting intermediate case).

One clue to understanding the relation between consciousness and nonconscious cognitive processes is systematically distinguishing between content and noncontent properties of conscious mental states. The content of a conscious mental state corresponds to an answer to the question, What are you thinking? However, understanding the role in cognitive activity of a particular state may require that we consider other properties of the state such as its duration or repeatability, or the degree of activation or evocative power (Dulany, 1991) of its informational content. Such properties are of course not reportable, or may be reportable only as second-order judgments about the original state in question. In Part II, I describe a framework for characterizing mental states that allows us to make this distinction in a principled way.

An Ecological Perspective on Cognition

Our everyday experience comprises primarily the experience of goal-directed activity in an information-rich environment. Consciousness is grounded in—and normally functions in the context of—purposeful, goal-directed action that is guided and supported by information currently available in the environment and picked up by the perceptual systems. To understand this experience thus requires an ecological perspective. In choosing the phrase *ecological perspective*, I am of course alluding to the work of James Gibson. Gibson (1966, 1979) saw his theory of visual perception as opposed to the information processing framework (and its predecessor, the unconscious inference view of perception), arguing that normal perception was not mediated by mental activity. This direct perception view has been elaborated by his followers (e.g., Mace, 1974), and has been the focus of much debate. In my opinion, however, the debate over the directness of perception (e.g., Fodor & Pylyshyn, 1981) has distracted attention from the most important insights embodied in Gibson's theory. It seems clear that there is a computational story to tell about the process by which proximal stimulation (e.g., events at the retina) plays a causal role in perception, and in this sense, perception is mediated rather than direct.

More important than Gibson's insistence on the directness of perception is his insight that the language used to describe the information available for perception embodies theoretical claims that are crucial in shaping theoretical accounts. This point is well summarized by Medin and Thau's (1992) statement, "By our reading, Gibson argued that inadequate analyses of the information available to the perceptual system may lead one to posit all sorts of complex computations to derive information that is actually already available" (p. 167). In many cases, these complex computations are postulated as parts of theoretical explanations, then attributed to unconscious mental processes because they cannot be logically or empirically viewed as conscious. On the other hand, I argue later that cognitive scientists often depend (sometimes implicitly) on descriptions that are in effect ecological, in exactly the sense intended by Gibson, and that correspond to the contents of conscious mental states.

The cospecification hypothesis described later follows from a central insight of Gibson's theory, an insight based on understanding perception as intrinsically linked to the activity of organisms embedded in natural environments. That insight concerns what Neisser (e.g., 1991) has labeled the *ecological self*, the self as specified by information picked up for visual perception. As Gibson (1979) put it, "The supposedly separate realms of the subjective and the objective are actually only poles of attention" (p. 116). That is, the same information available to perception specifies both subject—the experiencing self—and object, the perceived portion of the environment. Mental processes make use of both aspects of the available information, in order to control the activity of an organism embedded in an environment. The environment is usually perceived by exploration and resampling of continually available information, and ongoing activity continually changes the viewpoint from which the environment is perceived. Thus a snapshot, momentary view is specific to the perceiving self; in Gibson's (1979) words, "What we see *now* refers to the self, not the environment" (p. 234). I have much more to say about the specification of the self, and the implications of the ecological-self hypothesis for experienced cognition. Note, however, that this insight of Gibson's does not depend on whether or not perception is direct in some sense.

Another implication of the ecological perspective, in my view, is that mental representation is performatory. For example, when we mentally represent states of affairs in a verbal code, we do so by performing (at least some part of) the action of uttering appropriate speech. This performance changes the environment—including the internal environment of working memory—and thus affords further action. There are three important aspects of this emphasis on the performatory character of mental representation. First, keeping this point in mind will help us avoid the tendency to reify our theoretical descriptions by reminding us that mental representing involves activity that occurs and is patterned over time. Second, I argue that understanding mental representation as performatory helps us to understand how symbols and mental operations on them may be developmentally grounded in perceptual-motor activity (Chapman, 1988; cf. Harnad, 1982). I generalize the focus on perception as it functions in the guidance of purposive action to cognition generally. Third, we see the performatory character of mental representation reflected very directly in the empirical regularities found in some domains of cognitive research such as working memory (see chapter 8).

Finally, the ecological approach provides important guidance in thinking about the appropriate level of description for conscious contents—and thus for describing "stimuli" (J. J. Gibson, 1960) and other informational constructs in psychological research. Any psychological theory must begin by assuming (perhaps implicitly) a privileged level of description for the events to be explained, whether those events are characterized as stimuli or inputs to perception, mental states, behaviors, or computational goals. Indeed, it is exactly this issue on which one version of behaviorism foundered. In Chomsky's (1959) classic deconstruction of Skinner's (1957) behaviorist approach to language, a central point especially compelling to psychologists was that behaviors could not even be reliably identified without implicit reference to mental constructs or the informational content of responses. The concept of information remains problematic, and I argue that Gibson's view of information in terms of specificity relations is most appropriate for understanding experienced cognition. What we seem to ourselves to be doing or thinking is often a good starting point for psychological theory, and the ecological concept of information can help us to relate our informal phenomenology to more formal cognitive theory.

Cognition as Skilled Activity

Most cognitive activity is routine and thus skilled, and must therefore be understood by studying the acquisition of cognitive skill. Such routine activity makes up the bulk of our conscious experience, and its mundane nature makes it difficult for us to see the structure of consciousness, both in prescientific reflection on our experience and in the development of scientific theory.

The substantive topic of my empirical research, and of much of this book, is learning. In particular, I focus on the kind of learning most naturally described as *skill acquisition*—the development of abilities to perform routine, domain-specific, temporally extended, goal-directed tasks. It is a commonplace observation that practice produces dramatic changes in the experience and control of cognitive skills; compare, for example, a child just learning the "arithmetic facts" and an educated adult obtaining the sum of 7 and 9. Understanding these changes is critical to understanding experienced cognition in general; it will not do to contemplate the role of consciousness as if it were fixed across levels of experience.

It is also important to recognize that most of our conscious experience takes place in an environment that is familiar and stable in many respects. As many authors have noted, the control of and informational support for our cognitive activity is distributed between mental and environmental sources. For example, J. R. Anderson (1993) wrote that the declarative knowledge representations that support procedural learning in his theory are often "kept active in the environment" (p. 24). Performances of cognitive skills studied in the laboratory, as of everyday activities including perceptual-enactive skills, are thus embedded or situated within a medium (Neisser, 1991). For some skills—driving in real life, or pursuit tracking in the laboratory—the medium may be described primarily in terms of physical objects and constraints. On the other hand, a skill that we commonly consider mental—arithmetic, for example—is performed in a medium that must be described as symbolic.

Besides the ubiquity of skill in experienced cognition, studying mental activity from the point of view of skill acquisition lets us approach what Harnad (e.g., 1982) labeled the symbol-grounding problem. This problem is, roughly, to understand how it is that symbols can serve their representational function—for example, how words can be about, or refer to, their referents, states of affairs in the world. Harnad and others (e.g., Barsalou, 1993) have suggested that the symbols constituting mental representations are grounded in perceptual abilities, perhaps innate (also see Fodor, 1975). I argue that symbols are also grounded in skilled performances, and thus constructed in the course of development as suggested by Piaget.

THE COSPECIFICATION HYPOTHESIS

According to the *cospecification hypothesis*, the central feature of consciousness is that an experiencing self and experienced objects are cospecified in arrays of available information. This section is devoted to elaborating that hypothesis.

Consciousness Is Perspective

The idea of a perspective or point of view is central to our intuitive understanding of consciousness and subjectivity. A number of authors have recently made this point, although generally without pursuing the implications for a general theory of consciousness:

> Subjectivity has the further consequence that all of my conscious forms of intentionality that give me information about the world independent of myself are always from a special point of view. The world itself has no point of view, but my access to the world through my conscious states is always perspectival, always from my point of view. (Searle, 1992, p. 95)

> There can be no orientation (either spatial, temporal, or metaphorical) that does not involve a perspective from which the orientation is viewed. The very structure of orientation is perspectival. (M. Johnson, 1987, p. 36)

To have a sense of one's personal individuality is to have a sense of having a place or places in various manifolds, that is, systems of locations. To have sense of myself as a unique individual, I have a sense of a location in space, literally a point of view. (Harré & Gillett, 1994, pp. 103–104)

Wherever there is a conscious mind, there is a *point of view*. This is one of the most fundamental ideas we have about minds—or about consciousness. A conscious mind is an observer, who takes in a limited subset of all the information there is. An observer takes in the information that is available at a particular (roughly) continuous sequence of times and places in the universe. For most practical purposes, we can consider the point of view of a particular conscious subject to be just that: a *point* moving through space–time. (Dennett, 1991, pp. 101–102)

My suggestion is that this idea be taken quite literally and generally. By programmatically developing the notion of a point of view as an informational concept, we can see how the structure of consciousness fits into information-processing stories about cognition. Here, I briefly introduce this idea, elaborating it in chapters 4 through 7.

Neisser (1988, 1991, 1993) and E. J. Gibson (1993; E. J. Gibson & Adolph, 1992), following suggestions by J. J. Gibson, have noted that a point of view, an experiencing self, is specified by the information available to visual perception. Neisser labeled the self specified in this way the *ecological self* to distinguish it from other senses of the term *self* that refer to types of self-knowledge supported by memory, by information available in social interaction, and so forth. My contention is that the experiencing self as specified in perception is the foundational sense of self, and that the cospecification of self and environment in visual perception reveals the basic structure of awareness that characterizes a range of types or aspects of consciousness. The subjectivity of consciousness is exactly this informationally specified experiencing self. I begin, therefore, by considering what it means to say that self and environment are cospecified in the visual case.

Cospecification in the Ambient Optical Array

Cospecification of self and object by vision in an ambient array of light provides an illustration of the more general concept of cospecification. To understand this illustration, I must begin by considering the concept of an ambient optical array, and J. J. Gibson's (1961, 1966) specificity notion of information.

A number of authors have attempted to define the term *information*, but most theoretical discourse in cognitive science relies on relatively informal concepts of information (Haugeland, 1985; A. Newell, 1990; see Lachman, Lachman, & Butterfield, 1979 for a historical overview). These informal concepts are usually based on one of two models: the arbitrary reference and syntactic roles of symbols such as words, or the structural resemblances of pictures or diagrams to the scenes or objects depicted. More careful writers note that meaning or reference must be established within a complex theoretical network—for example, a truth-preserving symbol system (e.g., Haugeland, 1985). Nevertheless, most psychologists use the term *information* quite casually to refer to aspects of displays or of hypothesized mental representations.

More relevant for our purposes is Gibson's definition of information in terms of specification. In this view, any patterning in the energy available to sensory transducers may provide information for perception, if that patterning depends in a reliable way on the structure of the environment. For example, a texture gradient like that depicted in Fig. 1.1 is generally specific to a surface of a particular orientation relative to the observer's viewpoint. Dretske (1981) articulated a similar view of the concept *information* as a starting point for his philosophical analysis, "Roughly speaking, information is that commodity capable of yielding knowledge, and what information a signal carries is what we can learn from it" (p. 44). This commodity is carried by preserved patterns, in the sense that a pattern of depressions in the snow can yield knowledge about the path of someone walking across the yard in winter. "Yielding knowledge," of course, depends on the abilities of some user of the information. Furthermore, information in this sense can be transmitted by a series of objects or media, obeying what Dretske (1981) called, "*Xerox principle*: If *A* carries the information that *B*, and *B* carries the information that *C*,

FIG. 1.1. Texture gradients: Texture gradients, ubiquitous in real life, specify the orientation of surfaces and relative distance of points on the surface. Photograph copyright Corel Corporation.

then *A* carries the information that *C*" (p. 57). This account provides a relatively neutral definition of information that allows, but does not require, that information be represented symbolically.

Unlike the symbolic view of information suggested by the model of words and their referents, this view does not suggest an arbitrary relation between information and what it is about—the physics of our environment determines these specificity relations. However, unlike the resemblance view, according to the ecological view, "the information for something must specify it, but need not resemble it" (Reed, 1988, p. 275). For example, I see the computer screen in front of me, not the structured light that specifies or the retinal events that preserve and convey that information. Information is therefore not identical with the content of conscious mental states. For example, consider the content of a perceptual state: We see objects and surfaces, not the information that specifies them.

One way to understand the cospecific nature of the information available for perception is to consider the use of perspective technique in drawing. In realistic drawing, we depict things by abstracting information from our visual experiences, for example representing edges by line segments. A simple perspective drawing is shown in Fig. 1.2. This tech-

FIG. 1.2. Perspective drawing: Perspective technique in drawing captures some of the geometric invariants of the optical array for vision, specifying both the layout of the environment and a viewing point (a perspective) in that environment. Note that the same elements *cospecify* these aspects of the information captured by the drawing. Photograph copyright Corel Corporation.

nique captures some of the geometric characteristics of what J. J. Gibson (1966) called the ambient optical array. The idea of an ambient array, discussed in more detail in chapter 4, is that the information in light is structured by discontinuities (edges, borders, etc.) in the layout of environmental surfaces that reflect light to the eye. This structuring of light available to the eye can be thought of as a "sheaf of rays," a theoretical representation of the geometric lines of projection from environmental discontinuities. These rays surround the point of view (hence, ambient), preserving the adjacency structure (hence array) of the environmental features that structure light. Perspective technique in drawing can be described as the representation of these projective rays on a "picture plane" interposed between the viewpoint and the depicted scene.

Perspective drawings are often thought to be more realistic (and more advanced) than children's drawings that do not use such techniques. They depict the "monocular depth cues" described in introductory texts, such as interposition, relative size, and convergence. What makes such drawings realistic is that they capture the aspectual character of vision as experienced from a stationary viewpoint—for example, only surfaces oriented toward the viewpoint are visible. The drawing thus captures not only an environment populated by surfaces and objects, but also a particular point of view on that environment, a scene. This is what is meant by cospecification—the available information simultaneously specifies both an environment and the location of an experiencing self within that environment. It is not that some lines in a drawing depict objects and surfaces whereas others depict the point of view—the same lines simultaneously specify both. This cospecific character of the information available to perception is the starting point for understanding processes that distinguish self and object.

Again, it is important to note that the information depicted in such a drawing, like the information available for visual perception generally, cannot be identified with the content of awareness. For example, we are not typically aware of the convergence of lines or of texture gradients as such; instead these features of the ambient array carry information that allows us to be aware of surfaces and objects. This information thus supports, rather than constitutes, the content of our awareness. We can, with greater or lesser success, come to be aware of the information as such. However, as anyone who has seriously attempted to draw using perspective technique knows, this is a special and rather difficult attitude to adopt.

In perceiving real environments as opposed to drawings or photographs, the stationary viewpoint is of course a special case. Generally, our points of view are constantly shifting—small shifts associated with moving our eyes or heads, and larger shifts associated with moving around the environment. Furthermore, the environment itself is not static. It is well known that movement is important in perception, often allowing precise perception of objects that are perceived vaguely or with ambiguity when both object and observer are stationary (e.g., Johansson, 1975). Relative motion of parts of the optic array also contributes to distinguishing self-specific and object-specific information, and illusions of self-motion (vection) can be produced by appropriate manipulations of the kinetic optic array (J. J. Gibson, 1966).

These observations point to the importance of resampling and exploration in distinguishing self and object. In general, resampling or exploration of the available information over at least short time frames is necessary to unambiguously separate self-specific and object-specific aspects of the ambient array. In the limiting case of a stationary environment, stable environmental features correspond to invariant aspects of the ambient array, whereas aspects of the array that vary from moment to moment specify changes in point of view. Motion parallax—relative differences in movement of parts of the optic array—specifies separation of surfaces and objects in distance from the point of view (depth). Visual perception is characterized by exploration and resampling even for very young infants (E. J. Gibson, 1987), and infants quickly develop skills for distinguishing self and object (E. J. Gibson & Adolph, 1992). Such skills reflect the development of egolocative processes that serve to locate the self with respect to a surrounding environment. These observations bear a conceptual relation to Piaget's concept of *decentering* (Chapman, 1988), and are developed in more detail in chapter 4.

Generalizing the Cospecification Hypothesis

The cospecific nature of the ambient array for vision, and the role of resampling and exploration in distinguishing self and object, is one illustration of what I believe to be the general structure of consciousness in the sense of primary awareness. The cospecification hypothesis can thus be stated more formally like this:

> Consciousness is a feature of mental states, which are to be understood as comprising multimodal manifolds of informational arrays that cospecify self (viewpoint) and object and that support directed activity. Activity entails resampling and exploration of the informational manifold, allowing self- and object-specific aspects of the available information to be distinguished. The egolocative processes that accomplish or use the self-object distinction are the basis for conscious control of cognitive activity.

The information arrays that make up these multimodal manifolds include information provided by the environment-directed perceptual systems (e.g., vision and hearing), by kinesthesia and other bodily senses, by symbolic activity such as inner speech, and by memory in a variety of formats.

In contrast to most discussions of consciousness, I want to emphasize that various aspects of consciousness—perceptual-enactive awareness, symbolic awareness, and emotional awareness—are experientially and thus theoretically continuous. My claim is that the theoretical continuity of these various aspects of consciousness can be seen by recognizing that cospecification is a feature of informational arrays supported by other perceptual systems and by memory. This claim is developed in more detail in Part II (chapters 4–7).

THE PLAN OF THE BOOK

The book is organized into four parts, devoted to (a) providing a context for experienced cognition in information-processing metatheory and research on cognitive skill; (b) developing a framework for describing conscious mental states and the architecture of mind; (c) applying this framework to a number of theoretical issues, with a focus on cognitive skill; and (d) considering the implications of the framework.

Part I includes chapters 1 through 3. In chapter 1, I have tried to orient the reader to my approach to understanding experienced cognition, sketching what I see as the major issues, and introducing the cospecification hypothesis. In chapter 2, I review some basic elements of the information-processing approach to cognitive theory, providing some background for linking the experienced cognition framework to mainstream work in cognitive science. Chapter 3 is concerned with empirical phenomena revealed in research on cognitive skill, with special emphasis on those findings that are helpful for understanding the role of consciousness in the acquisition and performance of cognitive skills.

In Part II (chapters 4–7), I develop the cospecification hypothesis to provide a framework for describing consciousness, and I discuss this framework in relation to some architectural issues in cognitive theory. In chapter 4, I consider consciousness as it is involved in perception and unreflective physical activity. Chapter 5 is concerned with the kind of symbolic awareness that has received the most attention in discussions of consciousness, and briefly reviews some of the puzzles surrounding the intentionality or directedness of mental states. Chapter 6 presents an argument that the framework developed in earlier chapters can also encompass emotional awareness, providing a way to fit emotion and cognition into the same theoretical framework. Chapter 7 considers the implications of the cospecification hypothesis for the relations between consciousness and nonconscious but cognitively tuned systems such as memory.

Part III (chapters 8–13) considers a variety of central topics in cognitive theory from the point of view of the experienced cognition framework. This part of the book begins in chapter 8 with a discussion of working memory and private speech, topics often seen as central to consciousness. Chapter 9 is concerned with goals and goal structures, fundamental concepts for understanding the control of cognition. In chapter 10, I discuss causal thinking and problem solving, considering how causal knowledge is involved in experienced cognition and how we come to organize goals and basic actions into complex goal structures that guide extended episodes of purposive activity. Chapter 11 presents the application of the experienced cognition framework to prototypical thinking tasks, such as reasoning and judgment, offering an account of belief based on the description of conscious states presented in Part II. Chapter 12 includes discussions of research on expertise and everyday action, focusing on how such skilled activity is experienced and how it depends on regularities in the environment. Finally, chapter 13 presents a theoretical sketch of the conscious control of skilled mental activity, focusing on how the self is specified as a conscious agent.

Part IV (chapters 14–15) represents my attempt to place the experienced cognition framework in context. Chapter 14 examines the intuitions and phenomena that support current claims for a cognitive unconscious, considering the various senses in which current researchers have proposed that cognitive processes are unconscious and using the experienced cognition framework to assess these proposals. Finally, chapter 15 presents some of my hopes for the future of consciousness in cognitive theory, emphasizing my belief that we can and should develop cognitive theory that does justice to the fact that the subjects of our research are persons with conscious, first-person points of view.

2

Consciousness and the Information Processing Framework

The received view that guides most empirical research in cognitive psychology describes the mind as an information-processing system (Lachman, Lachman, & Butterfield, 1979; Massaro & Cowan, 1993). The information-processing (IP) framework has proved its heuristic value, guiding research that has generated many important insights into mental activity. The computer metaphor for the mind associated with the IP framework has also been fruitful, pointing the way toward solutions for (or at least useful approaches to) some perennial problems in the philosophy of mind (e.g., Dennett, 1991). However, as it is usually understood, the IP framework has also presented some obstacles to developing a satisfactory theory of consciousness. As I remarked in a commentary several years ago, IP theory shows us how representations can interact without an explicit first-person point of view (Carlson, 1992). Although this is promising in terms of developing satisfactorily objective cognitive theory, it leaves out the subjectivity that is central to understanding experienced cognition.

I believe that a useful, scientific theory of consciousness must make contact with what is good and useful in current cognitive theory. Furthermore, I believe that the core ideas of the IP framework are compatible with theory that acknowledges and accounts for the subjectivity of consciousness. In this chapter, I review those core ideas, arguing that they can be distinguished from several habits of thought that present obstacles to understanding consciousness.

MENTAL ACTIVITY AS COMPUTATION

Information-processing theories come in a variety of forms, but all share a common metaphor for cognition: At some useful level of description, mental activity is computation. In fact, for many cognitive scientists this position is not a metaphor but a fundamental commitment concerning the nature of the mind. In this section, I consider some of the reasons for its appeal.

Solving the Mind–Body Problem

The phrase *mind–body problem* refers to a classic set of issues in philosophy and psychology, at least some of which are likely familiar to anyone reading this book. A prototypical formulation of the problem might be something like this: How can mental events such as thoughts (or conscious experience) be reconciled with the scientific view of the individual as a physical system? Most if not all contemporary cognitive scientists would agree that the computational view of mind entailed by the IP framework solves this problem. The argument goes something like this: Thoughts (or ideas, or percepts, or concepts, or intentions, etc.) are *representations*. Representations have formal structures that allow them to be manipulated by the mechanical application of rules. Computers are obviously physical systems that do just this, and there is nothing mysterious about providing a physical account of how they do so. The computational view (which is also supported by a great deal of formal theory) therefore shows us how a physical mechanism—a computer or a nervous system—can also be a mind. As Pylyshyn (1980) put it:

> The most fundamental reason why cognition ought to be viewed as computation is that computation is the only worked-out view of process that is both compatible with a materialist view and that attributes the behavior of the process to the operation of rules upon representations. (p. 113)

The computational view of mind is of course neither monolithic nor as straightforward and unproblematic as it might appear in my sketch. Furthermore, the most basic claim—that mental activity is a variety (or several varieties) of computation—is not universally accepted (e.g., Searle, 1980, 1990). However, despite arguments to the contrary (by, e.g., Dreyfus, 1992; Searle, 1980), I see no fundamental problem with—and no satisfactory alternative to—the general claim that at some level of description, cognition is computation. Rather than argue for this position, I take it as a background assumption for my intended audience. The problem for a theory of experienced cognition, then, is how to account for conscious experience within the general IP framework. How can we accommodate the subjectivity of conscious awareness, and its causal role in cognitive activity, within the computational view of mind? Jackendoff (1987) argued that the success of the computational approach solves the mind–body problem (in his terms, the brain–mind problem) but leaves us with a mind–mind problem—how to reconcile the computational view of mind with conscious experience. My argument in this book could be read as a proposed solution to this mind–mind problem.

Varieties of Information Processing

The general IP framework, at least as viewed by psychologists, accommodates a variety of theoretical approaches that differ dramatically in their accounts of some mental phenomena but share the core assumptions discussed later. It is useful to briefly sketch some of these alternative approaches before turning to the core assumptions themselves. One way to identify alternative formulations within the IP framework is by considering the kinds of mental representations proposed, and I take that approach for two broad categories, symbol processing and connectionism. Massaro and Cowan (1993) have recently considered the range of theoretical possibilities in more detail.

The classical view of IP that has received the greatest amount of metatheoretical attention and discussion is the symbol processing paradigm associated with A. Newell and Simon (1972; Haugeland, 1985; A. Newell, 1981, 1990). In this view, mental representations are described as symbol structures, entities composed of symbols combined according to formal rules. (A *formal rule* is simply one that operates in virtue of the form of its operands rather than their physical realization or semantic content.) Mental activity is seen as the manipulation of these representations on the basis of such rules. An important feature of theories constructed within the symbol-processing approach is that the units (symbols) of which symbol structures are composed can have semantic interpretations (meanings) in the manner of words in natural language. Thus Fodor (1975) argued that the symbol-processing approach to cognition requires an innate language of thought that comprises the basic set of symbols. These elements are the tokens or operands manipulated in order to accomplish computation. As Chalmers (1992) put it, "In a symbolic system, the objects of computation are also objects of semantic interpretation" (p. 34).

For understanding experienced cognition, this point leads to an important implication of the symbol processing approach: In this view, the contents of conscious mental states are symbol structures, which have meanings or semantic interpretations. In order to account for at least some cognitive phenomena, however, it appears that symbol processing theories must also postulate symbol structures that are not plausibly contents of conscious mental states. For example, Marr's (1982) computational theory of vision treats events near the retinal level of the visual system as instances of symbol processing. However, the symbols involved are clearly not contents of visual experience but intermediate states in the computations responsible for visual experience. The symbol processing approach thus implies the existence of symbol structures that are not conscious, but are ontologically like the contents of conscious mental states.

Recently, an alternative approach known as connectionism (McClelland & Rumelhart, 1986) has received a great deal of attention. Connectionism is characterized by an emphasis on the parallel nature of computation distributed over a large number of units organized in networks, often on explicit analogy to the presumed operation of neurons in the brain (hence the term *neural network* for connectionist models). The individual units in connectionist models generally cannot be assigned semantic interpretations—it is said to be the activity of a network as a whole (or of a vector representing the input or output of a network) that constitutes a mental representation. Because of this feature, connectionist theory is sometimes said to be subsymbolic (e.g., Smolensky, 1988). Again, Chalmers (1992) concisely summarized the point, "In a subsymbolic system, the objects of computation are more fine-grained than the objects of semantic interpretation" (p. 34).

There is some debate as to whether connectionism should be understood as an alternative to symbol processing theories, or rather as reflecting a different level of description that can be regarded as an implementation of symbol processing (Broadbent, 1985; Rumelhart & McClelland, 1985). Although I am inclined toward the levels interpretation, many cognitive scientists working with connectionist models appear to regard them as a genuine alternative to (and potential replacement for) symbol-processing models. In either view, however, connectionist accounts allow an interpretation of the relation between conscious and nonconscious cognitive processes quite different than that implied by the symbol processing approach. That is, it seems compatible with the connectionist approach (at least in its popular subsymbolic form) to argue that only the contents of conscious mental states have intrinsic meanings or semantic interpretations, although those states might be supported by extensive subsymbolic processes (cf. Cleeremans & McClelland, 1991).

Massaro and Cowan (1993) recently argued that both symbol processing and connectionist approaches fit the general IP framework. They point out that IP psychologists have often made theoretical use of nonsymbolic notions of information, "IP theory has a history of nonsymbolic representations including discriminability, familiarity, memory strength, and even activation and inhibition among representations" (p. 416). These are noncontent properties of mental states, in the terminology developed in chapters 4 through 7. Others (e.g., Kosslyn & Hatfield, 1984) have also argued for nonsymbolic notions of information that are not specifically connectionist in nature.

In practice, many cognitive psychologists adopt a version of the IP metatheory that might be called eclectic activationism. They assume that the activation of representational units linked in networks is a (if not the) primary form of psychological causality. Usually the postulated units have semantic interpretations or labels—for example, much work on word recognition and semantic priming assumes units corresponding to individual words. The representational units postulated are thus symbolic, but (at least some of) the computation involved in processing is based on activation transmitted along weighted links among units, as in connectionist models. Models such as this are sometimes called localist connectionist models, but cannot be construed as subsymbolic (Chalmers, 1992). However, there is often no explicit analysis of the symbolic status of these units; in particular, the links that support the transfer of activation (and thus implement computation) are semantically rather than syntactically specified.

There are several lessons to be drawn from this brief sketch of the alternative approaches encompassed by the IP framework. First, the core assumptions of IP theory are not necessarily tied to the symbol processing approach. Second, many of the theoretical concepts that are labeled representations may not correspond to the content of conscious experience. However, alternative approaches may suggest different views of the relation between conscious and nonconscious processes. Finally, the core assumptions of the IP framework that are shared by cognitive scientists taking these different approaches are neutral with respect to the kind of representations postulated. The central point for understanding consciousness is that the IP framework can accommodate a number of alternative hypotheses about consciousness, including those embodied in the experienced cognition framework.

CORE ASSUMPTIONS OF THE INFORMATION PROCESSING APPROACH

A number of authors have reviewed the fundamental ideas of the information-processing approach to cognition (Haugeland, 1985; Lachman, Lachman, & Butterfield, 1979; Massaro & Cowan, 1993; A. Newell, 1990; Palmer & Kimchi, 1986; Pylyshyn, 1980). For example, Palmer and Kimchi (1986) characterized the IP framework in terms of five core assumptions:

informational description, recursive decomposition, flow continuity, flow dynamics, and physical embodiment. Palmer and Kimchi presented their overview as a characterization of the core ideas of information processing theory as understood and practiced by psychologists (in contrast to other cognitive scientists, such as artificial intelligence researchers). In this section, I take their discussion as the basis for sketching these core ideas.

Informational Description

The first assumption identified by Palmer and Kimchi (1986) is informational description:

> Mental events can be functionally described as "informational events," each of which consists of three parts: the *input information* (what it starts with), the *operation* performed on the input (what gets done to the input), and the *output information* (what it ends up with). (p. 39)

Developing informational descriptions depends on what Palmer and Kimchi called *mapping theories,* theories that systematize informational description but "make no psychological claims about what goes on 'inside the mental black box'" (p. 45). They went on to note that such theories are rare, at least for extensive domains.

In practice, most cognitive research depends on implicit mapping theories derived from common-sense analyses of relatively (often very) narrow domains. For example, experimental research on visual word recognition sometimes adopts an input description in terms of letter strings and (vaguely specified) prior knowledge of orthography, meaning, and so on. The output description is typically recognition, indexed by instructed responses such as naming or lexical decision. The informality and vagueness of such implicit mapping theories is in some ways very similar to the unscientific use of terminology for which Chomsky (1959) criticized Skinner's (1957) behaviorist approach to language. Of course, cognitive scientists are under no illusion that they are avoiding mentalism in starting with common-sense mapping theories.

In fact, researchers in many areas of cognitive science have made substantial progress by starting with common-sense, usually implicit, mapping theories (but see Schank, Collins, & Hunter, 1986). How can this be? Palmer and Kimchi pointed out that for sufficiently small domains, mapping theories are intuitively obvious because the complete set of possible input–output relations can be explicitly listed. More important, I think, is that our implicit mapping theories are also implicitly ecological in the sense of J. J. Gibson's (1966) "ecological optics." That is, both input and output are specified in a way that is implicitly but systematically related to the capabilities and possible activities of our research subjects

(and ourselves). Gibson argued that the information available for perception should be characterized in terms of invariants that specify affordances, the possibilities for action supported by objects and surfaces in
the environment. A texture gradient may thus specify the orientation of
a surface, (part of) the affordance for walking. Similarly, describing a
particular display as a letter string or a word is appropriate because the
display affords reading. Affordances generally correspond fairly well to
the units of phenomenal experience; which informational invariants specify an affordance is a matter for empirical investigation in particular cases.

To think clearly about consciousness in the IP framework requires that
we consider two kinds of causal relations that allow informational description. First, there are what might be called *operand–result relations*—as
in common-sense examples of symbol processing such as Marr's (1982)
cash-register example. Given informational inputs such as numbers and
an operation specification, the cash register produces a result (e.g., a sum).
In this case, operands and results are separately represented, and are
symbolic in the sense just discussed: They are both objects of computation
and representational units assigned semantic interpretations. Second,
there are what might be called *informational support relations*, as in the
relation between an invariant aspect of the optic array and the affordance
it helps to specify, or the relation between the activation of an element
in a connectionist network and the patterns in which it participates. Both
kinds of relations appropriately receive computational accounts in cognitive theory, but they differ in their implications for understanding
consciousness. The difference is like that between actually calculating the
area of a rectangle by multiplying measurements of its sides, and recognizing that the rectangle can be described in terms of both the length of
its sides and its area, which have an invariant relation and are simultaneously present.

Confusing these two types of informational relations leads to versions
of IP theory in which it is difficult to see a place for consciousness. I
believe it is a mistake, for example, to characterize a momentary, two-dimensional array of energy at the retina as the input to a process whose
output is perceptual experience (cf. Marr, 1982). Such a characterization
may serve as a heuristic starting point for some research purposes, but
it is systematically misleading with respect to understanding consciousness. As Dennett (1991) argued, this approach leads us to an insupportable
"Cartesian theater" view of consciousness as a stage in a linear flow of
information processing (also see Neisser, 1976).

Understanding experienced cognition within the IP framework thus
involves recognizing that (a) we generally work with mapping theories
based on an ecological level of description, and (b) not all informational
relations fit the operand-result model. Natsoulas (1992) argued that "con-

sciousness is what psychologists actually examine" (p. 364; also see Carlson, 1992), but consciousness cannot be understood as the output of a mental process. Certainly increasing the specificity, scope, and systematicity of our mapping theories is a worthy goal (and an awesome task). However, compatibility with the IP assumption of informational description requires that we systematize the terminology of experienced cognition and understand its relations to other theoretically important levels of description.

Recursive Decomposition

The IP framework entails a strategy for analyzing cognitive phenomena based on an assumption Palmer and Kimchi (1986) called *recursive decomposition*:

> Any complex (i.e., nonprimitive) informational event at one level of description can be specified more fully at a lower level by *decomposing* it into (1) a number of components, each of which is itself an informational event, and (2) the temporal ordering relations among them that specifies how the information "flows" through the system of components. (p. 39; italics in original)

One application of this assumption is simply to analyze temporally extended mental events into series of briefer events that are ontologically similar—that is, involving the same kinds of things. The familiar stage analysis of memory phenomena captured by the formula *encoding-storage-retrieval* is an instance of such analysis. The recursive character of the decomposition in this sense is simply that a particular analysis may itself be decomposed. For example, retrieval might be decomposed into stages such as cue encoding, search, verification, and response.

This analytic scheme generates hierarchical descriptions of mental events, with events at higher levels comprising assemblies of events at lower levels. This observation raises several issues. First, the decomposition cannot continue indefinitely. At some level, the events described will have no further decompositions in terms of smaller-scale mental events, but must be analyzed in terms of their implementations or physical realizations (e.g., neural processes). Although this issue of a stopping rule for decomposition has received much discussion (e.g., Palmer & Kimchi, 1986; Pylyshyn, 1980), there does not appear to be a general consensus on how to characterize the limits of decomposition from a cognitive point of view. Consider, for example, the analyses suggested by two of the most comprehensive cognitive theories currently available, the ACT theory proposed by J. R. Anderson (1983, 1993) and A. Newell's (1990) Soar theory. Newell argued, on the basis of the time scale of human activity, for a limited number of possible levels. Newell's argument is based on plausible assumptions about the time course of neural activity and about the speed with which simple, deliberative activities must be accomplished. Newell further suggested that events occurring at the rate of approximately 10 ms are symbolic, represented theoretically by the execution of productions (condition-action rules; see chapter 3). This may be contrasted with the production-system theory proposed by Anderson, which suggests that the grain size of cognitive activity is roughly an order of magnitude larger.

This contrast raises a second issue, that recursive decomposition typically generates analyses that involve mental processes below the level of consciousness. Dennett (1978) and others have discussed this feature as a virtue of the IP approach, noting that less "intelligence" is involved in each lower stage of decomposition. In Dennett's view, recursive decomposition thus holds the promise of explaining person-level phenomena by showing how they are composed of subpersonal processes that—at the implementation level—can be realized mechanically. From the point of view of understanding experienced cognition, the important point here is that recursive decomposition is usually taken to imply that there are levels of mental processes, qualitatively like conscious mental processes, that are subpersonal but above the implementation level. Thus, the IP framework appears to imply the existence of fast mental processes that are in principle unconscious and subpersonal but receive the kind of informational descriptions that are also appropriate for conscious mental processes (see chapter 15 for further discussion of this point).

A third issue concerns the so-called emergent properties of higher-level descriptions. The idea, a familiar one in all of the sciences, is that some properties exist only at higher levels of description. For example, at room temperature water is liquid, a property that cannot be attributed to the hydrogen and oxygen atoms (at least at room temperature) that constitute it. Analogously, none of the memory subprocesses suggested can itself be labeled retrieval. It is sometimes said that consciousness is such an emergent property, and in some sense it seems that it must be so. However, IP analyses typically begin with a highest-level description in which the point of view of an experiencing self is either absent or implicit, and it is not at all clear how consciousness might then emerge from the proposed mechanisms.

My point in raising these issues is not to argue that recursive decomposition is an inappropriate assumption for cognitive theory. However, as the assumption is usually applied, it entails postulating unconscious mental states that are similar in kind to conscious states, and such analyses make it difficult to develop a satisfactory account of consciousness. I argue in essence that the appropriate stopping rule for recursive decomposition is the smallest temporal scale at which conscious mental states can be (theoretically) identified, a position similar to J. R. Anderson's (1987a) argument that the appropriate level for cognitive theory can be identified with changes in the state of working memory.

Flow Continuity and Flow Dynamics

For my purposes, the next two assumptions identified by Palmer and Kimchi (1986) can be treated together. These assumptions are *flow continuity*—"All input information required to perform each operation must be available in the output of the operations that flow into it" (p. 39)—and *flow dynamics*—"No output can be produced by an operation until its input information is available and sufficient additional time has elapsed for it to process that input" (p. 39). These assumptions reflect a concern with the real-time character of cognitive activity and the completeness of causal stories about that activity. Flow continuity thus describes a completeness constraint on the specification of input–output functions. Flow dynamics captures the assumption that mental processes take time, and that the time required for a particular mental process is some (perhaps complex) function of the time required for its components.

We might call these the "no-magic" assumptions. They serve to establish the normative force of the IP framework, capturing the ideal of continuity and completeness in the causal stories developed for mental processes. These are the assumptions reflected in arguments for computational models, for example Johnson-Laird's (1983) insistence that cognitive theories should be cast as *effective procedures*, procedures that can be accurately captured in computer programs. The idea is that the specificity required to write a simulation program ensures that these assumptions are met, and the processes specified by the theory actually perform the activities for which theory tries to account.

Physical Embodiment

The final assumption discussed by Palmer and Kimchi (1986) is *physical embodiment*:

> In the dynamic physical system whose behavior is being described as an informational event, information is embodied in states of the system (here called *representations*) and operations that use this information are embodied in changes of state (here called *processes*). (p. 39)

The assumption is simply that the processes and entities proposed by cognitive theories are realized as physical activities of the nervous system. Cognitive scientists who take the view labeled by Searle (1980) as strong

AI would argue that mental processes can in principle be realized in a variety of media, including both nervous systems and computers. Others might argue that only nervous systems can implement some processes, but would agree that some physical embodiment realizes mental processes. There is little to say about the status of this assumption, as essentially all cognitive scientists would agree.

HABITS OF THOUGHT IN INFORMATION PROCESSING

The core assumptions of the information processing framework allow for a great deal of variability in the actual theories proposed (Massaro & Cowan, 1993), and there is of course some variability in the core assumptions adopted by individual cognitive scientists. For the purpose of understanding experienced cognition in the context of contemporary cognitive theory, the habits of thought that characterize much research in the IP framework are as important as the core assumptions. In this section, I describe several habits of thought that (a) are not necessarily entailed by the core assumptions already discussed, and (b) in my opinion, hinder our ability to develop a satisfactory theory of consciousness.

Linear Flow Thinking

Linear flow thinking derives from seeing the mind as an information channel flowing from stimulus to response, discouraging a truly reciprocal view of causality in individual–environment interactions. As Massaro and Cowan (1993) put it, "The basic notion of IP is that one must trace the progression of information through the system from stimuli to responses" (p. 386). This belief is reflected in the information-flow diagrams often seen in textbooks and in earlier research literature; such diagrams are less common in current research. Figure 2.1 presents a generic information-flow diagram. The important point about such diagrams is that the arrows suggest a unidirectional view of the causality of cognitive processes. Although few if any cognitive theorists would argue explicitly for such a view of causality in cognitive theory, I believe that such diagrams reflect a very common habit of thought that influences both the design of experimental research and the construction of theory.

One source of linear flow thinking is what has been called the sensory metatheory of the mind (Weimer, 1977; also see MacKay, 1987). This idea can be traced at least to the 18th and 19th century British philosophers who are sometimes characterized as *empiricists* because they argued that all of the contents of mental activity derived from sensory experience.

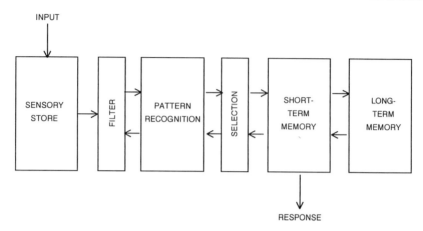

FIG. 2.1. A generic information-flow diagram: The habit of linear-flow thinking is often reflected in diagrams depicting the architecture of the information-processing system. This example is adapted from Reed's (1988) textbook.

The sensory metatheory suggests that a causal account of cognition should begin with a description of the events that stimulate the sensory systems (i.e., *stimuli*). This view can be seen in the earliest research on psychophysics, reaction time, and other topics. The general sensory metatheory is also reflected in Neisser's (1967) classic definition of the subject matter of cognitive psychology, "As used here, the term 'cognition' refers to all processes by which the sensory input is transformed, reduced, elaborated, stored, recovered, and used" (p. 4). Broadbent's (1958) conception of the mind as an information channel from stimulus to response was influential in establishing the research paradigms reviewed by Neisser, and may have been largely responsible for popularizing flow diagrams like that in Fig. 2.1.

A second source of linear-flow thinking in cognitive theory may be the general stimulus–response laboratory paradigm adopted from behaviorism. In this general paradigm, an experimental trial begins with a display, typically visual (and containing the stimuli) controlled by the experimenter, and ends with a response by the subject (and perhaps feedback concerning the degree to which the response corresponds to the goal presented by instructions at the beginning of the experiment). This general stimulus–response laboratory paradigm has the important advantage of allowing control of the content and timing of information available for the experimental participant to perceive. However, it tends to emphasize the stimulus as the effective cause of behavior while placing the individual's goals in the background. Furthermore, it abstracts from the ecological case of ongoing, reciprocal interaction with the environment, encouraging theoretical analysis that disregards that interaction.

Thinking about mental processes in terms of a linear flow of information from stimulus to response presents some obstacles to developing an understanding of conscious experience. First, this conception often leads researchers to adopt a knife-edge view of the timing of conscious experience (and other postulated mental events), implying that all persistence of information should be viewed as memory and that it is possible to locate consciousness precisely along the path of information processing. This account in turn suggests that mental processes occurring "before" (e.g., pattern recognition) and "after" (e.g., motor control) consciousness are unconscious (e.g., Broadbent, 1975). Dennett (1991) developed an extended argument against this view of consciousness, which he characterized as the *Cartesian Theater*, a place in the cognitive system in which the results of cognitive processes are displayed and conscious experience occurs.

Perhaps more important—because the linear-flow approach does have a valuable role as an empirical analytic technique—this habit of thought discourages a reciprocal view of the interaction between individual and environment. Neisser (1976) criticized IP theory for its reliance on linear-flow thinking, suggesting instead that cognition occurs within a perceptual cycle as illustrated in Fig. 2.2. This reciprocal, cyclic view of cognition is compatible with the IP framework (e.g., Vera & Simon, 1993), and is explicitly embodied in production-system models (see chapter 3). How-

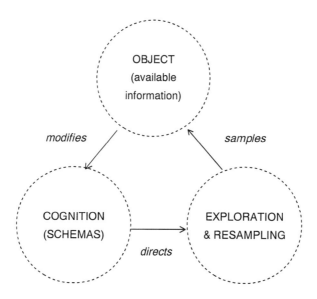

FIG. 2.2. The perceptual cycle: The perceptual cycle represents an attempt by Neisser (1976) to depict the reciprocal interaction of individual and environment. In Neisser's terms, *schema* refers to any patterned knowledge. This figure is adapted from the one presented by Neisser (1976, p. 21).

ever, few if any discussions of consciousness in the IP framework have carefully considered the implications of this reciprocity, and linear flow thinking seems to characterize most empirical research in cognitive psychology.

Methodological Solipsism

Fodor (1980a) used the term *methodological solipsism* (attributed to Putnam, 1975) to label a feature of typical research strategies in cognitive science. That feature is that the theoretical and empirical tasks of cognitive science are completely circumscribed by the informational descriptions of the phenomena to be explained. This approach follows from the assumptions of informational description and flow continuity sketched earlier. That is, the input description involved in defining a phenomenon is taken as a complete representation of the information available from the environment, and the theoretical account need not refer to the environment beyond that description. Discussing what he called "perhaps *the* basic idea of modern cognitive theory," Fodor (1980a) wrote:

> it's allowed that mental representations affect behavior in virtue of their content, but it's maintained that mental representations are distinct in content only if they are also distinct in form. The first clause is required to make it plausible that mental states are relations to mental representations and the second is required to make it plausible that mental processes are computations. (Computations just *are* processes in which representations have their causal consequences in virtue of their form.) (p. 68)

Therefore, if we adhere strictly to the computational model of mind, our theories cannot encompass the relation between mental representations and the environment. Hence solipsism—we make no reference to a surrounding environment, except in terms of representations.

In its precise form, methodological solipsism is not objectionable and may in fact be necessary to the conduct of at least parts of cognitive science (Fodor, 1980a). In practice, however, this solipsism often begins with implicit mapping theories derived either from common sense or from limited experimental paradigms. We then often fail to make explicit or revisit the theoretical assumptions involved in describing particular mental events. For example, it is commonplace to assume that the problem for vision is to construct three-dimensional experience from temporally punctate two-dimensional retinal images (Marr, 1982). A more obviously cognitive example is the tendency to characterize individuals' performance in thinking tasks on the basis of normative theories (such as logic or probability theory; see chapter 11) and assumed mappings of events to those theories. The tendency for methodological solipsism to produce paradigm-bound mapping theories is illustrated by Humphreys, Wiles, and Dennis' (1994) effort to provide a mapping theory for memory. They focus almost entirely on memory tasks defined with respect to a few experimental paradigms that have dominated laboratory research on memory (cf. Neisser, 1982).

For the purpose of understanding experienced cognition, the primary difficulty associated with methodological solipsism is the tendency to regard informational descriptions, particularly input descriptions, as pre-theoretically fixed and given. However, the ecological approach (chapter 1, chapter 4) emphasizes that one goal of psychological research is to discover appropriate descriptions of the information available for perception. This is similar to the point made by proponents of the situated cognition approach (e.g., Lave, 1988)—that to understand cognition, we must consider (and theoretically describe) agent-environment systems rather than individual agents.

Representationalism

A goal of cognitive theory is of course to account for regularity or systematicity in action and experience. A common style of explanation, which I call representationalism, is to propose mental representations that are patterned in a way that corresponds to the regularity to be explained. So, for example, abstract regularities in perceiving, remembering, or acting are explained by postulating schemas, said to be "precompiled generic knowledge structures" (Brewer, 1987, p. 189). These mental representations are said to be activated or instantiated when appropriate, thereby guiding the relevant mental activity. As with the other habits of thought associated with information-processing psychology, representationalism often captures important elements of truth about cognitive phenomena, but also leads many theorists to conclusions that make it difficult to understand experienced cognition.

The problems caused by this habit of thought stem in large part from ambiguities in the term *representation*. Palmer and Kimchi (1986) defined the concept as: "The prevailing notions are that representations are defined by (1) being *used* as a surrogate for some reference world and (2) preserving the abstract informational structure of that referent world" (p. 56). This definition is quite clear in cases of consciously manipulated symbolic representations, whether mental or artifactual. For example, it is obvious how a (physical, external paper) map fits this definition of representation. However, compare this definition with Palmer and Kimchi's description of the assumption of physical embodiment—that statement appears to identify representation with any state of the individual that preserves information. For example, consider Mandler's (1984) views on the topic of representation:

> The concept of representation is intimately tied to, and possibly identical with, the issue of useful theory. Representational systems are theoretical constructs that are postulated as responsible for (that cause or generate) the observable thoughts, actions, etc. of the organism . . . The representation of knowledge, in other words, is the theoretical system that is constructed in order to understand, explain, and predict the behavior of organisms. (p. 11)

The issue here is that cognitive scientists often fail to systematically (and empirically) distinguish between rules or representations that are consulted or considered by the individual in the guidance of cognition and those that represent the theorist's descriptions of rule-like regularities embodied in cognitive activity. For example, Chomsky (e.g., Chomsky & Katz, 1974) argued that the rules of grammar be considered as consulted, if unconscious, representations because the brain is the kind of thing that represents and consults rules.

However, it is not that easy to distinguish consulted rules and embodied regularities (Shepard, 1984). Furthermore, postulating unconscious rules often generates accounts that are parasitic on common-sense understanding of conscious mental activity, but are immune to empirical tests based on assessing individuals' conscious states (Dulany, Carlson, & Dewey, 1985). Consider Jackendoff's (1987) comment on the observation that individuals are apparently unaware of many of the representations postulated by cognitive theory:

> This observation, of course, does not undermine the claim of psychological reality for these information structures, for, as emphasized throughout, they are justified on the grounds of their power to explain the character of perceptual judgments, behavior, and understanding—not the character of introspection or awareness. (p. 287)

In contrast, Bandura (1986) commented:

> The notion that thought processes are inaccessible presupposes that valid methods exist for certifying what the nonconscious processes are. . . . The issue of who is unaware of what is not that easily resolvable. . . . The investigators' conjectures can hardly be regarded as the authentic process against which to judge whether or not others are unaware of the thoughts governing their actions. (pp. 122–123)

For many purposes, representationalism is a reasonable heuristic strategy. However, understanding experienced cognition requires that we distinguish in our theories between representations that paraphrase contents of mental states and the nonparaphrastic representations that describe information that is preserved by nonconscious processes (but not literally represented as contents of mental states). The basic idea is not to legislate the use of terminology, but to make a fundamental distinction between representations that involve the actual, occurrent point of view of the subject of the theory and those that do not.

Componentialism

Componentialism is in some sense the converse of representationalism. It is the tendency to explain abstract or very general regularities in activity or experience by postulating processing components or architectural features that embody those regularities. A classic example of componentialism is the so-called "modal theory" of short-term memory, which persists despite abundant evidence against it (e.g., Crowder, 1982, 1993a). The central claim of this modal theory (e.g., as exemplified in Atkinson & Shiffrin, 1968) is that a variety of limits on short-term remembering can be explained by a processing component defined as a *short-term store* with a number of slots corresponding to the short-term memory span (the number of items that can be briefly remembered and reproduced). Although this view of short-term memory still appears in many textbooks, it is now clear that remembering for brief periods of time is supported by a variety of processes (see chapter 8).

The habit of componentialism has led to a variety of attempts to identify consciousness with some processing component or other. For example, Baddeley (1993) suggested that consciousness might be identified with one of the components in his theory of working memory, the central executive. However, such approaches have produced little progress in understanding consciousness.

Implicit and Absent Agents

Perhaps the most pervasive habit of thought in IP theory, and the one most inimical to understanding experienced cognition, is the tendency to assume or ignore—rather than explain—agency in the control of cognitive activity (Bandura, 1989). The accounts of control adopted by IP theorists often are based on perspectives that can be characterized as *implicit agent* or *absent agent* stances.

The implicit agent stance is typified by the description of cognitive subsystems from the point of view of a user. For example, Logan (1989) discussed how individuals might control their automatic cognitive processes from the point of view of his Instance Theory of automaticity. One mechanism of control he suggested is thinking of appropriate retrieval cues to guide memory-based processes. Although his theory constrains the possible strategies an individual might adopt, the ability to choose retrieval cues (for example) is outside the theory. An agent—conceived as a user of the system described by the theory—is assumed.

The implicit agent stance is of course familiar to cognitive scientists as a version of the homunculus problem—postulating a "little person" in the head whose powers account for all of the difficult aspects of the phenomena to be explained. In many cases, an agent must be assumed implicitly for a theory to work at all. Searle (1992) put it this way: "*Without a homunculus that stands outside the recursive decomposition, we do not even have a syntax to operate with*" (p. 213). However, many cognitive scientists, sensitive to the homunculus problem, adopt an absent agent stance in which control is seen as external to the individual, much like some versions of behaviorism (Bandura, 1989). Connectionist theorists seem particularly susceptible to this stance, seldom including any account of goals or control of the activity they model. Theories that adopt an absent agent stance also tend to focus on small domains defined by particular experimental paradigms, perhaps because in these paradigms, the tasks given to experimental subjects are usually not controversial. Taking absent agent theories as accurately reflecting the ontology of mental processes leads to an understanding of consciousness as epiphenomenal (e.g., Jackendoff, 1987).

Theories that distinguish executive or control processes from the non-conscious or automatic processes that support them (e.g., Atkinson & Shiffrin, 1968; Baddeley, 1986; Norman & Shallice, 1986; Schneider & Detweiler, 1987) go some way toward making the agency involved in cognitive processes explicit. However, these theories usually fail to account for the subjectivity of consciousness, for having a point of view. As I (Carlson, 1992) wrote a few years ago:

> The information-processing framework provides an account of how representations can exist and interact, *from no particular first-person point of view.* Although this characteristic of the IP framework is often said to provide a solution to the problem of subjectivity of mental states, it is in fact the source of many of the problems ... This feature provides the basis for theories which seem to operate the same way with or without consciousness, and leads to the belief of many cognitive theorists that consciousness is an unnecessary feature added on to cognitive theory. (p. 601)

Summary

I generally share the core assumptions of the IP framework as outlined here. These assumptions provide a language for cognitive theory and identify a reasonable location within the space of philosophical debates about the mind and about the practice of science. The experienced cognition framework developed in this book thus fits within the broad IP approach to understanding cognition. The habits of thought associated with the assumptions of IP, however, present a variety of obstacles to developing a satisfactory theory of consciousness. Next I turn to some of the proposals for incorporating consciousness in the IP framework.

INFORMATION PROCESSING PROPOSALS
ABOUT CONSCIOUSNESS

Cognitive scientists concerned with consciousness have made a variety of general proposals for describing consciousness within the IP framework. These proposals include descriptions of consciousness as a processing component, as a processing function, as a processing stage, as epiphenomenal, and (most promising) as a dominant action scheme. In this section, I briefly review several of these proposals.

Consciousness as an Architectural Component

Some authors have explicitly identified consciousness with architectural components of an information processing system. For example, consciousness is often seen as part of the function of short-term or working memory. This approach focuses on the content of consciousness, presumed to be whatever information is active in this workspace portion of the IP system. Baars (1988) attempted to develop a comprehensive theory of consciousness based on this assumption. However, recent theories (e.g., Baddeley, 1986; Schneider & Detweiler, 1987) present a very elaborate view of working memory, so that it is almost synonymous with the IP system's activities as a whole (Crowder, 1993a, 1993b). On these more elaborate views of working memory, consciousness may be identified with some component of the working-memory system, such as a central executive (Baddeley, 1993) or control processes.

There seems to be something right about identifying consciousness with working memory, in that what we are aware of does seem to correspond with information that we are temporarily remembering or using. However, this approach (at least as it has been developed to date) does not deal with the subjectivity of consciousness, the agent or self who is experiencing the contents of working memory.

Consciousness as a Processing Function

An alternative is to identify consciousness with a processing function such as attention. For example, Velmans (1991) proposed that the concept of consciousness be replaced with the concept of *focal attention* (also see Carr, 1979; Posner, 1978). This approach focuses on the function of consciousness, based on phenomenological views of these processing functions (see Logan, 1995, for comments on the phenomenological nature of attention constructs). The version of this approach that identifies consciousness with attention (or the content of conscious states with information at the focus of attention) typically emphasizes the apparently selective character of consciousness—at a given moment, we are aware of only a small fraction of what is apparently available to consciousness. Similarly, resource views of attention (e.g., Kahneman, 1973) emphasize the need to select among activities rather than among contents, identifying consciousness with the activity or activities to which resources are currently devoted (also see later discussion). Others have identified consciousness with processing functions such as decision, planning, or dealing with novelty.

The approach of identifying consciousness with a processing function is unsatisfactory in two ways. First, it falls easily into the homunculus problem; attributing a particular processing function to consciousness can give a false sense that explanation has been achieved. Second, processing functions such as focal attention are hardly less mysterious than consciousness itself (Carlson, 1991). Finally, there is no consensus as to whether constructs such as attention designate explanatory primitives or label classes of phenomena to be explained (e.g., Johnston & Dark, 1986; Logan, 1995).

Consciousness as a Stage of Processing

Consciousness is sometimes identified with a stage of processing between input (stimulus) and output (response), implying a great deal of unconscious processing before and after that stage (e.g., Broadbent, 1975). This approach is at least partially coextensive with the two just discussed, but described in this way emphasizes the place of the component or function in the information-flow path from input to output. The processing stage approach is noteworthy because it makes explicit the assertion that the IP framework implies or supports the existence of a great deal of unconscious processing (e.g., Erdelyi, 1985). Perhaps more important, this is the perspective that implies what Dennett (1991) called the Cartesian Theater, a processing stage or bottleneck that constitutes consciousness and that imposes seriality on processing. The idea is that the variety of information processes, proceeding at least partially in parallel and perhaps in distinct modules, must come together to provide a unified conscious experience. Very often, this view is not made explicit but is implied by the use of interface concepts in the design, conduct, and explanation of experimental research. For example, research on word recognition often depends on assumptions about whether particular effects are preperceptual or postperceptual (e.g., compare Jenkins, 1992, and Massaro, 1992). The assumption (challenged by Dennett, 1991) is that mental contents are constituted or processed either before or after a particular processing interface.

Consciousness as Epiphenomenal

Consciousness is often viewed as *epiphenomenal*, a kind of nonfunctional side effect of information processing that plays little or no causal role in cognitive activity. Cognitive scientists with a wide variety of perspectives (e.g., Cleeremans & McClelland, 1991; Harnad, 1982; MacKay, 1990; Thagard, 1986; Velmans, 1991) have advanced essentially epiphenomenalist views of consciousness. Perhaps the most sophisticated such view has been developed by Jackendoff (1987). He described the hierarchically structured accounts of cognition developed in several domains (language, perception, and music), and argued that phenomenal experience was projected from an intermediate level in each hierarchy. Thus both higher (more abstract) and lower levels of theory describe unconscious mental processes. However, Jackendoff noted that conscious experience does not seem to be required for the operation of processes even at levels corresponding to phenomenal experience.

Several things should be noted about contemporary epiphenomenalist views framed within IP theories. First, the authors generally do not adopt a strong version of epiphenomenalism, allowing instead that consciousness has some causal consequences (e.g., in supporting verbal reports). However, they do regard consciousness as a side effect of the main business of cognition. Second, such accounts generally emphasize the presumed private, ineffable phenomenology of consciousness. Dennett (1991) offered a telling analysis of this form of phenomenology, arguing that *qualia* (the ineffable feels of conscious experience) do not exist. Finally, the epiphenomenalist approach to consciousness essentially represents a rejection or abandonment of the project of developing scientific accounts of consciousness or of first-person perspective (McGinn, 1991; Velmans, 1991). Although arguments against this aspect of the view could be developed, I believe it is more fruitful to simply make the opposite assumption—that consciousness can be approached scientifically—and hope that the results of doing so justify the assumption.

Consciousness as a Dominant Action Scheme

The most promising account of consciousness in IP theory identifies it with a dominant action scheme and associated control mechanisms (e.g., Carr, 1979; Norman & Shallice, 1986). The idea is that action should be understood in terms of organized patterns that compete for activation on the basis of available environmental and internal (e.g., goals) information. The most explicit development of this theme is in the work of Shallice and Norman (Norman & Shallice, 1986; Shallice, 1978, 1991, 1994); they also proposed an executive system that handles complex scheduling and selection issues. This approach is closest to the view to be developed in this book, emphasizing the role of action in experienced cognition.

Unconscious Information Processing

All of these approaches share the implication that much of cognition is unconscious. And although it does not seem to be a necessary implication, it is a short leap to infer from one of these approaches together with the core assumptions of IP (particularly recursive decomposition) that processes much like those that make up personal-level experienced cognition occur without consciousness. For example, Erdelyi (1985) used a similar argument to conclude that IP theory is compatible with a psychodynamic view of the unconscious:

> The concept of unconscious processes—if not the term itself—was not only *not* controversial but an obvious and fundamental feature of human information processing. The modern literature is replete with synonyms such as *automatic, inaccessible,* and *preattentive,* but only rarely does the unconscious itself make an appearance. (p. 59)

Others, notably Marcel (1983), argued instead that we should resist this inference and understand unconscious mental processes as qualitatively different from conscious processes. However, this suggestion has not really been fleshed out with a informational theory of consciousness.

In the remainder of this book, I use the term *nonconscious* to refer to processes supporting cognition but not themselves conscious, in order to emphasize the qualitative difference that I believe exists between those processes and conscious mental activity. In fact, I believe that such nonconscious processes are not, properly speaking, mental at all in several important senses to be discussed later. My argument is not that cognitive scientists should be concerned only with conscious mental processes, but that accounts of nonconscious processing should be framed with respect to clear hypotheses about consciousness.

FRAMING AN INFORMATIONAL THEORY
OF CONSCIOUSNESS

> Some scientists . . . are interested in only those theories that make testable predictions right now. This would be good hard-headed policy, except for the fact that all the testable theories so far concocted are demonstrably false, and it is foolish to think that the breakthroughs of vision required to compose *new* testable theories will come out of the blue without a good deal of imaginative exploration . . . (Dennett, 1991, p. 263)

I believe that a theory of consciousness should be framed in a way compatible with the core assumptions of IP psychology, to take advantage of its strengths, while avoiding the habits of thought that prevent really getting a grip on the phenomena of experienced cognition. The important point is not compatibility with any particular existing theory, but the construction of theory with an eye toward incorporating the insights achieved by cognitive science.

Computational Explanation as a Normative Standard

Computational explanation provides a normative standard for cognitive theory that is appropriate in many ways. The specificity and rigor demanded by simulation modeling has been discussed many times (e.g., Medin & Thau, 1992). Although I am not prepared to present a working computational model of experienced cognition, I believe that is a worthy ideal. The computational view of mind does seem to solve the mind-body problem, showing us how the same process can be described both in terms of physical mechanisms and in terms of mental activity. It is worth keeping in mind, however, that the assertion "all mental activity is computation" emphatically does not imply its converse, "all computation is mental activity"—even for all computation realized in a nervous system. That might in principle turn out to be the case, but it seems that enough examples of nonmental computation can be found that we ought to avoid assuming this converse a priori. I attempt to describe how nonconscious information processes can be seen to support experienced cognition. By describing mental activity in terms of mental states, characterized by variables identified on the basis of the cospecification hypothesis, we can see some important distinctions concerning the kinds of informational processes and relations involved in experienced cognition.

Perhaps equally important, the core assumptions of the IP framework point toward a focus on real-time aspects of cognition and on the continuity and completeness of the causal stories we tell about it. Cognitive theorists have scarcely tried to understand experienced cognition by describing the stream of consciousness with the kind of continuity and completeness demanded by the IP framework. We should not expect that doing so will be easy—there are many reasons to expect limits on introspection and on our ability to infer the experience of the subjects of our research—but the IP framework suggests an ideal to which we should aspire.

Information Processing and Theoretical Realism

Cognitive scientists have differed substantially among themselves with respect to *theoretical realism*, the view that theoretical constructs correspond to real features of the system under study. One of the attractions of cognitive neuroscience is that focusing on the nervous system provides some confidence that the objects of inquiry are really there. On the other hand, in the passage quoted earlier, Mandler (1984) expressed a common view in saying that representations are (merely) theoretical constructs. Kintsch's (1992) statement makes this stance very explicit, "I, however, prefer to take a lighter view of the scientific enterprise: The goal is not to find out the real truth about how the mind works but to find useful descriptions thereof" (p. 145). These statements reflect the ambivalence that many cognitive theorists seem to feel with respect to the ontology of cognitive theory. A thorough discussion of the pros and cons of theoretical realism is beyond the scope of this discussion (but see chapters 7 and 15). However, I do want to make my own position explicit: I believe that the heuristic, antirealist approach to cognitive theory is responsible for much of the confusion concerning the status of consciousness. If the representations and processes postulated by cognitive theory are only useful descriptions it is nonsense to declare that they are descriptions of unconscious processes because they fail to correspond to intuition, introspection, or reports. In particular, this view leads to a theoretical shortchanging of consciousness by failing to distinguish theoretical representations that capture (paraphrase) the contents of conscious experience and those that do not (cf. Block, 1995; Searle, 1990).

Framing an Informational Theory of Consciousness

I believe that theoretical realism is compatible with the core assumptions of IP theory as sketched previously. Ideally, then, a theory of experienced cognition will take advantage of the strengths of the IP framework while avoiding weaknesses of some particular theories. As a working hypothesis, I would suggest that the analysis of conscious states provides a principled stopping rule for recursive decomposition. This does not imply that no finer grain of analysis will be needed, but that nonconscious processes (such as those supporting visual perception) should be viewed as qualitatively different from conscious mental activity in ways to be described in Part II.

The habits of thought discussed earlier should be seen as occasionally useful heuristics, to be adopted as stop-gap approaches when we want to abstract from the perceptual cycle (Neisser, 1976) in which experienced cognition occurs. As such, they can have substantial heuristic value. The implications of these habits of thought for our understanding of consciousness are mostly negative, however, resulting in systematic denial or neglect of important features of experienced cognition.

Phenomena of Cognitive Skill

Life is largely mundane and routine, and therefore so is most consciousness and cognition. Despite the natural inclination to emphasize our novel
and surprising mental achievements, we will understand experienced
cognition more readily by recognizing that much of our activity involves
the routine use of well-learned cognitive skills. In this chapter, I review
empirical findings on cognitive skill and discuss typical approaches to
studying such skills in the laboratory. My goal at this point is not to
establish detailed links between the experienced cognition framework and
research on cognitive skill, but to acquaint the reader with basic methods
and phenomena from this literature. My review is highly selective, focusing on those aspects of the acquisition and performance of cognitive skills
that I find most relevant to understanding experienced cognition. Proctor
and Dutta (1995) have recently provided a broader overview of research
on skill.

THE STUDY OF COGNITIVE SKILL

Given the wide range of phenomena that might be labeled *learning*, it
may be helpful to begin by characterizing the range of phenomena with
which I am concerned. By *skill*, I mean the ability to routinely, reliably,
and fluently perform goal-directed activities as a result of practice with
those activities. As implied by this definition, I take skill to be a matter
of degree. However, skill need not imply optimality—individuals can and
do learn to skillfully perform inappropriate or suboptimal routines. And,

by this definition, I mean to exclude the everyday sense in which *skill* sometimes means innate ability that does not result from practice.

By *cognitive skill*, I mean to refer primarily to performances that are cognitive in two senses: They involve or embody knowledge, and they involve the generation or manipulation of mental representations. A prototypical example of a cognitive skill, discussed in more detail later, is mental arithmetic. Cognitive skill is studied primarily in formal, symbolic domains such as arithmetic, but is continuous with perceptual-enactive skills that are exercised in ecological domains. Although I see no theoretical or empirical reason to draw sharp lines between skill, memory, and expertise, my intention is to focus on those phenomena related to increasing fluency. Changes in fluency are associated with changes in the control and experience of mental activity, and thus particularly relevant for understanding experienced cognition.

Acquiring Knowledge and Acquiring Skill

A generation ago, cognitive psychologists working in the information-processing framework had little concern with learning and skill acquisition (Langley & Simon, 1981). For example, the classic 1979 text by Lachman, Lachman, and Butterfield has no index entry for skill and treats learning (at least under that label) only as an historical topic. However, the last decade or so has seen a large increase in research and theory concerned with cognitive skill, perhaps best represented by the work of Anderson and his students (e.g., J. R. Anderson, 1982, 1987b).

Of course, cognitive psychologists have had an ongoing concern with the acquisition of knowledge, studied in domains such as comprehending discourse and solving puzzle problems. In general, such studies focus on the representation of knowledge that can be consulted or reported—that is, declarative knowledge (see later)—rather than procedural knowledge that is revealed in the performance of skilled activity. Recently, research on so-called implicit memory phenomena (e.g., Schacter, 1989) has moved research on traditional questions of memory toward performance-oriented measures of knowledge. However, there is substantial disagreement over the relation between implicit learning and memory phenomena and skill. For example, Reber (1993) wrote, "Implicit learning theory says little or nothing about skill learning" (p. 16). Others, however, have argued that skill learning and implicit memory phenomena are intimately related (e.g., Berry & Dienes, 1993).

More important for present purpose is that the majority of research on memory has relied on intuitive, common-sense models of performance (for example, assuming that instructed report of recollective experience can be modeled simply as a signal-detection process). Furthermore, much memory research involves a single exposure to information to be learned or relies on well-established knowledge (e.g., of semantic categories). My focus is instead on research that (for the most part) directly examines improvements in performance with repeated practice of some task.

Laboratory Tasks for Studying Skill Acquisition

In most research on cognitive skill, participants learn to perform well-defined tasks in formal domains such as arithmetic, geometry, programming, games, or laboratory puzzle tasks. These domains are formal in the sense that they are composed of conventional symbols interrelated by well-defined rules (although these rules may not be explicitly communicated to experimental participants). Table 3.1 lists some of the tasks that researchers have used to study the acquisition of cognitive skill. The skills required for these tasks are clearly mental in the sense that the elements

TABLE 3.1
A Partial List of Tasks Used to Study the Acquisition of Cognitive Skill

---

Arithmetic calculation routines (e.g., Carlson & Lundy, 1992; Charness & Campbell, 1988; Elio, 1986)

Mathematics word problems (e.g., Mayer, Lewis, & Hegarty, 1992; Schoenfeld & Hermann, 1982)

Geometry proofs (e.g., Koedinger & Anderson, 1990)

Device troubleshooting (e.g., Brooke & Duncan, 1983; Carlson, Khoo, Yaure, & Schneider, 1990)

Computer programming (e.g., Adelson, 1981; J. R. Anderson, Farrell, & Sauers, 1984; McKeithen, Reitman, Rueter, & Hirtle, 1981; Pennington, 1987)

Computer text editing (e.g., Bovair, Kieras, & Polson, 1990; Card, Moran, & Newell, 1980)

Device control (e.g., Berry & Broadbent, 1987; Dixon & Gabrys, 1991)

Rule-based puzzles (Anzai & Simon, 1979)

Games (chess: e.g., Chase & Simon, 1973; bridge: e.g., Charness, 1979; GO: e.g., Reitman, 1976)

Video games (e.g., Fabiani, Buckley, Gratton, Coles, Donchin, & Logie, 1989)

Mental rotation (e.g., Kail, 1986)

Diagnosing x-ray pictures (Lesgold, Rubinson, Feltovich, Glaser, Klopfer, & Wang, 1988)

Decision making (e.g., E. J. Johnson, 1988; Mitchell & Beach, 1990)

Social science word problems (Voss, Greene, Post, & Penner, 1983)

Physics word problems (e.g., Chi, Feltovich, & Glaser, 1981; Simon & Simon, 1978)

Medical problem solving (e.g., Patel & Groen, 1986)

Note. This list excludes several categories of tasks also used to study skill: laboratory tasks without close real-world analogues, language-oriented tasks (reading, writing, discourse comprehension), and tasks that are primarily perceptual-enactive in nature (e.g., tracking, keyboarding, sports). See Proctor and Dutta (1995) for a broader review of skill research.

of the domains are symbolic, and intermediate states in performance may be instantiated as representations in working memory rather than as overt activities. For example, mental arithmetic involves manipulating symbolic tokens of numbers and holding intermediate results in working memory. Nevertheless, many cognitive skills in everyday experience are not as obviously symbolic, and rely on information available in the environment or embodied in overt performances rather than as intermediate states in working memory. For example, Larkin (1989) analyzed everyday tasks such as making coffee to demonstrate the importance of what she called display-based processes in problem solving.

Some have criticized researchers' reliance on formal tasks on the basis that they misrepresent everyday cognitive activity (e.g., Brown, Collins, & Duguid, 1989; Lave, 1988), so it is worthwhile to reflect on the costs and benefits of using such tasks. J. R. Anderson (1987a) argued that formal domains provide several methodological advantages for studying cognitive skill, including tractability in the laboratory. Essentially all research on cognitive processes relies on (at least implicit) normative models of performance (see chapter 11), so there is some advantage in using tasks that allow detailed and explicit formulation of correct performance. Furthermore, some aspects of experimental participants' experience can often be inferred from normative models (for example, that an individual is mentally representing a particular problem state). The cost of studying skills in formal domains is often thought to be that such skills are unrepresentative of cognition outside the laboratory.

Formal domains do provide conventional, thus shared, examples of skills that are primarily mental in the sense that representations encoded in artifacts such as language and arithmetic symbols are objects of manipulation. Conventional symbolic systems such as arithmetic provide relatively well-defined mediums in which skills are exercised. Symbolic skills exercised in formal domains are ubiquitous, and in my view, much of the research on everyday cognition demonstrates mostly that many such skills are exercised in symbolic mediums that are idiosyncratic (or in any case, less widely shared than the conventional skills often studied). Laboratory research on cognitive skill has many shortcomings, but the problem is not so much the use of conventional formal domains as disregard for the goals that symbolic skills serve in real life.

Mental and Perceptual-Enactive Skills

Skills that are primarily mental have much in common with skills that are primarily perceptual-enactive in character. Both categories of skill are cognitive, in the sense that knowledge is reflected or expressed in skilled performance. One thread of my argument in this book is that mental activity should be understood as grounded in perceptual-enactive per-formances, and I develop that theme at greater length in later chapters. First, however, let us consider some differences and relations between these two traditionally separate categories of skill.

Perceptual-enactive skills are those that involve movement in and physical action on the environment, guided by information currently available to perception. I use the term *enactive* rather than *motor* to em-phasize the cognitive, intentional character of such skills. Skills that are primarily perceptual-enactive differ from skills that are primarily mental in several ways. First, the normative standards by which perceptual-en-active performances are judged often involve more or different parameters than do the standards for mental skills. Consider skill in tracking tasks (e.g., Pew, 1966). In these tasks, participants manipulate an object—a pen, a computer mouse, joystick, or keys that control a computer-screen cur-sor—so that its movements (or the movements of a display it controls) correspond to a standard, which is usually continuously visible. A typical modern implementation might require individuals to keep a cursor dis-played on a computer screen centered on a moving target by manipulating a joystick. Performance quality is judged by the discrepancy between achieved and desired location of the cursor, usually monitored at frequent intervals (from the participant's point of view, monitoring may be effec-tively continuous). The standard of appropriate performance thus in-volves many intermediate states, rather than a single end state as in most problem-solving tasks (e.g., the goal of mental arithmetic is usually simply to get the correct answer at the end of the process). Or consider playing a musical instrument (or speaking)—not only is an appropriate sequence of states or actions required, so is appropriate timing within the sequence. The goal is not simply to play the final note as soon as possible! In many experiments with mental problem-solving tasks, participants are urged to respond as quickly as possible, but rarely to produce intermediate steps to some temporal criteria.

A second difference between skills that are primarily mental and those that are primarily perceptual-enactive is the degree and nature of concur-rent informational support from the environment. In many perceptual-en-active skills, performance is essentially continuously supported by infor-mation available to perception, which specifies the course of performance relative to standards defined over space and time. There are really two points here: First, in perceptual-enactive skills, feedback is usually available for many intermediate stages of performance, if not continuously. Second, perceptual-enactive skills are necessarily organized in space and time.

These differences between mental and perceptual-enactive skills are matters of degree. Larkin (1989), for example, emphasized the environ-mental support for everyday problem-solving tasks, and field research on everyday cognitive activities illustrates that in real life, problem-solving individuals often rely on properties of the environment rather than symbolic representations (e.g., Lave, 1988). More important, perceptual-enactive skills studied in the laboratory demonstrate many of the same phenomena discussed later for mental skills (Proctor & Dutta, 1995). Some work in my laboratory demonstrates that phenomena discovered in perceptual-enactive skills can also be found in mental skills (e.g., Carlson & Yaure, 1990).

I intend to focus primarily on mental skills, mostly those that involve multiple steps to achieve some symbolic result. A prototype example is mental arithmetic with multiple-digit numbers. Such skills are characterized by *cascaded* structure, in that the result of one step serves as an input to (operand for) a subsequent step. This in turn implies a hierarchical *goal structure* (see chapter 9), in which one step is performed in order to meet the conditions for performing another. Novice performance of such skills can be described in the classic *problem space* notation developed by Newell and Simon (e.g., 1972). This notation and the surrounding theory make essentially no reference, however, to issues such as timing and coordination that are very salient in the study of perceptual-enactive skills. In later chapters, I argue that these considerations are also important in understanding mental skills from the experienced cognition perspective.

Before beginning our brief survey of the phenomena of cognitive skill, it is worth distinguishing the notion of skill from that of expertise (also see chapter 12). Beginning in the 1970s, cognitive researchers published a great deal of work comparing expert and novice performance in a variety of (mostly formal, in the sense discussed) domains (Chi, Glaser, & Farr, 1988). For example, Larkin and her colleagues (e.g., Larkin, McDermott, Simon, & Simon, 1980) analyzed differences in the performance of experts (professors) and novices (beginning students) solving textbook physics problems. In these studies, experts differed from novices both in global performance measures (e.g., solution time) and in the organization of their performances.

Skill is a narrower and better-defined concept than *expertise*. We can probably do without a formal definition of *skill* (cf. Proctor & Dutta, 1995), but generally I use the term to refer to fluent performance within a fairly narrow task domain. In this sense, experts usually have a number of related skills, together with high-level strategic or metacognitive knowledge that may or may not accompany skill. The two concepts have in fact generated largely separate literatures. For example, the analysis of learning curves is rare in the study of expertise because researchers have generally taken a cross-sectional approach to comparing experts and novices. In the area of skill acquisition, however, examination of learning curves has been a major part of many researchers' empirical and theoretical efforts. Of course, many phenomena are common to both literatures, and I have occasion to refer to both.

Declarative and Procedural Knowledge

A basic distinction in cognitive theory (and elsewhere; e.g., Polanyi, 1958) is that between *declarative* knowledge that can be consulted and *procedural* knowledge that must be enacted to be used. Declarative knowledge is generally considered to be organized in terms of propositions (assertion-like units) that are distinct from their referents and from performances involving their referents. More simply, declarative knowledge can be more-or-less adequately paraphrased by sentences or (somewhat more controversially) depicted by images. Examples of declarative knowledge include the contents of my current beliefs that { *Today is Monday* } or { *Squirrels have bushy tails* }.

Procedural knowledge must be enacted rather than consulted or described. A classic example is knowing how to ride a bicycle. The distinction is sometimes described as the difference between *knowing that* (declarative knowledge) and *knowing how* (procedural knowledge). I argue later that declarative knowledge also has a performatory aspect (also see chapter 1), because symbols involve acts of representing. However, such acts of representing involve a distinction between knowledge and performances involving the objects of knowledge, allowing declarative knowledge to be consulted (see chapter 5). The classification of knowledge into procedural and declarative will provide a useful heuristic distinction, and it is hard to see how cognitive theory can avoid this or a similar distinction (J. R. Anderson, 1993).

I am concerned here primarily with the procedural knowledge that supports mental skill. Some theorists, notably J. R. Anderson (e.g., 1983), argue that performing a mental skill necessarily involves the interplay of declarative and procedural knowledge. From this point of view, practice involves changes in both declarative and procedural knowledge, and in their interaction. Others have argued that at least some skills need not involve declarative representation (e.g., Nissen & Bullemer, 1987), or that all mental activities should be seen as primarily procedural (e.g., Crowder, 1993b; Kolers & Roediger, 1984). In the remainder of this chapter, I assume (where it matters) that Anderson is correct on this point, that skilled performance generally involves both declarative and procedural knowledge.

HOW TO DO IT: STRATEGIES
AND COORDINATIVE MODES

The first issue for understanding cognitive skill concerns how individuals discover strategies or routines that allow cognitive tasks to be performed at all. This question is rarely studied as a skill acquisition issue in adults,

although it is the topic of much problem-solving research in which experimental participants solve one or two problems of a particular type.
Some research has addressed how children discover or construct strategies
for cognitive skills such as arithmetic that are routine for adults. It seems
obvious that over the course of a lifetime, most if not all cases of skill
acquisition involve assembling previously learned routines or component
skills into larger routines that accomplish more complex or more refined
tasks (e.g., Case, 1985). In this section, I consider how this might be
accomplished, considering the new routines as coordinative modes for
integrating already-learned component skills.

Mental Routines as Coordinative Modes

It is common to talk about the pattern of mental activity that solves a
problem or achieves a goal as a *strategy*, but this term carries the unfortunate connotation that the choice of subgoals or component skills follows
from a deliberate, metacognitive decision process. I therefore use the
phrase *mental routine* as a generic term for patterned, multistep mental
activities that accomplish goals. Mental addition of two-digit numbers
provides an example of a mental routine. One routine for this task goes
something like this: Add the ones digits, hold the result, carry if the result
is greater than 10, add the tens digit (plus the carry digit if there is one),
and place the results in the appropriate columns. This routine can be
described more precisely as a set of productions, or if–then rules, as shown
in Table 3.2. Other routines are possible, and most adults can use a variety
of routines to perform this task. For example, one might add the tens

TABLE 3.2
Production Rules for Multiple-Digit Addition

The set of rules presented here works only for problems with no carries; J. R. Anderson
presents a somewhat more complex set of rules that works for problems with or without
carries.

1.	IF		The goal is to solve an addition problem
		AND	Column x is the rightmost column without an answer digit
	THEN		Set a subgoal to write an answer digit in Column x
2.	IF		The goal is to write an answer digit in Column x
		AND	Digit A and Digit B are the digits in that column
		AND	The sum of A and B is C
	THEN		Set a subgoal to write C in Column x
3.	IF		The goal is to write C in Column x
	THEN		Write C in Column x
		AND	The goal to write an answer digit is satisfied

Note. Adapted from J. R. Anderson (1993, p. 5).

column first or begin by rounding one number to the nearest ten while holding the rounding amount.

As this example shows, a mental routine is an arrangement of component skills—here, using the addition facts and managing intermediate results in working memory—that accomplishes a goal. The routine may be theoretically represented as a goal structure, emphasizing that many of the steps are performed in order to make it possible to perform others. In chapter 9, I have much to say about goal structures and their psychological significance.

Here, I want to emphasize another aspect of mental routines that is especially relevant to their discovery or construction as a first step in skill acquisition. This aspect is that mental routines, much as movement routines, can be usefully viewed as coordinative modes, a concept drawn from the dynamical systems approach to movement skills (e.g., K. Newell, 1991). To begin with, consider why coordination is a central issue in the performance of movement skills. In order to perform a (phenomenologically) simple action such as reaching for a glass of wine, the movements of a number of muscles and joints must be coordinated in time, force, and extent. Furthermore, these movements must be coordinated with aspects of the environment. A central tenet of the dynamical systems approach to movement control is that some elements of the musculoskeletal system are joined in mutually constraining coordinative structures. A coordinative mode is a way of using a coordinative structure to perform an activity; for example, different gaits such as walking or running are alternative coordinative modes for locomotion. A more extensive discussion of the concept of coordinative modes is beyond the scope of this chapter, but this brief sketch is sufficient for our purposes.

My central point is that just as the elements of the movement system constitute a coordinative structure that must be used in some coordinative mode to accomplish a task, so too do the elements constituting a mental routine. The constraints that must be satisfied to perform a mental routine include limits on the availability of information in the environment and on the duration of working memory, as well as the rate and reliability of mental processes. For example, the routines used by adults to perform tasks such as, "Find the sum of 67 and 35," depend on the availability of the addends (e.g., to vision or hearing, then perhaps in working memory), the availability and speed of routines for performing individual steps (e.g., retrieving 12 as the sum of 7 and 5), and the ability to maintain intermediate results and their roles in the routine (e.g., 12 as the sum of the ones digits). To perform this task fluently requires also that such elements be temporally coordinated; for example, adding the tens column requires that the result of adding the ones column be available so that the carry can be performed.

In a moment we look at the example of routines for mental arithmetic in more detail. Our sketch so far should be sufficient to make the main point: In both perceptual-enactive and mental routines, the choice and timing of component skills constitute coordinative modes. These modes are patterns for performing mutually constraining elements so that the routine as a whole can be executed fluently—smoothly and quickly, without failures of placekeeping or loss of intermediate results.

An Illustration: The Medium and Routines for Arithmetic

The domain of arithmetic provides an illustrative case that will help us understand the idea that mental routines are coordinative modes. I focus on simple integer arithmetic, but the ideas developed are general to a variety of symbolic domains. First, consider the medium for exercising skill in arithmetic. Abstracted from its realization in the knowledge and skills of individuals, arithmetic may be viewed as a symbol system that is truth-preserving in the sense that operations on representations in the system correspond to operations on the represented states of affairs. For example, counting the numbers of men and of women in a room (thus symbolically encoding states of affairs) and adding the results (an operation in a symbolic domain) gives an answer that corresponds to the total number of people in the room. The symbol system that supports such operations may be described in terms of a vocabulary of symbols (the digits) and formal rules for composing them into complex representations (e.g., 327) and for operating on these representations (see Haugeland, 1985, for a more complete discussion of symbol systems).

From the point of view of cognitive theory, of course, a symbol system must be realized in the abilities of an individual. This observation implies that the truth-preserving character of the symbol system must be grounded in the evolutionary or developmental history of the individual (Harnad, 1990; also see chapter 5). More immediately, we can view the realization of the medium for arithmetic as a repertory of procedures for producing and manipulating the symbols involved. For example, adults can generally use the arithmetic facts (such as $5 + 3 = 8$) by performing single-step memory retrievals (e.g., Logan, 1988). The component skills for arithmetic thus correspond to particular operations within the symbolic medium.

We often perform complex, real-life arithmetic tasks—such as balancing a checkbook or calculating an average—with the aid of external devices such as calculators or pencil and paper. Nevertheless, adults typically have routines for performing mental arithmetic, in which operations are performed mentally and intermediate results are held in working memory rather than stored externally. One such routine was described earlier (see

Table 3.2). The constraints on these performances include the time required to execute component skills, the availability of operands at particular points in time, and the limited means available for remembering intermediate results and placekeeping information.

The point of describing a routine for mental arithmetic as a coordinative mode is that the routine constitutes an arrangement of component skills—arranged in terms of their temporal relations with one another—such that these constraints can be met and the routine fluently performed. Consider the routine specified by the rules in Table 3.2. These rules represent one kind of constraint on the organization of component skills, that the ordering of steps must be such that the information needed for a particular step be calculated before that step is performed. This is just the flow continuity assumption discussed in chapter 2, expressed at the level of conscious problem-solving steps. Less explicit are the constraints that such information must remain available in working memory at the time it is needed, and that the processes operating on it must correctly distinguish it from other information that is also available. And although the references to goals in the production rules of Table 3.2 make placekeeping explicit within this routine, placekeeping can be a significant difficulty even in very simple tasks. For example, Healy and Nairne (1985) documented placekeeping errors in simple counting tasks; the form of these errors (e.g., repeating or skipping a number) suggested that individuals failed to distinguish just-spoken numbers from intentions to speak numbers.

A successful mental routine thus serves as a coordinative mode in that it specifies the relative order and timing of component skills to meet a set of constraints on performance. Violations of well-learned routines—forced on experimental participants by, for example, requiring an unnatural or nonpreferred order of picking up information or of reporting results—create additional cognitive demands and may result in substantial decrements in performance. For example, Hitch (1978) demonstrated that forcing individuals to violate their preferred routines for multiple-digit arithmetic created additional working memory demands. In later chapters, I discuss several aspects of mental routines in detail.

How Mental Routines Are Generated

Routines for complex mental activities such as problem solving appear to be generated or discovered in two main ways. First, individuals may apply weak methods for problem solving, constructing routines on the fly by consulting declarative knowledge of the constraints on performance. Second, they may develop routines on the basis of examples, often called analogies when the surface content of problems differs.

Weak-method problem solving (Newell & Simon, 1972) captures the abstract structure of processes by which individuals discover coordinative modes in unfamiliar domains. The simplest weak method is trial-and-error—in some cases, individuals may simply perform an action or series of actions, abandoning them if the desired result is not achieved. More sophisticated, and much-analyzed, weak methods include *hill-climbing* and *means–ends analysis*. These strategies are weak in the sense that they do not make use of procedural knowledge of the problem domain, depending instead on very general notions of causal reasoning (see chapter 10).

More recent research suggests that much of the discovery or construction of strategies depends on the use of analogies or examples. For example, J. R. Anderson (e.g., 1993) demonstrated that novices learning to program in LISP base their performance on available examples of LISP code. In his view, the use of examples to generate new routines depends on the application of relatively general-purpose procedural knowledge to task-specific declarative knowledge. This view is consistent with a standard interpretation that relatively unskilled performance depends heavily on declarative knowledge (J. R. Anderson, 1982), a view that has been challenged (chapter 5; Karmiloff-Smith, 1994).

EFFECTS OF PRACTICE

The notion of skill is intimately related to the concept of *practice*, repeated performance of the same (or closely similar) routines. Although it was once commonly believed that practicing cognitive tasks resulted in the development of very general abilities or faculties, most cognitive theorists now believe that practice has relatively narrow and specific effects (Singley & J. R. Anderson, 1989). Most research has therefore focused on the effects of practice on specific tasks or task domains. This research demonstrates that practice has several kinds of effect on the performance of cognitive skills, resulting in (a) increases in fluency, (b) changes in the perceptual and cognitive units involved in task performance, and (c) changes in the control processes and structures that guide performance.

Consistency and Practice

Perhaps the most powerful variable influencing the acquisition of cognitive skill is the *consistency* of practice, the degree to which repeated trials evoke the same mental processes. Consistency can be manipulated (and thus operationally defined) in a variety of ways, which have in common the establishment of trial-to-trial correspondences between information available in the practice situation (e.g., the displays presented to experimental participants) and goal-directed actions based on that information (e.g., the answers or responses required by experimental instructions). These correspondences sometimes involve identity over trials in the particular display elements presented to, and physical actions required of, participants. However, the correspondences may also be more abstract, involving relational properties of display elements that vary from trial to trial (e.g., Fisk, Oransky, & Skedsvold, 1988; Kramer, Strayer, & Buckley, 1990), or sequences of operations performed on data that vary from trial to trial (e.g., Carlson & Lundy, 1992). The term *consistency* is perhaps best seen as describing a category of experimental manipulations that serve to establish regularities in task environments or in mental processes (also see chapter 12).

A series of studies conducted by Schneider and Shiffrin (1977; Shiffrin & Schneider, 1977) illustrates the notion of consistency and has stimulated a great deal of research on the topic. Schneider and Shiffrin demonstrated that individuals performing *search tasks*—searching for a particular symbolic element such as a letter or digit in an array of such elements displayed or held in memory—improved much more with practice if the task was consistently mapped (CM). In one version of this task, the individual is told to press a key when a particular letter appears among other letters in a series of rapidly changing visual displays. Consistent mapping means that a particular element—say the letter *T*—always plays the same role in the task, serving on every trial as the *target* element to be detected or as a *distractor* element to be ignored. In a task that is *variably mapped* (VM), in contrast, the same element may appear on some trials as a target and on others as a distractor. A CM search task thus involves a correspondence from trial to trial between a display element and a response, whereas this correspondence does not hold for a VM search task.

The most important conclusion of these and related studies (see Shiffrin & Dumais, 1981, for a review) is that consistent mapping results in search performance that appears to be automatic. Shiffrin and Schneider (1977) contrasted automatic processes, said to be fast, effortless, and parallel, with controlled processes, said to be slow, effortful, and serial. A variety of evidence supported this characterization. For example, novice performance and performance after VM practice shows *set size effects*—the time to detect a target increases systematically with the number of items being searched, suggesting that individuals examine items one by one. After CM practice, however, set size effects are dramatically reduced, suggesting that subjects examine all items at the same time, in parallel. In addition, automatic processes are sometimes said to be unconscious, whereas controlled processes are conscious; I return to this issue in chapter 15.

The neat picture presented by Schneider and Shiffrin has since become much more complex, and their concept of automaticity has been challenged (e.g., Cheng, 1985) and elaborated (e.g., Bargh, 1989, 1992). However, their work established the importance of consistency in determining the effects of practice. Furthermore, they showed that the concept of consistency can be distinguished from the simple frequency with which a particular display–response relation is practiced, a result that also holds for much more complex and abstract definitions of consistency (e.g., Wenger & Carlson, 1995).

Practice Increases Fluency

Perhaps the most ubiquitous effect of practice is increased fluency. In laboratory tasks and many real-life situations, fluency is reflected largely in speed of performance. Practice typically results in a speedup in performance that follows approximately a power function, with large speedups from trial to trial early in practice and smaller speedups with additional practice. Figure 3.1 shows a fairly typical learning curve in terms of time to perform a cognitive task, illustrating this speedup with practice, with a power function fitted to average data points.

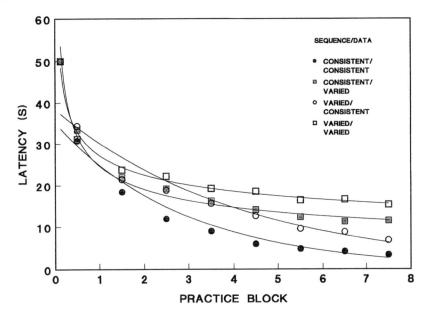

FIG. 3.1. Typical learning curves: This figure presents the average time required for learners to perform arithmetic routines in an experiment conducted by Carlson and Lundy (1992). The sequence in which participants performed the steps of a routine was consistent or varied over trials, as were the data on which they performed calculations. The curves fitted to the results from varied-data conditions are based on power functions, whereas the steeper curves fitted to consistent-data conditions are based on exponential functions.

A. Newell and Rosenbloom (1981) argued that this typical result should be viewed as a general law of learning. This, the power law of practice, is described by the equation

$$T = a + bN^{-c},$$

where T is time to perform the task, a is the asymptotic (i.e., shortest possible) time required, b represents the total amount of speedup possible, N is the number of practice trials, and the exponent c represents the rate of learning. They surveyed evidence from a variety of domains, concluding that the general power law described the effects of practice better than alternatives such as an exponential function. Power-law speedup has been explained in a variety of ways, and Newell and Rosenbloom surveyed the range of abstract possibilities. Their own explanation, essentially similar to the more sophisticated account developed in Newell's (1990) Soar theory, was based on *chunking*. The general idea is that practice results in the creation of larger chunks—knowledge units of greater scope—and that the speed of performance depends largely on the number of independently specified chunks to be executed. At the other extreme, MacKay (1982) described mechanisms for speedup that depend entirely on faster execution of the components making up a routine. The available accounts of speedup can thus be classified on the basis of whether they emphasize changes in the content or noncontent properties of cognitive units, a distinction to be elaborated in Part II. Some theorists (e.g., J. R. Anderson, 1983, 1993) suggest that the speedup in performance with practice results from a combination of content and noncontent changes.

There is little doubt that speedup is a very common result of practice in both mental and perceptual-enactive tasks. However, the generality of Newell and Rosenbloom's (1981) power law of practice has been challenged on a variety of grounds. K. Newell (1991), for example, argued that in many cases of perceptual-motor skill, performance improvements must be described in terms of parameters other than speed, and that the improvement noted in these parameters often does not obey a power function. For example, discovering a coordinative mode for a movement skill such as shooting baskets may result in a sudden improvement in performance. In a problem-solving domain, troubleshooting simulated electronic circuits, Carlson et al. (1990) noted continuing improvement in performance parameters such as simulated cost after solution time was essentially asymptotic. And in a study of the effects of practice on mental arithmetic routines, Lundy and I (Carlson & Lundy, 1992) found evidence that the mathematical form of the speedup may depend on the conditions of practice. Specifically, under conditions in which the data to be manipulated were consistent—allowing replacement of the multiple-step calculation routine with memory retrieval—the learning curve was better fit by the steeper exponential function than by a power function. The power function provided a better fit than the exponential in conditions in which a consistent sequence of operations was performed on data that varied from trial to trial, however.

Some form of negatively accelerated speedup is common, then, but there is reason to doubt the generality of the power law. Perhaps more important, there are many skills for which faster is not necessarily better—consider public speaking or musical performance, for instance. There is every reason to think that practice produces increased fluency in these tasks as well, but less easily measured characteristics such as smoothness of performance—maintaining appropriate timing and rhythmicity—are more appropriate than simple speed. Research on cognitive skill has almost always employed speed as a goal parameter, however, and the general finding of negatively accelerated speedup is sufficient to raise the issue of the units of cognitive skill and how they can support particular coordinative modes.

Practice Changes Cognitive Units

A great deal of evidence points to the conclusion that practice changes the cognitive units into which skill is organized. For example, children just learning the addition facts organize their performance around counting steps, adopting routines to coordinate these component skills with task demands (Resnick, 1989). After a moderate amount of practice, children typically adopt a *min* strategy for addition, counting on from the larger addend for the number of steps specified by the smaller (min) addend and reporting the last number they reach as the solution. Adults, however, organize their addition performance around steps corresponding to single-step memory retrievals of the addition facts (although these single-step retrievals may have internal structure; see chapter 13).

Generally, then, practice results in the *restructuring* of mental routines. The stepwise organization of naive performance is replaced by more efficient organizations that may comprise larger units of knowledge. The concept of *chunking* is a general and classical approach to understanding changes in performance (Miller, 1956; A. Newell, 1990). Some researchers have presented relatively direct evidence for chunking. For example, Chase and Ericsson (1982), following earlier work by DeGroot (1965), demonstrated that expert chess players organized their perception of and memory for board positions on the basis of configurations meaningful in terms of chess games.

Some authors (e.g., J. R. Anderson, 1982; Rosenbloom & Newell, 1987) have suggested that restructuring is an automatic consequence of practice.

However, much evidence suggests that restructuring is not inevitable (e.g., Carlson & Schneider, 1989b; Carlson, Sullivan, & Schneider, 1989b; Elio, 1986; Lewis, 1981). Other evidence suggests that many cases of restructuring are strategic, based on deliberate consideration of how possible organizations of component skills are related to parameters of ideal performance (e.g., Carlson et al., 1990). It seems likely, on the basis of the range of evidence currently available, that restructuring is strategic except in some cases in which a multistep algorithm can be replaced by memory retrieval. In such cases, both learning and using solutions that can be retrieved from memory may be a relatively automatic consequence of practice (Logan, 1988; Logan & Etherton, 1994).

Regardless of the precise mechanism by which it occurs, it is clear that skilled performance depends on different units than does naive performance. This conclusion is supported by a number of observations that *transfer*—the effect of practicing one task on performance of another—is very narrow. For example, Anderson and his colleagues have reported that learning to evaluate LISP code results in little if any transfer to generating LISP code (J. R. Anderson, 1993; McKendree & J. R. Anderson, 1987; Singley & J. R. Anderson, 1989). Positive transfer, the beneficial effect of practicing one task on performing another, generally depends on partial identity (or at least close similarity) between the tasks (see Cormier & Hagman, 1987, and Singley & J. R. Anderson, 1989, for reviews). The narrow scope of transfer found in many cases demonstrates that skill depends on changes in the units of knowledge or activity, and suggests that these units are procedural in that they are use-specific.

Practice Changes Control Processes

Practice also results in changes in the control processes and control structures that guide performance. (By *control structure*, I just mean the organization of whatever processes control performance.) Some of these changes correspond in a straightforward manner to changes in the units of skill—for example, different control structures are obviously required for addition by counting and by memory retrieval. Some changes in control may result from noncontent changes in the cognitive units that make up a skilled routine. For example, the apparent shift from serial, item-by-item comparison to parallel consideration of all items with practice in consistently mapped search tasks reflects a major change in how performance is controlled. Schneider (e.g., Schneider & Detweiler, 1987) suggested that this shift may be possible in part because consistently mapped target elements come to automatically attract attention, obviating the need for controlled search.

There is also evidence that some processes that serve as component skills for higher-order skills become autonomous or ballistic in character.

For example, Logan and his colleagues (Logan & Cowan, 1984; Zbrodoff & Logan, 1986) used a *stop-signal paradigm* to study the control of processes such as simple arithmetic and word recognition. In this paradigm, subjects are instructed to generate answers (e.g., sums) to displayed items as quickly as possible, unless a signal to stop the response appears. As the delay between the display of an item and the stop signal increases, it becomes increasingly difficult to stop the response. By assessing memory for the displayed items and their answers, Logan adduced evidence that in some cases participants can stop their overt responses but not the thoughts guiding those responses. And in some cases, even a prior intention is insufficient to stop a mental process. For example, in the well-known *Stroop task*, individuals are asked to name either a color word (e.g., green) or the color in which the word is displayed. When asked to name the color in which an incongruent word appears (e.g., "green" printed in red ink), individuals apparently cannot avoid reading the word, which interferes with the color-naming task.

A process such as word recognition can thus be described as *autonomous*, in that it is apparently initiated without (or against) intention. Although this conclusion is not without its difficulties—for example, the evidence for it usually comes from tasks in which a to-be-ignored item has obvious relevance to the instructed task—it seems likely that at least some mental processes are autonomous in this sense, and that in at least some cases, this autonomy is acquired rather than innate. Perhaps more important from the point of view of real-life skill is that some processes can be completed ballistically once they are intentionally initiated. That is, conscious control is required only to begin the process, not to complete it. It is important to note two versions of this idea: In the stronger version, the notion is that once initiated, the process cannot be controlled or stopped (e.g., Logan, 1985, 1989). A weaker version that is likely more relevant to the assembly of complex routines is that although the process could be controlled once initiated, it is not necessary to do so. These changes are often interpreted as a reduced involvement of consciousness, but should be viewed as changes in how individuals are aware in skilled performance (I return to these issues in chapter 13).

CONSCIOUSNESS AND COGNITIVE SKILL

Intuition and common sense suggest a link between consciousness and learning, and that the role of consciousness in performing particular tasks changes with practice. Thus we exhort our students or children to pay attention in order to learn, and talk about the unconscious performance of highly skilled activities such as driving a familiar route. Although the topic of learning without awareness has appeared in the literature repeatedly over at least the past 40 years (e.g., Brewer, 1974; Carlson & Dulany, 1985; Dulany, 1957, 1968; Dulany, Carlson, & Dewey, 1984; Eriksen, 1962; Shanks & St. John, 1994), I know of no comprehensive treatment of the role of consciousness at various stages of learning. In later chapters, I address these issues in a variety of ways after developing the experienced cognition framework in greater detail. Here I sketch a preliminary approach, adopting a relatively nonanalytic stance toward consciousness (i.e., considering consciousness only in the sense of accessible content).

Researchers have often failed to distinguish between awareness during learning and retrospective awareness of what was learned, or between awareness of information being learned and metacognitive awareness that something is being learned. The phenomena of cognitive skill briefly reviewed suggests that it is important to understand the role of consciousness in cognitive skill by considering consciousness during acquisition, consciousness of acquired skills, and consciousness during fluent performance.

Consciousness in Early Skill Acquisition

Many authors have noted the intuitive link between consciousness and early stages of learning. As MacKay (1990) put it,

> The close relationship between consciousness and novelty has frequently been noted ... Consciousness seems necessary and sufficient for learning novel information: we normally become conscious of what is new, and what is old or frequently repeated drops out of awareness, as in habituation. (p. 279)

Later we examine this link in more detail, on the basis of the understanding of consciousness to be developed in Part II. For now, note that there are at least two questions about the role of consciousness early in learning. As Dulany and I (Carlson & Dulany, 1985) put it, "Intuition tells us that consciousness plays an essential role in learning: We learn when we pay attention and when we can consciously represent the regularities in our world" (p. 45). That is, acquisition of cognitive skill is conscious in the sense that appropriate environmental information must be attended, and we must be conscious of the relations or contingencies among environmental events and our actions in order to learn them. A third sense of consciousness in early phases of skill acquisition is intention to learn; that is, that learning requires not just consciousness of environmental information and its role in a goal-directed process, but also an intention to learn on that basis.

Researchers have addressed each of these senses of consciousness in learning, often concluding that learning without awareness in one or more senses is possible. The first two conclusions—that learning may occur without awareness of relevant environmental information, and that learning may occur without awareness of relevant contingencies—remain controversial. The third conclusion—that learning may occur without a corresponding intention to learn—is, in my view, clearly established. On my reading of the evidence, however, neither of the first two conclusions is established (for reviews, see Brewer, 1974; Eriksen, 1962; Shanks & St. John, 1994). In fact, I believe that both are likely false, for reasons that are easier to discuss later in the book (see chapter 15). Not only has most research on these questions failed to meet appropriate methodological criteria (Carlson, 1994; Carlson & Dulany, 1985), most research has not been based on sufficiently clear conceptions of consciousness to make clear exactly what hypotheses are being rejected.

More important at the moment is that even researchers who have concluded that learning without awareness is possible have demonstrated that consciousness is critical in determining the course of early stages of skill acquisition. In attempting to demonstrate learning without awareness, researchers have shown that subjects' beliefs, intentions, and strategies have substantial effects on the knowledge and skills they acquire.

Metacognitive Awareness of Acquired Skills

Another sense of consciousness in cognitive skill involves individuals' metacognitive awareness of acquired skills. Such awareness is often possible, and presumably necessary for strategic restructuring of cognitive routines (e.g., Carlson et al., 1990). However, it is notoriously difficult to extract reliable introspections from experts, and it seems very unlikely that cognitive skill is necessarily accompanied by any detailed metacognitive awareness. In at least some cases, laboratory research supports the conclusion that the knowledge supporting skilled performance is accessible only by performing the skill, and cannot otherwise be consulted. For example, Nissen and her colleagues (e.g., Willingham, Nissen, & Bullemer, 1989) demonstrated that subjects at least have great difficulty in accessing their knowledge of perceptual-motor sequences for instructed report rather than by performing those sequences in the context in which they were learned. This lack of metacognitive access is sometimes taken as evidence for unconscious learning.

Streamlining Conscious Control

A final sense of consciousness in cognitive skill is concerned with conscious control of mental routines. With increasing skill, it appears that conscious control is streamlined as performance depends on different or larger units of information. In my view, experienced cognition is best understood by asking not whether this or that is conscious or not, but by asking how an individual is conscious in the course of a particular performance. As the units of knowledge and performance change with practice, the experience of skilled performance also changes. Researchers are beginning to realize that even so-called automatic processes are in fact under control in some sense (e.g., Bargh, 1989; Jacoby, Ste-Marie, & Toth, 1993; Logan, 1992).

In chapter 13, I sketch a theory of conscious control that emphasizes the performatory character of skilled cognition and describes consciousness during skilled performance in terms of the conditions for cospecification and egolocative processing. First, however, I develop the experienced cognition framework in much greater detail.

THE STRUCTURE OF CONSCIOUSNESS AND THE ARCHITECTURE OF THE MIND

The experienced cognition framework draws together a means of describing awareness that shows the continuities among perceptual-enactive, symbolic, and emotional experience. The purpose of this part of the book is to make the case that the same formal structure characterizes each of these aspects of experienced cognition. That formal structure describes the intentionality of conscious mental states—that each mental state comprises an individual self experiencing some content in some psychological mode, directed at some object or state of affairs. Analyzing the intentional structure of conscious mental states provides a set of variables for theoretical descriptions of experienced cognition. The co-specification hypothesis guides this analysis, suggesting approaches to understanding how states with symbolic content are grounded in perceptual-enactive experience and how emotionality and cognition can be integrated in a single theoretical framework. The analysis of experienced cognition in terms of intentional structure can be reconciled with standard information processing theory by considering the relations of conscious mental states to the nonconscious information systems that support them, a topic addressed in chapter 7.

The account sketched in these chapters is an attempt to address the homunculus problem while avoiding the absent-agent or implicit-agent approaches critiqued in chapter

2. The central idea is that the cospecification hypothesis provides an informational account of the experiencing self. This account is integral to the analysis of intentionality that provides a theoretical context for describing conscious mental states.

Perceptual and Enactive Awareness

People perceive in order to move and move in order to perceive. What, then, is movement but a form of perception, a way of knowing the world as well as acting on it?

—Thelen, 1995, p. 89

EXPERIENCE AND PERCEPTUALLY GUIDED ACTION

Surely a primary fact about human consciousness is that each of us is bodily present in an environment with which we are constantly in reciprocal interaction. The primary form of experienced cognition is thus a perceptually guided action in a natural environment (e.g., Thompson, Palacios, & Varela, 1992). In this chapter, I discuss the structure of conscious states that are primarily perceptual and enactive, rather than symbolic, in character. These states exhibit the structure that supports cospecification and other properties of conscious states generally, allowing us to see how more complex, symbolic forms of experienced cognition are grounded in perceptual-enactive experience. Understanding this structure also requires that we address some fundamental issues about the description of the mental states that make up our experience. A starting point is a long-standing debate concerning the relation between perceptual experience and the information that supports it.

Ecological and Establishment Stories About Perception

When James Gibson wrote his classic books (1966, 1979), presenting his ecological theory of perception, the standard theory of perception with which he contrasted his approach was derived from a long philosophical

69

tradition by way of Helmholtz (Rock, 1983). This traditional story about perception began with *sense data*, the presumed basic input from the sense organs (the eye, the ear), and described a process of unconscious inference that produced *percepts*, conceived essentially as conscious experiences of the environment. For example, the momentary two-dimensional retinal image was said to provide premises for a reasoning process yielding as a conclusion visual perception of *depth* (that is, distance from the observer). A modern version of this approach can be found in Rock (1983). Although current computational approaches to perception (e.g., Pinker, 1984) vary in how well they fit this caricature, such approaches generally have more in common with the unconscious inference tradition than with Gibson's ecological approach. In particular, these approaches generally assume that the perceptual systems must derive perceptual experience by computation that begins with input that is spatially and temporally *punctate* (point-like)— for example, the computational task of the visual system is said to begin with a spatially two-dimensional array of momentary light intensities and end with a description of a three-dimensional scene (e.g., Marr, 1982).

The general information-processing story about perception thus describes computational processes that are often characterized as inferences. The conclusions of these chains of inference are perceptual beliefs or experiences. As Fodor and Pylyshyn (1981) put it:

> The current Establishment theory (sometimes referred to as the "information processing" view) is that perception depends, in several respects presently to be discussed, upon *inferences*. Since inference is a process in which premises are displayed and consequences derived, and since that takes time, it is part and parcel of the information processing view that there is an intrinsic connection between perception and memory. And since, finally, the Establishment holds that the psychological mechanism of inference is the transformation of mental representations, it follows that perception is in relevant respects a computational process. (pp. 139–140)

Barrow and Tenenbaum (1986) characterized the starting point and goals of the computational study of vision like this:

> Vision is an information processing task with well-defined input and output. The input consists of two-dimensional arrays of brightness values, representing projections of a three-dimensional scene . . . The desired output is a concise description of the three-dimensional scene depicted in the image, the exact nature of which depends upon the goals and expectations of the observer. It generally involves a description of objects and their interrelationships but may also include such information as the three-dimensional structure of surfaces, their physical characteristics (shape, texture, color, material), and the locations of shadows and light sources.
>
> Vision is necessarily a constructive process. Since the input can be represented merely as arrays of numbers, the production of descriptions in

terms of surfaces and objects must involve the imposition of structure on the sensory data by the perceiver. (chap. 38, p. 2)

I have dwelled on this characterization of the information-processing approach to perception because it is often associated with habits of thinking about cognition (described in chapter 2) that make it difficult to place conscious experience in the resulting theory. All intermediate stages and states in perceptual processing are taken as symbolic and contentful, but unconscious except for a final stage. This approach thus seems to assume a linear-flow view of information processing, suggesting that consciousness be conceived as an information processing stage. Furthermore, computational vision theorists often adopt an implicit-agent stance with respect to experience and control of activity.

In contrast, the ecological approach advocated by Gibson (1966, 1979) differs in its assumptions about the function and informational basis of perception. First, Gibson took the primary function of perception to be the guidance of action, not the delivery of perceptual beliefs or descriptions of the environment. Surfaces and objects in the environment are therefore said to be perceived in terms of their *affordances*, those aspects that support action. So, for example, a crucial aspect of large surfaces is whether they afford locomotion—is the surface sufficiently horizontal, flat, and rigid to walk on? Second, the information available to perception is said to specify affordances. This is the basis of Gibson's claim that perception is direct rather than inferential (more about this in a moment). Third, the information available to an active organism for perception specifies both the environment and the self. To return to Gibson's (1979) statement of this point (also see chapter 1), "The supposedly separate realms of the subjective and the objective are actually only poles of attention" (p. 116), and "What we see *now* refers to the self, not the environment" (Gibson, 1979, p. 234). The basic idea, again, is that perceptual experience is necessarily perspectival in character, providing information both about the environment and about the current location of the self experiencing that environment. This is of course the basis for the cospecification hypothesis described in chapter 1, and for the comments of Neisser (1988, 1993) and E. J. Gibson (1993) on the ecological self.

The contrast between Establishment and ecological views of perception is often drawn—by both sides—primarily in terms of the directness of perception (e.g., Fodor & Pylyshyn, 1981; Turvey, Shaw, Reed, & Mace, 1981). In my view, this is unfortunate because it has obscured more important issues. It seems beyond doubt that there is a computational story to tell about the relation between the transduction that occurs at receptor surfaces (e.g., the retina) and the brain processes that support cognitively tuned perception. The nature of that computational story will depend on the grain size and character (a) of our starting descriptions of the environment to be perceived, (b) of the information-conveying events at the sensory surfaces and in the nervous system, and (c) of perceptual experience and action (Fowler & Turvey, 1982). The computational story will describe information-support relations among various theoretical descriptions of the information for perception. However, I would prefer to emphasize other aspects of Gibson's (1966, 1979) insights, and to state the "directness" issue in this way: The Establishment view suggests that there are extensive, detailed, and literal parallels to be drawn between the operation of perceptual systems and the operation of conscious, symbolic cognition. For example, Pomerantz and Kubovy (1986) explicitly drew parallels between visual perception and problem-solving strategies. The ecological view suggests instead that the computational view of perception describes processes that are qualitatively different from those of symbolic cognition. In my view, this is the important sense in which we might say that perception is direct—it is not mediated by processes that are like conscious, symbolic reasoning or problem solving. The intermediate states in perceptual processing—for example, states of the nervous system between the retina and the visual cortex—are not characterized by an intentional structure like that described next for conscious mental states.

At stake in this debate are several very fundamental aspects of cognitive theory, notably the concepts of *information* and *representation*. Many cognitive scientists have pointed to the cognitive, or knowledge-based, character of perception—or at least the phenomenally seamless interface between perception and cognition—as evidence that the information for perception should be described in symbolic terms and that the intermediate stages of computation involved in perception should be characterized as mental representations. As Marr (1982) put it, "vision goes symbolic almost immediately" (p. 343) as we trace its course from the retina to the cortex. However, Kosslyn and Hatfield (1984) argued for a sense of representation in computational models of vision that is not symbolic in character, and which thus has an explanatory force that is not parasitic on our common-sense understanding of conscious symbolic cognition. Developing a theoretical understanding of experienced cognition will require an account of these concepts in terms that can show the relation between nonconscious informational processes and conscious representational states. Our starting point is the old philosophical issue of intentionality.

The Intentionality of Perceptual-Enactive Awareness

The philosophical puzzles about consciousness (and mentality generally) have often been stated in terms of intentionality: How can mental states be directed at or about nonmental states of affairs?[1] Intentionality in this sense—which should not be confused with the everyday sense synonymous with purposiveness—is most clearly evident in the case of symbolic representations. For example, my current belief that it is cloudy is about the weather, a state of affairs that is "outside my head." Searle (1983) defined *intentionality* like this:

> Intentionality is that property of many mental states and events by which they are directed at or about or of objects and states of affairs in the world. If, for example, I have a belief, it must be a belief that such and such is the case; if I have a fear, it must be a fear of something or that something will occur; if I have a desire, it must be a desire to do something or that something should happen or be the case; if I have an intention, it must be an intention to do something. (p. 1)

What is traditionally difficult about understanding intentionality centers on the question: How can a physical state (such as the state of one's nervous system) also have (or be, or support) a content that is intentional, about something (e.g., Haugeland, 1985)? In my view, this difficulty stems

---

[1]The modern source of the term *intentionality* seems to be Brentano (1874/1973), who attempted to distinguish between mental and physical phenomena on the basis that mental phenomena were about something other than themselves, unlike physical phenomena. On my reading, Brentano meant by *phenomena* something like "appearances in experience," rather than our more modern sense that makes *phenomenon* nearly synonymous with *event*. This interpretation suggests that Brentano would not have ascribed intentionality to instances of direct perception. This position is countered by the argument sketched in chapter 4, that perceptual information is multimodal and the sensory modalities reflect skilled attributions rather than fundamental distinctions in the nature of awareness. Newell (1990) argued that there is no problem with the intentionality or references of symbol systems:

> Within the framework set out here, the matter seems straightforward. Start out with knowledge systems. Knowledge is about its domain, which is external to the system being characterized. To have the knowledge that the block is on the table is to have knowledge about the block and about the table. Knowledge is a way of describing a system whose behavior can be computed (by an observer) with respect to an external environment. Symbol systems realize knowledge systems. At least some of them do, and these are the ones of interest here. They do so only approximately, of course, a matter to which we will return. Hence, symbol systems are about the same external things that the knowledge systems they realize are about. After all, it is the same system that is being described, just in two different ways. Symbol systems realize knowledge systems by implementing representation laws so that the symbol structures encode the knowledge about the external world.
>
> That's all there is to intentionality, except for the details of how to build symbol systems that approximate knowledge systems closely enough. (pp. 78–79)

From the experienced cognition perspective, of course, there is indeed more than that to intentionality.

primarily from recognizing the subject-content-object distinction while ignoring the cospecificity of information that supports mental states. I argue that the intentional structure of conscious mental states can be described as psychological variables in the context of cospecific information arrays. This psychological structure of intentionality can be found in perceptual-enactive awareness, as well as in clearly symbolic states such as verbally expressed beliefs. In this section, I describe how perceptual-enactive awareness exhibits the major features of consciousness: subjectivity, purposiveness, and intentionality. My discussion draws heavily from Searle (1983, 1990), but I have freely adapted his analysis and other notions in the philosophical literature to my purposes.

Let me begin with some observations about perceptual-enactive awareness. The term *perceptual-enactive awareness* is intended to remind us of Gibson's insight that perception always accompanies and guides action, and that perception should be regarded as (in large part) a process of actively seeking and picking up information from the environment rather than as passive reception of information or as inferential construction. I focus on visual perception for a couple of reasons: Vision is the dominant perceptual modality for humans with intact perceptual systems, and the points I wish to make are more easily expressed in relation to vision than other modalities.

The first point to make is that perception establishes a (typically moving) point of view, the fundamental basis of primary awareness according to the cospecification hypothesis. As already discussed, vision alone appears to be sufficient to specify an experiencing self in this sense. There is much evidence to suggest, however, that information from vision and other sources (e.g., the vestibular system) is integrated to establish orientation and thus a point of view (e.g., Owen, 1990). Because of the central role of activity in vision, orientation also depends on the ability to move oneself and thereby control one's point of view. Spatial orientation is clearly an acquired skill or developmental achievement (Pick & Lockman, 1981), and for infants this development depends on the developing ability to control posture and locomotion (E. J. Gibson, 1993). As Thelen (1995) noted, experience is perceptual-enactive from the beginning. Second, perceptual awareness presents aspectual or perspectival views of objects and surfaces—when looking at (for example) a tree, from a particular location and at a particular time, we may say that the tree presents us with one view of the many views possible from different vantage points. Third, our visual experience is characterized by focus—of the many objects and surfaces in our field of view at a particular moment, one (or at most a very few) stands out as figure against the ground of other perceptually available objects and surfaces. This focus is likely related to currently active goals for manipulation or egomotion, and Pick and Lockman (1981) suggested that spatial orientation may depend on multiple egocentric frames of reference. For example, the frame of reference involved in perceiving a small object may be based on the body as a whole or on the arm, depending on whether and how the object is to be manipulated. Ballard, Hayhoe, Pook, and Rao (in press) recently argued that the deictic character of a visual focus is instrumental in controlling cognition generally.

These linked aspects of perceptual-enactive awareness already show the major features of intentional structure—experience is directed, presenting objects in relation to the experiencing self. Next consider some parallel observations about action. As a number of authors (e.g., E. J. Gibson, 1993; Lee, 1993) have noted, even infants engage in organized activities guided by perception. Some of these activities—looking, searching with head and facial movements for a nipple—may be described as primarily exploratory (J. J. Gibson, 1966). Others might be described as primarily manipulatory—for example, sucking—and with development during the first year or so of life, more and more actions can be described as primarily egomotive, serving to move the self with respect to the environment (E. J. Gibson, 1993). Two points should be noted here: First, even very primitive, apparently innate, activities are characterized by internal structure and are probably best described in terms of coordinative structures and modes (Thelen, 1995). Second, these actions are guided by perception and in that sense directed at aspects of the environment. We might say that even early actions are *prehensile* (grasping), some of them literally so and some in an extended sense that refers to informationally grasping aspects of the environment.

Related observations led Piaget (see Chapman, 1988) to describe early activity in terms of what he called the primary circular reaction. This pattern, observed at least as early as one month of age, is characterized by the tendency of infants to attempt to repeat nonreflex movements apparently first made by accident. Because of their apparently intentional repetition, nonreflex character, and apparent goal of achieving a perceptual consequence, Piaget described these reactions as schemes. That is, primary circular reactions are intentional, organized, and prehensile (or in Piaget's, 1972, terms, "assimilatory").

So even in very young infants, perception and action show the beginnings of an organized perceptual-enactive cycle, in which perception and action are closely linked as individuals interact with the environment. We can see in the activities of infants the beginnings of deliberate goal-directed activities, and describe infants as agents acting in an information-rich environment (E. J. Gibson, 1993; Thelen, 1995). The information-processing approach suggests that understanding this cycle should begin with informational descriptions of the bases for perception and action, and for that we must consider the concept of *information* itself.

Information and Awareness

> The notion of information has been taken to characterize a measure of physical organization (or decrease in entropy), a pattern of communication between source and receiver, a form of control and feedback, the probability of a message being transmitted over a communication channel, the content of a cognitive state, the meaning of a linguistic form, or the reduction of an uncertainty. These concepts of information are defined in various theories such as physics, thermodynamics, communication theory, cybernetics, statistical information theory, inductive logic, and so on. There seems to be no unique idea of information upon which these various concepts converge and hence no proprietary theory of information. (Bogdan, 1994, p. 53)

As noted in chapter 1, one of Gibson's major insights was that the starting point of perceptual research and theory depends critically on the language used to describe the information available for perception (see Gibson, 1961, for a foundational discussion of this point). Gibson argued that the perceptual systems were prepared by evolution to directly pick up invariant patterns of information specific to the affordances for action of surfaces and objects in the environment. Such invariants may be spatially and temporally extended, requiring theorists to generate complex descriptions (e.g., in geometric or mathematical terms) to capture these invariants in physical language (Fowler & Turvey, 1982). However, the need for a complex theoretical description need not imply a correspondingly complex perceptual process; it is not the task of the perceptual system to reassemble what a cognitive theorist has taken apart. Gibson (1979) cast this point in terms drawn from older, philosophical discussions of the basis of perception, "Phenomenal objects are *not* built up of qualities; it is the other way around" (p. 134). His biographer, Reed (1988) put it this way, "Surely, Gibson taught, we perceive the world in which we live and infer the world of the physicist, not the other way around" (p. 285).

Given the assumption (see chapter 2) that the task of cognitive theory is to describe how an informational description of input (e.g., the environment) is transformed into an informational description of output (e.g., action), the starting point for those informational descriptions is obviously critical in determining the nature of the theories we develop. One starting point is to take symbolic representation as our model for informational description. From this point of view, for example, patterns of neural activity occurring very early in the path from the retina to the cortex are taken to be symbolic (Marr, 1982). This characterization suggests such properties as arbitrary reference—aside from causal history, there is no reason that a particular pattern of activity must refer to a particular state of affairs—and participation in formal relations that support compositional structure (e.g., Fodor & Pylyshyn, 1981, 1988). This view of information often leads us to think of mental representation on the model of natural language, and to rely on written language as a model for theoretical notation meant to paraphrase the contents of mental states. The processes that operate on information in this sense are computational in that rules can be applied to manipulate symbols on the basis of their formal or syntactic properties.

A second possible starting point is to think of information in terms of resemblance or correspondence. This is the sense in which a photograph carries information about a scene and the sense in which mental images are sometimes said to be "depictive" (Kosslyn, 1981). The processes that operate on information in this sense are analogous to processes that manipulate objects in the world (including moving the body, head, or eyes). In fact, neurophysiological evidence suggests that the processes involved in mental imagery are supported by the some of the parts of the brain that support visual perception (Farah, 1988; Kosslyn, 1994). Like the symbolic view, this approach to understanding the concept of information suggests parallels to a common type of artifact—pictures rather than written language in this case.

A third alternative is provided by Gibson's view of information, summarized by Reed (1988) like this, "The information for something must specify it, but need not resemble it" (p. 275). The idea is something like this: Any patterning of energy (e.g., light) over space and time that corresponds to the structure of the world carries information about the world. As developed by Gibson and his followers, this view suggests that not all processes or structures that preserve information should be described as representing it. As noted in chapter 1, Dretske (1981) developed a cognitive-philosophical analysis of information compatible with this view, although his theory of cognitive processing is more similar to the unconscious inference approach than to Gibson's view of perception. Two aspects of Dretske's view are relevant for my argument, "Roughly speaking, information is that commodity capable of yielding knowledge, and what information a signal carries is what we can learn from it" (p. 44). This definition is compatible with the formal information-theory definition of information in terms of uncertainty reduction (see Quastler, 1955, for early efforts to apply information theory to psychological issues, and Dretske, 1981, for theoretical development of this point). More important, Dretske's definition is sufficiently abstract to remind us that information is a concept independent of any particular view of representation. If we understand knowledge to include not just declarative knowledge, but also procedural knowledge that is performed rather than consulted, Dretske's definition is also compatible with Gibson's view of information as a commodity that guides action by specifying the environmental affordances that support that action.

The propagation of information in a medium is captured by Dretske's (1981) "*Xerox principle*: If *A* carries the information that *B*, and *B* carries the information that *C*, then *A* carries the information that *C*" (p. 57). For example, if activity at the retina carries information specific to the structured light constituting the ambient array for vision, and that ambient array carries information specific to the environmental surfaces that structure the light, retinal activity carries or preserves information specific to the environment. A pattern of activity may be said to carry, contain, preserve or constitute information when changes in that pattern are correlated with changes in some state of affairs. From a third-person or reflective point of view, the specificity relation may of course be uncertain, as in the case of optical illusions.

The important point here is that both the symbolic and resemblance views of information conflate the concepts of *information, representation,* and *content*. In those views, items of information are the kinds of things of which we can be aware, that can be contents of conscious mental states. In the ecological view, information may be said to support contentful states, as it supports action directed toward objects in the environment. In this sense, processes or structures may preserve or transmit information without representing it, although our *theoretical descriptions* of those processes or structures represent the information those processes or structures preserve.

In fact, most cognitive research not concerned with early perceptual processes is implicitly based on ecological input and output descriptions. As experimentalists, we generally give action- or ability-relative descriptions of the displays we present to participants in our experiments; for example, we describe the content of visual displays as words or digits rather than in terms derived from optics or other branches of physics. And we tend to use the term *information* as a category label for these descriptions. Similarly, we describe participants' activities, including their responses, in terms that reflect an intentional interpretation of those activities. For example, participants in reaction-time experiments may be instructed to press one key to indicate that an element of one (target) category was displayed, and another key (or no key) to indicate that an element of an alternative (distractor) category was present. These keypresses are typically, if implicitly, interpreted as intentional (purposive) communicative acts expressing the participant's state of mind. Only when consciousness itself is at issue (e.g., Greenwald, Klinger, & Schuh, 1995) is the intentional character of such responses questioned (also see chapter 14).

As Dretske's (1981) analysis makes clear, causal relations among patterns—for example, among environmental surfaces, the ambient array of structured light, and retinal events—allow for the preservation of information. Theoretical descriptions of these patterns will be related computationally, for example by geometrical transformations. However, not all instances of preserving information constitute representation in the sense that something is "*used* as a surrogate for some reference world" (Palmer & Kimchi, 1986, p. 56; see chapter 2), or in the sense of having intentional content.

Perceptual-enactive awareness thus occurs in the course of organized activity supported by informational arrays that are preserved by patterns in the environment and by activity in the nervous system. The information making up these arrays should be described at an ecological grain, as we usually do for research purposes, keeping in mind that not all computational relations among descriptions correspond to computational processes operating on representations. It is in this context that we can elaborate the ideas of cospecification and egolocation.

COSPECIFICATION AND EGOLOCATION

Chapter 1 introduced the *cospecification hypothesis*, that concurrent specification of self and environment is the basis of conscious awareness. In this section, I elaborate that hypothesis, first providing greater detail on cospecification in visual awareness. A central point is that self and object are not just cospecified but may be actively distinguished from one another by processes that I call *egolocative*. Understanding egolocative processing requires us to consider how the informational array available for vision evolves in the course of action. I then generalize the cospecification hypothesis to other modalities, arguing that in general the perceptual and action systems sample an informational manifold in which self and objects are cospecified. The case of cospecification in vision is thus an illustrative example of a general feature of the structure of experienced cognition.

Cospecification in the Ambient Array

J. J. Gibson (1966) described the information available for vision as an ambient array of light. The essential idea is that the light striking the retina, which is primarily reflected from surfaces in the environment, is structured by discontinuities in the texture and layout of those surfaces. We can think of the static array of information available from a stable environment to a particular viewpoint as a sheaf of rays originating at edges and borders in the environment and converging at the viewpoint. As noted in chapter 1, perspective technique in drawing is based on a similar concept, the projection of edges and borders to a picture plane between the viewpoint and the depicted surfaces.

The structured light that surrounds us in illuminated environments constitutes the ambient array of information for vision. If we consider this array from a particular point of view and frozen at a particular moment in time, we can abstract a description of the information available for visual perception that corresponds (more or less) to the information captured in a photograph or perspective drawing. The more general case, however, is a dynamic or kinetic array, evolving over time with the movement of objects in the environment and movement of the point of view (because of eye and head movements, and locomotion through the environment). Motion of the self and of the objects of perception is critical to many perceptual phenomena (J. J. Gibson, 1979; Johansson, 1975). It is in the context of this dynamic array that self and environment may be said to be cospecified in the information available for vision. For example, optical flow—correlated motion of the entire visual field—specifies motion of the self with respect to a stable environment: "It is only a *total* motion of the structured ambient array that specifies movement of the self, not a part motion of the array. The latter specifies the motion of an object in the world" (J. J. Gibson, 1966, pp. 200–201). If we move with our eyes directed toward a spatial goal, that goal is specified in the kinetic array as the center of optical flow. Even in the more complex case in which we look around while moving (rather than continually fixating our spatial goal), flow of the ambient array specifies (and thus can guide) the movement of the self (Cutting, Springer, Braren, & Johnson, 1992).

Egolocation, Resampling, and Exploration

As developed so far, cospecification is an abstract characteristic of the information available for perception. In the simplifying static case, the point is simply that the information available in the ambient optical array is specific to both an environment and the vantage point or perspective from which that environment is viewed. This characterization tells us about the circumstances in which experienced cognition can occur, and not about the cognitive processes themselves. To understand cognitive processes, we can begin with the idea of egolocative processing that distinguishes self and object (more generally, objects and surfaces in the environment). Consider the kinetic array for vision in a stable environment, in which changes in the available information are caused only by movement of the viewpoint—typically as a result of goal-directed action—with respect to the environment. The changes in the array will specify the direction and rate of the viewpoint's movement, while invariant aspects of the array will specify the (stable) layout of the environment. Resampling of the array is involved in achieving clear perceptions of objects in the environment (Underwood, 1982). We can thus describe the perceptual processes that pick up these aspects of the optic array as depending on resampling and exploration of the array. I mean to imply no sharp distinction between resampling, which implies picking up information at brief intervals with small changes in viewpoint, and exploration, which implies sampling over larger temporal and spatial intervals. An important feature of this analysis is that relative rates of change of aspects of the optic array provide the basis for distinguishing self-specific and object-specific aspects of the available information. As J. J. Gibson (1966) noted:

> Now the remarkable fact about visual scanning is that awareness of the succession of temporary retinal impressions is completely absent from the perceptual experience. There is awareness of the simultaneous existence of all the objects in the world, or all the parts of a picture, despite the fact that the objects, or parts, are fixated one after another—at least with our kind of vision. The whole physical array seems to coexist phenomenally although it has been looked at sequentially. No one has ever been able to count his eye fixations while inspecting the world, or a picture, although it is easy to count the number of objects in the array. The retinal-impression theory of perception has an elaborate explanation of this puzzling fact in terms of a presumed *internal canceling* of the retinal motions and an unconscious combining of retinal impressions. . . . But it might be accounted for as a case of the equivalence of successive sampling and simultaneous grasping. (p. 252)

The stability of the environment thus allows resampling of invariant aspects of the ambient array, a condition for perceiving objects and surfaces as distinct from the self. There is, of course, a complex computational story to be told about how the nervous system preserves information across samples, and there are alternative theories of visual egolocation (e.g., Cutting et al., 1992). However, it is the informational conditions for egolocative processing that are of greatest interest for my purposes.

The dynamic patterning of visual perception in terms of resampling and exploration is largely built in to the nervous system by evolution. It is well known that even for a stationary observer, the information available to vision is sampled at rapid intervals as the eyes perform a continuing series of brief fixations and movements (saccades and tracking movements). The relative motion of points in the visual field—parallax—generated by movements of the point of view, provides a source of information not available in a (hypothetical) static array. This information is important both for the perceptual achievements most studied by cognitive scientists, such as shape recognition, and for egolocation (e.g., Cutting et al., 1992). Understanding these processes in detail depends on generalizing the concept of an ambient array to incorporate nonvisual sources of information. For example, nonvisual information about one's body contributes to orientation and egolocation.

A final point concerning resampling and exploration concerns is that information specifying one's viewpoint typically changes faster than most of the information specifying the environment. For example, saccadic eye movements occur three or four times per second while the environment typically remains mostly stable. Many mental processes appear to be temporally linked with eye movements (Ballard et al., in press; Just & Carpenter, 1976), suggesting that symbolic cognition is also characterized by rapid changes in self-specific information in the context of relatively stable object-specific information. This observation is important in understanding how emotional awareness is related to other aspects of experienced cognition.

THE INTENTIONAL STRUCTURE
OF PERCEPTION AND ACTION

Perception and action have intentionality primarily in virtue of their directedness, not because of relations of reference or aboutness, as in the case of symbolic contents. In this section I attempt to spell this out, relying heavily on Searle's (1983) analysis although differing from his account in some respects.

Conditions of Satisfaction

There are some well-known problems concerning how mental states can be about things or states of affairs in the world. One of these problems is that mental states can fail to be satisfied. For example, I might believe that the refrigerator contains adequate supplies for dinner and plan some of my activities on the basis of that belief, finding out only later that my belief was false. In some sense, the content of my belief was about the nonexistent food in the refrigerator, and functioned in my mental processes in virtue of the content. Yet the belief, like my hunger for dinner, has gone unsatisfied.

This example is intended to illustrate two points: First, the contents of mental states must be systematically distinguished from the objects that those states are about. Not only did the refrigerator contain no food, neither did my mental states contain food in any literal sense. Second, objects in this sense should not be confused with real objects (in the ordinary sense) in the nonmental world. So what can the contents of mental states be about in general? According to Searle (1983), mental states are about their *conditions of satisfaction*, the states of affairs that must exist if the mental states are to be satisfied. For example, my belief about the food in my refrigerator would have been satisfied had the food actually been present. Conditions of satisfaction is thus a theoretical device allowing us to talk about the contents of mental states in a coherent manner that corresponds to common sense, which recognizes no particular conceptual problem in talking about false beliefs, unfulfilled hopes, and failed intentions (although it does appear that the ability to do so is a skill developed during childhood; e.g., Perner, 1991). Thinking about the conditions of satisfaction for our mental states also suggests that the contents of a particular mental state can be specified only with respect to a network of other states and abilities.

Searle (1983) also noted that mental states are characterized by *directions of fit* with their conditions of satisfaction. A belief has a *mind-to-world* direction of fit. For the belief to be satisfied, the mental state must be fit to the world—the content of the belief must be true, must represent an actual state of affairs. A desire, on the other hand, has a *world-to-mind* direction of fit. If my desire to have dinner is to be satisfied, the world must somehow come to fit the content of that desire. In actual cognitive activity, of course, there is reciprocal causality and interaction—for example, some of my beliefs play a role in how I carry out actions related to my desire. Nevertheless, the idea of direction of fit is a useful analytic device for considering the intentionality of mental states. Furthermore, it helps us to understand the causal relations among mental states and their conditions of satisfaction. For example, if my desire is satisfied through intentional action, the desire itself is one of the causal precursors of the world coming to fit that desire.

Beliefs and desires are perhaps the prototypical mental states, and are easily described in terms of symbolic contents that refer to conditions of satisfaction. However, perception and action are much more fundamental examples of experienced cognition; as Searle (1983) put it, "it is a mistake to think of belief and desire as the primary forms of cognition and volition, wrong because they both lack the internal causal self-referentiality which connects cognition and volition to their conditions of satisfaction" (pp. 104–105). That is, belief and desire are often indirectly related (for example, by chains of inference) to their conditions of satisfaction, whereas, "Biologically speaking, the primary forms of Intentionality are perception and action, because by their very content they involve the organism in direct causal relations with the environment on which his survival depends" (Searle, 1983, p. 104). Perceptual-enactive awareness thus shows the basic intentional structure of mental states: The experience of a self acting in an environment can be described as a series of mental states in which self and environment are specified, and the manner in which they are specified can be described in terms of the mode and content of the state. As a first approximation, we can think of mode as identified by direction of fit, and content as identified by conditions of satisfaction. In the remainder of this chapter and the next two, I elaborate this analysis of intentional structure.

Causal Self-Reference

Perception is to action roughly as belief is to desire, in that perception has a mind-to-world direction of fit, whereas action has a world-to-mind direction of fit. Normally these are intermingled and closely coordinated, as perception guides action and action helps to determine the information available to perception. Searle (1983) pointed out that perception and action are also causally self-referential; for example, "the sense in which the visual experience is self-referential is simply that it figures in its own conditions of satisfaction" (p. 49). That is, for a state of visual awareness to be satisfied, it must be the case that the state is caused by its object. My visual experience of the keyboard in front of me is not satisfied unless the keyboard is among the causes of the experience; otherwise I am experiencing a hallucination rather than a state of perceptual awareness. Resampling information from a stable environment normally allows this causal relation to be confirmed; in fact, Dennett (1991) argued that "strong hallucinations" that cannot be distinguished from normal perception are impossible because of the resampling and exploration characteristics of normal perception. Action is similarly causally self-referential—if I intentionally turn my head, the turning must be caused in part by the intention if the intention is to be satisfied.

These essentially philosophical observations are supported primarily by logical analysis of phenomenal experience. However, they can be "cashed out" in cognitive-theoretical terms by placing them in the context of the cospecification hypothesis. Perception and action normally take place in a perception-action cycle (cf. Neisser, 1976) in which perception guides action and action determines what information is available to perception. In this cycle, self and object are cospecified by evolving information arrays and distinguished by resampling these arrays as self-specific and object-specific aspects of the information change at typically different rates. This cospecification provides the informational basis for the intentional structure described by Searle (1983), a structure that we will see is characteristic of experienced cognition generally.

An interesting implication of this analysis is that our experience of perceptual modality (e.g., vision versus hearing) might be characterized as skilled attribution, in the sense that we may learn that certain kinds of experience are based on certain kinds of exploratory activity. For example, visual experience is based on active looking (Thelen, 1995).

Jackendoff (1987) commented on the modality-specificity of conscious experience—that is, our usually very accurate ability to attribute the source of our experience to, for example, vision or hearing. What does this modality-specificity tell us about conscious experience? Primarily, I think, it should remind us that perception is active, as emphasized by J. J. Gibson (1966, 1979). That is, looking and listening are two different activities. Because conscious experience is also generally performatory in character, and these activities of looking and listening involve quite different performances, it should not surprise us that they produce different self-specifying information, resulting in different egolocative processes, and the experience of receiving information from distinct perceptual modalities.

THE ORGANIZATION OF ACTION SCHEMES

In order to understand the intentionality of perceptual-enactive awareness more deeply, and to build toward an account of the conscious control of cognitive activity, we must also consider some aspects of the action side of the perception-action cycle. In particular, we must consider that action is patterned in terms of schemes that are to some degree self-organizing and typically prehensile (grasping) with respect to physical and informational objects. I use the term *scheme* rather than *schema* because I want to emphasize organization or patterning over time rather than mental representation of that organization.

Organization of Simple Action Patterns

As noted earlier, even the reflexes and action patterns present at birth are often best described as organized systems rather than simple responses (e.g., Easton, 1972; Thelen, 1995). In particular, many reflexes are internally patterned—the movement consists of detectable parts—and may be literally prehensile—for example, the grasping and sucking reflexes. Understanding the basis for voluntary action thus begins with seeing these innate movements as embedded in a perceptual-enactive cycle—they have consequences that affect objects in the world and the information available to perception. In Piaget's (1972) terms, they are schemes to which objects may be assimilated; furthermore, they may be adapted or accommodated to the environment in which they are performed.

Constraints on Sensorimotor Activity

Action in an environment, and the information available to support such action, is constrained by the physical laws of the world. Piaget (e.g., 1972) saw these constraints as fundamental to the development of mental operations. Although Piaget's work is presented in textbooks largely in terms of developmental stages, Chapman (1988) pointed out that his "genetic epistemology" is primarily about the conditions for, or grounding of, knowledge. Consider, for example, the group structure found in the system comprising possible displacements in space. Group structure is one way of describing the set of constraints on operations within a domain. Following Poincaré (1914), Piaget (1954) pointed out that the system of possible displacements of an object in space showed these properties that together constitute group structure (paraphrased from Chapman, 1988, pp. 108–109):

1. *Composition under closure* (any sequence of displacements results in a position also belonging to the system);
2. *Associativity* (any location can be reached by different routes);
3. *Identity* (an object that is not moved remains where it is);
4. *Inversion* (reversing any sequence of displacements returns the object to its point of origin).

Piaget (1954, 1972) saw this structure as the developmental grounds for, and thus the formal patterning of, symbolic cognition. In Chapman's (1988) summary:

> The psychological reality corresponding to the group of displacements is simply the manner in which the actions belonging to the system are organized among themselves.
>
> Roughly the same is true for the additive system of whole numbers, except that the operations belonging to this system (i.e., addition and subtraction) are actions that have become interiorized. (p. 131)

The physical constraints captured in this description of group structure guarantee noncontradiction in the actual displacements (movements) that can be performed. Noncontradiction, of course, is also the fundamental principle of logical reasoning and thus the underlying constraint on a *truth-preserving* symbol system (Haugeland, 1985; also see chapter 2). It is important to note that these properties are constraints on relations among actions, not rules that must be consulted in order to perform those actions.

Cospecification in the ambient optical array is of course subject to these constraints because the array preserves a system of spatial relations. The resampling and exploration that make possible egolocative processing of course are (or correspond to) displacements in space. Perceptual-enactive awareness is thus constrained by physical laws in a manner whose abstract structure may also characterize a variety of symbolic mental activity. This observation, together with finding the same formal structure in analyzing the intentionality of both perceptual-enactive and symbolic awareness, supports the hypothesis that symbolic awareness is grounded in perceptual-enactive awareness. This grounding may account for the truth-preserving character of symbolic representation, especially if we adopt a performatory view of mental representation.

ACTION AND THE CONTENT OF AWARENESS

The preceding analysis indicates that action commonly serves as the means or vehicle rather than the content of awareness. This observation points toward the performatory nature of experienced cognition generally.

The Several Senses of Representation

Contemporary cognitive science approaches the mind as a container full of representations, informational vehicles that serve as surrogates for the environment. I believe that, despite a great deal of bold talk, much confusion surrounds the concept of representation. In particular, the descriptions that figure in computational theories (or information-processing theories intended to be translatable into computational terms) are often characterized as representations. This terminology provides a useful metaphorical link to understanding the theories because representation brings to mind common-sense examples such as acts of representing (e.g., speaking) or artifactual representations such as writing or pictures. Unfortunately, this metaphorical link is not helpful—in fact, is harmful—when it comes to understanding conscious experience and how it is related to the terms of our computational theory. As Searle (1992) noted, cognitive science is guilty of "anthropomorphizing the brain." In chapter 7, I consider the status of nonconscious informational states in more detail. Here, let us consider the various senses that might be given the term *representation*.

In one sense, any process or structure that preserves information—that obeys Dretske's (1981) Xerox principle previously stated—may be described as a representation (Kosslyn & Hatfield, 1984). In this sense, my footprints in the snow represent my trip up the driveway, preserving some information that might be described (by an observer or theorist) in propositions referring to the direction of my walk and my approximate shoe size. However, this sense of representation is relative to an observer, and not intrinsic in the representational system itself. Some of the activity of our nervous systems must be representational in this sense—preserving information in a way that can be described symbolically but is not itself necessarily symbolic. Shepard's (1984) resonance metaphor captures this sense of representation and points out its cognitive character. For example, a piano can be said to represent middle C by virtue of the tuning of a string, which may therefore resonate in sympathy to a nearby tuning fork, thereby perceiving the active state of the tuning fork. Similarly, our perceptual systems are tuned (by evolution and by experience that allows skill acquisition) to resonate to some environmental events. One consequence of resonance is to preserve information, to extend in time the availability of some property (e.g., frequency) of the initiating event. Some connectionist modelers describe the activity of neural networks as resonance (for example, see the discussion of Grossberg's work in Fischer, Bullock, Rotenberg, & Raya, 1993).

In a second sense, the term *representation* is reserved for structures or processes that can be manipulated independently of the objects about which they preserve information. Artifacts such as written language, mathematical symbols, or pictures are representations in this sense. So are performances of routines in the absence of their objects—speaking is a complex, socially grounded example, but so are some simpler activities. In this sense, it might be more accurate to speak of acts of representing than of representations. In general, representation in this sense is performatory, and it is performatory representation that constitutes the content of conscious mental states. From this point of view, agency is central to the concept of representation.

Agency and Perceptual-Enactive Awareness

Agency, the self as cause, is central to primary awareness because causal directionality is inherent in perceptually guided action. We can see this in the causal self-reference of perception and action previously described. As Dennett (1991) noted, the cyclical, reciprocal causal relations between self and environment can be seen in the nonmental interactions between the simplest organisms and their environments. In particular, moving within the environment and distinguishing through action parts of the environment that are not self (and thus might, for example, be food) reflect the beginnings of the perception–action cycle. Dennett pointed out that such reciprocal causality is the evolutionary ground for human selves, although as he pointed out, the activities of simple organisms are not very "selfy" from our point of view. Nevertheless, perceptual-enactive awareness arises evolutionarily, and perhaps developmentally, from activity in a relatively stable environment.

Egolocation is critical in the guidance of action insofar as that action occurs with respect to the spatial layout of the environment. Visual egolocation (or visual proprioception) provides a model for understanding primary awareness that is not just an analogy or metaphor. Symbolic consciousness is grounded in spatially constrained perceptual-enactive experience. It follows that conscious mental activity—for example, reasoning—is also grounded in spatially organized activity. Johnson (1987) observed that movement or path metaphors are ubiquitous in natural-language discussions of reasoning.

The intentional structure characteristic of symbolic awareness is already present in perceptual-enactive awareness. Within a cospecific array of available information, we can see how modes of awareness emerge in activity, distinguishing self and objects through a content that can be identified by the mental states' conditions of satisfaction. The examples presented here come mostly from vision, but this analysis can be extended to informational arrays in any modality. In general, conscious mental states arise in the context of multimodal manifolds of informational arrays. In the next chapter, I elaborate the analysis of intentional structure in terms of theoretical variables by considering the structure of symbolic awareness.

5

Symbolic and Representational Awareness

Perceptual-enactive awareness is the primary form of experienced cognition, but symbolic awareness characterizes states and processes that are prototypically mental, such as verbal reasoning. In this chapter, I consider symbolic awareness and how it is related to perceptual-enactive awareness. Using explicit instantiated belief as an illustration, the analysis of intentional structure begun in the last chapter can be developed further. In such states, the distinctions among self, mode, content, and object are clearer and have been the subject of much prior analysis (e.g., by Searle, 1990). The cospecification hypothesis also applies to symbolic and representational awareness, showing the theoretical continuity between perceptual-enactive and symbolic awareness, and clarifying the concept of conscious representation. The result of analyzing the intentional structure of mental states is a framework for describing conscious mental states and their relations in mental processes.

THE INTENTIONAL ANALYSIS
OF CONSCIOUS SYMBOLIC STATES

The previous chapter introduced the basic concepts needed to analyze the intentional structure of conscious mental states. Applying these concepts to the analysis of symbolic awareness will lead us to understand conscious mental states in terms of variables that can provide a basis for cognitive theory. This is an important step toward a theoretical framework because on most accounts of what it means to do scientific research, or to construct scientific theories, we can refer to entities in our theories only by means of variables associated with those entities. The variables identified in this analysis will help us to understand mental processes in terms of conscious mental states, and to see the relations among perceptual-enactive, symbolic, and emotional awareness in terms of a common intentional structure.

Explicit Instantiated Belief

Explicit, instantiated beliefs provide an informative caricature of typical states of symbolic awareness. By explicit, I mean that the content of such a belief can be accurately expressed by a sentence in the believer's natural language, interpreted literally. By instantiated, I mean that the content is realized in a current mental state—as opposed to the many beliefs that we might say are implicit or potential in our long-term knowledge. This point is important, because a hypothesis of the experienced cognition framework is that beliefs must be instantiated in current mental states to control activity. So, for example, my belief that I must lecture tomorrow morning influences my behavior only insofar as I actually think so—as I experience a mental state with the content of that belief. A belief that does not come to mind is only potential or dispositional, not actual. There are interesting senses in which one might say that implicit, uninstantiated beliefs can affect activity; that is one form of the hypothesis of a cognitive unconscious (which I take up in chapter 14, although I disagree with it). Let us begin, however, with the intentionality of conscious beliefs.

The Speech Act Analogy.   Consider first Searle's philosophical theory of intentionality (briefly discussed in the previous chapter). Searle (1983) developed his theory of intentionality by analogy to his earlier theory of speech acts (Searle, 1969). A *speech act* is simply an action accomplished by speaking, by making an utterance. Speech act theory is an attempt to understand language by understanding not just linguistic structure, but also the uses and functions of speaking. It also provides a basis for understanding some distinctions that are critical for understanding the intentionality of mental states generally.

In talking about speech acts, we must begin by distinguishing between the *propositional content* (which we can think of as the literal meaning of the spoken words) and the *illocutionary force*, the intended meaning or function of the utterance. We can see this distinction most clearly in what are known as indirect speech acts. For example, if you say to a companion at the dinner table, "Can you pass the salt?" and she responds, "Yes, I think I can," something has gone wrong—the literal propositional content of an utterance is clearly distinct from its intended meaning or illocutionary force (here, "I ask that you pass me the salt"). A variety of factors, including context and convention, help to determine illocutionary force; for the present purpose, it is sufficient to understand that content and illocutionary force are distinct.

The function served by a speech act thus depends on both its propositional content and its illocutionary force—that is, {you pass the salt} and its force as a request (determined by context and convention). Similarly, the function served by a mental state depends on both its propositional content and its psychological mode. Believing that a conservative is Speaker of the House of Representatives is quite different from desiring that he or she fill that role, although both the belief and the desire might have the same propositional content {a conservative is Speaker of the House}. The mode of a mental state is thus a noncontent property with implications for the role of the state in mental processes.

The content of a state, defined by its conditions of satisfaction (see chapter 4), also must be distinguished both from its vehicle and from its object. By *vehicle*, I simply mean that which carries content. For example, spoken language is a performatory vehicle that carries the content of an utterance; later I argue that private speech serves as one vehicle for thought. This distinction is easier to see in the case of symbolic awareness than in the case of perceptual-enactive awareness because we are familiar with the idea that the same content can be expressed in language—and thus experienced in thought—in various ways, for example by paraphrases. It is difficult to see, however, how the content of a particular state of perceptual-enactive awareness could be expressed or experienced differently. That is because the contents of such states are so immediately tied, causally and temporally, to their conditions of satisfaction.

The distinction between content and object is also in some ways easier to appreciate in the case of symbolic awareness. Content is aspectual and abstractive, in that an object is thought of or represented only under certain descriptions. So, for example, when I see the tree outside the window, my immediate visual experience is of the tree from my perspective, including only that aspect or view of the tree available from my current point of view (e.g., the side that is toward me). Furthermore, my visual experience abstracts some properties of the physical object responsible for that experience. Returning to the speech act analogy, this point is familiar as the characteristic of linguistic meaning sometimes referred to as *opaque reference*. The idea is that an individual's words need not support translation into synonymous words or phrases. For example, imagine that I say, "Professor Leibowitz would know the answer to my question." It happens that he is also the tallest member of my department, so that "Professor Leibowitz" and "tallest member of my department" refer to the same object. However, it would be false to say that the statement, "The tallest member of my department would know the answer to my question," is a correct translation or paraphrase of the meaning of my utterance. Rather, the two statements represent different aspects or views of the same object. And the same is true of the corresponding beliefs: Believing that Professor Leibowitz could answer my questions is not the same as believing that the tallest member my department could do so. The point is exactly parallel to the point made in chapter 4 concerning the perspectival nature of visual experience: The content of a mental state presents one of many possible views of its object.

The speech act analogy thus illustrates two important points about symbolic awareness: First, like the contents of perceptual-enactive awareness, the contents of symbolic awareness are aspectual or perspectival, necessarily involving a point of view. Our theoretical thinking must therefore carefully distinguish between the contents and objects of mental states. Second, just as we must distinguish the propositional content and illocutionary force of a speech act, we must distinguish the content and mode of a state of symbolic awareness.

Content and the Concept of Representation. The analysis of intentional structure thus suggests a principled distinction between content and noncontent properties of mental states. Both content and noncontent properties must of course be described in cognitive theory. All of these theoretical descriptions are often discussed as representations involved in mental processes (chapter 2). However, only some of them—those that represent content properties of mental states—capture aspects of mental activity that can be properly construed as representations for the human subject described by a theory. There is potential for great confusion here on several counts. First, it is not widely accepted that all contentful states described by cognitive theory are experienced by subjects. Standard practice in cognitive science thus denies the importance of conscious experience as a criterion for theory. Second, it is well known that representational systems differ in how they divide information-processing tasks between representations and processes that operate on those representations. Theoretical realism requires that this division in cognitive theory correspond to the content-noncontent distinction in experienced cognition.

Finally, and perhaps most responsible for the difficulty of developing theories that do justice to experienced cognition, the noncontent properties of a particular mental state may be represented in the content of a subsequent, metacognitive state. For example, having a degree of belief in (or conversely, a degree of uncertainty about) some proposition does not require the representation of some scalar quantity in the content of the same belief. However, individuals can reliably report their degrees of belief (see chapter 11), which seems to require a higher order state that takes the belief state as an object, thus representing what is a mode variable in the original state as a content variable in the higher order state.

Content and Noncontent Properties of Mental States

Both content and noncontent properties of mental states contribute to psychological function. Mental processes can be described in part as functions whose arguments are mental states. This kind of functional description differs from the common description of mental processes (e.g., in computational vision or production-system models of problem solving) in that it involves computing both representations that capture mental contents and variables that capture noncontent properties of mental states. For example, the belief that it is almost time for dinner plays a quite different role in my mental life than does the wish or desire that it is almost time for dinner—mental states that differ in mode but not content.

Contents and Their Relations. Much of cognitive psychology is concerned with possible mental state contents and their relations. For example, models of semantic memory address such questions as how concepts are combined, how conceptual categories are formed or understood, or how new experiences can be assimilated to existing knowledge (e.g., reference). More abstractly, both normative (e.g., logic) and descriptive theories of reasoning are concerned with syntactic relations among possible mental contents. Considering specific theories of symbolic content is beyond the scope of the present discussion, but the central point is that theories of meaning and its representation are concerned primarily with the structure and organization of possible mental state contents. The contents of mental states may be described, and the contents of multiple states related, in terms of both semantic and syntactic variables. A list of such content variables would include at least all those variables needed to distinguish one sentence from another. In particular, these variables must allow description of the propositional structure (subject-predicate form) of symbolic contents that allows those contents to be related in reasoning processes.

Noncontent Intentional Properties. Noncontent variables include those that follow directly from the analysis of intentional structure and those that do not. For example, degree of *commitment* is a noncontent intentional variable related to psychological mode, reflecting how strongly an individual believes, desires, or is otherwise committed to a particular content. Degree of commitment is often available as a metacognitive judgment, as shown by the many psychological studies demonstrating high degrees of systematicity in the relations among scaled judgments. According to the analysis offered here, all mental states are characterized by degrees of commitment associated with particular modes of entertaining content. It is important to keep in mind that these are not variables of content, although contents can certainly express matters of degree. The distinction is like that between (a) being 50% certain that it will rain this afternoon, and (b) being 100% certain that there is a 50% chance of rain. In many cases, of course, degree of commitment may be functionally at ceiling. For example, in our ordinary, nonreflective activity we are functionally certain of—completely committed to—the contents of our perceptual awareness.

An implication of this point, developed at greater length in later chapters, is that reports of degree of commitment—for example, belief or subjective likelihood—reflect metacognitive judgments rather than direct access to mental processes. In some cases—such as degrees of belief in linguistically represented propositions—such judgments may be highly accurate, or at least very systematic. In other cases, such as judgments of degree of desire (usually reified as desirability of some state of affairs), metacognitive access may be very difficult and reports consequently highly labile (e.g., Fischhoff, Slovic, & Lichtenstein, 1980; Slovic, 1995).

Noncontent Implementation Properties. Some noncontent variables follow not from the analysis of intentional structure but from concerns with implementation properties (J. R. Anderson, 1987b) such as the time course of information processing. For example, mental states presumably have duration (Pöppel, 1988), even if the beginning and end of a particular state cannot be fixed with indefinite precision (Dennett & Kinsbourne, 1992). Mental state contents may also vary in their durability; some things are hard to keep in mind. Other noncontent variables include the evocative powers (often described in psychological literature in terms such as *strength* or *availability*) of current mental state contents. For example, the reliability or speed with which thinking the concept *cat* evokes the concept *dog* depends in some manner on content relations and may be important for modeling mental processes, but these variables are not themselves part of the intentional structure of the corresponding mental states.

A complete theory of cognition must encompass relations among mental states in terms of all of these categories of variables. For example, to understand even a simple case of everyday reasoning, we must understand the contents of mental states in which premises and conclusions are considered, the psychological modes (e.g., belief) and degrees of commitment involved in considering those contents, and implementation properties such as the durations of the mental states involved. In the next sections, I consider some observations about content and noncontent variables that follow from analyzing the intentional structure of mental states from the experienced cognition point of view.

SYMBOLIC CONTENTS AND MENTAL REPRESENTATION

Activity is critical in the generation of perceptual-enactive experience, for example by changing one's point of view. Activities that can be reliably performed without immediate, concurrent support from the environment serve a more elaborate role in generating symbolic awareness. Such performances can come to serve as surrogates for the environment, thus constituting acts of representing. For example, private speech can serve as a vehicle for the content of an instantiated belief. Such instances of symbolic representation are therefore performatory in character. When memory allows some performances to be dissociated from immediate environmental support—a commonplace observation—there can be intentional distance between the content and object of an experienced mental state, expanding the ways that state can participate in mental processes.

The Performatory Character of Symbolic Representation

There are many ways to present the notion of symbolic representation, and it is not clear that there is a consensus among cognitive scientists concerning the basic concept. For many purposes, a rough functional characterization is sufficient, and we can point to clear examples of symbols and the representational systems in which they participate. Language and mathematics are the prototypes, each exhibiting such characteristics as arbitrary reference, formal structure that supports syntactically based composition of symbol structures, and operations that perform truth-preserving transformations of those structures (e.g., Haugeland, 1985). These symbol structures are representations, we might say, because they can be manipulated as surrogates for the states of affairs they represent (Palmer & Kimchi, 1986; also see chapter 2).

Many cognitive scientists have argued (or assumed) that all of the information processes in cognitive theory should be characterized as symbol processing (e.g., Fodor, 1975; Fodor & Pylyshyn, 1981; Marr, 1982; Newell, 1990), although this assumption is not universal (e.g., Massaro & Cowan, 1993). Many of these information processes, if they existed, would have to be unconscious. The explanatory force of this unconscious symbol-processing relies on analogies to the conscious manipulation of symbols like those of language or mathematics. One might argue that the existence of computational machines demonstrates that symbol manipulation does not require consciousness (or indeed mentality of any sort). Conscious symbol manipulation, however, involves a point of view, a perspective from which the representational vehicle (speech, written symbols, or electrical states) serves its representational function. This is the central point of Searle's (1980, 1990) famous Chinese room parable—that the standard account of representation in the IP framework results in theories that have no place for a point of view. In this example, Searle asked readers to imagine a room in which an individual with no access to the outside world translates Chinese sentences into English by consulting explicit rules, and argued that no understanding of Chinese is thereby produced. Despite its weaknesses as an argument (see the commentaries accompanying Searle, 1980, 1990), the example does pose an important challenge. The common "systems response" to Searle's argument is that a point of view, from which understanding can occur, is somehow emergent in the activities of the information-processing system as a whole. Proponents of the system's response, however, have the burden of proof to show how this is possible. There is no reason to assume, as cognitive scientists often have, that consciousness arises simply because a system is sufficiently complex. In chapter 7, I consider the status of nonconscious information processes at greater length. I believe, however, that Searle is correct in asserting that cognitive theorists have generally anthropomorphized the brain (Searle, 1990), relying on analogies to conscious cognition for explanatory force and failing to show how conscious experience can emerge from nonconscious symbol processing.

I propose instead to begin with experienced cognition, considering the structure of conscious mental states that clearly involve symbolic representation. For example, for at least some mental states, the vehicle of content is quite literally language in the form of private speech. Symbolic representation in this sense is grounded in performances that do not require continuous, concurrent environmental support.

In perceptual-enactive awareness, performances such as looking or manipulating serve as vehicles of content by virtue of being directed at objects or states of affairs that figure in conditions of satisfaction. The same observation is true in many clear cases of symbolic awareness, even though the performance may be covert (as in the case of private speech). Consider, for example, the use of covert (or sometimes overt) speech to code information to be remembered in a short-term memory task. In a typical study, participants are asked to view or listen to short lists of verbal items (digits, letters, or words), then to demonstrate by recall or recognition that they have remembered the list. The results of many experiments converge on the conclusion that the mental representations used to retain these lists are speech-like (see Baddeley, 1986, for a review of this work). The performatory character of these representations is shown by observations like those of Zhang and Simon (1985), who demonstrated that memory for lists longer than about three items depended on the time required to pronounce the items (more items could be remembered when they could be spoken quickly). By *performatory character*, then, I mean to emphasize the temporal (and sometimes spatial) organization of, and constraints on, activities that serve a representational function.

Language and Private Speech as Vehicles of Content

Intuition suggests a strong link between verbalization and the concept of consciousness. Much of the thinking that we experience and remember can be characterized as inner speech, and the ability to verbally report aspects of our experience is often taken as an index of awareness. I think that the commonly assumed linkage between consciousness and verbal reportability is seriously misleading, and that perceptual-enactive forms of awareness are more fundamental. Nevertheless, those conscious mental states whose contents are linguistic (or can be accurately paraphrased by natural-language sentences) are clear cases of consciousness that might be labeled symbolic awareness.

Cognitive scientists generally agree that language plays a crucial role in cognition, but also generally reject or disregard the view that private speech actually constitutes (some) thinking. The specialness of language—its complex syntactic structure, the universality of many of its features across cultures and native language groups, its rapid acquisition by children, and thus its presumed innateness—is almost an article of faith among cognitive scientists influenced by linguistics. On the other hand, a number of prominent theorists (e.g., J. R. Anderson, 1983; Newell, 1990) have expressed the opinion that language will ultimately be explained in the same theoretical terms as other aspects of cognition such as problem solving. My point here is independent of this argument. However we ultimately account for language, its primary realization is in the performance of speech. And speech serves as a vehicle of content, both for social interactions and for individuals; I pursue this point at greater length in chapter 8.

The philosophical literature on intentionality is mostly concerned with the analysis of mental states with linguistic or language-like contents. An example of an intentional state prototypical of cases analyzed in the literature, if not of actual experienced cognition, is the kind of mental state expressed by a sentence like, "I believe that x," where x is a proposition making an assertion about a state of the world. Mental states that can be described in this way are sometimes called propositional attitudes, to indicate that the state comprises an attitude (e.g., belief) toward a proposition. Philosophers have often assumed that "mental states are relations to mental representations" (Fodor, 1980a, p. 68; see chapter 2), but this is often a philosophical version of the implicit-agent stance in which the agent (who has the attitude toward some content) stands outside the domain of theoretical explanation. Sentences describing such states are often indexical or deictic; for example, the truth values of, "I believe that it is Wednesday" or, "I believe that my computer is in front of me" depend on a viewpoint, the location in space and time of the speaker. To have a belief like this of course does not require saying such a sentence; however, it might involve actually saying (to oneself) a sentence expressing the content of the belief. That is, covertly uttering, "It's Wednesday" might be part of entertaining the corresponding belief.

Philosophers (and sometimes cognitive scientists) have discussed the intentionality or aboutness of states primarily in terms of the referents of their language-like content. For example, Fodor (1980b, commenting on Searle, 1980) said:

> The main point about the treatment of intentionality in representational theories of the mind . . . is this: intentional properties of propositional attitudes are viewed as inherited from semantic properties of mental representations (and not from the functional role of mental representations, unless "functional role" is construed broadly enough to include symbol-world relations). In effect, what is proposed is a reduction of the problem *what makes mental states intentional* to the problem *what bestows semantic properties on (fixes the interpretation of) a symbol*. This reduction looks promising because we're going to have to answer the latter question anyhow (for example, in constructing theories of natural language); and we need the notion of mental representation anyhow (for example, to provide appropriate domains for mental processes). (p. 431)

From my point of view, of course, Fodor had this backwards: The intentional structure of mental states can be seen in perceptual-enactive awareness, which is not symbolic in the same sense that states with linguistic content are symbolic.

Intentional Distance and the Content–Object Distinction

Intentional distance refers to the feature of some mental state contents that they can be functionally dissociated from their objects or conditions of satisfaction. In the case of perceptual-enactive awareness, the possibility of such dissociation is extremely limited—one generally cannot experience perceptual contents or intentions in action without the ongoing support of information available in the environment. Two implications follow: First, such contents are not truly representations in the sense that they are temporally and causally closely bound to their objects and thus cannot be manipulated as surrogates for those objects in the sense that symbolic contents can be. Second, metacognitive access to the content–object distinction is correspondingly limited. In contrast, an explicit, instantiated belief that we experience in part as a covert verbal performance (i.e., saying to ourselves) has greater intentional distance from its object than does a state involving nonreflective perceptual experience of an object presently in view in the environment.

To summarize: When activities serve as vehicles of content, and can be reliably performed in the absence of immediate environmental support, awareness can be symbolic and representational in the sense that content and object can be temporally and functionally dissociated. This dissociation is the intentional distance made possible by memory. Linguistic representation realized in private speech constitutes the prototypical example of symbolic representation, although I do not wish to claim that symbolic thinking is only private speech.

NONCONTENT PROPERTIES
AND MENTAL PROCESSES

The experienced cognition framework suggests that mental processes be understood as series of causally related mental states described in terms of their intentional structure. Some of these relations can be described in terms of content variables, but others must be described in terms of noncontent variables. This requires considering the noncontent properties of mental states in somewhat greater detail.

Degrees of Commitment and Mental Processes
as Functions

Mental processes may be characterized by the types of mental states they relate—where *type* refers primarily to the mode in which content is entertained. For example, reasoning generally relates multiple states in the mode of belief, states whose contents are premises and conclusion related in an argument structure. The theories of reasoning known as mental logic theories (e.g., Rips, 1994) describe these content relations, as do some forms of nonpsychological logic. Intention formation, in common-sense, cognitive explanations, is usually thought to involve the generation of a state in the mode of intent on the basis of prior states in the modes of belief and desire. Dulany's (1968) Theory of Propositional Control (Wilson & Dulany, 1983) describes the formation of intentions by subjects in some experimental paradigms. In both reasoning and intention formation, which might be viewed as fundamental categories of cognition, we can analytically distinguish generation of content (described in terms of content variables) from transfer of commitment (described in terms of mode variables).

The syntax of mental processes thus describes relations among both content and mode variables, describing paths for the transfer of commitment. For example, we might represent the reasoning schema *modus ponens* as follows:

$$B(q) = f[B(\text{if } p, \text{then } q), B(p)]$$

indicating that degree of belief in the conclusion (the truth of the consequent q) is some function of degree of belief in the premises. In chapter 11, I elaborate on this approach to analyzing mental processes, discussing in detail examples of such analyses by Dulany and me (Dulany, 1968; Carlson & Dulany, 1988). Note, however, that existing theories typically address either the generation of content or transfer of commitment, but rarely both at once. For example, research on deductive reasoning has typically been concerned with how individuals generate conclusions given sentences representing premises (e.g., Johnson–Laird, 1983), whereas degrees of belief in those premises are rarely considered. On the other hand, research in the information integration tradition (e.g., N. H. Anderson, 1981) has generally focused on how continuously scaled variables—which can sometimes be construed as degrees of belief—describing particular fixed contents, are integrated.

In the experienced cognition approach, *mental operations* are characterized as functions relating mental states. The operations are thus not themselves states, and not the kind of thing we expect to be conscious or unconscious. The distinction between content and noncontent intentional variables thus helps us to understand what hypothesis might be rejected when a process is described as unconscious: the hypothesis that the relevant contents include only the contents of conscious states, related by nonconscious operations (Dulany, 1991).

Implementation Properties and Evocative Powers

A number of authors have noted that part of what it means to be a symbol is to provide access to knowledge beyond that carried by the symbol itself (e.g., Newell, 1990). This property of symbolic contents is what Dulany (1991; see next) has described as the evocative power of mental contents—their capacity to bring to mind other mental contents. The evocative power of a particular content may be described along content or semantic lines: Which possible contents are likely to be brought to mind by a particular instantiated content? However, it must also be described in terms of speed and reliability, the observable consequences of theoretical constructs such as strength of association or degree of activation. As discussed in chapter 2, such constructs are central to many of the explanations offered by cognitive psychologists trying to account for their experimental results. From the present perspective, these constructs are best understood as reflecting noncontent, implementational properties of mental states. Typically, content relations are assumed and experimental manipulations are aimed at varying these noncontent variables, which may be correlated with content relations. For example, the use of priming techniques in cognitive research is based on the assumption that semantically related contents are also related by associative links allowing the spread of activation. We should not suppose, however, that such variables are part of the content of the experimental participant's conscious experience—not because they are unconscious contents, but because they are not content variables at all.

Understanding experienced cognition as a sequence of conscious mental states thus entails finding functions that relate those states in terms of their contents, modes, and implementation properties. The first two of these categories of variables follow from the analysis of intentional structure, and neither intentional nor implementational noncontent variables describe contents of conscious experience. By understanding experienced cognition in this framework, we can clarify issues concerning what is and is not conscious about cognition.

THE GROUNDING OF SYMBOLIC COGNITION

Understanding symbolic representation as performatory suggests an approach to the symbol grounding problem. This problem is essentially the question of how symbols come to have their symbolic or representational status. As Harnad (1990) noted, this is a critical problem for symbol-processing versions of information-processing theory (see chapter 2) because the computations carried out by mental processes must result in representations that are useful to the individual acting in an environment, presumably by accurately representing aspects of that environment. Of course, any theory that allows symbolic representation, even as a subset of cognitive activity, must confront this problem. Harnad's solution is based on the idea of *categorical perception*, that the perceptual systems act to identify patterns in categorical terms rather than preserving the unique and continuous nature of the available information. For example, we appear to hear speech sounds as instances of phonetic categories rather than in terms of their auditory characteristics (but see Massaro, 1992). Harnad's approach is similar to Dretske's (1981) account of the transition from analog preservation of information to symbolic representation—according to Dretske, when information is transformed into discrete (thus, digital) categories, it becomes symbolic. These approaches suggest that we must ultimately account for the symbolic character of mental activity in evolutionary terms; from the point of view of a given individual, the capacities that support symbolic representation are innate. This is the *language of thought* hypothesis, that a basic vocabulary of symbols underlies our cognitive capacities (Fodor, 1975).

Piaget offered an alternative to the language of thought account, suggesting that the capacity for symbolic representation is constructed in the course of development. On this view, symbols are *developmentally grounded* in the formal structure of sensorimotor activity. I noted in the previous chapter that the physical constraints on activities such as movement (displacement in space) exhibited a formal structure corresponding to the group structure of symbol systems such as integer arithmetic. To form more general logical structure, we need add to group structure only the features of class identity and set inclusion (Chapman, 1988). The asymmetry or temporal ordering of activities such as counting, which depends on memory (i.e., knowing which of a set of items have been counted), allows for this generalization. Gallistel and Gelman (e.g., 1992) also argued that nonverbal abilities provide the basis for simple arithmetic skills that become symbolic with development. Their account is very different from Piaget's in a number of ways, particularly in assuming preverbal abilities that are specific to arithmetic. Nevertheless, it shares the feature that symbolic skill is developmentally grounded in the characteristics of nonsymbolic activity. And in the case of arithmetic, we have a wealth of developmental observations of children as they acquire skill in symbolic performance.

Consider the typical course of development of arithmetic ability. The first skill that is clearly a component of adult arithmetic is counting. Counting, in turn, depends on the ability to produce verbal items—the names of numbers—in one-to-one correspondence with objects to be counted. The ability to place objects into one-to-one correspondence with one another, or with simple actions such as pointing, is itself a skill that must be acquired. One of the first arithmetic operations beyond counting to be learned is addition, which is usually acquired on the basis of examples in which visually presented sets of objects are spatially grouped. Children initially add by counting, inventing and discarding several algorithms before settling on the *min* strategy in which they count on from the larger addend the number of times specified by the smaller, or min, addend, reporting the endpoint of the count as the result (Groen & Parkman, 1972; Groen & Resnick, 1977; Resnick, 1989).

There is considerable debate among developmental psychologists concerning the best way to characterize this developmental course. For example, Siegler (e.g., 1991) argued that children acquire procedures for performing arithmetic operations, then use the ability to reliably perform these procedures as a basis for learning the principles underlying their performance. Karmiloff-Smith (1994) proposed a similar account of cognitive development in general, arguing that the knowledge implicit in procedural skills is gradually made explicit, thus coming under greater control, "A fundamental aspect of human development is the hypothesized process by which information that is *in* a cognitive system becomes progressively explicit knowledge *to* that system. I call this the 'representational redescription' hypothesis . . ." (p. 694). On the other hand, Gelman (e.g., 1990) argued that principles precede, and support the acquisition of, procedures.

It seems likely that neither of these alternatives is correct, and that the acquisition of complex symbolic skills follows a course that could be described as *bootstrapping*—as routines are learned and practiced, they become sufficiently reliable to be combined into higher order skills. More important, however, it seems that actions constrained by physical laws and supported by environmentally available information (e.g., the physical presence of objects to be counted or sets to be added) form the basis of operations that can later be performed mentally—that is, without such concurrent environmental constraint and support. This is the essence of Piaget's account of the formal structure of arithmetic (and of logic), and helps us see how the truth-preserving character of symbolic mediums for skilled performance can be developmentally grounded. Actions come to serve a symbolic function, which can be taken over by artifacts (e.g., written digits) that come to have conventional symbolic meaning. The availability of conventional symbol systems may then allow more complex symbolic skills that are grounded only very indirectly in actions on the environment.

Symbolic Representation and Cognition

Symbolic representation is often said to be essential for the generative character of cognition (e.g., Fodor & Pylyshyn, 1988). For example, language is said to be generative because skilled users of a language can produce and understand an indefinite number of novel (to them) but well-formed sentences. Similarly, although perhaps less impressively, the symbol system constituting integer arithmetic is generative—for example, it appears that we can always (in principle, at least) count one number higher than we have before. The standard account of how generative symbolic skills are realized psychologically goes something like this: Mental operations corresponding to syntactic rules operate to compose and transform mental representations that are realized as symbol structures. Thus, for example, the rules of arithmetic allow us to indefinitely compose symbol structures representing new numbers.

A second role of symbol representation in cognition is supposed to be in providing access to knowledge. Newell (1990) argued that providing distal access is a defining feature of symbolic representations, and that the need for such access is the fundamental reason for postulating symbolic representation. The idea is that some computational tasks—guiding actions or making inferences, for example—require the use of more information than can be stored locally to the processes making a computation. For example, Newell (1990) pointed out that, "the structure of the token 'cat' does not contain all the needed knowledge" (p. 74) to comprehend its use in a sentence or to support inferences. Activating or producing a token of *cat* must therefore (at least according to Newell's localist view of symbol representation) have the activation or production of related symbols among its consequences. A particular symbol thus participates in cognition in virtue of its relations to other symbols.

Dulany (1991) noted that proposals about the nature of symbolic representations are critical for understanding the contents of conscious mental episodes. He argued that cognition involves three kinds of symbolic representation: reference, signification, and evocation. In the first sense, something is a representation if it refers—if it denotes or stands for something. This is our ordinary sense, in which, for example, the word *clock* stands for a category of things. The second sense of representation is signification—something represents by virtue of its functional role in a representational system. Consider function words like *by*, *of*, *in*, and so on. These words do not refer in the sense of standing for objects in the world. However, they participate in representations by virtue of their functional role in the system of language. Together with other words they can represent, thus serving as symbols. Finally, Dulany argued that a symbolic representation may be simply something that can evoke other representations; that is, by its presence in consciousness can cause other representations to come to consciousness, to be activated or constructed. In this sense, the content of perceptual awareness might be seen as symbolic, because we can formulate sentences (for example) on the basis of perceptual experience. From my point of view, this final sense of *symbolic* does not capture all of perceptual-enactive awareness, whose content need not be symbolic. However, it does identify one role of performatory representation—the act of producing a symbol token (e.g., a word) changes the information available, much as movement in an environment changes the optic array for vision.

Inner speech is one example of symbolic representation that should be seen as a kind of performance, symbolic representing that can occur without the environmental presence of an object toward which the performance is informationally directed. This view is similar to Piaget's (as represented in Chapman, 1988) in some ways, emphasizing the grounding of symbols in action and thus the embodiment of formal constraints that correspond to physical laws. Understanding symbolic representation in this way allows us to see the continuity of perceptual-enactive and symbolic awareness. In both types of mental states, action supported by currently available information allows for exploration and resampling, providing the opportunity for egolocative processing and the emergence of intentional structure.

The performatory view of symbolic representation sketched here is useful in several ways. It provides a solution to the symbol grounding problem that grows naturally out of the intentional analysis of perceptual-enactive awareness, illustrating the continuity between perceptual-enactive and symbolic awareness. It helps us to understand how symbolic activity can be cognitively useful by providing an account of the constraints that enable truth-preserving mental representation. Finally, understanding symbolic representation as performatory helps us to understand the parallel roles of activity in perceptual-enactive and symbolic awareness.

COSPECIFICATION IN SYMBOLIC AWARENESS

Cospecification is central to the intentionality of symbolic awareness, as it is for perceptual-enactive awareness. Just as the information available to perception is cospecific and supports (and constrains) resampling and exploration, so too does the information made available by symbolic representation. In this section, I consider cospecification and egolocative processing in the context of symbolic mental states, concluding with a discussion of how the variables of intentional structure help us to understand the potential for reflective awareness of mental states.

Symbolic Media as Informational Arrays

I argued in chapter 4 that egolocative processes that distinguish self and object in perceptual-enactive awareness involve resampling and exploration of informational arrays supported by a stable environment. Egolocation in turn allows consciousness to serve its function of guiding activity.

In the case of symbolic awareness, it is remembered information that provides the basis for resampling and exploration. Just as the information available for vision constitutes an array, defined (for the simplifying case of a static visual field) by spatial adjacency relations, the information available for symbolic thinking constitutes an array defined by adjacency relations. Adjacency relations in an array are of course interdefined with a traversal process, such as scanning in the case of the visual array. In the case of mental representation by language, the adjacency relations may be temporal (as in articulatory rehearsal of a list of items in a short-term memory experiment) or semantic (as in the reminding or priming that occurs when we think a word). This is how private speech, or other performances in the absence of current environmental support, serves a representational function. Thus information from memory, whose object or referent may be past experience, constitutes an array that can be resampled and explored just as a visual array can, although perhaps with a different set of constraints. For example, research on mental imagery demonstrates that processes that constitute imagery have perspectival character and sequential traversal, as does visual perception (Kosslyn, 1994).

In addition to its great representational flexibility, an advantage of language as a vehicle for thought is that the availability of information can be extended by repeated performatory representation—that is, rehearsal. By extending the availability of information, rehearsal supports the resampling and exploration of remembered information, allowing stability and repeatability for egolocative processing. This reliability or stability of performatory representations whose objects are past experienced also constitutes the basic condition for intentional distance and symbolic representation. The gist of this idea is that both the performatory representation and the information supporting it are subject to resampling.

Mode and Content

Like perceptual-enactive states, symbolic mental states take place within an informational manifold, a collection of available information organized in arrays that simultaneously specify the experiencing self and the objects of awareness. The aspects of intentional structure referred to by *mode* and *content* correspond to the two poles of this cospecific relation. Briefly, cognitive mode describes the manner in which the self is specified, whereas content characterizes how an object of cognition is specified. The mode of a mental state depends on the activity being performed. For example, the characteristic mode of the mental states experienced by an individual engaged in reasoning is belief. The aspectual shape or perspectival character of a mental state content indicates how the object of that state is specified. For example, a particular object may be thought of as an exemplar of a category, supporting some kinds of inference (e.g., to possible uses of the object).

Is Consciousness a Matter of Degree?
Agency and Intentional Distance

A common way of thinking about consciousness is in terms of reflective or metacognitive access to mental states. The preceding discussion suggests two ways in which the possibility of reflective awareness may be a matter of degree. The first is related to the intentional distance between content and object, involving the manner in which a symbolic mental content specifies its conditions of satisfaction, or object. Acts of representing may differ in the degree to which they can be reliably performed in the absence of concurrent environmental support of their intentional objects. The importance of language to thought lies in part in the fact that linguistic vehicles can, under some circumstances, be very reliably reproduced in the absence of their referents. Imagining, especially dynamic imagining of extended events, is on average somewhat less reliable. In both cases, artifacts—written language or various kinds of depictions— can effectively off-load the burden of reproducing acts of representing. To the extent that an act of representing can be performed without the current informational support of its object, effective intentional distance is increased because (a) the representing can itself become the object of (metacognitive) thought, and (b) an individual can therefore distinguish the aspectual view of an object provided by its representation from the object itself.

A second way in which the possibility of reflective consciousness may be a matter of degree concerns *agency*, the manner in which the mode of a mental state reflects specification of the self. Again, this variable depends on the extent to which an activity relies on the informational support of the current environment. To the extent that the activity is independent of such concurrent support, the mode of awareness and the content of awareness can be discriminated by metacognitive processes that take the mental activity as object.

The degree of agency corresponds to the extent to which egolocative processes can separate self from content and object, and thus provides an important variable for cognitive theory. For example, agency will likely depend on the opportunity for resampling and exploration of an informational array, an opportunity that is reduced in the case of rapidly changing arrays. We should therefore expect that highly skilled activities, in which rapid performance results in rapid change in informational arrays, to be characterized by reduced metacognitive access, a subjective mindlessness.

Another expectation based on these considerations is that increased agency should provide greater opportunities to link activities to goals in new ways. A goal can be conceived as a metacognitive state whose content relates the self and some desired state of affairs; to the extent that self and object can be distinguished, it should be easier to form a mental state with corresponding content that can be linked with the content of the goal. Social-cognitive research involving manipulations of self-awareness (e.g., Carver & Scheier, 1981, 1982, 1990; Duval & Hensley, 1976; Duval & Wicklund, 1972) supports this prediction. For example, asking subjects to perform a novel task in front of a mirror—which increases the salience of visual information specifying the self—may lead to better performance. On the other hand, as I discuss in the next chapter, circumstances can emphasize self-specific information in a way that interferes with performance, as when high levels of arousal prevent the rapid changes of viewpoint characteristic of perceptual-enactive and symbolic awareness. The role of goals and agency in cognition, and particularly in skill acquisition, is considered in more detail in chapter 9.

In general, then, mental states can be characterized in terms of their degree of agency. Although individual states can be so described, the more important point is that processes that distinguish self from object— perhaps over a series of individual mental states—are critical for understanding the role of consciousness in the control of activity. Self-awareness, in the sense of agency produced by egolocative processing, provides the opportunity to link activities with goals in new ways.

Rather than classifying mental states and the processes in which they participate as conscious or unconscious, then, we can understand variations in the possibility of reflective awareness as determined in part by the values particular mental states take on these dimensions of intentional distance and agency. The analysis of intentional structure provides a basis for understanding some of the limits on reflective access without postulating a separate domain of unconscious mental states.

SUMMARY: VARIABLES FOR DESCRIBING
MENTAL STATES

The analyses of experienced cognition offered in chapters 4 and 5 represent an elaboration of the cospecification hypothesis in terms of the intentional structure of mental states. This intentional structure provides a number of variables for describing mental states, and thus for developing scientific theories of cognition as it is experienced.

Figure 5.1 summarizes this analysis in terms of the informational manifold in which experienced cognition occurs. Informational arrays made available by the perceptual and memory systems cospecify an acting, experiencing self and objects of experience. The contents of experience reflect the manner in which activity involves the self in reciprocal interaction with the environment. As I argued in chapter 4, the fundamental intentional structure of experienced cognition is present even in nonreflective, nonsymbolic perceptual-enactive awareness.

Figure 5.2 summarizes the variables I have discussed for describing conscious mental states. Although in the figure I have associated these variables with particular aspects of intentional structure, it is important

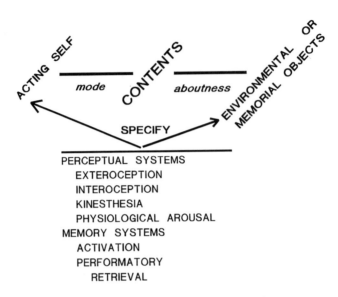

FIG. 5.1. The informational manifold: The perceptual and memory systems support a manifold of informational arrays in which self and objects are cospecified.

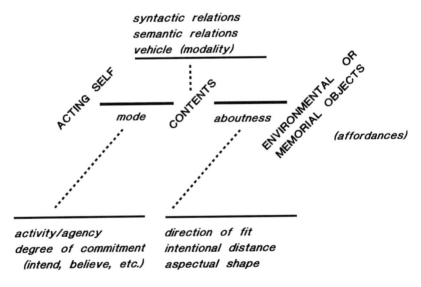

FIG. 5.2. The intentional structure of experienced cognition: Conscious mental states have intentional structure that provides a set of variables for describing mental processes.

to remember that variables that are analytically distinct may be logically or empirically linked. For example, we noted in chapter 4 that alternative modes of commitment such as *intend* and *believe* are associated with different directions of fit between content and object. Furthermore, actual episodes of experienced cognition generally involve many mental states in rapid succession. Pöppel (1988) estimated that mental states may have durations in the range of 30 milliseconds to 3 seconds, and that states in the upper part of this range are quite uncommon. Newell (1990) argued on the basis of neural and computational considerations that the cognitive band of human action includes events of approximately 100 milliseconds to 10 seconds, with simple operations occurring at a time scale of about 1 second. It is at about this grain of analysis that I believe the analysis of intentional structure can be applied.

Emotion, Bodily Awareness, and the Unity of Consciousness

> *The mind is embodied, in the full sense of the term, not just embrained.*
> —Damasio, 1994, p. 118

Integrating theories of emotion and theories of cognition is a longstanding challenge. Although there is a great deal of evidence that emotion affects cognition in a variety of ways, the most comprehensive theories of cognition available (e.g., J. R. Anderson, 1983, 1993; Newell, 1990) have essentially nothing to say about emotion. And the conceptions of cognition assumed by theories of emotion are generally not very detailed. In this chapter, I argue that the cospecification hypothesis provides a basis for achieving this integration. The central idea is that the bodily information central to emotional experience has characteristic effects on egolocative processing, and that these effects constitute the experience of emotionality. Considering how it is that self and object are cospecified in emotional experience will also help to clarify the general cospecification hypothesis.

EMOTION AS AROUSAL PLUS COGNITION

There is widespread agreement that emotion involves components of physiological arousal or bodily awareness together with evaluative cognition. This idea is expressed in different ways in the early proposals known as the James–Lange and Cannon–Bard theories (Strongman, 1978), and is a central tenet of contemporary theories (e.g., Lang, 1995). However, exactly how arousal and cognition combine to yield emotional experience is unclear. Some authors write as if arousal and cognitive evaluations serve as premises in inference-like processes whose conclusions constitute emotional experience. This approach, like other attempts to treat emotion in primarily content terms, seems to miss the essence of emotional experience. By understanding the roles of arousal and cognitive content in mental states construed according to the experienced cognition framework, we can develop an alternative view of this relation.

Sources and Functions of Arousal

The physiological arousal accompanying emotion involves increased activation of the autonomic nervous system. There is a broad consensus that the conditions for this activation include disruption of ongoing activity or discrepancies between expectations and reality (Lang, 1995; Mandler, 1984). The actual pattern of neural (and glandular) activity may be quite general to a variety of emotional experiences, as suggested by Mandler, "The resulting affective event is the perception of autonomic activity, which—except for some special states such as sexual arousal—is registered as undifferentiated arousal, varying primarily in intensity" (p. 118). Recently, some authors (e.g., Levenson, 1992) have argued that more detailed measurements demonstrate some specificity of patterns of autonomic arousal to particular categories of emotional experience.

Whether autonomic arousal is undifferentiated or specific to particular emotions is less important to my argument than is a more global observation about this arousal: The arousal accompanying emotion has an informational aspect, constituting part of the informational manifold in which experienced cognition occurs. Autonomic arousal provides a source of primarily self-specific information, which changes slowly relative to the pace of mental activity. The core of my hypothesis about emotional awareness is this: The difference, compared to less-emotional episodes, in the relative rate at which self-specific and object-specific aspects of informational arrays change, is largely responsible for the distinctive character of emotional awareness. In contrast to the rapid changes in point of view characteristic of perceptual or mental activity, the bodily awareness supporting emotional experience contributes to relatively slow changes in self-specific information.

A number of theorists, noting the role of discrepancy or disruption in generating the arousal associated with emotion, have suggested that the function of emotion is to trigger or modulate self-awareness or control functions. For example, Mandler (1985) described autonomic arousal as "a signal to the mental organization for attention, alertness, and scanning of the environment" (p. 118). In Mandler's view, this signaling function is mediated by imagery and participates in cognitive processes in the same way as any other kind of information: "The role of imagery in emotion is not special; it functions in emotional construction as it does in all other conscious states" (Mandler, 1984, p. 93). Similarly, Laird and Bresler (1992) proposed what they called a self-perception theory of emotion, arguing that the informational elements of arousal function in emotional experience as visual features do in visual experience.

This general approach to the role of arousal in emotional experience appropriately indicates the informational function of that arousal. It also addresses the question of the adaptive function of emotion, suggesting that emotion indicates a need for more active control (because ongoing, goal-directed activity has been disrupted or is not progressing satisfactorily). These considerations have led Lang (1995) to suggest that emotions are action dispositions, tendencies toward certain kinds of activity. This approach is generally compatible with the experienced cognition framework, but we need to see how these ideas can be elaborated in that framework.

Affective Valence and Egolocation

Particular emotions can be identified in terms of the degree of arousal and the affective valence associated with each (e.g., Lang, 1995; Ortony & Turner, 1990). *Affective valence* refers to the positive–negative dimension of emotional experience, and is often linked with primitive, biologically based motivational systems. For example, Lang (1995) suggested that emotion is based on appetitive and aversive systems that underlie consummatory and escape or avoidance activities.

The affective valence of emotional cognition thus involves assessing the relation of the self to some (real or imagined) state of the world. The term *valence* itself suggests approach or avoidance, a metaphor grounded in the perceptual guidance of egomotion. Lang (1995) noted that, "The behavior of very primitive organisms can be wholly characterized by two responses—a direct approach to appetitive stimuli and withdrawal from nociceptive stimuli" (p. 373). I want to suggest that the role of emotionality in experienced cognition is tied to the idea of egolocative processing—in order to approach or avoid something, the self must be located with respect to that something. The processes triggered by the onset of emotion—startle, orienting, scanning the environment—are just the sort of processes that should be associated with egolocation, rapidly changing an individual's viewpoint, and thus the self-specific aspects of the informational manifold available to that individual. At the same time, the arousal component of emotion is relatively slow, providing a stable set of self-specific cues. The longer-term, less-intense emotional experience often referred to as *mood* may serve to provide self-specific information over even longer time spans. Considering how these processes affect cospecification and egolocative processes will provide a framework for understanding the complex mixture of perceptual-enactive and metacognitive experience that constitutes the experience of emotionality.

BODILY AWARENESS AND COSPECIFICATION

We can understand the place of emotionality in experienced cognition by considering the role of bodily awareness in cospecification and egolocative processing. By *bodily awareness* here, I mean primarily what might be called the inner senses of the body—that is, information that specifies the inner state of the body rather than its location in environmental space or the arrangement of the limbs, for example. And although the state of our bodies can become the object of a mental state—that is, we can think about the body and its varying states—that is not the normal contribution of bodily awareness to experienced cognition. That normal contribution is instead to the cospecific manifold of information available for egolocative processes, in particular contributing stable, largely self-specific information. In terms of content, we might say that this information serves to establish the viewpoint from which an object is regarded, thus influencing the aspectual shape of content that is about that object. For example, if one is hungry, thoughts about the kitchen are likely to focus on its status as the location of food.

Body-Specific Information

A variety of information specifying the state of the body is available at any given moment. This information comprises kinesthesia (including visual and auditory kinesthesia; Gibson, 1966; also see chapter 4) and position sense, and the drive senses—pain, hunger, thirst, and so on—as well as information specifying the states of arousal associated with emotion. Some portion of this information is essential to emotional experience. However, in my view it is not necessary that the state of the body as such constitute an object of awareness for body-specific information to make its contribution to emotional experience. This hypothesis is thus contrary to several current proposals. For example, Laird and Bresler (1992) wrote, "we are asserting that the experience of an emotion is a cognition" (p. 228). Similarly, Damasio (1994) claimed that, *"feelings are just as cognitive as any other perceptual image"* (p. 159, italics in original). In these views, emotional arousal makes its contribution to experience by constituting part of the content of awareness.

In order to understand my hypothesis concerning the role of body-specific information, consider in more detail this self-perception view in which information about a body state constitutes the content of emotional experience. Damasio (1994) expressed this view forcefully and concisely:

> If an emotion is a collection of changes in body state connected to particular mental images that have activated a specific brain system, *the essence of feeling is the experience of such changes in juxtaposition to the mental images that initiated the cycle.* In other words, a feeling depends on a juxtaposition of an image of the body proper to an image of something else, such as the visual image of a face or the auditory image of a melody. (p. 145)

> Receiving a comprehensive set of signals about the body state in the appropriate brain regions is the necessary beginning but is not sufficient for feelings to be felt. As I suggested in the discussion on images, a further condition for the experience is the correlation of the ongoing representation of the body with the neural representations constituting the self. A feeling about a particular object is based on the subjectivity of the perception of the object, the perception of the body state it engenders, and the perception of modified style and efficiency of the thought process as all of the above happens. (pp. 147–148)

> Those who believe that little of the body state appears in consciousness under normal conditions may want to reconsider. (p. 152)

Damasio is correct to argue that the juxtaposition of body-specific information with object-specific information (e.g., "the visual image of a face") is central to emotional experience. However, distinguishing systematically between self-specific and object-specific information, and between content and non-content properties of mental states, lets us see that these types of information may play quite different roles in supporting emotional experience.

In contrast to the widely held view that perception of bodily states constitutes part of the content of emotional experience, the experienced cognition framework suggests that body-specific information contributes to emotional experience not as content per se but in a manner parallel to the contribution of perspective information to visual awareness. Just as perspective information specifies not the objects of visual awareness, but the vantage point from which they are viewed, body-specific information specifies not the objects of emotional awareness but the (emotional) vantage point from which they are experienced. How can this be?

Temporal Relations and Egolocation

In visual awareness, the self-specific information—information that specifies the viewpoint or viewpath from which the environment is seen—changes very rapidly relative to environment-specific information. This is obviously true in the ecological case of action within a relatively stable environment, and in the resampling associated with eye movements even when we are not moving around the environment. This difference in relative rates of change allows egolocative processing. In emotional awareness, the temporal and relative stability relations between self- and object-specific information typical of perceptual awareness are reversed.

In emotional awareness, the self-specific information corresponding to physiological arousal changes very slowly relative to changes that are due to changes in point of view that result from egomotion or other action, and thus relative to those affordances that guide action. For example, Frijda, Ortony, Sonnemans, and Clore (1992) reported estimates of 1.5 to 4 seconds for the minimal duration of emotional experience, and much longer time courses for some aspects of emotionality. In contrast, the duration of eye fixations during which visual information is sampled in skilled activities ranges from about 0.3 seconds in reading (Carr, 1986) to about 0.6 seconds in other skilled activities (Moray, 1986). These temporal relations help to account for the phenomenal experience of the projection of emotion (e.g., when you are angry, everyone is annoying), because the reversal of temporal relations interferes with cognitive aspects of egolocative processing. That is, we cannot distinguish our selves from the environment as effectively when we are in highly emotional states because we resample the environment with less moment-to-moment change in point of view. Rather than experiencing objects from a rapid succession of perspectives, we may experience a succession of objects from a single perspective established largely by emotional arousal. For example, when angry we may experience a succession of events as annoying or provoking.

Action Tendencies in Emotional Awareness

Emotions have been described as *action tendencies* or dispositions (e.g., Frijda, 1986; Lang, 1995; Shaver, Wu, & Schwartz, 1992). For example, the experience of anger may involve awareness of readiness to fight or perform other violent acts. This is one sense in which we might say that the cognition involved in emotion is performatory. These action tendencies are of course associated with the valence of emotional experience, likely pointing toward evolutionary elaboration and refinement of simple approach and withdrawal tendencies.

From the point of view of the intentional structure of emotional experience, two points about action tendencies should be noted. First, the informational aspects of an action tendency presumably constitute self-specific information, as does the bodily awareness associated with emotional arousal. Second, action tendencies suggest a direction of fit between the emotional states and their conditions of satisfaction. In particular, the action tendencies most commonly associated with emotion (e.g., to fight or flee) entail states with a world-to-mind direction of fit. Emotion may be triggered, according to Mandler (1984), because the world is failing to fit to the mind. Whatever action scheme was being pursued is not proceeding smoothly, and the consequences of actions are failing to correspond to intentions. Emotion is thus associated with the category of states that can be described as *desires*, which according to the analysis sketched in chapters 4 and 5 have a world-to-mind direction of fit.

Emotionality as a Global Descriptor

According to this analysis, emotions are not themselves conscious mental states. Although emotion per se can become the content of a metacognitive state—for example, when I notice that I am angry, { I am angry } is the content of a higher order state. Awareness of emotion in this sense—as a content—is not essential, however, to emotional experience. Despite the arguments that emotions can be represented as nodes or tags in a semantic network (e.g., Bower, 1981), the hypothesis that emotions are simply types of content can be rejected.

Could the emotional aspect of experience be described as the mode of a mental state, on the model of belief? Believing can become the content of a metacognitive state, as can being angry. Furthermore, the linguistic frames we use to report (some of) our mental states seem to be similar for emotions and belief. Compare "I believe that the conservatives have a great deal of political power" with "I am angry that the conservatives have a great deal of political power." It would appear that these sentences report two states with the same propositional content, entertained in different psychological modes. However, I believe that this hypothesis is also incorrect. In this case, analysis of the language in which we report mental states is misleading, obscuring the distinction between states as experienced and states as objects of reflection.

Instead, I think that the most appropriate way to view emotionality is as a global descriptor of a mental state or series of states, a property of the informational manifold in which conscious mental states occur. Just as a visual point of view determines the aspectual shape of visual experience—the "angle" we have on the objects we see—emotionality determines the aspectual shape of cognitive contents. For example, when angry, we tend to see the provocative aspects of situations.

I do not mean to deny that emotional experience can include reflective states whose content includes the emotion, nor do I mean to argue that such reflective states are atypical of emotional episodes. However, I do mean to claim that the fundamental feature of experienced cognition described by the term *emotion* is best understood as a characteristic of the informational manifold in which mental states occur, rather than as a content of those states. I hope to show that this analysis provides some insight in to how emotion is involved in the control of activity.

EMOTION AND THE CONTROL OF ACTIVITY

Emotion is involved in the control of activity. This is obvious from intro-spection and casual observation, and theorists concerned with emotion concur on this point. Lang and his colleagues (e.g., Lang, Bradley, Cuth-bert, 1992), for example, presented a theory relating motivational systems and the valence of emotion. The sometimes disruptive effects of emotion are perhaps best documented (e.g., Mandler, 1984), but Damasio (1994) and others pointed out the importance of emotionality for the normal control of activity. For example, patients with frontal-lobe damage are characterized by both abnormal (diminished) emotionality and failures of normal control of long-term goal-directed activity. The experienced cognition framework provides a means of understanding these relations between emotion and control.

Emotion and Egolocative Processing

One way in which emotion affects the control of activity is that emotional arousal serves to prompt and sustain egolocative processing. By changing the typical temporal relations between changes in self-specific and in object-specific information, emotional arousal provides increased oppor-tunities for self-consciousness. In visual experience, for example, taking the (usually constantly changing) point of view as an object of awareness involves adopting a special reflective attitude. This is achieved by the application of metacognitive skills for reflection, which must be highly developed to support activities such as drawing complex objects in accu-rate perspective technique. A somewhat less-specialized skill is the ability to reflect on one's spatial perspective in developing knowledge of the layout of a particular environment (Easton & Sholl, 1995; Sholl, 1995). In emotional experience, the self-specific information provided by autonomic arousal is much longer-lasting, remaining relatively stable over a period of seconds or longer. This stability provides the opportunity for resam-pling and exploration, making it possible to take the (emotional) self as an object of cognitive activity.

The egolocative processing allowed by this situation is exactly what is needed to allow the establishment of new goals or to reconsider the goals guiding ongoing activity. As discussed in more detail in chapter 9, goals are best conceived as egolocative states that specify the self achieving some state. Emotions may serve to evoke information that allows the present, experiencing self to be linked to the future self who will perform the activities specified by a new goal. Such links might be described as allowing commitment to future intentions and actions. The cospecific nature of informational arrays implies that current states may be linked to goal states by virtue of associative relations among both self-specific and object-specific information.

Emotion and the Transfer of Commitment

An interesting, and sometimes troubling, aspect of emotion is the phenomenon known as transfer of excitation. The core of this phenomenon is the observation that arousal produced by one event can be transferred to another, resulting in increased emotionality in the experience of the second event. For example, in Schachter and Singer's (1962) classic study, they provided evidence that arousal produced by injection of a drug (epinephrine) could contribute to the emotionality of an experience engineered by the experimenters. In ecological situations, the emotional arousal engendered by one event cause us to experience a subsequent event from a similar emotional point of view.

Mauro (1992) summarized the evidence on excitation transfer like this, "It appears that excitation transfer is the combination of cognitions concerning one event with the physiological arousal from another event" (p. 161); and "The emotional response to an event depends on the complex of cognitive and physiological processes that are active when that event occurs—whatever their original source" (p. 162).

Like the application of judgment heuristics (Kahneman, Slovic, & Tversky, 1982), we notice the phenomenon of excitation transfer primarily when it produces inappropriate results. For example, many of us have had the experience of snapping at an annoying family member, then realizing that the anger or annoyance being expressed really originated with an incident at work (although of course we may be more likely to recall those cases in which we were the victims rather than the agents of inappropriate emotional expression). More generally, the transfer of excitation is often appropriate insofar as the action required by an emotion-provoking situation typically extends over some period of time.

Excitation transfer in emotional experience (as it is usually identified) may be a special case of the transfer of commitment involved in mental processes such as reasoning, decision making, and intention formation. Again, consider a nonnormative case, the effectiveness of emotional appeals in persuasion. Emotional appeals sometimes succeed in inducing individuals to transfer belief from initial premises to some conclusion, even when the logical relations among the assertions do not support the reasoning. In decision making, the emotional consequences of how choices are framed may affect which choices are preferred (Tversky & Kahneman, 1981). These phenomena suggest that the arousal associated with emotional experience sometimes contributes to the degrees of commitment associated with beliefs. Transfer of commitment is of course also necessary in normative cases of rational thinking. For example, Dulany's Theory of Propositional Control (Dulany, 1968; Wilson & Dulany, 1983) describes the transfer of commitment from beliefs about contingencies and the strength with which outcomes are desired to intentions to act. Similarly, one aspect of reasoning is the transfer of commitment from premises to conclusions, resulting in lawful relations among the degrees of belief associated with the contents representing premises and conclusions. A reasonable hypothesis entailed by the present account is that the stability of self-specific information associated with emotion contributes to transfer of commitment by allowing the contents of several mental states to be considered from a partially invariant perspective. That is, we come to believe conclusions when we can reliably consider them from a point of view consistent with the perspective from which we consider their premises (chapter 11).

Emotionality and Long-Term Control

Consistent with this suggestion, emotionality appears to be critical for long-term control. Damasio (1994) argued that the lack of emotionality characteristic of frontal-lobe patients is related to their inability to effectively construct and carry out long-term plans. Damasio argued further that this long-term function of emotionality is central to the subjectivity of consciousness; for example, "I see self and the subjectivity it begets as necessary for consciousness in general and not just for self-consciousness" (p. 238); and "Our experiences tend to have a consistent perspective, as if there were indeed an owner and knower for most, though not all, contents. I imagine this perspective to be rooted in a relatively stable, endlessly repeated biological state" (p. 238). Stable information about the self is thus provided by biological states of the body, allowing us to sustain long-term goal-directed activity by allowing egolocative processes to distinguish information specific to the self from information specific to the immediate environment or activity. Lacking this stability, frontal-lobe patients are often captured by current affordances of the environment (or of what comes to mind from memory), appearing impulsive and uncontrolled.

Overall, then, the normal adaptive role of emotion in the control of activity can be seen as allowing the self to be distinguished from the immediate affordances of the environment. The salient and stable (over the course of relatively many distinct mental states) self-specific information provided by physiological arousal facilitates this distinction. When a situation calls for changing goals, as in the disruption of an ongoing action scheme, or for sustaining goals over long periods of time, as in the long-term planning so difficult for frontal-lobe patients, emotion serves an adaptive function. However, when close attention to currently available object-specific information is required, emotion is likely to be disruptive. This account is similar to Easterbrook's (1959) cue-utilization explanation of arousal-performance relations (see next), and suggests an approach to accounting for some aspects of emotional experience.

EMOTION AND THE STRUCTURE
OF MENTAL STATES

I have argued that emotionality need not appear as content to influence experienced cognition, but that the physiological arousal associated with emotion is a source of body-specific (and thus self-specific) information that contributes to cospecification. This arousal changes slowly relative to the course of thought and action, shaping the (emotional) perspective on objects of awareness. The link between this arousal and the goal-directedness (motivational character) of emotional valence should be understood in terms of egolocative processing—distinguishing self-specific from object-specific aspects of the informational manifold is central to the informational guidance of action. Although emotional arousal can be taken as object by metacognitive processing, this is not essential to the experience of emotion.

How Can We Be Angry and Not Know It?

A striking feature of emotion is that it can appear to be unconscious in the sense that an individual may realize that he or she is in an emotional state, and has been for some time, apparently without knowing it. Furthermore, it may not be obvious what event has caused the emotional state. If emotions are construed as cognitive contents, as many theorists have argued, this observation may be taken as evidence for unconscious processing. Because cognitive appraisal and perception of states of arousal are presumed to be precursors to emotional experience, such episodes appear to be unconscious in the sense of trains of thought occurring outside of awareness.

The present analysis suggests an alternative account of this phenomenon. The informational contribution of emotional arousal to experienced cognition need not appear as content, but provides what might be called perspectival information that affects which aspects of information specific to the object of thought make up the content of the experienced mental state. To put it another way, in the absence of metacognitive or reflective mental processes, physiological arousal need not appear as part of the content of experience even though it influences the values of the variables that describe experienced states. For example, the arousal associated with anger may affect experience in part through increasing the degree of commitment associated with a mental state with the mode *desire*, although the content of that state is not about the arousal. This implies, of course, that some informational influences on experienced cognition are nonconscious in the sense of influencing content without themselves appearing as content. This implication is taken up in more detail in the next chapter.

Effects of Emotion on Cognition

Much of the research on emotion and cognition has been concerned with how cognitive processes might differ, depending on an individual's emotional state. The effects that have been demonstrated fall into two categories: *content effects* such as the apparent mood-specificity of memory, and *noncontent effects* such as the disruption of cognitive (or other) performance by extreme emotional arousal. A review of these effects is beyond the scope of this chapter (see Isen, 1984); however, the analysis of emotionality in experienced cognition suggests approaches to understanding these effects. First, of course, on the present analysis a mixture of content and noncontent effects is exactly what we should expect. The present framework also implies some specific suggestions about particular effects.

Perhaps the most-studied content effect of emotion is mood-specific memory. The basic finding is that individuals often recall more mood-congruent than noncongruent information, particularly for negative moods (Isen, 1984; Rinck, Glowalla, & Schneider, 1992). One proposed explanation for this phenomenon is the network proposal suggested by Bower (1981). This explanation suggests that emotion is mentally represented in terms of nodes and links in a memory network, just like other mental contents. An emotional state thus activates portions of the network associated with information to be retrieved, increasing the likelihood or speed of retrieval. This is essentially a version of the more general encoding specificity account of memory retrieval (Tulving & Thomson, 1973), which suggests that memory is most effective when the information available at the time of retrieval matches that present during learning. The experienced cognition framework suggests a slightly different account that does not assume either that the emotional state present at learning or that at retrieval must become a content of consciousness in order to produce mood-specific effects. Rather, mood is part of the constellation of self-specific information that contributes to a particular perspectival or aspectual view of information to be learned or of retrieval cues. The similarity of this informational contribution between learning and retrieval episodes may generate corresponding similarities in the content of experience by contributing to similar aspectual views of the learned information and the retrieval cues. For example, considering some object from the perspective of sadness may be associated with contents that represent particular aspects of that object, without the sadness itself appearing as content. This account may be compatible at an implementation level with the network account, but has different implications for the phenomenal experience associated with this phenomenon.

Consider next the effect of emotional arousal on performance. The well-known Yerkes–Dodson law suggests that for a particular task performed by an individual, there will be an optimal level of arousal (see Proctor & Dutta, 1995, for a brief review). Although the generality of this law has been questioned (e.g., Christianson, 1992), it does seem to capture an empirical generalization for many situations. The experienced cognition framework suggests that such effects follow from the role of arousal in affecting the salience and stability of self-specific information. A degree of stability is needed to sustain the egolocative processing that allows goal-directed activities to be pursued. On the other hand, extreme arousal may make it difficult to flexibly change goals and to attend to environmental information necessary to guide task performance.

My point here is not to develop detailed accounts of emotion–cognition interactions, but to point out that the present analysis of emotionality can provide the beginnings of such accounts. Recognizing the informational, but not necessarily content-constituting, contribution of emotional arousal to experienced mental states lets us see that emotion and cognition are not separate domains but theoretically separable aspects of experienced cognition.

THE UNITY OF AWARENESS

The analysis presented in chapters 4 through 6 shows us how awareness arises in, and influences, the reciprocal interaction of organism (self) and environment. Experienced cognition occurs in an informational manifold comprising informational arrays whose availability is supported by the perceptual systems, by memory, by acts of performatory representation, and by systems responsible for bodily awareness. The experiencing self and experienced objects are cospecified in this informational manifold, and the perception–action cycle provides the opportunity for egolocative processing that distinguishes self and object. This activity can be characterized as a sequence of conscious mental states with intentional structure (as depicted in Figs. 5.1 and 5.2), which may be described in terms of variables appropriate for computational, information-processing theory building.

The Continuity of Consciousness

The experienced cognition framework shows us how the experiential unity and continuity of conscious experience correspond to a theoretical unity and continuity. James (1890) described the experiential unity and continuity of consciousness in his famous description of the stream of consciousness, and we generally take these features of consciousness for granted in our everyday, pretheoretical experience.

Recently, however, some cognitive theorists have argued that consciousness is neither unitary nor continuous. Jackendoff (1987), for example, argued against viewing consciousness as unitary, on the basis of observations such as the division of perceptual experience into the sensory modalities of vision, hearing, and so on. This position is countered by the argument sketched in chapter 4, that perceptual information is multimodal and the sensory modalities reflect skilled attributions rather than fundamental distinctions in the nature of awareness. More important, I have tried to show that the same intentional structure is characteristic of awareness in a variety of modalities.

More seriously for the project of constructing a theory of experienced cognition consistent with the core assumptions of the information-processing framework, Dennett (1991) argued against the unity and continuity of consciousness on the basis of the structure of the mind conceived as an information processing system. Noting the many parallel, subpersonal processes postulated by current cognitive theory, he gave this thumbnail sketch of his theory of consciousness:

> There is no single, definitive "stream of consciousness" because there is no central Headquarters, no Cartesian Theater where "it all comes together" for the perusal of a Central Meaner. Instead of such a single stream (however wide), there are multiple channels in which specialist circuits try, in parallel pandemoniums, to do their various things, creating Multiple Drafts as they go. Most of these fragmentary drafts of "narrative" play short-lived roles in the modulation of current activity but some get promoted to further functional roles, in swift succession, by the activity of a virtual machine in the brain. The seriality of this machine (its "von Neumannesque" character) is not a "hard-wired" design feature, but rather the upshot of a succession of coalitions of these specialists. (p. 253)

This account suggests that the apparent temporal continuity of conscious experience is a kind of illusion. As Dennett noted later in his book, "One of the most striking features of consciousness is its *dis*continuity . . . The discontinuity of consciousness is striking because of the *apparent* continuity of consciousness" (p. 356). The idea is that conscious mental processes examined from an information-processing perspective—from a third-person point of view—do not have a one-to-one correspondence with events in the environment or in the perceptual systems. Dennett's examples included the sampling nature of visual perception and the so-called filling-in inferences involved in both normal perceptual phenomena and strikingly abnormal phenomena such as blindsight (Weiskrantz, 1980,

1986, 1993). Dennett's own response to such phenomena is to point out that in the normal case no such inferences are needed because no process expects the information that is not provided (e.g., no information has ever been available from the normal retina's blind spot; therefore, no process expects to receive such information).

The positions taken by Jackendoff and by Dennett illustrate a common theme of current cognitive science that poses an apparent difficulty for theories of consciousness: Cognitive processing is seen as distributed over many subsystems, but our common-sense view of consciousness suggests a kind of unity apparently not present in the systems that support cognition. The experienced cognition framework suggests both a diagnosis and solution for this difficulty. Though Jackendoff and Dennett both pointed to interesting and important phenomena, both play on the ambiguity of mental processes considered from no particular first-person point of view. This ambiguity results in shifting time scales and grains of analysis while interpreting theoretical representations as contentful states that involve no conscious subject. This in turn leads to a question that I believe is ill-formed: How do some of these states come to constitute conscious experience, and where does that happen?

Instead, we should ask how a point of view is constituted—the question addressed by the cospecification hypothesis. Cospecification and the corresponding intentional structure of conscious mental states are formally similar across modalities of perception and of awareness, pointing toward the theoretical continuity of consciousness. Consciousness is not an architectural component, subsystem, or location in the brain, but an organizing principle of information processing by individuals acting in environments. Furthermore, much self-specific information is, as Damasio (1994) put it, stable and endlessly repeated. And, as Gibson (1966) pointed out, many perceptible features of the environment are also stable and endlessly repeated. And, as Ballard (1996) pointed out, cognition is continually grounded in one's literal point of view, which changes location and focus sequentially, supporting the serial character of experienced cognition. The experiential unity of conscious experience is, on this analysis, an ecological fact that is a consequence of these stabilities.

Cospecification and Egolocative Processing

Cospecification and egolocative processing are general principles of consciousness that apply to all aspects of subjective experience. Mental states occur in an informational manifold comprising arrays supported by perceptual systems and by memory, and the succession of mental states in an episode constitutes activity guided by the information available in these arrays.

My starting point was cospecification and egolocative processing in visual perception, as described in Gibson's (1966, 1979) ecological theory of perception and developed by Neisser (1988, 1991, 1993), E. J. Gibson (1993), and Lee (1993). We saw that an elaboration of this analysis, recognizing the contributions of informational persistence and performatory representation, could be applied to symbolic and representational awareness. In the present chapter, I argued that the cospecification analysis can also be applied to emotional awareness. In particular, the intentional structure of conscious experience can be found in all of these aspects of awareness. Taken together, these analyses provide a sketch of an informationally based account of consciousness that can be applied across a range of types or aspects of awareness. This account lets us see how experienced cognition can be fit into the general computational theory of mind, and provides variables for developing theoretical descriptions.

The Performatory Character of Cognition

By emphasizing the performatory character of cognition, the experienced cognition framework shows us "the body in the mind" and how cognition can be developmentally and evolutionarily grounded in perceptual-enactive experience. Mundane although it may be, we are essentially always doing something, and that activity is the basis for our experience. Recognizing the performatory character of experienced cognition helps us solve the symbol-grounding problem by showing how cognition can be developmentally or evolutionarily grounded in physical constraints on perceptual-enactive experience. This is also where the grain of truth lies in Turvey's (1992) physics of intention. In the next chapter, I conclude my discussion of the experienced cognition framework by describing how to understand the contribution of nonconscious information systems to experienced cognition.

7

Awareness and Nonconscious Information Systems

Conscious mind is like the tip of the iceberg; most of our mental activity goes on nonconsciously. Yet nonconscious mind is not like an alternate, hidden consciousness, carrying out the same sort of mental activities you do consciously.
—Farthing, 1992, p. 16

The only occurrent reality of the mental as mental is consciousness.
—Searle, 1992, p. 187

Experienced cognition may be described as a sequence of conscious mental states, each characterized by the intentional structure discussed in chapters 4 through 6. I believe that this level of analysis has a special status in psychological theory, and that the framework sketched here suggests appropriate variables for constructing consciousness-centered theories of particular cognitive phenomena. Nevertheless, any serious general theory of cognition must consider what I call the nonconscious information systems that support experienced cognition. Cognitive scientists tell many computational stories about the information processes involved in perception, action, and memory that fail to plausibly (or even remotely) correspond to conscious mental processes. Yet these computational stories do increase our understanding of cognitive phenomena. Although one might argue with any specific theoretical formulation, it seems clear that cognitive theory must deal with the relation between experienced cognition and nonconscious information processes.

Because many of the representations postulated in computational theories fail to plausibly correspond to the contents of conscious mental states, evidence for these theories is often said to constitute evidence for unconscious mental activity (e.g., Jackendoff, 1987). In fact, the empirical discovery of such unconscious processes is highly valued by many and often highly touted as evidence of scientific progress in understanding cognition (e.g., Greenwald, 1992; cf. Carlson, 1992). In chapter 14, I consider the status of such claims at greater length.

How should we think about nonconscious information processes in the experienced cognition framework? To understand experienced cognition in relation to current cognitive theory, we must answer this question, and in this chapter I attempt to do so. Rather than taking the more or less standard approach of asking how consciousness might emerge from a complex, multilayered story about information processing, as the tip of the iceberg of cognitive processes, I instead begin with the analysis of experienced mental states developed in the preceding chapters. I believe, with Searle (1990), that cognitive scientists have tended to anthropomorphize the brain, implicitly attributing to postulated unconscious processes the kind of intentional structure described in chapters 4 through 6. However, this is not just a theoretical mistake, but follows from the stance that we, as individuals experiencing our own cognition, adopt toward both external and internal processes that preserve and make available information. Just as we take external artifacts such as maps or written language as symbolic because they support certain kinds of mental activity, we take the internal states of memory, perceptual, and action systems as representational because of their role in supporting experienced cognition.

This stance can be contrasted with other possible views, which range from understanding the mental representations postulated in cognitive theories as just notation (e.g., J. R. Anderson, 1990, chapter 1) to a theoretical realism in which such representations are seen as the real entities involved in mental activity, with consciousness viewed as an epiphenomenal projection of this activity (e.g., Jackendoff, 1987; Thagard, 1986). My view is that we can and should be theoretical realists, striving for theories that organize the ontology as well as the functions of mental events.

In order to discuss how nonconscious information processes contribute to experienced cognition, I begin by briefly considering the kinds of causal relations involved in mental activity. I then consider the theoretical and ontological status of representations postulated in theories of memory, the cognitive character of perception and action systems, and several implementation issues raised by recent work in cognitive neuroscience. I conclude the chapter by discussing the relation of the experienced cognition framework to architectural thinking in cognitive science.

MENTAL STATES AND MENTAL CAUSALITY

Intuitively, we often understand the causality of physical events on a kind of impetus model, the prototype of which is perceiving the movement and collisions of objects. The deeper nature of our concepts of causality is more complex and controversial (e.g., Mackie, 1974), and a discussion of these issues is beyond the scope of this book. We can start, however, by making two kinds of distinctions: between content and noncontent properties of mental states, and between causal sequences and causal support. The first of these distinctions follows from the analysis of intentional structure of mental states, and serves to remind us that not all of the variables causally relevant to cognition are content variables. For example, as discussed in chapter 5, an account of reasoning must trace causal relations among degrees of belief as well as among the contents of mental states. The distinction between causal sequences and causal support follows from recognizing that some cognitive explanations provide a kind of causal account that traces a sequence of events at a consistent level or grain size, whereas other explanations provide accounts that relate levels of analysis or description (Fowler & Turvey, 1982). Accounts of relations among levels describe the causal support of one level for another.

Computation and Causality

The information-processing framework prescribes a particular kind of causal story about particular processes, in which certain aspects of a system are described as realizing computations. Cognitive scientists have advocated computational description for processes ranging from early vision (Marr, 1982) to deductive reasoning with verbal premises (Johnson-Laird, 1983). There are many examples of artifacts that can also be described in computational terms, ranging from a cash register calculating sales totals (Marr, 1982) to general-purpose digital computers that perform a wide variety of functions. It therefore seems clear that nonmental systems can realize computations, providing a kind of proof by demonstration that a computational story about a phenomenon is also a causal story about physical causes and effects. This is the sense in which the computational view of the mind is often said to solve the mind–body problem (chapter 2): We can see a mechanical device both as realizing computations and as a physical mechanism. And it seems clear that neurons can implement computational functions, indicating the plausibility of computational stories as causal accounts of the activity of the nervous system.

Cognitive scientists have therefore generally accepted the assumption that cognition must, at some appropriate level of description, be computation. I agree with this assumption, but I believe it is important to add this caveat: The assertion "mental activity is (necessarily) neural computation" does not imply the converse "neural computation is (necessarily) mental activity," where *mental activity* refers to events that can be described as series of mental states. An important feature of the examples typically used in presenting arguments for the computational mind is that they seem to be cases in which physical mechanisms realize computational functions without invoking an intelligent agent to perform the computations—there seems to be no homunculus or ghost in the machine (Ryle, 1949). However, as Searle (1990, 1992) and others have noted, artifacts such as computers can be described as realizing computational functions only from the point of view of some user or observer. And this conclusion holds, even for neural computation that supports cognition. In an important sense, neural computation is mental or representational, only from the point of view embodied in a current conscious state.

It is at least as much an observation about us, as individuals with points of view, as it is about computers, that we can understand (and design) these devices as machines for performing computations by manipulating representations. As Dennett (1987) put it, we can adopt an *intentional stance* toward a system (a computer or another person), interpreting it as if it were engaged in mental activity that comprises mental states with intentional structure. And we do this all the time, understanding devices and other inanimate objects in terms derived from common-sense psychology: A red light tells me that my laptop computer wants its battery recharged, and I can make progress in fixing my malfunctioning heating system by realizing that the thermostat believes it is already warm enough in the family room.

Of course, we do not believe that the computer or the heating system really have beliefs or desires in the same sense that persons do. And one attitude toward these observations is to argue that neither do persons have beliefs, desires, or other mental states in the way suggested by common-sense psychology. Thus we should work toward reducing such accounts to a subpersonal level that entails no first-person point of view (Dennett, 1987, 1991).

An alternative consistent with the experienced cognition framework is to recognize two kinds of causal relations that can be described in computational terms. First, there are relations among conscious mental states with intentional structure, as discussed in chapter 5. These relations can be described in terms of computations defined over both content and noncontent properties of mental states, for example premises and degrees of belief for the states involved in a reasoning process. Some terms in these computational descriptions will thus correspond to, or paraphrase, experienced contents, whereas others will not (or will correspond only to the contents of the metacognitive experience of the process). These causal relations link mental states in causal sequences described at a consistent grain size, the grain of experienced cognition. Second, there are relations among descriptions of informational states, as between the array of intensity values of light on the retina and the three dimensional character of visual experience. These relations cross grain sizes, describing relations of causal support among levels of analysis.

Causal Sequences and Causal Support

To tell a causal story about mental activity, then, we must describe a series of mental states in terms that show the lawful regularities embodied in the sequence. This is of course a familiar statement—temporal succession is causally described when the description captures causally relevant variables and supports counterfactual statements (had A not happened, B would not have happened), in terms of lawful regularities (e.g., Mackie, 1974). In the case of mental activity, the sequence to be described is a sequence of states with intentional structure as described in the preceding chapters; in particular, each state comprises a content held in some psychological mode.

My central point here is that more than one kind of causal relation can be found in a sequence of conscious mental states, and the types of causal relations correspond to the intentional structure of mental states. Relations among mental state contents, and between contents and the environmental or neural events that make available informational arrays, may be seen as computational in the standard sense—new representations are computed from current representational contents or from information (described at an appropriate grain size) available from perception or memory. These computations constitute part of the causal sequence of mental activity, the traditional subject matter of psychology. Any intermediate states in these computations will constitute contents of mental states intermediate in the sequence. However, the rules that govern these computations, and that are made explicit in cognitive theory, describe relations among contents and are not themselves contents of experienced cognition.

A complete description of an episode of mental activity also requires consideration of the psychological modes associated with the states that make up the episode. The relations among psychological mode variables can also be described in computational terms, but here the description is more like a computational description of a physical phenomenon—the computations do not capture the generation of new content, but regularities embodied in the process. For example, suppose it should turn out empirically that the transfer of belief in simple conjunctive reasoning—concluding that {A and B} from premises {A} and {B}—can be computationally described as a simple multiplicative relation, as suggested by probability theory (i.e., $p(A\&B) = p(A) \times p(B)$). We would not expect that multiplying was one of the mental contents manipulated to accomplish the reasoning, nor that numerical values corresponding to degrees of belief were contents of relevant mental states (Dulany, 1991).

To summarize, both of these kinds of relations among mental states—the relations among contents described by logical schemas, and the relations among degrees of commitment just discussed—are reasonably described as rules. And both kinds of rules describe regularities in causal sequences of mental states. However, neither is the kind of thing we would expect to be the content of a mental state, to be consulted by individuals in order to carry out mental activities.

Another aspect of causal description of mental activity is involved in understanding how information is made available by memory or perception. This is a question of what might be called the causal support for mental activity. It corresponds to what are sometimes called implementation issues—that is, how does a physical process preserve information and allow its manipulation? As suggested in chapter 6, not all informational support for mental states is reflected in the content of those states. We might say that such information is implicit in cognition, although explicit in cognitive theory.

Spatial Metaphors in Information Processing

Our intuitions about the causal relations among physical objects embody some aspects of the spatial relations among objects. "No action at a distance" is an assumption of both intuitive and (at least until recently) scientific physics, and intuitively identified causes and effects often involve movement of objects in space (Michotte, 1963). Information-processing psychologists have often used spatial metaphors to describe the causal relations involved in mental activity (Roediger, 1980). For example, introductory psychology students are still often taught that information will remembered if it is moved from short-term to long-term memory. Spatial metaphors like this serve to reinforce the habit of componentialism (see chapter 2), of capturing systematicity in observations by ascribing corresponding properties to components of the information-processing system.

Although box models are now rare in serious cognitive theory, the attraction of spatial metaphors continues. For example, many cognitive psychologists talk about whether a particular piece of information is in working memory or in long-term memory. The spatial character of causal description in cognitive science is clear in Newell's (1990) definition of symbols as providing distal access necessary because not all of the information needed for a computation may be available locally (i.e., at the site of the computation). Much recent research in cognitive neuroscience is dominated by a localist perspective, which emphasizes discovering where in the brain particular computations are performed, or where certain information is represented. The kind of spatial thinking that results from this perspective is sometimes quite different from that in standard information-processing psychology. For example, a number of neuroscientists have suggested that the brain is organized in terms of multiple maps. These maps are neural structures that are topographically organized on the basis of ecological or bodily space, and are supported by spatially distinct neural structures. The functional organization of neural structures is sometimes referred to as the neural architecture underlying cognition.

Cognitive scientists, notably Newell (1989, 1990), have argued that we should frame cognitive theories in terms of cognitive architectures. In Newell's words, "An architecture is the fixed structure that realizes a symbol system. It is what makes possible the hardware-software distinction—a structure that can be programmed with content (encoded in some representation) which can itself control behavior" (p. 404); and, "An architecture provides a boundary that separates structure from content" (p. 82). It is often said that the fixed structure constituting cognitive architecture can itself only be explained in biological terms (e.g., Pylyshyn, 1980). However, many theorists believe that there are several (or many) levels of mental representation between conscious experience or ecologically described behavior and the level of biologically fixed cognitive architecture.

For my purposes, the most important point is that the architectural distinctions critical to understanding experienced cognition are those that support our analysis of mental states as informational arrays in which cospecification, and thus intentional structure, can occur. Before attempting to discuss the experienced cognition framework in architectural terms, however, let us consider how to think about the so-called underlying representations that make up these intermediate levels of cognitive analysis. I focus on memory representations because of the central place of memory research in cognitive psychology and in the information-processing framework generally.

DISPOSITIONAL REPRESENTATIONS IN MEMORY

What is in memory? According to current theories, memory is populated with schemas, prototypes, instances, lexicon entries, nodes, propositions, episodes, concepts, and so on—depending, of course, on which theory we choose. Generally, although not always, these memory representations are interpreted as symbols or symbol structures, on the intuitive model of symbolic contents of conscious mental states. As discussed later in this chapter, many memory theorists have recognized that it is not appropriate to think of memory as literally storing representations like these. Instead, memory may be said to store *dispositional representations* (Damasio, 1994) that support the construction of contents of conscious experience (e.g., Mandler, 1992). I argue that these dispositional representations constitute informational arrays toward which we take an intentional stance, and which we retrieve by a constructive process of performatory retrieval.

The Generalized Network View of Memory

There seems to be a more or less standard view of memory adopted by many researchers, especially those who are not themselves memory theorists. This standard view is a generic version of associative network theory, in which the concept of activation is used to describe causal relations. What is activated are memory representations, with content often corresponding to potential contents of conscious mental states. How activation functions in cognition is based on some concept of strength, of representations or of associative links among them. The stronger a representation or link, the more effective that element of memory is in guiding thought or action. Strength increases with use, providing a mechanism for learning. The causal story about a particular mental episode is told in terms of a sequence of activations determined by associative links among representations. The work of Collins and Quillian (1969) and Collins and Loftus (1975) is often cited as a source of this idea, and MacKay (1982, 1987) has proposed an unusually comprehensive network theory of cognition generally.

As actually used by most cognitive psychologists, this view represents an interpreted node architecture in which at least some nodes in a network are assigned individual semantic interpretations. For example, a node might correspond to a concept or a word, and activating the node constitutes thinking the corresponding idea. Activation is often taken as a continuous variable, and it is sometimes said that a node (or the content it represents) becomes conscious when some threshold of activation strength or duration is reached (e.g., MacKay, 1990; Underwood, 1982). Fodor and Pylyshyn (1988) among others (e.g., Johnson-Laird, Hermann, & Chaffin, 1984) have criticized this approach to understanding memory, arguing that labeling nodes in a network does not really address the issue of semantic interpretation. Nevertheless, variations on this approach have allowed psychologists to systematically discuss a wide range of memory phenomena, involving both deliberate remembering and unintentional uses of memory such as priming. A wide variety of alternative process models (e.g., Gillund & Shiffrin, 1984; Hintzman, 1986) fit this general framework in virtue of postulating separately stored and semantically interpretable memory representations, and operation on the basis of activation of representational units.

It has, however, been widely recognized by memory theorists and other cognitive scientists that what is stored in memory does not consist of mental contents as such; for example, "Engrams are dispositions, potentialities, processes held in abeyance" (Tulving, 1983, p. 169); "Memory is not a storage process as such; it is simply the property of information processing that extends in time afterwards" (Crowder, 1989, p. 272); "But we should think of memory rather as a *mechanism* for generating current performance, including conscious thoughts and actions, based on past experience" (Searle, 1992, p. 187); and, "Human memory does not, in a literal sense, store anything; it simply changes as a function of experience" (Estes, 1980, p. 68). These comments suggest that memory representations—whether described as items, schemas, episodes, or whatever—should be seen as theoretical constructs whose only reality consists in their role in theories of memory, rather than as real entities. That these authors and others have been moved to make this point explicitly is testimony to our habit of reifying representations postulated by cognitive theorists. In his 1990 book, John Anderson put the point directly and forcefully:

> There is no convincing evidence or argument that there is any real level between the biological and the algorithm level. (p. 18)

> Under the ACT* theory and many other theories, steps of cognition at the algorithm level correspond to points of discrete changes in working memory. (p. 20)

> However, when we are inducing a scientific theory from behavioral data, we should not lose track of what we are doing. We are inducing an *abstract* function that maps input to output. We need a notation for codifying that function so we can communicate it to others, reason about it, and derive predictions. This is what our cognitive architectures and implementation theories provide us with—a system of notation for specifying the function. We should not ascribe any more ontological significance to the mechanisms of that architecture than we do to an integral sign in a calculus expression. If two theorists propose two sets of mechanisms in two architectures that compute the same function, then they are proposing the same theory. (p. 26)

Although not all memory theorists would likely agree with these statements, these comments indicate that contemporary memory theory generally implies what has traditionally been called a constructivist view of experienced cognition. That is, the contents of conscious states—experienced as recollections or implicitly informed by memory—do not correspond to pre-existing memory representations, but are constructed online as they are experienced. In fact, some theorists have abandoned the idea of distinct semantically interpretable representations in memory altogether. For example, Pribram (e.g., 1986) has long argued for a holographic view of memory storage, in which experienced contents are based on information distributed over many elements of a neural system for memory, like optical holograms. A variety of such composite-storage models of memory have now been proposed (e.g., Eich, 1985; Humphreys, Bain, & Pike, 1989; Murdock, 1982), and of course the distributed representations in many connectionist models do not allow semantic interpretation of individual computational units (Chalmers, 1992).

Memory as an Informational Array

Perhaps the best way, then, to characterize the representations postulated by theories of memory is to say that they are dispositional. This is the term Damasio (1994) used to talk about the neural substrate for memory; in his words, "What dispositional representations hold in store in their little commune of synapses is not a picture per se, but a means to reconstitute 'a picture' " (p. 102).

From the point of view of experienced cognition, the important point about dispositional representations in memory is that their activity constitutes an informational array, as does the information available to visual perception. At a given moment, this array may be seen as preserving information specific to previously experienced episodes, perhaps inextricably mingled with one another because of their similarity (Hintzman, 1986). As in the case of the information available to visual perception, memory constitutes an array because it preserves adjacency relations. Some of these adjacency relations may be spatial, but they may also be temporal or semantic (as when a chain of associations allows us to retrieve particular information; e.g., Reiser, Black, & Abelson, 1985). Formally, the critical point about an array is that adjacency relations are defined with respect to some traversal process such as scanning. Given this characteristic, a memory system can support cospecification and egolocation, as does the optical array available through the visual system.

Understanding memory representations as dispositional also helps us think about how the nonconscious processes that preserve information over time are related to conscious mental processes. As Searle (1990, 1992) argued, memory representations have no occurrent existence as mental states except as they support the construction of conscious mental states. Nevertheless, as individual cognizers, we can adopt an intentional stance toward these dispositional representations, acting as if they constitute a store of possible conscious contents. This is effective in part because many acts of representing are analogous to speech acts in which the intended audience is ourselves. This intentional stance toward our own cognitive support systems unfortunately also leads us as theorists to talk in a way that anthropomorphizes the brain (Searle, 1990).

We can also state abstractly some of the other requirements for a memory system, in addition to providing informational arrays specifying past rather than current experience. These requirements are familiar and include content addressability (cuing on the basis of semantic or similarity relations), automatic abstraction and categorization, and operation on the basis of minimal control signals. Each of these memory functions can be described *anthropomorphically*—that is, by describing series of states and operations that are like conscious mental processes. However, recent efforts to model the operation of memory have demonstrated that each of these functions can be achieved by a variety of computational methods that appear to be quite different than conscious mental processes. For example, Hintzman (1986) described a model that assumes all experiences are encoded as separate instances, and abstraction results from the activation and blending of multiple traces at the time of retrieval. Abstractions are stored as such when the retrieval echo that combines traces of previous experiences (thus abstracting from the individual experiences) becomes "the object of conscious reflection" (p. 422), and the experience of that abstract echo is stored. Other models realize these and other memory functions on the basis of distributed representations, in which the units of computation in memory do not correspond to the units of experienced cognition (e.g., Grossberg & Stone, 1986; Murdock, 1982).

This is the sense in which memory may be described as a nonconscious information system: The units of computation that constitute dispositional representations need not be viewed as copies of, or even qualitatively similar to, conscious contents. What is in memory is representational only from the point of view of some conscious state supported by the information that memory preserves. This point is not intended to diminish the accomplishments of memory theorists; however, it does present a quite different perspective on the relation between conscious and nonconscious processes than the common view that consciousness is merely an attribute of some subset of the representations in a complex system (Jackendoff, 1987). In the next section, I consider one way of thinking about the use of memory that is especially apt for understanding experienced cognition.

Performatory Memory Retrieval as a Cognitive Primitive

Memory researchers have generally made minimal assumptions about how memory supports cognitive activities, focusing on tasks intended to reveal memory functions in a relatively pure form. Probably the majority of memory experiments involve examining participants' recall or recognition of words, rather than (for example) the role of memory in problem solving or reasoning. Retrieval is usually defined in terms of tasks in which the individual's goal is to remember items as defined in an earlier study phase. Recent research on implicit memory (Schachter, 1987) is often specifically concerned with the effects of prior experiences when the goal is not to remember but to make some judgment that may be influenced by a task earlier in the experiment, but even in this approach, the focus is usually on effects of studying individual items such as words.

My emphasis on the performatory character of representation suggests that the basic unit of cognitive activity involving memory as representational be characterized as performatory retrieval. What we might call occurrent or instantiated representations—as opposed to the dispositional representations in memory—are performances such as covert speech or visual imagining that serve a symbolic function. This emphasis is similar to that of Newell's (1990) Soar theory, in which all memory is modeled as productions, or to the proceduralist view of memory articulated by Kolers and Roediger (1984) and Crowder (1993b). To think or bring to mind a studied word in response to a retrieval cue involves performing some part of the act of uttering that word. In this view, memory is seen as guiding an activity, much as information available in the environment guides perceptual-motor activity. Because the emphasis is on the activity and the information that supports it, rather than the nature of the dispositional representation in memory, this view is also consistent with a view of memory as a single system that can be cued or used in various ways (Humphreys et al., 1989).

Resampling and Exploration of Memory

The memory system also supports resampling and exploration, as does information in the ambient optic array. In the case of recollection, the conditions of satisfaction for the recollective state include some past experience. Furthermore, recollective states are causally self-referential in the same way that perceptual awareness is: Part of the conditions of satisfaction for a recollection is that it be (at least partially) caused by the earlier experience. Recollection is thus a metacognitive state that has as its object some earlier mental state or episode.

Just as we can explore the environment, and resample information specifying environmental objects, we can explore and resample memorial objects. As Tulving (1985) put it:

> A normal healthy person who possesses autonoetic consciousness is capable of becoming aware of her own past as well as her own future; she is capable

of mental time travel, roaming at will over what has happened as readily as over what might happen . . . (p. 5)

Because the information available always includes self-specific information that changes as a result of current activity, and because memorial objects are relatively stable, egolocative processes that distinguish self and object can operate in a manner formally similar to egolocation in visual perception. Egolocative processing with respect to memory provides a temporal orientation (a now referent) for experienced cognition. In the words of James (1890), "There is thus a sort of *perspective projection* of past objects upon present consciousness, similar to that of wide landscapes upon a camera-screen" (p. 593).

It is clear that memorial information can also guide activity without producing recollective awareness, and research on implicit memory has been largely concerned with documenting this. It is also the case that much of our awareness of past experiences is fleeting, lacking the stability that would support resampling or exploration. In such cases, performatory representation may serve to provide working memory, in that the performance itself—covert speech, for example—provides a new and at least temporarily stable memorial object (also see chapter 8). This seems to be what Baddeley (1986) had in mind in describing the recency effect as a basis for orientation, "I would like to suggest that [the recency effect] may play a central role in the crucial, but poorly understood process of orienting ourselves in space and time" (p. 164); and, "It is a process that appears to tell us where we have just been and what we have just done, thereby linking us with a continuous flow of conscious experience" (p. 165).

To summarize this material on memory: Theorists have postulated a wide variety of mechanisms and representations to account for memory functions, but many theorists (at least when writing carefully) are not committed to an ontology that implies that these representations are real but unconscious mental contents. It therefore seems more appropriate to think of memory representations as dispositional states of a nonconscious information system, states that are not like contents of mental states. This nonconscious system serves to provide informational arrays that support cospecification, and at least sometimes support egolocative processes that depend on resampling and exploration. Conscious mental processes guided by this information allow us to adopt an intentional stance toward memory, much as we can toward external artifacts that function as symbols. Like perceptual-enactive states, states whose content is based on memory are causally self-referential.

The constructivist view of memory discussed here might seem incompatible with the perceptual realism associated with the ecological view of perception discussed earlier. In fact, however, I believe that these views are complementary. Recall the Gibsonian view that "the information for something must specify it, but need not resemble it" (Reed, 1988, p. 275). Just as the objects of perception must be distinguished both from the information that specifies them and from the contents of perceptual experience, so must memory be understood in terms of the objects and contents of recollective experience, both of which must be distinguished from the information that specifies memorial objects. It is this information, not the contents or their objects, that is preserved by the memory system. Because the information preserved in memory can serve in the construction of recollective contents (which are representations of past experiences), it can be seen as comprising dispositional representations. For both perception and memory, failing to maintain these distinctions—a failure that often entails talking about information as if it were itself content—leads to an implausible brand of constructivism that must suppose unconscious contents and unconscious inferences. In contrast, keeping these distinctions in mind lets us see how the relation between conscious contents and nonconscious information processes is the same for perceptual-enactive and symbolic awareness.

PERCEPTION AND ACTION SYSTEMS

The preceding observations suggest that the representational status of memory is virtual, present only from the point of view that emerges with conscious mental activity. I have considered memory at some length because of the central role of memory research in cognitive psychology. However, many of the same points can be applied to perception and action systems: Perceiving and acting are supported by cognitively tuned, but nonconscious, systems that have a kind of virtual representational status.

Affordances and Cognitive Tuning

There is abundant evidence that perception and action systems are tuned to environmental affordances, and that this tuning is in part a consequence of experience. Perceptual learning is perhaps most dramatic in examples of skills that seem virtually impossible for novices, such as determining the sex of recently hatched chicks (Biederman & Shiffrar, 1987; Lunn, 1948) or diagnosing heart and lung abnormalities from X-ray pictures (Lesgold, Rubinson et al., 1988). In these cases, skilled judges can reliably extract information that is practically invisible to the novice. The dramatic performances of gymnasts, divers, jugglers, and other athletes illustrate this point for skills that emphasize action rather than (or in addition to) perception.

Several points concerning perceptual-enactive skills are important for understanding their relations to nonconscious information processes. First, such skills are clearly cognitive in the sense that they embody knowledge. Second, very often this knowledge is available only procedurally: Perceptual-enactive skills are performed, not consulted. Some skills that have large perceptual-enactive components—such as speaking, reading, or writing—are suited for symbolic functions such as communication and arbitrary coding for working memory. However, this is not true for skills such as tying one's shoes. Performances that we think of as artistic (dance, music, etc.) provide an interesting intermediate case, analysis of which is beyond the scope of this chapter (but see Jackendoff, 1987, on music). Third, there is much evidence that acquiring perceptual-enactive skills is a matter of learning to select appropriate information, information that affords achieving particular goals (E. J. Gibson, 1993; Lee, 1993; Proctor & Dutta, 1995, chapter 2). Instruction that directs learners' attention to this information can dramatically speed the acquisition of perceptual-enactive skills (e.g., Biederman & Shiffrar, 1987).

It seems appropriate to describe perceptual-enactive learning as *cognitive tuning*, the development of knowledge by adjusting activity to environmental and bodily affordances. The result of cognitive tuning may be described as mental representation in exactly the same sense that nonconscious states of memory are so described. As discussed in chapter 4, Shepard (1984, 1993) developed J. J. Gibson's (1966) metaphor of resonance to describe the representation of perceptual knowledge (some memory theorists have also used the resonance metaphor to describe the representation of knowledge, notably Grossberg in his adaptive resonance theory; e.g., Grossberg & Stone, 1986). And although computational theorists of vision generally distinguish between early vision and later (or higher) processes that are more cognitive in character, for my purposes there seems no need to draw a sharp distinction between memory and the cognitive tuning of perception and action. Several striking examples illustrate the theoretical continuity between memory phenomena that we conventionally call mental and phenomena of perceptual-enactive skill. For instance, MacKay (1987) reviewed evidence that mental practice— covertly rehearsing a performance that is later made overtly—can increase the fluency of skill. And Kosslyn (1981), Farah (1994), and others have documented the dependence of visual imagery on neural systems involved in visual perception. These lines of evidence support what Crowder (1993b) called a proceduralist view of memory, "The idea that memory storage for an experience resides in the same neural units that processed that experience when it happened in the first place" (p. 139). As he put it a little later in discussing working memory, "the continuing *activity itself* is the agency of retention" (p. 140, italics in original).

Nonsymbolic Accounts of Cognitive Tuning

Just as theorists have developed nonsymbolic (or subsymbolic) models for many memory phenomena, a number of cognitive scientists have developed nonsymbolic accounts of perceptual-enactive phenomena. Connectionist models postulating distributed representations (Cohen & Huston, 1994) fit this category, as do dynamical systems accounts of action (K. Newell, 1991; Turvey, 1990, 1992). These accounts are, of course, just as computational in nature as are symbol-processing accounts, and in general fit the broad information-processing framework as outlined in chapter 2 (also see Massaro & Cowan, 1993). For my present purpose, the importance of these theoretical efforts is their status as existence proofs: Some cognitive phenomena do not require explanations in terms of symbol processing, unconscious or not. Fodor and Pylyshyn (1988) argued convincingly that cognitive theory needs symbolic representations for some purposes (e.g., to support inference and generativity). However, their argument does not establish that all processes exhibiting cognitive tuning require such explanations. In particular, there seems to be no reason to think that the nonconscious information processing involved in much of perception and action requires representations that are compositional on the basis of formal syntax. Rather, the organization of these information processes is continually supported by the physical structure of the environment and of the body.

EXPERIENCED COGNITION
AND COGNITIVE ARCHITECTURE

Developments in cognitive neuroscience in recent years have led many cognitive scientists to seek neurophysiological evidence for hypotheses that are essentially cognitive in nature, framed in terms of the information-processing framework. We have known for a long time that the central nervous system is organized into subsystems that correspond to some degree to cognitive functions (see Shallice, 1988, for a review). It is an exciting time for cognitive neuroscientists, and there seems to be reason to hope that neurophysiological evidence will let us choose among implementational hypotheses that J. R. Anderson (1990, p. 26) described as different notations for the same theoretical claim. For the time being, however, I believe that cognitive psychologists will continue to make theoretical progress by developing implementation-level theories in cognitive rather than neural terms.

One theme in some recent neurophysiological theory seems especially relevant to understanding experienced cognition, given the framework developed in chapters 4 through 6. This is the view that multiple mapping is a basic principle of neural organization in the brain, a view developed in different ways by Edelman (1989), Damasio (1994), and others. In Edelman's version of this hypothesis, cognition arises through reentrant signaling that serves to coordinate multiple temporally and spatially organized neural maps that preserve the information generate by perception and action. In his more readable discussion, Damasio wrote about cognition and consciousness emerging from the juxtaposition of images whose (dispositional) neural representations remain separate. Although not universally well-received (e.g., see Dennett's 1991 comments on Edelman, 1989), a version of this multiple-mapping hypothesis seems just the kind of neural organization suitable for supporting cospecification and egolocation in a manifold of informational arrays.

I have spent much of this chapter developing my view of the representations proposed in cognitive theories about the implementation of mental activity, and many of the same comments could be applied to architectural distinctions. Nevertheless, as Newell (1990) argued, architectural thinking can lead to more unified theories of cognition. In that spirit, although without Newell's rigor or detail, I offer Fig. 7.1, an almost-serious depiction of the architecture of experienced cognition. The major points to be drawn from this sketch are that experienced cognition is supported by mutually interacting nonconscious information systems, and that our

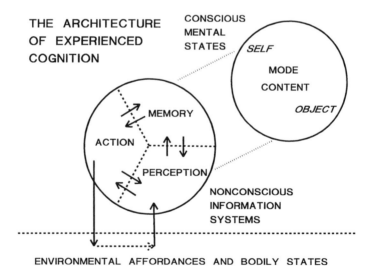

FIG. 7.1. The architecture of experienced cognition: The primary architectural distinction in the experienced cognition framework is between conscious mental states with intentional structure and the nonconscious information systems that support those states.

experience of environmental affordances and bodily states is mediated by these systems as we engage in cyclical interaction with the environment. Perhaps most important, the figure reflects my opinion that neither componentialism nor representationalism will tell us much about the relation between experienced cognition and nonconscious information systems. In the next section of the book, we return to what J. R. Anderson (1990) would call the algorithm level (corresponding to discrete changes in working memory; see previous argument)—the level at which we understand cognition as a sequence of experienced mental states.

III

CONSCIOUSNESS AND SKILLED COGNITIVE ACTIVITY

In earlier chapters, I described a perspective on consciousness and developed a theoretical framework for encompassing consciousness in cognitive theory. This part of the book, chapters 8 through 13, is concerned with several topics central to cognitive theory. My goal is to show how the experienced cognition framework can be applied to understanding the kinds of mental activity prototypical of everyday cognition, and how we can understand the control of cognition as individuals become more experienced in particular domains. Chapters 8 and 9 are concerned with topics important for understanding a wide range of phenomena. In chapter 8, I discuss working memory, arguing that it is best seen as a collection of performatory strategies for temporarily maintaining information. In chapter 9, I consider the concept of *goal structures*, the patterns of goals and subgoals needed to guide complex activities. Chapters 10 and 11 are concerned with traditional categories of higher mental processes, problem solving and reasoning. In chapter 10, I discuss the links among causal thinking, problem solving as the generation of goal structures and coordinative modes, and our experience of ourselves as agents. In chapter 11, I develop a view of reasoning as relations among mental states, characterized in terms of their intentional structure. Chapter 12 is concerned with expertise and skill acquisition; my central theme is that the alleged mindlessness of expert performance can be understood by considering the restructuring that leads individuals from reflective problem solving to skilled routine performance. Chapter 13 provides a theoretical sketch of cognitive control that represents an attempt to link theory and observations of cognitive skill with the experienced cognition account of agency.

8

Working Memory:
Private Speech and Other
Performatory Vehicles of Thought

Language and inner speech are central to our commonsense ideas about consciousness. And in current cognitive theory, working memory often plays a central role as a system that maintains information—often in linguistic form—so that it can be used to accomplish cognitive tasks. Limits on working memory are thus a major constraint on the coordinative modes that we can adopt in performing mental routines. In this chapter, I examine these topics from the vantage point of the experienced cognition framework.

Most individuals would agree that their conscious experience very often includes a kind of internal monologue, and the ability to report experience in verbal form is often taken as a mark of its conscious status (e.g., Nisbett & Wilson, 1977). It seems that language has a special status with respect to consciousness, and many cognitive scientists have argued that language ability is supported by specialized cognitive modules. The supposed specialness, and at least partially innate character, of language is almost a dogma of linguistics and psycholinguistics, although some cognitive theorists (e.g., J. R. Anderson, 1983; Newell, 1990) have argued that language can be understood in the same theoretical terms used to describe cognition generally. Some theorists (e.g., Whorf, 1956) have argued that language strongly shapes thought. Most cognitive scientists do not support a strong version of this linguistic relativity hypothesis (Scholnick & Hall, 1991). However, it is clear that language (or "verbal coding") accompanies much cognitive activity, and Hunt and Agnoli (1991) summarized the evidence that language does shape thinking in some respects. It thus seems clear that private speech is one important medium of cognitive activity.

The concept of short-term or working memory also has important intuitive links to the concept of consciousness, as discussed in chapter 2. Consciousness is sometimes identified with the contents of working memory (e.g., Baars, 1988), and working memory is viewed as the center of the cognitive system. As Haberlandt (1994) put it in his recent text:

> Working memory is the cognitive center responsible for problem solving, retrieval of information, language comprehension, and many other cognitive operations. Depending on task demands, information is maintained in a phonological loop, a visuo-spatial sketch pad, or an abstract conceptual form. Working memory also schedules the component processes involved in each skill and makes intermediate results available for other component processes. (p. 246)

And although the components attributed to the working memory system have multiplied in recent years (Baddeley, 1986; Crowder, 1993a), there is a historical link between the concept of short-term memory and verbal contents. For example, textbook accounts of Atkinson and Shiffrin's (1968) seminal work on short-term memory often describe verbal coding as one criterion of short-term memory, as opposed to the literal coding of sensory memory and the semantic coding of long-term memory.

In this chapter, I argue that we should view private speech as a real, although not all-inclusive, medium of thought. Working memory should be viewed not as an architectural component of the cognitive system, but as a collection of strategies for preserving information and for controlling its application. Many of these strategies—such as verbal rehearsal—are performatory in character (that is, rely on performatory representation). We might say that working memory is a *function*, one that juxtaposes mental contents so that cognitive activities supported by nonconscious information systems can take place. This function may be served in a variety of ways, in cognitive routines that make use of distributed capacities for working memory. Because speech is among the most flexible of our performances and has a clearly symbolic and representational function, private speech is the most important working memory strategy in many situations.

WORKING MEMORY IN COGNITIVE THEORY

Working memory and related concepts have often served as surrogates for consciousness in cognitive theory. The most widely discussed attribute of working memory is its limited capacity for storing information, starting with Miller's (1956) famous account of the "magic number 7 (plus or minus 2)" (p. 81). It seems undeniable that our mental processes are in some sense limited in their capacity, in the sense that the amount of mental activity possible during a period of time is limited. Some authors (e.g., Lachman et al., 1979) have attributed this limited capacity to consciousness itself, and the most common general understanding has been that some stage in the flow of information from stimulus to response (see chapter 2) constitutes a bottleneck that limits cognitive processing (e.g., Pashler, 1994).

In this section, I briefly review the concept of working memory in cognitive theory (for more thorough reviews, see Baddeley, 1986; Cowan, 1993; Crowder, 1982, 1993a). I argue that we can understand capacity limits on cognition largely in terms of constraints on the performatory aspects of thinking, together with properties of systems that passively preserve information.

Short-Term Memory as an Architectural Component

Historically, short-term or working memory has been viewed as an architectural component of the cognitive system. Initially, the theoretical debate about how to account for short-term memory phenomena focused on whether memory was unitary or consisted of two systems, one specialized for short-term remembering and one for long-term retention. Following the work of Waugh and Norman (1965) and Atkinson and Shiffrin (1968), most psychologists accepted that short-term memory was supported by a distinct architectural component, and attention turned to studying the characteristics of short-term memory. More recently, Crowder (1982, 1993a) and others have rejected this architectural view of short-term memory on a variety of grounds. Crowder (1982, 1993a) and Baddeley (1986) provided historical reviews of research on short-term remembering.

Most important for my purposes, Miller's magic number and a variety of subsequent empirical and theoretical work suggested that most or all limits on mental processes could be attributed to a single source, the limited ability to hold information while using it in the course of mental activity. Atkinson and Shiffrin (1968) popularized the idea that short-term memory served as a cognitive workspace, analogous to a chalkboard or message board—or to the active memory of a computer. According to their model, short-term memory could be described as a buffer containing a limited number of slots. A memorable image from a film narrated by Gordon Bower (*Human Memory*, 1978) depicts items in memory as blocks lined up on a workbench, with one block being knocked off the bench as another is added.

Although this memory was presumed to constitute a kind of mental workspace, it was rarely studied as such. Instead, most research focused on short-term remembering tasks, often based on variations of the digit-span or other serial recall tasks. Baddeley and Hitch (1974; Hitch & Baddeley, 1976) demonstrated in a series of studies that the idea of short-term memory as a unitary workspace with a limited number of slots was untenable. In these experiments, they demonstrated that either a memory preload (giving participants a series of digits to remember) or requiring them to continuously repeat the digits aloud (a technique known as *articulatory suppression*) slowed but did not prevent performance of a variety of tasks that required working memory. Because some of the digit sequences approached or exceeded the memory span attributed to short-term memory, no slots should have remained available for the primary tasks. They therefore proposed the concept of *working memory*, a system for holding and manipulating information in the performance of mental activities. Over the past two decades, Baddeley, Hitch, and many others have conducted many experiments designed to reveal the structure and properties of this proposed system (see Baddeley, 1986, 1993, for reviews of this work).

Working Memory as the Center of Cognitive Activity

Working memory has therefore come to be viewed as the center of cognitive activity, as described in the passage from Haberlandt (1994) quoted earlier. In order to serve this theoretical role, working memory must be seen as a system of (at least partially) separable components, supporting what are sometimes called *distributed capacities*. The system proposed by Baddeley (1986) consists of a central executive responsible for control and active processes, and slave systems responsible for storage that is relatively passive in the sense that the only dynamic process not involving the central executive is rehearsal. A variety of evidence supports the distinction between active processing and passive storage; for example, Klapp, Marshburn, and Lester (1983) demonstrated that individuals could maintain a near-span memory load while performing cognitive tasks, if they had time to consolidate the memory load before beginning a task. Baddeley (1993) suggested that consciousness is one of the functions of the central executive; however, he has also acknowledged that the operations of the central executive are largely mysterious. A number of other authors have discussed the distributed character of working memory capacities, including Carlson et al. (1990), Monsell (1984), and Schneider and Detweiler (1987, 1988).

Other theorists (e.g., J. R. Anderson, 1983; Cowan, 1993) have suggested that working memory be identified with the active portion of a more general memory system, described by some kind of network representation. This approach focuses more on the content of working memory than on the processes that operate on that content, but maintains the view of working memory as the center of cognitive activity.

Crowder (1982, 1993a, 1993b) noted that these approaches broaden the concept of working memory to the point that the concept itself plays little theoretical role. As he put it:

> Baddeley and Hitch see both components [the articulatory loop and the central executive] as participating in the short-term memory system. But such an attitude is almost superfluous: once the short-term memory system has been jammed with different codes, different forms of rehearsal, and executives with associated slave loops, then it is clear that we are just using the term "short-term memory system" as a stand-in for "information-processing system." All the interest is in the precisely-formulated assumptions about components *within* the overall system. (pp. 308–309)

Crowder's conclusion seems appropriate, especially considering the complexity of a proposal like that of Schneider and Detweiler (1987), which includes modules corresponding to cognitive domains with labels such as *visual*, *verbal*, and *semantic*, a separate control system modulating communication among modules, and three levels of description for the components and their interactions.

The idea of a working memory system that is in some sense unitary remains pervasive, however, in both textbook presentations and empirical research. For example, a great many studies have employed dual-task techniques similar to those used by Baddeley and Hitch (e.g., 1974), in order to demonstrate that various manipulations of a primary task affect the demands on working memory or attentional capacity (e.g., Kahneman, 1973). The logic of these techniques has been reviewed by Fisk, Derrick, and Schneider (1986–1987) among others; the central idea is that as a task demands more of a limited workspace, it becomes more difficult to perform two tasks concurrently. The literatures on working memory, attentional capacity, and dual-task performance are vast and controversial, but certainly demonstrate the complexity of understanding working memory (e.g., Pashler, 1994; Schneider & Detweiler, 1987, 1988). Despite attempts to account for a variety of phenomena in terms of a single working memory capacity, it is clear that understanding our ability or inability to manage multiple tasks in brief periods of time requires that we consider the form of information in the environment, various strategies for short-term remembering, the nature of actions required by the tasks, and details of the temporal relations among information pickup and the mental and physical activities involved in achieving task goals.

For understanding experienced cognition, however, the most important point may be this: The pervasive belief in an architecturally based working memory seems to be in part a surrogate for what Dennett (1991) labeled the Cartesian Theater view of consciousness. The idea is that there must be some place in the information processing system where the various sources of information and activities based on that information come together to provide coherence and unity to mental activity. Baars (1988) proposed a general theory of consciousness based on this view. It does seem that mental contents must be juxtaposed to accomplish many cognitive activities. For example, to (mentally) add the digits 7 and 9, we must think these digits in close temporal proximity with the goal of obtaining their sum. And limits on our capacity for working memory do constrain our ability to juxtapose the appropriate contents for accomplishing some tasks. The experienced cognition framework suggests that this function is served by a variety of mechanisms that preserve information over time, rather than by a single, architecturally defined system.

Sources of Capacity Limitations in Cognition

I want to argue that in fact there are a variety of sources or loci of capacity limitation in cognition. Some theoretical unity can be achieved by understanding these as performatory limitations, with constraints that depend on the structures supporting the performances.

Consider the "general workspace" view of working memory and consciousness. We have seen that a limited-slot buffer model of short-term memory cannot serve this function. However, some authors (e.g., J. R. Anderson, 1983; Cowan, 1993) have made the plausible suggestion that the presence of information in working memory is a matter of degree, depending on the state of activation of portions of long-term memory. Only 7 ± 2 items might be reportable, based on activation strength and duration, but more items might be sufficiently active to support ongoing cognitive activity. For example, J. R. Anderson (1983) estimated that his ACT* theory would require about 20 cognitive units to be active at a given time to support ongoing cognitive processes. In Anderson's version of this general workspace account, sources of activation include perception, current goals, spreading activation in a declarative-knowledge network, and explicit actions of productions. Anderson suggested that the limited capacity attributed to working memory results from limits on the total amount of activation available, a suggestion analogous to Kahneman's (1973) account of attentional resources. In this view, the content of consciousness might be identified with only a subset of the information currently in a state of activation that constitutes working memory (Cowan, 1993).

One problem with this modified general workspace account of working memory is that (as developed so far) it fails to account for a class of phenomena characterized by relatively slow access to information already in working memory. According to this account, perceptual encoding makes information available to cognitive processes by activating appropriate elements of long-term knowledge—that is, by placing information in working memory. Once there, the information can participate in mental processes, for example integration with information activated (retrieved) by means other than current perception. However, in a number of studies, my colleagues and I (e.g., Carlson et al., 1990; Carlson, Sullivan, & Schneider, 1989b; Carlson, Wenger, & Sullivan, 1993) have shown that individuals are slower to perform a variety of simple tasks when they must use information already in working memory rather than (or in addition to) information available to perception. For example, Carlson et al. (1989b) asked participants to apply Boolean rules (e.g., AND) with operands held in working memory or available on a computer display, responding with a keypress indicating that the result was 0 or 1 (in this study, digital electronic symbols for logic gates represented the Boolean operators, and operands and results were coded as *0* or *1* rather than *true* or *false*). Even after extensive practice, it took considerably longer (e.g., 1.7 seconds compared to slightly less than 1 second) to answer when operands were remembered rather than currently displayed. Although this particular study required selection—on memory-access trials, the display cued participants to retrieve a subset of the remembered information—we found very similar results in other studies that did not require selection (and that included other control conditions to rule out experimental artifacts).

These results pose something of a challenge to general-workspace views. If information available to perception must be brought into working memory (by encoding that results in appropriate activation), processes based on information already present in working memory should have an advantage in processing time. However, the opposite is the case. Researchers sometimes write about retrieval from working memory, but that implies separate spaces for working memory and processing. This is a fairly natural account in a model like Baddeley's (1986); for instance, the central executive might have to execute some procedure to make use of information from an articulatory loop. Similarly, Carlson et al. (1993) suggested an account based on the Schneider and Detweiler (1987) model, proposing that additional autoassociative processing within a connectionist network might be required to establish a representation of remembered information adequate to guide additional activity (report by keypress, in the Carlson et al. study).

More generally, the single-capacity view suggested by these general-workspace models has failed to account for a variety of results in dual-task paradigms. This large literature (for reviews, see Broadbent, 1982; Pashler, 1994; Schneider & Detweiler, 1988) leads to the general conclusion that, when overall difficulty is taken into account, the degree to which concurrent tasks interfere with one another depends on the nature of the tasks, not just their overall difficulty. One theoretical response to this conclusion is to postulate a variety of mental resources that are to some degree domain-specific (e.g., verbal or visual) and independently capacity-limited. Baddeley's (1986) working memory model is an example of this approach; Wickens (e.g., 1984) offered an alternative that emphasizes perceptual and action processes rather than memory. In this spirit, Pashler (e.g., 1990) argued that response selection is the source of many phenomena taken as evidence of capacity limitation.

Some order can be brought to this research domain by viewing capacity limitations as performatory limits that depend on the characteristics of the particular performance; examples include speed of execution, information constraints, and the need for coordination. This view suggests that the selective aspect of attention should be seen as a consequence of the pickup of information by activities. Johnston and Dark (1986) summarized a variety of arguments that selective attention generally should be seen as an effect or consequence of processing, rather than as a cognitive function in its own right.

DISTRIBUTED CAPACITIES
FOR WORKING MEMORY

The previous discussion suggests that the function of working memory—holding information so that it can be used in mental activities—is distributed over a variety of capacities or abilities. I have also suggested that some of the most-studied phenomena of short-term memory, such as the limited memory span for verbal items, depend on individuals' performatory strategies for remembering rather than reflecting the properties of an architectural component of the mind. In this section, I argue that working memory abilities are distributed over three kinds of capacities or abilities: (a) performatory strategies for remembering, such as verbal rehearsal; (b) persisting availability of information in the form of mental activation or environmental availability; and (c) strategies for the coordination and control of performatory remembering and informational persistence. Each of these capacities is skill-based, in senses to be discussed.

Performatory Strategies for Working Memory

Verbal rehearsal was one of the control processes for short-term memory discussed by Atkinson and Shiffrin (1968), and has probably received the most research attention. Several lines of evidence point to the performatory character of this strategy. First, secondary tasks involving speech disrupt short-term memory for verbal information (see Baddeley, 1986, for a review of this work). Second, verbal rehearsal seems especially important in tasks that emphasize remembering the order in which items were encountered (Healy, 1982); presumably the serially organized character of speech is implicated in this phenomenon. Third, and perhaps most dramatic, a number of studies demonstrate that the short-term memory span for verbal items depends on the time required to pronounce the items. For example, Stigler, Lee, and Stevenson (1986) demonstrated that differences between speakers of Chinese and of English in memory spans for digits could be explained on the basis of the time required to name the digits in the two languages.

Ericsson and his colleagues (e.g., Chase & Ericsson, 1982; Ericsson & Kintsch, 1995) argued that working memory capacity can be functionally expanded by domain-specific coding that allows individuals to rehearse short-hand codes rather than individual items. When retrieval is required, these rehearsed codes can be expanded on the basis of permanent knowledge to recover the original items. For example, Chase and Ericsson described a dramatic increase in digit span with practice by a subject who used knowledge of typical or exemplary times for running events to recode strings of digits to be remembered. These results demonstrate that strategies for using private speech to support working memory are skill-based.

Other performatory strategies have also been documented. Reisberg, Rappoport, and O'Shaugnessy (1984) taught experimental participants to extend their digit span by combining verbal rehearsal with what they called the finger loop—rehearsal by serially tapping with fingers to which digits had been assigned. A number of studies have shown that experts in abacus calculation perform mental arithmetic using routines that correspond to routines for manipulating the abacus. For example, patterns of confusion errors and of memory for intermediate results both correspond to states of the abacus (Hatano & Osawa, 1983; Miller & Stigler, 1991; Stigler, 1984).

There has been relatively less research on short-term memory for items that are difficult to represent in speech. Kirby and Kosslyn (1992) reviewed evidence that short-term memory for visual images is in many respects like that for verbal material, including dependence on rehearsal. Smyth and her colleagues (e.g., Smyth & Scholey, 1994) reported results indicating that memory for motor routines is not organized such that the duration of motor activities determines short-term memory span. However, other performatory properties of motor activity may constrain short-term memory. For example, Kosslyn (1981) reviewed a variety of evidence that the use and maintenance of mental images are constrained in a manner consistent with looking strategies such as scanning and serial fixation of parts. Recently, a number of researchers have documented the importance of visual and manipulatory strategies that distribute working memory functions over internal and external means of preserving information (Ballard et al., in press; Kirsh, 1995; Kirsh & Maglio, 1994; Zhang & Norman, 1994, 1995). For example, Kirsh (1995) described what he called complementary strategies such as pointing and arranging objects to reduce cognitive loads, similar to the strategies for working memory in arithmetic demonstrated in my laboratory (Cary & Carlson, 1995) and discussed later.

This brief sketch of research concerned with rehearsal strategies suggests two conclusions. First, a variety of performances—private speech, motor activity, covert looking—can support short-term memory. Second, at least some constraints on performance in short-term memory task seem to correspond to constraints on these performances—for example, the time required to pronounce verbal items or the visual angle subtended by mental imagery. Reisberg, Rappaport, and O'Shaughnessy (1984) summarized their similar view in this way:

> Rather than being storage places or even memories in any strict sense, the "holding zones" of working memory are activity-based strategic processes, processes we will call *scratch-pad strategies*. Thus, when we use the articulatory rehearsal loop, for example, we are not choosing to employ some already-existing memory component. Instead, we are *creating* a temporary memory component by taking an activity that is not intrinsically memorial, and temporarily recruiting that activity for short-term storage. (pp. 203–204)

These strategies are clearly based on performatory skills, and their deployment also depends on metacognitive skills. If we grant, as most cognitive theorists seem prepared to do, that information in working memory constitutes contents of conscious mental states, we can draw two conclusions from the work reviewed here. First, as argued in earlier chapters, contents of symbolic mental states may be instances of performatory representation in which a (possibly covert) activity serves as the medium or vehicle of representation. Second, because the performances in question are skills, we can seen that increases in skill change the possibilities for experienced cognition, because they change the possibilities for symbolic representation.

Persisting Activation, Permanent Knowledge, and Environmental Availability

Some theorists (e.g., J. R. Anderson, 1983; Cowan, 1993) have suggested that working memory be conceived in terms of activation of portions of long-term memory. In one sense, this view is logically entailed by the widely accepted general activationist view of mental causation—in order to use long-term knowledge, for example to encode items presented in a short-term memory experiment, that knowledge must be activated. Once an item is activated, that activation has some time course, declining over time to a tonic level (perhaps zero). Until that time, the persisting activation can be detected using experimental techniques such as repetition priming. For example, faster identification of words relative to a baseline is taken as evidence that the corresponding memory representations have been activated. This persisting activation presumably supports the continuing availability of information for cognitive processes. Thus, whether or not activation in this sense is viewed as definitive of working memory, the persistence of activation provides support for at least some short-term remembering.

Activation in this sense is often considered separately from working memory, reflecting a continuing belief in the architectural status of working memory. Rather than treating activation as support for working memory, many theorists appear to regard it as a function of long-term memory and thus part of separate research domain. In this view, the content of working memory is considered as separate from long-term knowledge, and items in working memory are considered tokens or copies of items also stored in long-term memory. Recently, however, Ericsson and Kintsch (1995) presented a general theory of the relation between long-term and working memory. Their theory emphasizes that information in working memory serves to provide direct access to related permanent knowledge.

Understanding long-term memory as a nonconscious system that provides informational support for conscious activity (chapter 7) suggests a somewhat different view of this issue. From this perspective, the relation between conscious mental activity and long-term memory is similar to the relation between consciousness and perception. Both long-term memory and perception make available informational arrays that support cospecification and, under certain conditions, egolocative processing. Both also serve to support working memory by maintaining these informational arrays over time; in the case of long-term memory, information maintenance depends largely on neural structures and activity. In the case of perception, it depends as well on the persisting availability and reliable transduction of information from the environment—on the stable world in which we experience cognition, and on the reliable operation of our perceptual systems.

In many instances, informational persistence in the environment and in memory function in much the same way. For example, Carlson, Wenger, and Sullivan (1993) demonstrated a number of qualitative parallels in the performance of subjects reporting verbal items (assigned to keypress responses) while alternating between two lists. Performance in this task appeared to be organized in much the same way, regardless of whether both lists were remembered, both available to perception, or divided between memory and perception. Processes such as *sequential readout, buffering,* or *traversal* apply equally well to making use of remembered or of perceived information. This insight is captured in Schneider and Detweiler's (1987) model of working memory, in which modules for various types of information (e.g., visual, semantic) support the same kinds of control processes and information transmission constraints.

Individuals in fact often make strategic use of the persistence of information in the environment to offload the demands of working memory while engaged in cognitive activity. For example, Larkin (1989) analyzed what she called *display-based problem solving,* demonstrating that problem solvers make use of perceptually available states of the environment to represent intermediate results in problem solving. She described the process of making coffee—a process that has the kind of complex, hierarchical goal structure typical of problem solving (see chapters 9 and 10, this volume). In this task, the state of the environment preserves information about position in the problem space—for example, whether or not the coffee grounds have been placed in the filter basket is readily checked by visual perception. Strategies such as note-taking or the use of pencil and paper in performing arithmetic are also examples of offloading working memory demands into the environment. The use of external memory aids is ubiquitous, although it has received relatively little research attention, especially in the context of working memory. Recently, however, researchers have begun examining such strategies from a variety of perspectives (Ballard et al., in press; Donald, 1993; Hertel, 1993; Intons-Peterson & Fournier, 1986; Kirsh, 1995; Kirsh & Maglio, 1994; Zhang & Norman, 1994, 1995).

Environmental support for working memory is of course coordinated, and at least partially coextensive, with performatory strategies for remembering. For example, my students and I informally observed participants in experiments using a variety of strategies for using manipulatory space for working memory in mental arithmetic and spatial problem-solving tasks. Cary and Carlson (1995) documented the effectiveness of an external spatial placekeeping strategy in mental arithmetic. We asked participants in our study to obtain the sum of digits presented on dice-like plastic markers. When we allowed participants to manipulate markers containing digits to be added, all did so, usually moving to one side those that had already been added. When participants were not allowed to manipulate the markers, we observed increases in talking aloud, which we interpreted as alternative means for placekeeping.

Social conventions, such as the conversational maxims identified by Grice (1975), also appear to have evolved to distribute working memory demands. For example, the *given-new contract* is a conversational convention requiring that each utterance refer to both previously mentioned (given) information and new information. This convention distributes the working memory demands of conversation over participants. However, means by which mutual knowledge is established—for example, the extent to which given information is explicitly uttered—depends on the expertise of the conversational participants (Isaacs & Clark, 1987). Thus, if long-term knowledge of a conversational partner can be assumed or efficiently evoked, less given information need be explicitly mentioned. Similarly, in teamwork settings, participants often provide working memory support to one another.

This discussion of the various means by which information is kept available—held in working memory—implies that working memory should not be viewed as an architectural component of the mind. Instead, working memory is better viewed as a collection of strategies and skills for extending and utilizing the availability of information, which is supported by both mental resources and the stable character of the environment available to perception. From this perspective, it is important to consider the various functions served by working memory. Rather than simply holding information that serves as data for mental processes—for example, the operands and results of mental arithmetic—working memory also involves the instantiation of goals, placekeeping, and other coordinative processes.

Coordination and Control in Working Memory

"If we're to understand how language works, we must discard the usual view that words *denote*, or *represent*, or *designate*; instead, their function is to *control*: each word makes various agents change what various other agents do" (Minsky, 1986, p. 196).

Many, perhaps most, tasks require that we coordinate information being held in working memory by rehearsal or activation with information currently available to perception. Consider solving the arithmetic problem $68 + 17$ without pencil and paper. A variety of strategies are available for obtaining this sum, but except for direct memory retrieval (for most of us, not an option for this particular problem), each involves performing two or more additions, maintaining intermediate results, and integrating those results. Furthermore, in executing these strategies we must encode and segregate the display elements appropriately (for example, interpreting the 7 as occupying the ones rather than the tens place). This may involve resampling the display; in more complex problems such as $68 + 17 + 35 + 46$ or $325 + 1983$ such resampling is almost certainly necessary. If we do use pencil and paper, thus offloading the working memory demand to the environment, the symbols we generate must also be appropriately coordinated with the provided display, with one another, and with mental operations for calculation.

These considerations suggest that the operation of working memory, at least when it is working in the service of goals other than simply remembering, should be seen primarily in terms of strategies and routines for the coordination and control of multiple sources of short-term remembering. Schneider and Detweiler's (1987) model, for example, suggests that there are multiple memory modules, each of which can serve as a sequentially organized buffer. Each buffer can be triggered to produce its contents sequentially, corresponding to a kind of performatory retrieval. The working memory system as described by Schneider and Detweiler consists of the interconnections among these buffers and the control processes that coordinate the maintenance and sequencing of these retrievals. Schneider and Detweiler identified a number of constraints on coordination and control, such as the time course of processes to be controlled and the reliability of (ballistically completed) memory retrieval.

This view of working memory is illustrated in a series of experiments conducted by my students and me (Carlson, Wenger, & Sullivan, 1993; Wenger & Carlson, 1995). As previously mentioned, participants in these studies performed the relatively simple task of reporting (by keypresses) series of six digits, alternating between two lists of three digits each. Two results from these studies are important here. First, individuals responded more slowly when one or both of the lists was no longer visible, requiring that those items be remembered rather than perceived in the course of generating the sequence of keypresses. This result is consistent with other findings concerning the additional time and effort required to use information in working memory, compared to information available to perception (e.g., Carlson, Sullivan, & Schneider, 1989b). Second, the serial position function for keypress latencies (see Fig. 8.1) showed a pattern in which individuals made two responses very quickly, then paused before making two more responses, and so on. Although overall speed varied depending on the source of information (memory or perception), the serial position pattern was similar regardless of the sources of information on a particular trial. This finding was very robust and could be observed in the data for each participant and for almost all individual trials. This result appears to be diagnostic not of the architectural structure of a short-term memory system or of switching attention between memory and perception (Dark, 1990; Weber, Burt, & Noll, 1986), but of the organization of control processes needed to perform the task. Consider those cases in which one list is available for perception and one is held in working memory. In this case, a participant must coordinate three streams of sequentially organized activity, each of which is almost trivially easy by itself: (a) reproducing the sequence of remembered information; (b)

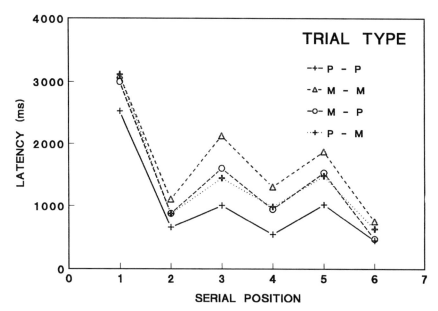

FIG. 8.1. Serial position function from Carlson, Wenger, and Sullivan (1993): This figure depicts the time to enter each keypress as subjects reported items from two lists, alternating between the lists. Each point represents the time between successive keypresses; for example, the latencies indicated at serial position 2 reflect the time between the first and second keypresses. Although more time was required when items were held in memory (M) rather than immediately available to perception (P), the pattern of responding is very similar: pairs of keypresses separated by short intervals, with longer pauses between pairs.

extracting information from the display in a conventional left-to-right manner, and (c) producing a series of keypresses.

The central point of this study for present purposes is that using so-called "working memory" depends on the coordination of performatory strategies and other sources of available information. The critical role of private speech in working memory follows from the flexibility and availability of linguistic skills—anything that can be coded in linguistic terms can be rehearsed by private speech, and private speech provides a reliable medium for temporally organized performances.

PRIVATE SPEECH AS A MEDIUM OF THOUGHT

Much of our experience of cognition includes private, usually covert, speech. For example, Klinger and Cox (1987–1988) attempted to study the contents of the stream of consciousness by asking participants to record the content of their experience when prompted at random intervals by a beeper.

They noted that "most thought samples contained some interior monologue largely independent of other variables" (p. 105). Contemporary
cognitive scientists tend to view this private speech as an expression of
underlying, perhaps inaccessible, mental representations rather than as a
genuine medium of thought (but see Barsalou, 1993; Polk & Newell, 1995).
However, in my opinion, this attitude stems from an overgeneralized
rejection of the behaviorist view that identifies thought with covert speech.
Although thinking is not simply talking to oneself, private speech serves in
many instances as a genuine, performatory vehicle of mental activity.

The Baby and the Bathwater

As a number of authors (e.g., Lachman et al., 1979) have pointed out, the
cognitive psychologists of the 1950s, 1960s, and 1970s went to great lengths
to reject behaviorism. This rejection included not just the metatheoretical
principles of behaviorism such as the denial of mental concepts, but also
some of the topic matter of behaviorist psychology. For example, Langley
and Simon (1981) commented on the neglect of learning theory in cognitive psychology. In the case of private speech, the tendencies to reject
behaviorism's metatheoretical constraints and to reject its topics correspond, resulting in a major blind spot in cognitive theory. In rejecting the
behaviorist account of thinking as covert speech (Watson, 1930), cognitive
science has neglected a research topic that seems to me critical to understanding experienced cognition.

Our everyday experience of our cognitive processes includes a great
deal of private speech, and this intuitive observation undoubtedly lent
credence to Watson's (1930) claim that thinking was nothing more than
covert speech. The standard textbook response to Watson's claim is to
cite the dramatic experiment of Smith, Brown, Toman, and Goodman
(1947). Smith et al. demonstrated that an individual paralyzed by a cu-
rare-based drug and provided with artificial respiration could think despite being unable to perform any activity (such as subvocal speech) that
requires muscle movements. J. R. Anderson's (1985) textbook summary
of the implications of this research is fairly typical:

> Thus, it seems clear that thinking can proceed in the absence of any muscle
> activity. For current purpose, the relevant additional observation is that
> thought is not just implicit speech but is truly an internal, nonmotor activity.
>
> Additional evidence that thought is not to be equated with language
> comes from the research on propositional memories ... people tend to
> retain not the exact words of a linguistic communication, but rather some
> more abstract representation of the meaning of the communication. (p. 316)

Note the shift here from the evidence—"absence of any muscle activity"—
to the conclusion, "not just implicit speech," which begs the question

whether covert speech might be supported by the same neural structures that support overt speech, even in the absence of muscle activity. Rosenbaum (1991) offered a more careful discussion of the Smith et al. experiment, noting that it speaks directly only to the issue of speech sufficiently overt in that it involves muscle movements. Anderson and others also pointed to the experience of searching for words to express our thoughts, and evidence that memory for verbal material is often not verbatim, as evidence that thinking cannot be identified with private speech.

Certainly the accumulation of data and theory since Watson's time indicates that we need a more complex view of language than behaviorism can provide (e.g., Chomsky, 1959). However, we ought to reconsider the possibility that private speech is a genuine medium of thought that retains the performatory character of overt speech, even when no muscle movements are involved (or possible). Results from research using articulatory suppression to demonstrate speech-based coding in problem-solving and short-term memory tasks (e.g., Baddeley & Hitch, 1974) provide evidence for this possibility, but has generally included little consideration of the performatory character of linguistic expression. By performatory character, I refer to the temporally extended, sequentially organized nature of linguistic acts of representing.

Language as Medium and Expression of Thought

Consider what it would mean for language to serve as a medium of thought, as opposed to an expression of thought. It is common in cognitive theory to distinguish between underlying representations that perform the real work of cognition, and the (presumably partial) appearance of those representations in phenomenal experience or overt communicative activity. The idea is that the mental representations that are causally functional in generating and guiding activity are different in both content and format from the representations that appear in consciousness (e.g., Jackendoff, 1987). From this point of view, verbal reports—perhaps even those made to oneself (Dennett, 1991)—are expressions of thoughts whose causally functional representations underlie mental activity.

The behaviorist view, in contrast, suggests that performances—of speech or other activities—actually constitute thinking. Rather than expressing underlying representations, the performances are the representations, serving for example to substitute for environmental events as prompts to action. Such substitution for environmental events is often offered as part of the definition of representation (e.g., Palmer & Kimchi, 1986; see chapter 4, this volume). Although many aspects of the behaviorist approach disqualify it as a general theory of mind, the idea that performances—including speech—can serve literally as a medium for thought ought to be taken seriously. One area in which this idea has been explored is the analysis of verbal reports of mental processes.

Private Speech and Verbal Protocols

One method for obtaining evidence about the course of mental processes is the collection of *verbal protocols*. In this technique, experimental participants are asked to talk aloud as they perform cognitive tasks, usually puzzle-type problems. The resulting protocols may serve as the basis for generating and testing simulation models of mental activities (e.g., Anzai & Simon, 1979). However, the general use of verbal protocols has been criticized on the grounds that individuals often report bases for their behavior that fail to correspond to researchers' experimentally based accounts. For example, Nisbett and Wilson (1977) argued that participants in many experiments gave reports based on common-sense theories about mental processes rather than on their experience of those processes.

Ericsson and Simon (1980, 1983) analyzed verbal protocol methodology from an information-processing point of view. They made a number of distinctions that helped to clarify both the evidential status and relation to consciousness of verbal protocols. First, they noted that retrospective reports are subject to all of the gaps, errors, and distortions that are well-documented in the study of memory. We should expect—for non-controversial reasons—that concurrent reports are less susceptible to (at least) these sources of error than are retrospective reports. Second, Ericsson and Simon pointed out that the information required to perform some tasks—for example, short-term remembering of easily named items such as digits, letters, or words—is likely to already be in (covert) verbal form and thus directly reportable without recoding. They review evidence supporting this possibility, evidence that can also be read as supporting the hypothesis that private speech is a medium of thought. On the other hand, much of our experience is in other modalities such as visual or spatial imagery and thus must be described within the limits of our vocabulary, rather than directly reported. Third, they noted that some researchers have instructed subjects to report not simply the content of what they are thinking, but reasons for what they are doing. Such instructions are likely to require subjects to reconstruct or infer what to say, rather than to directly report the content of their current thought.

Recent research on the phenomenon of *verbal overshadowing* demonstrates the importance of this issue. For example, Schooler, Ohlsson, and Brooks (1993) demonstrated that asking experimental participants to verbalize their problem-solving strategies reduced their chances of success in solving insight problems. This result illustrates two points: First, private speech is not always useful in supporting mental activity. Second, and more important, this finding demonstrates the power of private speech in thinking; for example, Schooler and his colleagues suggested that verbalization served to direct their subjects' attention to inappropriate information. In other cases, of course, private speech is helpful (for example, Schooler et al. suggested this will be true for non-insight step-by-step problems).

These comments refer mostly to the role of private speech as a vehicle of content. However, other, implementational properties of private speech as performance are important in allowing it to serve as means of controlling activity. Next, then, let us consider the role of private speech in controlling mental activity.

PRIVATE SPEECH AND CONTROL OF MENTAL ACTIVITY

In one sense, it is quite obvious that speech can control behavior. One major reason for speaking is to control the behavior of others—speech act theory (Austin, 1962; Searle, 1969) emphasizes that many of our utterances have extralinguistic, perlocutionary effects. For example, the intended effect of saying "give me the wrench" is not primarily to convey information but to evoke a particular action on the part of the listener. Perhaps less obviously (or at least less studied by cognitive scientists), speech can also serve a role in the temporal coordination of activity. Consider, for example, cases of social coordination by worksongs or by the count with which a quarterback in American football begins a play. In these cases, the activities of several individuals are coordinated with respect to a temporal referent provided by stereotyped speech.

These examples are of course instances of public speech, and the effects involve control or coordination across individuals. It seems reasonable to suppose, however, that private speech can serve analogous control functions within individuals. This hypothesis was developed at some length by Vygotsky (1934/1986), although without the level of detail required by the information processing approach. In this section, I discuss the hypothesis that private speech serves to control mental activity in three ways: (a) by supporting working memory for goals and contents, (b) by providing temporal markers for the coordination of mental activity, and (c) by providing a mechanism for metacognitive monitoring of mental activity.

Private Speech and the Development of Self-Regulation

It seems beyond doubt that social speech can control activity. It is also obvious that social speech plays an important role in language development, including the development of covert speech. Human infants may come prepared to learn a language, and perhaps even to count (Gallistel & Gelman, 1992), but representing the number {2} by uttering "two" or "zwei" is surely dependent on an interactive, social language community.

It is a short step from these observations to the hypothesis that private speech plays a role in self-regulation, or the conscious control of activity. Theorists as diverse as Skinner (1957) and Vygotsky (1934/1986) argued for versions of this hypothesis. The basic idea is that private speech (whether overt or covert) represents an appropriation of social speech, as in commands from parents or language that coordinates the activity of several individuals, for the function of self-regulation.

Developmental work inspired by Vygotsky has supported this general hypothesis that private speech plays a role in self-regulation (see Berk, 1992, for a review). There are formidable methodological problems in this work, and most of the research has focused at a broader, less precise level of analysis than we need for cognitive theory. Some research motivated by cognitive theory suggests that verbalization can support the learning by adults of effective problem-solving strategies (Ahlum-Heath & Di-Vesta, 1986). However, I know of no systematic discussion of the range of functions that private speech might serve in the moment-to-moment control of mental activity. The following discussion is therefore largely speculative.

Functions of Private Speech

It should be uncontroversial that some mental activities depend on verbal coding; examples include rehearsal of verbal items for short-term memory tasks and coding elements of mental arithmetic tasks. What is more controversial for some of these cases is the assertion that these activities require performatory use of private speech. Cary and Carlson (1995) argued that performatory aspects of private speech—the sequencing and timing of speech elements—serves a placekeeping function in simple mental arithmetic tasks.

Because it allows generation of serial performances that have reliable properties such as duration (of parts as well as of entire utterances), repeatability, and evocation of related information, private speech is well-suited to serve a variety of controlling functions. In many anecdotal examples, speech serves to control perceptual-motor activity—for example, counting may serve to control the rhythm of an activity such as dancing. Often, such instances begin with social speech provided by a coach or activity leader; the coaching speech provides a scaffold that is withdrawn as skill is acquired. Introspection and casual observation suggest that individuals spontaneously adopt speech-based strategies for coordinating activities. To my knowledge, however, there is no laboratory documentation of these phenomena, beyond the limited demonstration conducted in my laboratory.

Working Memory and Monitoring Cognitive Performance

An important aspect of experienced cognition is the ability to monitor ongoing performances, in order to evaluate progress toward goals or maintenance of performance parameters. In addition to its other functions, private speech—and performatory representation generally—provides a means for monitoring cognitive performance (Scholnick & Hall, 1991). In the case of mental arithmetic, for example, verbalizing the elements— numbers and operations—may provide informational support for placekeeping and for monitoring performance speed. For example, Carlson and Cary (1993) demonstrated that individuals performing a simple running addition task responded to an instruction to emphasize speed (rather than accuracy) by dramatically increasing their rate of ver- balization, speaking a greater proportion of the elements involved in addition (primarily displayed digits, *plus*, and *equals*). The actual speed with which they accomplished the addition task changed little, however. This result suggests that individuals monitored their compliance with the instruction by monitoring the rate of private speech. Similarly, production fluency might provide information for metacognitive assessment of the quality of representation in working memory or the availability of answers by retrieval (perhaps indicating the need to recruit an algorithmic backup strategy; Siegler, 1988).

COSPECIFICATION AND EGOLOCATIVE PROCESSES IN WORKING MEMORY

In chapters 4 through 6, I discussed cospecification and egolocative proc- essing in informational arrays provided by vision, memory, and bodily awareness. In this section, I develop that discussion specifically in the context of working memory. My central theme is that cospecification of self and object by informational arrays constructed in the course of work- ing memory activity provides a major means of egolocative processing that serves to orient us in time and space.

Working Memory and the Informational Manifold

In the extended sense I described, working memory might be identified with the portions of the informational manifold guiding current activities, including information currently available in the environment and information whose availability is supported by persisting mental activation. Conventionally, of course, *working memory* is used more narrowly to refer to that part of the informational manifold that both lacks current environmental support and is represented by a current performance (e.g., verbally rehearsing an item or refreshing an image). In the broader conception, the term working memory picks out those aspects of available arrays that are serving functions in ongoing goal-directed activity. This view is consistent with effect views of attention that regard the selection of information as a consequence of cognitive activity rather than the result of an attentional mechanisms that causes information to be selected (Johnston & Dark, 1986).

This conception bears some similarity to the view advocated by Cowan (1988, 1993). Cowan identified working memory with currently active information and suggested that the active information be subdivided into that which is at the current focus of attention and that which provides a background or surround for the focal information. It would be generally compatible with Cowan's view and similar approaches (e.g., J. R. Anderson, 1983) to identify currently active information broadly enough to include not just clearly symbolic contents such as verbal codings or mental images, but also information available to perception and information about current bodily states. In this view, working memory would then constitute the "field of view" for experienced cognition, and the focal information would constitute the contents of current conscious states. As in the case of visual kinesthesia (Gibson, 1966; chapter 4), systematic changes in the array of available information provide information that specifies an acting self.

Performatory Strategies and Egolocative Processing

This field of view conception of working memory may be seen as an architectural hypothesis concerning the relation between mechanisms that support cospecification in an informational manifold and between contemporary theories of working memory and active cognition. In this conception, working memory serves a crucial role in the egolocative processing that serves to orient us in time and space (cf. Baddeley, 1986, pp. 164–165). In particular, performatory routines such as verbal rehearsal serve to extend the availability of information, thus providing or enhancing the conditions for egolocative processing. Such extended availability allows for resampling and exploration, as does the stability of perceptual information provided by the persisting environment. The egolocative processing thereby made possible provides the structure needed to link currently available information with instantiated goals.

Working Memory and Goal Instantiation

This account implies that a primary function of working memory is the formation of intentions, a process I call *goal instantiation*. A goal is instantiated when the content of a conscious mental state specifies the self as achieving some result by engaging in some activity. My students and I (Carlson & Shin, 1996; Carlson & Yaure, 1990) have investigated this process in the context of *practice schedule effects*. Participants in these experiments learned rule-application skills based on a pseudo-arithmetic presentation of simple Boolean rules (e.g., AND) operating on data represented as *0* or *1*. A consistent finding is that practicing these rules in a random schedule, in which any of four rules may appear on a particular trial, leads to poorer performance during practice than does practicing in a blocked schedule in which the same rule appears repeatedly within a block of trials. However, transfer performance—the fluency with which the rules are applied in multistep problems—is significantly superior following random practice. A series of studies converged on the conclusion that the critical factor in this effect is that random practice requires individuals to reinstantiate a goal (to apply a particular rule) on each trial. This ability, in turn, supports superior performance in transfer to problem solving. Additional evidence indicates that advance knowledge of the rule to be applied at each step speeds performance, demonstrating the distinct nature of goal instantiation (Carlson & Shin, 1996; also see Carlson, Shin, & Wenger, 1994; Sohn & Carlson, 1996).

This view of goal instantiation in working memory is generally compatible with the role attributed to working memory in the recognize–act cycle of production-system models of cognition, such as ACT (J. R. Anderson, 1983, 1993) and Soar (Newell, 1990). In the next chapter, I consider goals and goal instantiation in greater detail in order to link this analysis with the analysis of conscious mental states outlined in Part II.

9

Controlling Cognitive Activity: Goals and Goal Structures

A striking feature of experienced cognition is the sense of agency, the experience of ourselves as actors in control of our own activity. This phenomenon has always been problematic for scientific psychology, and psychologists with theoretical inclinations ranging from behaviorism (e.g., Skinner, 1971) to contemporary cognitive science (e.g., Jackendoff, 1987) have rejected it as a kind of illusion or epiphenomenon. But cognitive theory cannot do without some concept of internal control, and in current theory, that idea is most often identified with the label *goal*. In this chapter, I consider the role of goals and goal structures (organized patterns of goals) in experienced cognition. My central theme is that we should understand intentions, or instantiated goals, as instances of egolocative processing that function in the control of cognitive activity and that constitute the experience of agency. I thus consider the structure of intentions in terms of the variables of intentional structure discussed in previous chapters.

Intentions in this sense are a special case of intentional mental states. I often refer to *instantiated goals* rather than to intentions in order to minimize possible confusions produced by this terminological correspondence, but use the more colloquial term *intention* when possible. Also, intentions as instantiated goals should be distinguished from *desires*, in that a desire does not by itself imply action. Together with beliefs, desires may be precursors of instantiated goals (Dulany, 1968), as discussed in chapter 6. In this chapter, however, my focus is not on the generation of intentions, but on their structure and role in experienced cognition.

172

GOAL INSTANTIATION AND EGOLOCATION

Each of us is almost always engaged in some kind of goal-directed activity. Although the goals involved may be trivial or mundane, it seems obvious that they play a central role in organizing our experience and behavior. The concept of goal is therefore central to cognitive science. In other areas of psychology, goals have received much theoretical and empirical attention (e.g., Austin & Vancouver, 1996; Latham & Locke, 1991). One might think that the cognitive science literature would contain a number of foundational discussions. In fact, however, the idea that individuals' activities are goal-directed is a background assumption (Newell, 1990), left implicit in most cognitive research and theory. We set goals for participants in our experiments—and for our computational models—largely in common-sense terms, and the representation of goals in computational models often appears to be largely a matter of intuition and convenience rather than the result of detailed psychological analysis.

As a preliminary definition of *goal*, we may begin with Mandler's (1984) observation that there are "no goals without means" (p. 82). That is, a goal specifies the self as achieving a desired state by engaging in a particular activity (perhaps specified abstractly or vaguely). This represents an elaboration of the point made in chapter 4, that describing a mental state as an intention in action involves specifying both an action and its conditions of satisfaction, which include that the action be causally functional in bringing about these conditions. Similarly, when a goal is instantiated as an intention to act, the conditions of satisfaction include some desired state of affairs, and that the intention functions causally in bringing that state about. Instantiating a goal thus involves taking self-specific information as an object of cognition. This view of goals contrasts with the view that goals do not specify behaviors (Austin & Vancouver, 1996), and can be compared to the typical treatment in cognitive science.

Goal Concepts in Cognitive Theory

Cognitive scientists have generally assumed without much discussion that human activity is goal-directed (Newell, 1990). In Newell's (1980) view of cognition, goals are identified with states in a problem space—possible arrangements of mental or physical elements that respect the constraints of the problem domain. A particular desired arrangement of elements is known as the goal state, and the arrangement of elements at the beginning of the problem-solving episode is the initial state. For example, the much-studied (e.g., Kotovsky, Hayes, & Simon, 1985) Tower of Hanoi problem in its most common form presents problem solvers with a physical apparatus consisting of three poles and several rings of

Tower of Hanoi

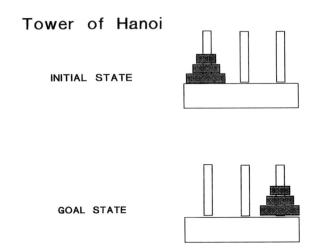

INITIAL STATE

GOAL STATE

FIG. 9.1. Tower of Hanoi apparatus: The apparatus consists of three pegs, with rings of different sizes. The goal is to move the stack of rings from the leftmost to the rightmost peg, respecting the constraints that (a) only one ring may be moved at a time, and (b) a larger ring may not be placed on top of a smaller one.

various sizes that can be fit onto those poles. In this simple problem, states of the psychological problem space can be identified with states of the physical apparatus. Figure 9.1 depicts this apparatus. One operator, or possible action, is available to individuals solving this problem: moving one ring at a time from one pole to another. The primary constraint on possible states is that no ring may be placed atop a smaller ring. The problem begins with all of the rings stacked on one pole, and the goal state is defined as a similar arrangement but with the rings stacked on a different pole.

Notice the contrast between this definition of a goal as a desired state of a problem space, and Mandler's observation cited earlier. Whereas Mandler's comment points to a mental state somehow involving the self as agent, the problem-space definition refers only to the conditions of satisfaction of such a state—the conditions that must be met if the goal is to be satisfied. Although a problem-space definition of goal states is often sufficient to address particular empirical issues, it also reflects the implicit agent stance discussed in chapter 2. The problem solver stands outside the theoretical account. Furthermore, actual goals often include process parameters among their conditions of satisfaction—for example, part of a problem solver's goal may be to solve a problem quickly or with minimal effort.

In most experimental research, participants are assumed to adopt goals (including parameters such as speed or average accuracy) provided by the experimenter's instructions. Articles reporting experimental research often describe instructions only in general terms, and procedures to explicitly examine participants understanding of the experimental task are rarely used or reported. It is often difficult, therefore, to know exactly what goals participants have adopted in response to instructions and other experimental demands. Similarly, the mapping of answers or responses to presumed mental representations they express is rarely analyzed in detail (a major exception is research based on Anderson's *information integration* approach; e.g., N. H. Anderson, 1981). Very often, of course, this common-sense approach is effective in addressing the researcher's empirical concerns, and there seems little more to say than (for example), "Participants were asked to recall, in writing, as many words as possible from the studied list."

For my purposes, however, the common-sense approach to instructions, tasks, and goals in much cognitive research is unfortunate. Considered together with the substantive conclusions of typical experiments, this nonanalytic approach to goals reflects the implicit agent stance already discussed—experimental participants are treated as users of the cognitive system under study, and their points of view (as they might be revealed in a careful analysis of goals) are outside the domain of explanation.

There are also exceptions to the generalization that cognitive scientists have adopted a (merely) common-sense approach to participants' goals in empirical research, and this work demonstrates the critical role of goals in cognitive performance. Perhaps the most widely known exception is the study of speed–accuracy tradeoffs, in which instructions or incentives are manipulated in order to vary participants' goals to maximize speed or accuracy as they perform perceptual or cognitive tasks. The central phenomenon is that individuals can trade accuracy for speed in many tasks, performing more quickly at the cost of lower accuracy. Instructions or incentives can be effective experimental manipulations, encouraging participants to adjust their goals for performance. It also appears that with practice, individuals can learn to perform at an optimal point, finding a tradeoff that allows fast, accurate performance (Rabbitt, 1981). Similarly, individuals can choose or be instructed to emphasize particular aspects of performance as they practice complex tasks (Gopher, Weil, & Siegel, 1989). In multiple-task situations, individuals can often deliberately choose particular tradeoffs between tasks (Proctor & Dutta, 1995). Analyses of these phenomena tend to be pragmatic rather than theoretical, or at least focused on behavioral consequences rather than experiential variables. The wealth of empirical data on these tradeoffs does indicate the importance of understanding how goals control performance in both simple and complex tasks.

A number of cognitive researchers have used the concept of goals to account for phenomena in the domain of memory. For example, R. C. Anderson and Pichert (1978) reported a very interesting manipulation of as-if goals for reading and for recall. In their study, participants read brief passages with instructions that specified a particular perspective or role to be adopted. For example, the investigators asked participants to read and later recall a story that described a home, adopting the perspective of either a home buyer or a burglar. Participants recalled more perspective-relevant than perspective-irrelevant information (e.g., the condition of the roof versus the presence of an expensive television). When asked to shift perspectives and again recall the story, they could recall information relevant to the new perspective but not included in the first recall attempt. More recently, Albrecht and his colleagues (Albrecht, O'Brien, Mason, & Myers, 1995) showed that comprehension and memory for stories is organized around the goals of characters in the story. Furthermore, readers focus on these goals particularly when they are encouraged to adopt the perspective of the story's protagonist.

A third domain of research relevant to understanding the role of goals in cognition is concerned with memory for intentions. A number of authors have suggested that goals or intentions have a special status in memory (e.g., J. R. Anderson, 1983, 1993). Perhaps the best known empirical example is the *Zeigarnik effect*, the finding that individuals are often better able to remember unfulfilled intentions than intentions that have been completed (Goschke & Kuhl, 1993; Seifert, Meyer, Davidson, Patalano, & Yaniv, 1995). Recently, researchers have devoted considerable attention to the general topic of *prospective remembering*, remembering to act on intentions formed some time before the action is required (for example, to take medicine at a particular time). McDaniel and Einstein (1993; Einstein & McDaniel, 1990) provided reviews of some of this research, and Kvavilashvili (1987) reviewed older research on memory for intentions generally.

Two main findings from the research on memory for intentions are relevant here. First, there is evidence that individuals can better remember verbally presented material if it is encoded as an intention to act; for example, memory is improved when experimental participants are asked to act out items in a list of words (Engelkamp & Cohen, 1991; Engelkamp, Zimmer, Mohr, & Sellen, 1994). Second, there is evidence that content and intending can be dissociated in memory. That is, sometimes we can remember that we intended to do something, but not what we intended to do (Goschke & Kuhl, 1993; Kvavilashvili, 1987). These results suggest that the self-specific information involved in an instantiated goal has a special status in memory, distinct from that of object-specific information, perhaps serving as a source of activation (J. R. Anderson, 1993; Goschke

& Kuhl, 1993). However, this literature provides little insight into the function of goals in guiding cognitive activity.

Careful analyses of learners' goals have been rare in research concerned with the acquisition of cognitive skill. Generally, researchers have assumed that participants follow instructions and attempt to perform their instructed tasks as quickly and accurately as possible. This assumption underlies the focus of much research on the power-function speedup discussed in chapter 3. However, there are many instances of skills in which faster is not necessarily better, and greater speed does not always indicate greater fluency—consider the skills of playing a musical instrument or delivering a lecture.

A study conducted in my lab (Carlson et al., 1990) demonstrates the complexity of relating goal parameters to measures of performance in the acquisition of a problem-solving skill. In this study, participants learned a relatively complex problem-solving skill, troubleshooting simulated digital electronic circuits displayed on a computer screen. They could choose a variety of actions, such as testing the output state of a component or replacing a component. We instructed participants to minimize the simulated cost (in dollars) of repairing each circuit, which was determined by summing the costs assigned to various actions. Solution time was also assigned a cost, but this cost was low relative to the costs of problem-solving actions. We found that participants continued to restructure their actions to reduce simulated cost after solution time was nearly asymptotic. The standard learning curve in terms of solution time therefore concealed a major aspect of skill acquisition in this case. On the basis of both behavioral data and participants' reports, we can conclude that their goals specified not just correct solution but noncontent parameters of the solution process.

Production system models of cognitive performance, notably ACT (J. R. Anderson, 1983, 1993) and Soar (Newell, 1990), make the role of goals very explicit. In the ACT theories, for example, each step in cognitive performance depends on matching a goal active in working memory to the condition of a production. The actions of many productions explicitly manipulate goals, removing them from or adding them to the information active in working memory. However, these theories do not provide much deep analysis of the goal concept itself. In particular, these theories do not address how goals are involved in the experience of cognitive activity. It is worth noting, however, that Anderson's English translations of ACT productions generally express goals as verbs representing actions, which naturally have the person as agent. For example, consider the production rules for addition discussed in chapter 3 (Table 3.2). The goal clauses of these productions specify actions: "to solve" or "to write out." Implicitly, then, Anderson's view of goals embodies Mandler's (1984) point that "there are no goals without means" (p. 82).

To summarize this brief review of literature concerned with goals: Although I have undoubtedly overlooked some important research, there is relatively little in the cognitive science literature that is directly relevant to understanding the function of goals in the moment-to-moment control of cognition. (J. R. Anderson's work, e.g., 1983, is a major exception.) Furthermore, there is little theory in either the cognitive science literature or in other areas of psychology (e.g., Austin & Vancouver, 1996) that addresses the role of instantiated goals in constituting individuals' experience of agency. However, there is substantial evidence pointing to the importance of goals not just for understanding action but for understanding how knowledge is organized and for predicting the outcome of memory processes. There is also some evidence consistent with the view that the psychological mode *intend* and the content of the intention can be dissociated. In the next section, I consider the structure of intentions.

The Structure of Intentions

How should we think about goals in the experienced cognition framework? First, as in the ACT theories, we should understand goals in informational terms. In particular, instantiated goals, or intentions, specify the self as achieving a state by engaging in an activity. We are essentially always engaged in goal-directed activity, however mundane or brief; the specification of the self as engaged in goal-directed activity is thus typical of experienced cognition. The information carried by the content of an instantiated goal is also egolocative—because the intended outcome has not yet been achieved, it must be distinguished from the self whose action is aimed at achieving it.

Instantiated goals correspond to basic intentional actions, which may be accomplished in a single cognitive step and correspond to units of causal knowledge. Typically, of course, our activities require a series of subgoals to be instantiated, and I discuss such extended episodes of purposive activity next. Consider the (relatively) simple case of a goal location in visually guided locomotion. To walk across the room to the stereo requires that I get up, walk around the table in front of me, and take several steps to cross the room. The goal location is more-or-less continuously available to my visual perception, and my approach is specified by optical flow variables discussed by Gibson (1966) and others. In addition, my action must be guided by information that specifies the aperture between my seat and the table in front of it, the location and orientation of the floor, the orientation and disposition of my body, and so on. E. J. Gibson (1993) referred to such information as constituting a set of *nested affordances* for action. We can see in this brief sketch some important distinctions. For example, the goal object (location) may be said to guide the episode of reaching it throughout. Intermediate intentions-in-action (see chapter 4), however, have contents based on information that becomes available as my action proceeds, but which is not necessarily implied by the content of the beginning intention.

The mental state corresponding to an instantiated goal may be described by the formula *self-mode-content* (see chapter 5), spelled out something like this:

I intend that [*x* be accomplished by (my) doing *y*]

This formula makes explicit the egolocative character of instantiated goals—the distinction between the goal conditions (*x*) that would satisfy the mental state and the active self ([my] doing *y*) is an aspect of the content of the mental state. Generally, *x* will be a state of affairs in the world, and *y* will be an action in the individual's repertoire. Both may allow (or require) decomposition, as when a subgoal hierarchy is needed to achieve a top-level goal. The *instrumental* or by-means-of relation is also explicit in the content of the state. These features allow instantiated goals to be organized in hierarchies that describe the control of extended episodes, as discussed later. Note, however, that in the case of intentions-in-action (chapter 4), we often perform purposeful actions whose content is supported by immediate activity and information available from perception. For example, my action in reaching for the glass of water next to my keyboard is goal-directed, but the content of the state in which that goal is instantiated is carried by the action itself rather than by a prior, symbolic representation. There is thus little intentional distance between content and object (chapter 5), limiting my metacognitive access to the goal-directed nature of the action.

This analysis lets us untangle some common confusions in standard conceptions of goals, alluded to in Mandler's (1985) discussion. Two points are especially important: (a) the distinction between a goal state or object in the world (considered apart from an agent's point of view) and an instantiated goal as a mental state with the mode *intend* and a structured content specifying action and consequence, and (b) the recognition that goals must be instantiated as mental states to be functional in the control of cognition. This account thus helps to bridge the gap between existing theoretical accounts of the control of cognition and cognition as we experience it. In the next section, I consider performances that require (as most do) multiple goal-directed steps organized to achieve some overall goal.

GOAL STRUCTURES

Describing mental and physical activity seems to require some kind of hierarchical description, and cognitive theorists have offered a wide variety of such descriptions. One kind of hierarchical description especially relevant to understanding experienced cognition can be framed in terms of the goal structures, or arrangements of subgoals, that individuals adopt for particular tasks. A goal structure represents a decomposition of the problem of controlling an episode of cognitive activity. Cognitive tasks are typically defined in terms of an overall goal (e.g., "obtain the sum of 537 and 128") that picks out a reasonably coherent mental episode. This task-defining goal serves as the top-level goal for purposes of theoretical analysis, although it may serve as a subgoal for some other, higher-level goal (e.g., "determine the balance in your bank account" or "satisfy the experimenter's requests"). Working down, the task may be decomposed into a series of subgoals (e.g., "obtain the sum of 7 and 8"), perhaps requiring several levels. Often, achieving subgoals serves to satisfy ena-bling conditions for achieving higher level goals. When the enabling condition achieved is the availability of data (i.e., an *intermediate result*) for subsequent mental operations, I refer to the task as *cascaded* (Carlson & Lundy, 1992). Similarly, in multiple-step verbal reasoning processes, the conclusion of one step may serve as a premise for a subsequent step (Carlson, Lundy, & Yaure, 1992; Schum, 1977, 1980). All of these obser-vations are of course familiar from Newell's (1980) *problem space* analysis of mental activity, although I have presented the ideas to emphasize those aspects important for understanding experienced cognition.

Goal Structures Support Plans

Most cognitive tasks in real life (as opposed to the laboratory) do involve multiple, cascaded steps and intermediate results. This implies a need to manage working memory—in the extended sense that includes perfor-matory strategies and offloading information into the environment—and to coordinate the performance of multiple steps with the availability of information on which they depend. The goal structure adopted for a cascaded task thus specifies a plan or routine for instantiating subgoals and managing working memory. A particular goal structure can of course be identified only with respect to a particular individual performing a task in specified circumstances. It is often easier to speak as if a goal structure were a property of the task itself, leaving the agent implicit as in Newell and Simon's (1972) description of goals as states in a problem space. Assuming an overall goal and certain constraints on the available information and mental operations, we can thus describe particular tasks in terms of their goal structures, abstract characterizations of the organization of goals and relations among intermediate results and subgoals. However, returning to the analysis of intentional structure, we can make the role of the agent, or acting self, theoretically explicit.

Performance of a task may then be described as traversal of its goal structure. This traversal may be constrained by limits on the availability of information in the environment or in memory. For example, Rosenbaum (1987; Rosenbaum, Hindorff, & Munro, 1987) described simple motor performances in terms of traversal of a hierarchical control representation. Performance of routine cognitive skills can therefore be described as skilled traversal of goal structures. Describing performance in this way highlights the parallel structure of cognitive and perceptual-enactive performance. Just as we traverse a medium (the physical environment) to reach a visually specified goal location in the case of egomotion, in routine problem solving we traverse a medium (for example, a conventional symbol system such as arithmetic, supported by permanent knowledge) to reach a cognitively specified goal state (M. Johnson, 1987). In both cases, action changes self-specific information in relation to relatively stable object-specific information, giving rise to the experience of activity in an environment. In this sense, *traversal* may be a more useful general term for skilled cognitive activity than is *search* in the standard sense that derives from Newell and Simon's (1972) work on problem solving. This is because goal structures may continue to organize experience and performance of skilled routines long after those goal structures have been constructed by weak-method search processes (chapter 2).

Goal Structures and Learning

A variety of evidence indicates that goal structures are important in learning cognitive skills. In research concerned with analogical transfer—transfer of problem-solving skills based on one or a very few prior experiences—Catrambone (1994, 1995; Catrambone & Holyoak, 1990) demonstrated that transfer performance is much better when an initial (practice) problem is presented so as to emphasize its goal structure. For example, in one series of experiments, Catrambone (1995) taught participants to perform arithmetic routines with the goal of determining statistical quantities based on the Poisson distribution. Some participants solved a practice problem in which labels indicated intermediate results that reflected the achievement of subgoals, whereas others solved a practice problem without such labels. Although there was little difference between groups in solving test problems very similar to the practice problems, the label group was much more successful at solving test problems that required modification of the practiced calculation routine. Catrambone concluded that it is the identification of steps as subgoals that allows individuals to see mathematical routines as meaningful.

Wenger and Carlson (1996) drew a similar conclusion based on research using a many-trial practice paradigm. In these studies, participants practiced 12-step cascaded arithmetic routines. The sequence of arithmetic operations (addition, subtraction, etc.) was either consistent or varied over trials. The goal structure, defined abstractly in terms of the relations among intermediate results and subsequent steps as shown in Fig. 9.2, was also consistent or varied. As shown in Fig. 9.3, practicing with a consistent goal structure substantially increased the speedup observed with practice, compared to practicing with varied goal structures. Learners practicing with consistent goal structures also achieved much higher accuracy. Consistent sequences of operations also led to somewhat faster performance compared to varied sequences, but this effect was smaller than the effect of consistency in goal structures. There was no benefit in accuracy for a consistent operator sequence. These results suggest that individuals learned a routine for applying a goal structure to coordinate information in working memory with displayed information and mental operations.

Goal Structures and Causal Knowledge

Goal structures (or their abstract forms) also govern thinking about much of our causal knowledge, as shown in studies of event and discourse comprehension and memory. For example, Lichtenstein and Brewer (1980) asked experimental participants to recall filmed goal-directed activities such as setting up a slide projector. The recall protocols demonstrated that individuals regularized their recall with respect to goal structures, often reporting that events occurred in an order corresponding to the goal–subgoal structure of the activity rather than preserving the actual presented order from the film. For example, subjects tended to recall the action of plugging in the projector at a logical point in the sequence of actions, rather than at the point it actually occurred. Similarly, Trabasso and his colleagues (Trabasso, Secco, & van den Broek, 1984; Trabasso & Sperry, 1985; Trabasso & van den Broek, 1985) demonstrated the importance of causal structures organized along goal–subgoal lines in the comprehension of written discourse.

Researchers concerned with causal knowledge and causal judgments have emphasized the distinction between effective or focal causes and enabling conditions (e.g., Cheng & Novick, 1991; Einhorn & Hogarth, 1986; Hilton & Slugoski, 1986). For example, touching a lit match to a newspaper might be viewed as the focal cause of the resulting fire, whereas the presence of oxygen is seen as an enabling condition. Both categories of cause support counterfactuals—had either the lit match or the oxygen not been present, the fire would not have occurred. A number of theoretical proposals concerning the psychological status of this distinction are available; for example, Einhorn and Hogarth (1986) argued that causal judgments that distinguish causes from conditions depend on *cues to causality* such as covariation and temporal order, whereas Hilton and Slugoski (1986) emphasized counterfactual and contrastive reasoning. An alternative view, developed in more detail in the next chapter, is that

Given A = 9,

	TRAVERSAL STEP	INTERMEDIATE VALUES IN WM
B = MAX (A,5)		
C = DIF (2,7)	(1)	A
D = MIN (B,8)	(2)	B
E = SUM (C,D)	(3)	B,C
F = MIN (6,3)	(4)	C,D
G = DIF (E,9)	(5)	E
H = SUM (F,G)	(6)	F
I = MAX (H,3)	(7)	F,G
J = DIF (2,5)	(8)	H
K = MIN (J,7)	(9)	I
L = MAX (I,K)	(10)	I,J
M = SUM (L,5)	(11)	I,K
	(12)	L

ENTER ANSWER: M = ?

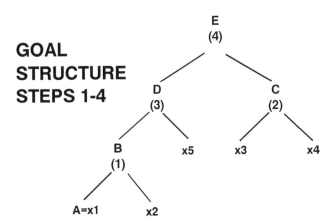

GOAL STRUCTURE STEPS 1-4

FIG. 9.2. Task and goal structure used in Wenger and Carlson (1996): An example of the task is shown at the top left. The steps appeared sequentially on a computer display, at the subject's keypress request. The intermediate values that must be held in working memory at the beginning of each step are shown at the top right. At the bottom is shown the goal structure for the first four steps of this task. Letters indicate variables, and numbers in parentheses indicate the sequence in which the goal structure is traversed.

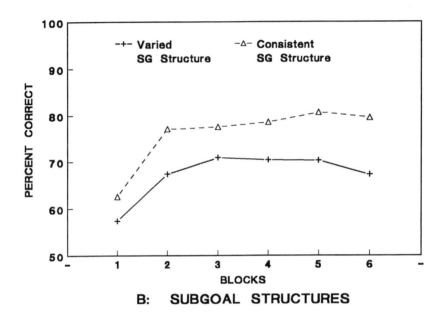

B: SUBGOAL STRUCTURES

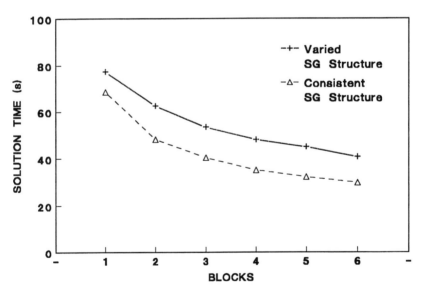

FIG. 9.3. Results from Wenger and Carlson (1996): The figure displays percent correct (top) and solution time (bottom) for subjects practicing with consistent and varied goal structures, as a function of practice block. The benefit of practicing with a consistent goal structure is substantial on both measures.

causal knowledge is grounded in the experience of causality in perceptual-enactive awareness. This view suggests that the distinction between focal causes and enabling conditions depends on the structure of mental states that instantiate goals, and is consistent with evidence that causal knowledge is patterned along the lines of goal structures.

THE HIERARCHICAL STRUCTURE OF ACTION

Goal structures capture only one aspect of the hierarchical structure of action. Understanding our experience of goal-directed cognitive activity requires that we recognize two types of hierarchical relations among actions, decompositional and instrumental. In addition, we must consider the internal structure of goal-directed actions that constitute the units in which goal structures are described. It is at this level of analysis that we can approach an account of cognitive control at the grain of individual mental states.

Decompositional and Instrumental Hierarchies

Two of the many possible conceptions of hierarchical organization in cognitive activity are especially relevant to understanding experienced cognition and its control. *Decompositional hierarchies* describe the relations among instantiated subgoals, representing goal structures that are traversed over time in the course of performing activities. *Instrumental hierarchies* relate alternative descriptions of activity that are concurrently available and appropriate, and represent various scales or grains at which goal-directed activity may be described. The goal structure embodied in a particular performance is a decompositional hierarchy that describes the organization of control, the decomposition of a top-level goal into subgoals that achieve portions of the desired end state or that achieve enabling conditions for other subgoals. The stopping point or bottom level of a decompositional hierarchy is at the level of a basic action that can be directly intended, a goal that can be instantiated in a single mental state.

The notion of an instrumental hierarchy is less familiar in cognitive theory, but equally critical for understanding experienced cognition. Vallacher and Wegner (1987) developed this idea in their *action identification theory* (although they do not use the term *instrumental hierarchy*). The basic idea is that any episode of activity admits of multiple true descriptions, from the point of view of either the actor or an observer or theorist. For example, consider the activity that might be described (with suitable elaboration) as "seeing if someone is home," "ringing the doorbell," or "pressing a button with the right index finger." At some levels of description, the relation between adjacent levels captures the by-means-of, or instrumental relation, inherent in instantiated goals. Furthermore, circumstances may systematically influence the level of description most available or salient to actors (see chapter 12, this volume). Two points are important here: First, it is not clear that the description of instrumental hierarchies has a psychologically principled stopping point—certainly as theorists, and sometimes as actors, we may continue almost indefinitely to accept finer-grained descriptions of the realization of actions. Second, although instrumental hierarchies can be important in understanding the control of activity, they do not describe the sequence of mental states involved in the experience of goal-directed activity. Confusing the two notions of hierarchy can thus lead to mistaken efforts at theoretical reductionism.

Both decompositional and instrumental hierarchies are important for understanding experienced cognition because we need to understand both the actual sequence of events that we experience in skilled performance and the interesting phenomenon that we as actors can accept alternative descriptions of our experience as correct. In chapter 14, I return to this second point in considering the appeal of unconscious mental processes to psychological theorists. The two notions of hierarchy are linked, in that subgoals at different points in a decompositional hierarchy or goal structure will likely have contents that correspond to different levels of an instrumental hierarchy for the task. This is the point that ecological theorists (Flach, Lintern, & Larish, 1990; E. J. Gibson, 1993; J. J. Gibson, 1966) make in talking about "nested affordances." Looking at the hierarchical organization of action in terms of the environmental support for an activity, affordances must be described at multiple temporal and spatial grain sizes. For example, that a portion of the floor affords support (because it is flat, solid, etc.) is nested in the affordance of the room for navigation by walking (because it is sufficiently uncluttered, of appropriate scale, and has a floor, etc.). Unfortunately, ecological theories of action developed to date do not provide corresponding descriptions of the cognitive control based on those affordances, emphasizing descriptions of the environment while acknowledging but not explaining the performing self.

Planning

One of the most remarkable achievements of human cognition is planning—representing often complex courses of action in advance of performing them. The more complex instances of planning generally depend on external artifacts as representations and memory aids—for example, blueprints and schedules—but planning on a smaller scale is characteristic of experienced cognition. Planning has been considered in greater detail by artificial intelligence researchers (e.g., Hayes-Roth & Hayes-Roth, 1979) than by cognitive psychologists; however, J. R. Anderson (1983) offered the following characterization of

> A litmus test for planning: the system sets forth a sequence of intended actions, notes a conflict in the sequence, and reorganizes it. If it can be shown that a system reorders a preferred sequence of actions in anticipation of goal conflict, then that system is engaging in planning. (p. 167)

Of course, not all instances of planning generate goal conflicts and Anderson's point concerns empirically identifying the ability to plan. More important for the present discussion, this observation indicates that goal structures, taken as metacognitive objects of thought, provide the basis for planning. Planning thus epitomizes the metacognitive control of activity, involving mental states whose contents represent the self as engaged in extended, purposive activity.

The Structure of Component Skills

Describing cognitive activity in terms of goal structures as just sketched entails that the elements of cognitive activity be described as component skills. For example, procedures for using arithmetic facts serve as component skills for multistep mental arithmetic. Component skills are often viewed as automatic and encapsulated, lacking internal structure or dynamics. For example, Siegler's (1988, 1989) account of skill in using arithmetic facts treats simple problems (e.g., $5 + 3$) as cognitive units associated with possible answers. However, both empirical and theoretical considerations suggest that component skills must have internal structure. Empirically, a number of studies from my laboratory suggest that even with extensive practice, rule-application skills retain some of the sequential structure observed early in practice (Carlson & Schneider, 1989a; Carlson, Sullivan, & Schneider, 1989a, 1989b; Sohn & Carlson, 1996). Theoretically, it seems that goals and data must be represented separately in order that component skills can be linked into goal structures.

Some current theories of skill acquisition recognize this in various ways. For example, the units of cognitive skill in J. R. Anderson's (1983, 1993) ACT theories are productions, if–then or condition–action rules whose conditions include separate clauses representing goals, data, and other conditions for execution. Logan's (1988) instance theory suggests that skill is based on remembered episodes that include goals, stimuli, and answers (goal-relative interpretations of stimuli). These theories incorporate separate representation of goals and other aspects of component skills, and

Anderson's theory provides substantial detail on how component skills are organized into extended episodes of goal-directed activity. Neither theory, however, considers in detail the internal temporal structure of single steps of conscious mental episodes. The present analysis of goals and goal structures suggests that goal instantiation is a separable aspect of component skills, preceding the processing of data. For example, in performing mental arithmetic an individual instantiates a goal to add, then applies an addition procedure to specific digits. This account is captured in the GOER model developed by my students and me. This model suggests that component skills for mental arithmetic have an internal temporal structure of the form illustrated in Fig. 9.4. The basic idea is that individuals first instantiate a goal—for example, intending to add—then consider operands from the perspective, or procedural framework, specified by that goal.

The GOER model and evidence for it are discussed in more detail in chapter 13. Several general points are relevant to the present discussion, however. First, this model is consistent with production-system theories (J. R. Anderson, 1983, 1993; Newell, 1990) in suggesting that the basic unit of cognitive performance is a procedural or performatory retrieval. Second, it is consistent with the recent recognition that automatic processes are in fact conditional (e.g., Bargh, 1989) and closely controlled (e.g., Logan, 1989, 1992). For example, research has demonstrated that some automatic processes can be voluntarily inhibited or initiated. Although early summaries of research on automaticity (e.g., Shiffrin & Dumais,

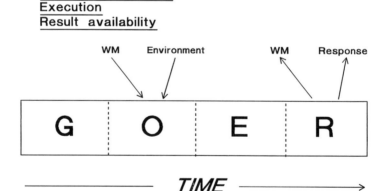

FIG. 9.4. The GOER model: The figure depicts the basic assumptions of the GOER model of calculation steps. Goal instantiation provides a perspective from which operands are considered. The GOER model is discussed in more detail in chapter 13.

1981) drew a very strong contrast between controlled and automatic processes, a careful reading of the original research (e.g., Shiffrin & Schneider, 1977) shows a recognition that most tasks require a mix of controlled and automatic aspects.

Most important, the present analysis and the GOER model suggest an alternative to the implicit-agent stance, and suggests hypotheses about the content of experienced cognition. As previously discussed, goal instantiation—the first element of performing component skills, according to the GOER model—is an egolocative process establishing a distinction between the experiencing self and the objects of cognition. The G component of the GOER model thus reflects specification of the self as performing an operation such as adding. The operands, encoded with respect to the instantiated goal, constitute contents of the mental state corresponding to performance of a component skill. In other terms, encoding operands in terms of a goal represents assimilation of (mental) objects in terms of their affordances for the basic action represented by the goal. However, the *execution* of a procedure (e.g., retrieval of the appropriate arithmetic fact) does not constitute a mental content in this sense. The result—for example, the retrieved answer to a simple arithmetic problem—makes information available to a subsequent mental state, but need not constitute part of the content of the performatory state. To make the moral of this story explicit: The GOER model suggests that the mental state in which a step of mental arithmetic is performed has the structure

I intend that [I add A and B].

The mode of the state that instantiates a goal is *intend*, and the content makes explicit reference to the acting self. In chapter 13, I return to this point to discuss the time course of such activities in more detail, in terms of the relations between the structured content of the state and noncontent properties such as the time course of the state.

COSPECIFICATION IN EXTENDED EPISODES

The GOER model thus describes an egolocative process based on cospecification in an informational manifold that specifies the self as engaged in an activity (e.g., adding) with respect to particular objects (e.g., displayed digits). Over an extended episode—for example, performing a multiple-step arithmetic routine—a goal structure describes the cospecification of self and medium. In this section, I am concerned with how we experience our cognitive activity in the course of relatively extended, goal-directed episodes.

Plausible Regularities

Because an instantiated goal specifies the self as engaging in an activity that achieves some state of affairs, the ability to form an intention depends on what Searle (1983) called *plausible regularities*. These regularities reflect the most fundamental level of causal knowledge—knowledge that an intended action can be expected to have some (likely) effect. The pieces of this type of causal knowledge are first experienced as intentions-in-action, whose consequences are in some degree learned. We see this structure in the primary circular reaction of young infants, in which the infant appears to intentionally repeat some action that was first initiated accidentally, in order to observe the repeated consequence of that action. This point is in part terminological, serving to clarify what is meant by *intention*—an expected consequence is part of the content of a mental state that instantiates a goal. This is necessary because, as we see in the next chapter, possible actions must be indexed by their consequences if problem-solving strategies other than trial and error are to be used.

The learning involved in establishing causal knowledge in this procedural form need not be metacognitive. Although the intended action and its consequence must enter awareness together (so that they can participate in the content of a single mental state representing the intention), learning does not require an additional state that represents the link as such. However, this analysis implies that to function as instantiated subgoals in hierarchically organized action, these regularities must become objects of metacognitive thought. This is the point made by developmental theorists such as Siegler (1991) and Karmiloff-Smith (1994), who argued that procedures precede principles (Siegler) or that knowledge is initially implicit in procedural skills, then later made explicit by reflection on those skills (Karmiloff-Smith). This point is of course linked to the idea that mental representation is performatory: When a performance is sufficiently reliable to allow resampling—the performance can be repeated "at will"; it can also be consulted, allowing procedural knowledge to also function declaratively.

Self in Action

Instantiated goals serve to specify the acting self and to distinguish self from object in the course of goal-directed activity. In other words, what we experience is what we are trying to do. This point may be elaborated by returning to the link between purposive cognitive activity and emotion (chapter 6).

A number of theorists have argued that emotionality serves a function in sustaining extended goal-directed activity (e.g., Carver & Scheier, 1990;

Damasio, 1994; Weiner, 1987; also see chapter 6). For example, Damasio argued that the difficulties faced by frontal-lobe patients—who seem quite rational in conversation or in performing routine activities but are often quite unable to organize their activity in terms of long-term goals—follow from their diminished emotionality. On the analysis offered here, there is an important structural parallel between emotionality and (relatively) long-term goals: Both are characterized by self-specific information that changes slowly relative to the pace of cognition and perception. In the case of pure emotionality, it is the relatively slow course of physiological arousal that most clearly serves this function. In the case of goals, consider the high-level goals at the tops of hierarchical goal structures—such goals specify the self as engaged in a single activity that may require many steps. It seems a reasonable hypothesis that some persisting aspects of the available information continue to support specification of the self as performing the activity described by the content of the top-level goal. That is, emotion serves to sustain activity directed at long-term goals.

My hypothesis, then, is that emotionality and goal-directedness are linked in function and in experience on the basis of their parallel roles in the structure of mental states. The evolutionary history of this link is presumably along the lines sketched by Damasio (1994) and others; the emotional and cognitive aspects of cospecification evolved together because sustained purposive activity allows numerous adaptive advantages. Developing this link allows us to interpret a number of specific phenomena often described as implicating emotion–cognition interactions. For example, Mandler (1985) suggested that emotional experience may be triggered by the disruption of an ongoing action plan. On the present account, this is because a mental state instantiating a goal fails to be satisfied. The contrast between the self specified as completing an action and the environment specified as not fitting the state serves as a basis for egolocative processing.

Multiple Tasks

The information-processing conception of limited cognitive capacities (Broadbent, 1957) has spurred a huge research literature based on so-called dual-task paradigms. Although the term *dual task* is usually given a common-sense rather than a formal definition, the research literature suggests that an individual is in a dual-task (or more generally, multiple-task) situation when two logically independent goals are to be satisfied in the same period of time, and environmental constraints require that both tasks begin before either goal is satisfied. For example, Baddeley and Hitch (1974) asked participants in their experiments to satisfy two goals—to correctly perform a reasoning or calculation task, and to remember lists of digits or letters (to satisfy a goal of later ordered recall) during that performance. In one of the most ambitious (at least from the participants' point of view) dual-task studies reported, Allport, Antonis, and Reynolds (1972) asked experienced musicians to sight-read music and play the piano while shadowing (quickly repeating aloud) spoken words. These individuals appeared to succeed in performing these tasks concurrently, and after some practice, without interference. More typical, however, is Baddeley and Hitch's (1974) finding that participants asked to recite digits while performing verbal reasoning tasks could do so, but at some cost in accuracy and speed. Since these early studies, researchers have concentrated on relatively small-scale tasks and on theoretical issues concerning the number and type of mental resources that might be shared among tasks.

The experienced cognition framework suggests an analysis of dual-task situations in terms of goal structures, suggesting that true concurrence is rare or impossible over extended episodes. Based on the model of egolocation in visually guided locomotion, it seems reasonable to suggest the hypothesis that simultaneous egolocative processing with respect to separate goal structures is not possible. This analysis leads me to suggest that true concurrence of tasks is possible only for very short periods corresponding to the ballistic completion of component skills. That is, another goal may be instantiated during the execution of an activity specified by a just-instantiated goal. However, my claim is that it is not possible to simultaneously instantiate two or more goals. Therefore, the issue for performance in multiple-task situations is the coordination of multiple goal structures by switching or integration; some data is available to support this conception (e.g., Gopher, in press).

CONTROL OF EXTENDED EPISODES

I have mentioned extended episodes in several connections so far in this chapter. I am now prepared to be more specific about this notion, and to consider some of its implications for the organization of experienced cognition. Briefly, I mean by *extended episodes* instances in which a single top-level goal serves to guide a many-step mental process (where "many" could be taken to mean "a number exceeding the conventional limit on the number of elements in working memory"). Most of our everyday experience involves extended episodes in this sense. The conscious control of activity in extended episodes depends on coordinating reliable causal regularities in both action and the environment, linking self, action, and object. Goal structures reflect the coordinative modes that allow us to perform routine cognitive activities. The acting self is specified in the course of this activity, and the changing availability of information reflects the reciprocal, cyclic nature of interaction with the medium for the skilled performance.

Maintaining Goal Structures

In the abstract, the notion of a goal structure allows for indefinite elaboration and specificity. In reality, the goal structure involved in a particular episode is realized in a series of mental states dependent on the information available from memory and from the environment. The actual control of a specific extended episodes requires that a goal structure be preserved in memory or the environment to allow placekeeping and coordination. Most theorists have assumed that some special knowledge structure such as a schema (e.g., Norman, 1981) or goal stack (e.g., Anderson, 1983) is required to maintain the organization of subgoals in extended episodes. These theories are prescriptive in K. Newell's (1991) sense—the course of activity is prescribed by a preexisting information structure, rather than controlled in the course of ongoing interactions between self and environment.

As an alternative to the prescriptive view, extended episodes may be conceived as multiple perception-cognition-action cycles, in which organism-environment causality is reciprocal (Neisser, 1976). In this view, at least for routine activity supported by already learned affordances of the environment, a goal structure is generated online in the course of performance. Simon (e.g., 1992) argued that the ubiquity of environmental support makes such structures unnecessary, "The chaining is accomplished by the continually changing problem situation that evokes the appropriate chain of productions. The productions do not have to be strung together in memory" (p. 132). As we see in chapter 12, consistent with Simon's argument, a central feature of highly skilled performance is reliance on information in the environment to support goal-directed activity.

Our research on routines for mental arithmetic—using a paradigm analogous to RSVP (Rapid Serial Visual Presentation; Just, Carpenter, & Woolley, 1982) in an attempt to build a laboratory model of the perception-cognition-action cycle—suggests that individuals do acquire knowledge of subgoal sequences as such (Carlson & Lundy, 1992; Lundy, Wenger, Schmidt, & Carlson, 1994; Wenger & Carlson, 1996). However, experimental participants have great difficulty in describing these sequences outside the context of performing the task. This suggests that there is minimal symbolic representation involved in controlling performances based on learned subgoal structures. The minimal-control nature of the knowledge that guides well-learned sequences can be seen in the difficulty of coordination and placekeeping in dynamic task situations that minimize external support. For example, Healy and Nairne (1985) demonstrated errors in simple verbal counting, such as skipping or repeating numbers, that suggested failures of placekeeping. In such skilled activities, it appears that the contents of goals instantiated to guide performance are carried by performances and the perceptual information made available by those performances, as in perceptual-enactive awareness.

Cospecification and Purposive Activity

As a theoretical device, goal structures provide a description of how the self is specified in the course of purposive activity directed at environmental objects. In understanding this point, it is important to recognize that not all consequences of our actions are intended. It may be difficult to distinguish intended from incidental outcomes even in the first person, due to the availability of multiple descriptions and the constructive nature of remembering. Generally, traversing a goal structure (a metaphor appropriate because the process itself is literally grounded in perceptually guided egomotion) specifies the self as initiating a sequence of actions that have, as one consequence, the selection of information. Understanding the role of goal structures in controlling experienced cognition, and understanding instantiated goals as mental states in which an acting self is specified, lets us link the experience of agency and the phenomena of cognitive control without adopting an implicit-agent stance. Applying the analysis of intentional structure to instantiated goals begins to make agency explicit in cognitive theory.

10

Causal Thinking and Problem Solving

A person is confronted with a problem *when he wants something and does not know immediately what series of actions he can perform to get it.*
—Newell & Simon, 1972, p. 72

Much of our everyday thinking is about cause-and-effect relationships.
—Zechmeister & Johnson, 1992, p. 21

The study of problem solving is concerned with how individuals choose actions to achieve desired outcomes, and the study of causal thinking is concerned with how we understand domains in terms of cause-and-effect relations among their elements. The link between these topics is our experience as causal agents, intervening in the world. As we acquire skill in a domain by solving problems, we shift from testing hypotheses about causal relations in order to generate goal structures to developing sub-routines organized around the affordances for action of objects in the domain. Problem solving seems to require metacognitive awareness of our roles as causal agents, but this awareness depends on the more fundamental causal knowledge embodied in our procedural skills, which serve as operators in problem solving. Clarifying the ways in which the experience of causal agency is involved in problem solving and causal thinking sets the stage for deeper consideration of complex skills in the following chapters and helps us to understand how the notions of consciousness and causal relations are often entangled.

PROBLEM SOLVING AND CAUSAL THINKING

Research on problem solving and on causal thinking often dissociates the self as problem solver from causal relations among events in which the self does not participate. Cognitive psychologists have usually studied problem solving either with puzzle problems (such as the Tower of Hanoi; e.g., Anzai & Simon, 1979) or with school-like problems in formal domains such as mathematics or physics (Mayer, 1992). Even these simple problem-solving situations require causal thinking because the problem solver must choose actions that have as their consequences particular states of the problems. As J. R. Anderson (1990) noted:

> It is peculiar that causal inference does not get more play in mainstream cognitive psychology because it has to be one of the key organizing constructs of human cognition. It is central to problem solving, and some of us (J. R. Anderson, 1983; Newell, 1980, Tolman, 1932) see problem solving as particularly central to human cognition. In solving a problem, we are basically trying to do something that will cause a particular state of affairs. Surely, how we reason about causality must be central to how we organize our problem solving. Still, the standard practice, of which I have been guilty, is to talk about problem solving and ignore causality. (p. 150)

This "standard practice" reflects a failure to theoretically integrate the "poles of attention" (Gibson, 1979) to self and object discussed in chapter 4. The reason for this standard practice is, I think, that psychologists interested in problem solving have focused on the organization of problem-solving strategies, taking for granted the causal structure of the domain and adopting an implicit-agent stance toward the intentional nature of problem-solving actions. Thus, for example, goals are often discussed in a manner that dissociates actions and their intended outcomes (Austin & Vancouver, 1996).

When causality itself is the focus of research (e.g., Sperber, Premack, & Premack, 1995), experimental paradigms usually focus on causal relations among events in the world, not causal relations involving the self as agent, again consistent with the implicit-agent stance. This research often makes use of paradigms based on real-world thinking, ranging from simple causal attributions for the behavior of persons (e.g., Kelley, 1973) to operating or troubleshooting mechanical or electronic devices (e.g., Carlson et al., 1990; Lesgold & LaJoie, 1991) and medical diagnosis (e.g., Patel & Groen, 1986). Research participants typically make causal judgments as observers of events (which are often described rather than displayed or enacted). The causal relations evaluated are thus relations among events in which the judge does not participate. Although research in social psychology has considered attributions to persons, the attributions studied are often to individuals' traits rather than to their intentional actions. Theoretical discussions of such causal thinking (e.g., Kahneman & Tversky, 1982b; Kelley, 1973) often assume that it is guided by very abstract causal schemas that specify cause-to-effect directionality (cf. Carlson & Schneider, 1989) and support counterfactual inference (that is, the inference that had a cause not been present, an effect would not have occurred). Some researchers have suggested that such causal schemas are innate (e.g., Premack, 1992).

Intentional Action and Causal Knowledge

The most fundamental way in which we experience causality is in the causal self-reference of perceptual-enactive awareness (chapter 4). The causal self-reference of action—the agency or self-efficacy experienced in intentional action—can be mapped to the notion of operator knowledge in problem-solving research. These fundamental units of causal knowledge correspond to answers to the question, "How can I intervene in or influence the course of events that I experience?" In the classic Newell and Simon (1972) view of problem solving, an operator is defined as an action that changes the state of a problem space, and Newell (1990) identified operators with deliberate goals. Operator knowledge in this sense can be captured in the language of production-system models as discussed in chapters 3 and 9, emphasizing several structural aspects of causal knowledge: goals specifying action by the self as agent, situational knowledge specifying enabling conditions, and expected consequences of action. For example, productions for a task as simple as mental arithmetic (see Table 3.2) specify an action (e.g., to add) and enabling conditions (the availability of operands), and imply an outcome (e.g., a sum). The conditions of satisfaction of a mental state corresponding to such a production include that the result be obtained by a process involving the self as a cause: I add (by memory retrieval, by counting, etc.) to obtain the sum. This analysis suggests the hypothesis that the units of causal knowledge correspond to basic actions and their anticipated consequences. In reflecting on events to make causal attributions, however, an individual might appropriately identify either an intentional action or its enabling (or constraining) conditions as causal precursors of an outcome. For events at larger time scales, this corresponds to identifying either a longer-term disposition to perform certain kinds of actions, or relatively broad properties of the environment. For example, students may attribute exam grades to their own intelligence or study habits, or to the difficulty of the material or of the exam itself.

It is not clear whether the causal self-reference of intentional action should be viewed as innate, inherent in the structure of awareness from the first moment, or as constructed in the course of development. It is clear, however, that an appreciation of causality in some sense is present very early in the life of human infants (Premack, 1992). And despite substantial theoretical disagreements, current research on infant cognition converges on the conclusion that very young children can and do distinguish between physical and intentional causality (Baillargeon, Kotovsky, & Needham, 1995; Carey, 1995; Premack & Premack, 1995). It also seems likely that very young infants experience themselves as causal agents, performing some actions intentionally at least in the sense of deliberately repeating actions that occur by chance or in (reflex) response to external events. Which comes first—a primitive appreciation of causality or the experience of agency—is a question beyond the scope of the present discussion. However, some observations concerning the nature of causal knowledge will help us to understand how basic intentional actions are assembled by problem solving into more complex routines.

PROCEDURAL KNOWLEDGE AND CAUSAL TEXTURE

The procedural knowledge that constitutes problem-solving operators need not be accessible for explicit, reflective causal judgments. For example, it is widely agreed that much procedural knowledge (such as how to ride a bicycle) can be accessed only by performing it, not by verbal description. Yet this knowledge is clearly causal in nature, involving relations between actions and their consequences. And when an individual selects or chooses a problem-solving operator, he or she is evoking procedural knowledge, apparently on the basis of some form of metacognitive access. To understand the relation between causal knowledge and problem solving thus requires that we consider the structure of intentional actions in terms of their accessibility to the egolocative processes that link them into goal structures.

Procedural Versus Metacognitive Experience of Causal Relations

Earlier we noted that intentions-in-action can be described as mental states with the mode *intend* and content that is informationally supported by the action itself (chapter 4). Because the contents of these states are so closely tied to the vehicles of their informational support, there is little of the intentional distance that would allow these contents to be manipulated independently of their objects—rather than first "thinking" such contents, our experience is that we "just do it." Typically, however, such mental states are embedded in goal structures, as described in chapter 9, which seems to require metacognitive access based on egolocative processes that distinguish self and object. How can this be? That is, how can procedural knowledge be the basis of problem-solving activity that generates goal structures?

Consider an example: Imagine that you form the goal of writing a comment (perhaps "huh?!") in the margin of this paragraph. In the service of this goal, you reach for a pencil on a table in front of you. This action is presumably realized as a mental state that is an intention-in-action, a basic action because it relies on well-established skill. If not alerted to reflectively consider this action as an example, your experience of it likely would be nonreflective and fleeting. According to the analysis offered in previous chapters, however, its content would be egolocative: something like *that I get the pencil by reaching for it*. The vehicle of this content, however, need not be a mental representation separate from the performance of the action, and in the course of that action the self is specified as intentionally reaching for the pencil. And recall that the content specifies its conditions of satisfaction—the desired outcome, that you in fact get the pencil.

In the example as described so far, everything has proceeded smoothly, with little need or basis for reflective awareness (and thus for autobiographical memory). Imagine now that your reach for the pencil fails: The mental state, the intention-in-action, fails to be satisfied. This is the circumstance that, according to the analysis presented earlier, triggers emotion (presumably mild in this case) and prompts additional egolocative processing. At this point, you are likely to engage in what intuitively seems more like problem solving, reflecting on the mental state realizing your intention to reach for the pencil.

There are two major points to be drawn from this example. First, even in the fluent, nonreflective case described first, the content of the intention-in-action specifies its conditions of satisfaction. As discussed in chapter 4, these include the desired outcome, and that the intention function causally in achieving that outcome. The dispositional representation supporting the action can thus be indexed by its consequence, as required for problem solving (see next for further discussion). Furthermore, the state specifies the self as engaged in intentional action, as a causal agent. Second, in the normal case in which all goes well and the action is successful, little reflection is involved. Yet the obvious embeddedness of the mental state in a goal structure—you reach for the pencil in order to achieve some further goal—tells us that this is a case of (admittedly minimal) problem solving. We might describe such cases as involving a kind of implicit metacognition, due to the causal self-reference of the intention-in-action.

Another way of understanding these points comes from recognizing that procedural knowledge of causal relations forms the basis of so-called operant or instrumental behavior. For example, Shanks (e.g., 1993) explicitly explored this relation, arguing for an associative model of causal knowledge. As Dickinson and Shanks (1995) noted, "cognitive resources for representing causality should be intimately tied to the behavioural capacity for goal-directed instrumental action—action by means of which we manipulate and control the environment to serve our needs and desires" (p. 5). In a series of studies, they showed that some biases in human causality judgment are paralleled by phenomena in the instrumental conditioning of laboratory rats. Dickinson and Shanks argued that much of our causal knowledge is of a "weak" form (Kummer, 1995) that supports practical inference (performing an action when it is likely to yield desired consequences), without knowledge "about the specific generative processes that instantiate the causal association" (p. 19).

The structures of individual mental states realizing intentions-in-action thus have the properties needed for such states to serve as problem-solving operators: contents that specify desired outcomes, and the distinction between self and object that provides the basis for more reflective problem solving when necessary. The starting point for problem solving is a repertoire of such basic actions, which embody an individual's causal, procedural knowledge of how to effectively intervene in the environment.

Discovery of Possible Actions and Causal Relations

Discussions of problem solving generally presuppose the availability of operators and the ability to foresee (perhaps with some uncertainty) the consequences of performing the corresponding actions (e.g., J. R. Anderson, 1987b; Newell & Simon, 1972). Even the weakest of problem-solving methods, trial and error, assumes a repertoire of possible actions whose consequences are discovered in the course of problem solving. Presumably many of the basic actions that can serve as problem-solving operators are acquired or constructed in the course of development, on the basis of innate perceptual-motor schemes (Case, 1985; Chapman, 1988; Thelen, 1995). Others may be learned by imitation or example (J. R. Anderson, 1993), although this learning process also assumes a repertoire of possible actions.

Considering in detail how repertoires of basic actions are acquired is beyond the scope of this chapter. However, several observations about these repertoires are important. One is that constructing new operators— in the sense of possible basic intended actions—is one consequence of the restructuring involved in skill acquisition (chapter 2; Case, 1985). For example, in learning to type, an individual must acquire skills for particular keystrokes on the basis of prior skills for moving the hands and fingers. Second, naive problem solving often involves elaborating our knowledge of both the conditions and consequences of basic actions. For example, in learning new word processing software, I learn that a particular keystroke (which I already know how to make) in a particular context has a particular result. This kind of learning can of course proceed by a kind of trial and error. More typically, however, such learning involves reasoning about our actions and their consequences in the context of relatively high-level goals for problem solving. Although the discovery of possible actions is important to problem solving, it is using some repertoire of already-available operators to generate a goal structure that is the starting point of interesting novice problem solving.

NOVICE PROBLEM SOLVING: GENERATION OF GOAL STRUCTURES

In chapter 3, I described problem solving as the generation or discovery of coordinative modes, goal structures that make use of causal regularities embodied in basic actions (operators). A problem solver who is a novice in a particular domain must generate goal structures on the basis of some beginning repertoire of possible actions. The character of these possible actions as instantiated goals, with the intentional structure described in earlier chapters, allows the connection between the self experienced as a causal agent and knowledge of a domain's causal texture as a medium for problem solving.

Causal Knowledge as a Medium for Problem Solving

Causal knowledge of a domain provides the medium for problem-solving activities in that domain. In the classic Newell and Simon (1972) account of problem solving, discussed in more detail later, problem solvers' knowledge is characterized in terms of operators (possible actions) that change the state of a problem space. The enabling conditions and consequences of operators are specified in terms of arrangements of elements that constitute states in the problem space, and applying an operator constitutes a causal event within the domain of the problem space.

Several considerations are important for understanding the relations between operator knowledge and the causal texture of a problem-solving domain. First, at least in nonreflective activity, operators are units of procedural knowledge that the problem solver performs rather than consults. Second, the enabling conditions that make an operator applicable are simply the affordances for action of a particular state of a problem space. Third, when a problem solver metacognitively consults operator knowledge by imagining the consequences of particular actions, he or she is reflectively considering a state whose content corresponds to the content of an instantiated goal or intention. As discussed in the previous chapter, this content has the form *that [x be accomplished by (my) doing y]*, representing an instrumental relation. Causal knowledge of the domain considered apart from the individual problem solver is often implicit in such contents because our actions often rely on distal effects. For example, if I solve the problem of how to increase the temperature of my living room by adjusting the thermostat, I am relying on a causal chain of events involving the thermostat, furnace, and heat registers. Knowledge of this causal chain may be useful in choosing the action, but is not essential. In fact, we can be quite mistaken about how a particular causal chain works, and yet succeed (more or less well) in achieving our goals. For example, many individuals hold the incorrect theory that a thermostat works like a valve, regulating the amount of heat produced (Kempton, 1986), yet succeed in warming their rooms (see the discussion in Baron, 1994, pp. 95–97).

What is explicit in the content of mental states involved in choosing operators need be only the action to be performed and its goal-relevant consequences. Sometimes, of course, our incorrect causal theories are inadequate to support solving new problems in a domain. For example, the valve theory of thermostats is not very useful in diagnosing a malfunctioning heating system. In such cases, successful problem solvers extend their causal knowledge of a domain by reflecting on previously successful actions, treating their procedural knowledge as declarative by explicitly consulting it, and by finding new ways to causally intervene in the domain (Karmiloff-Smith, 1994). Researchers have investigated this process of hypothesis-testing—choosing actions in order to determine their consequences—both in simple laboratory tasks (e.g., Bruner, Goodnow, & Austin, 1956) and in more complex realistic or real-life situations (e.g., Dunbar, 1995; Klahr & Dunbar, 1988; Klayman & Ha, 1987). A review of this literature is beyond the scope of this chapter, but two points are worth emphasizing. First, the structure of mental states—intentions or instantiated goals—involved in discovering causal knowledge or in using that knowledge is essentially the same. Second, a careful consideration of the information available in problem solving and in hypothesis testing helps us to understand both how we experience problem solving and the common shortcomings of our causal thinking (Einhorn, 1980; Einhorn & Hogarth, 1985, 1986). In particular, we experience ourselves as agents whose actions have goal-relevant consequences in the problem domain, and this experience implies knowledge of the causal texture of the domain only at the grain size of our intended actions. So, for example, the knowl-

edge that provides a basis for solving a particular word-processing problem such as moving a block of text need not support troubleshooting a
problem with the software. At this grain size, however, the causal knowledge embodied in our repertoire of basic actions must support the generation of goal structures if problem solving is to succeed.

Problem Solving as Generation of Goal Structures

Newell (1980) described problem solving as the fundamental category of
cognition. According to his *problem space hypothesis*, cognition generally
can be described as a search in problem spaces that represent states of
the world (including goal states) organized around the operators that
serve to change the state of the problem space. In a novel domain in
which an individual has little domain-specific procedural knowledge,
search of the problem space is organized on the basis of so-called *weak
methods*, general strategies that can be applied to any problem space. Weak
methods depend on the ability to recognize the desired (goal) state of the
space, and to apply operators that may serve to bring that state about.
The weakest problem-solving method of all is trial-and-error, which in
its purest form involves applying operators at random until the goal state
is achieved.

More powerful weak methods involve choosing a series of operators
that result in moving through the problem space in a series of steps that
approach the goal. These methods can be described as the generation of
goal structures, constrained by the availability of primitive operators. The
most general of these methods is means–ends analysis. Newell and Simon
(1972) described means–ends analysis in their General Problem Solver
(GPS) system:

> This kind of analysis—classifying things in terms of the functions they serve
> and oscillating among ends, functions required, and means that perform
> them—forms the basic system of heuristic of GPS. More precisely, this
> means-ends system of heuristic assumes the following:
>
> 1. If an object is given that is not the desired one, differences will be de-
>   tectable between the available object and the desired object.
> 2. Operators affect some features of their operands and leave others un-
>   changed. Hence operators can be characterized by the changes they pro-
>   duce and can be used to try to eliminate differences between the objects
>   to which they are applied and desired objects.
> 3. If a desired operator is not applicable, it may be profitable to try to
>   modify the inputs so that it becomes applicable.
> 4. Some differences will prove more difficult to affect than others.

It is profitable, therefore, to try to eliminate "difficult" differences, even at
the cost of introducing new differences of lesser difficulty. This process can
be repeated as long as progress is being made toward eliminating the more
difficult differences. (p. 416)

The central point here is the correspondence between this classic account
of weak-method problem solving and the language of the experienced
cognition framework: First, operators correspond to basic actions that can
be intended; as noted, Newell (1990) identified operators with "deliberate
goals." Second, operators must be indexed or organized in terms of their
consequences, and thus represent units of causal knowledge relating the
problem solver's actions to their effects. In Baron's (1994) words, to apply
means-ends analysis, "we must have knowledge about which operators
reduce which differences" (p. 62).

The heuristic of means–ends analysis thus serves to generate a goal
structure that (a) represents a path through the problem space, at each
step of which a goal to apply an operator is instantiated; and (b) reflects
causal knowledge of the domain, at a level of description that relates the
individual's actions (as causes) to changes in the problem state (as effects).
The instrumental, "by-means-of" relation is thus central to the definition
of an operator.

This process of generating a goal structure involves egolocative processing, in the sense that self and object are distinguished—consider, for
example, the verbal protocol collected by Anzai and Simon (1979). In this
study, Anzai and Simon studied a single participant as she learned to solve
the Tower of Hanoi problem. The transcript of this subject is included as an
appendix to their paper, and shows that she is explicitly constructing a goal
structure, planning moves, and considering enabling conditions and problem constraints. In addition to the constraints imposed by the rules of the
problem, the problem solver is also choosing actions that satisfy constraints
on working memory. In this case, the presence of the physical Tower of
Hanoi apparatus (see chapter 9) provides substantial external support for
working memory. Nevertheless, the protocol also contains evidence of the
maintenance or recovery of goals in working memory.

In general, problem solvers simultaneously construct goal structures
and sequences for traversing those goal structures, constructing or discovering both logical relations among subgoals and orders for achieving
those subgoals. However, although a goal structure constrains the possible
sequences of action, it need not determine them completely. For example,
Carlson and Lundy (1992) demonstrated that individuals could learn
alternative sequences for traversing the same goal structure in performing
arithmetic routines.

The use of means–ends analysis by problem solvers is well documented. With only a small shift in terminology, we can also see means–

ends analysis as a strategy for diagnostic reasoning. In diagnostic reasoning, an individual begins with an effect and reasons about possible causes (e.g., Carlson & Dulany, 1988). In the case of problem solving, such reasoning serves the subgoal of finding an appropriate action that can cause a desired outcome.

Diagnostic Reasoning and Hypothesis Testing

Diagnostic reasoning and hypothesis testing are central to problem solving in this sense of discovering or generating a goal structure to accomplish a task. The desired end state may be conceived as an effect, an outcome of a causal sequence that is determined at least in part by the problem solver's actions. At each step in means–ends analysis, the problem solver might be seen as testing the hypothesis that each operator being considered will accomplish the desired effect.

The basic structure of diagnostic reasoning and causal attribution is a matter of much dispute, perhaps indicating that diagnostic reasoning can be accomplished in a variety of ways, but hypothesis testing of some sort seems central. Some authors (e.g., Kelley, 1973; Kahneman & Tversky, 1982b) have suggested that causal thinking is guided by causal schemas that facilitate thinking forward from cause to effect, rendering diagnostic reasoning more difficult than predicting an effect given its cause. Research in my laboratory (Carlson & Schneider, 1989a) suggests, however, the context in which causal knowledge is acquired is more important than any inherent directionality. In our study, participants learned causal rules governing the operation of digital logic gates. They practiced applying these rules either to make predictions of the gates' outputs given information about their inputs, or to make verification judgments given both input and output information. Consistent with research in other domains (see J. R. Anderson, 1992), we found evidence that the knowledge subjects acquired was at least partially use-specific, in that practicing prediction judgments resulted in poorer verification performance than did practicing verification.

Symbolic and Nonsymbolic Problem Solving

This use-specificity of the causal knowledge embodied in problem-solving operators is one basis for the claim that cognition must be understood as situated in real-life settings, rather than as symbolic activity that applies across domains. Cognitive psychologists have concentrated largely on understanding problem solving in symbolic domains such as geometry and arithmetic. However, some authors have argued that problem solving in these "schooled" domains is not representative of everyday problem solving (e.g., Greeno, 1989; Lave, 1988). The present analysis allows us to see similar abstract structures for problem solving in symbolic and nonsymbolic domains.

Problem solving has often been described in terms drawn from visually guided locomotion: searching, solution path, seeing a solution, and so on. Johnson (1987) argued that these and other such terms for mental activity reflect the "body in the mind," the status of mental operations as derived from bodily actions. For example, he wrote, "Metaphorically, we understand the process of reasoning as a form of motion along a path—propositions are the locations (or bounded areas) that we start out from, proceed through, and wind up at" (p. 38). I share Johnson's hypothesis that our mental activity is in fact grounded in our bodily experience, and thus shares important structural characteristics with it (chapter 1). Let us consider how this hypothesis is relevant to understanding the relation between problem solving in symbolic and nonsymbolic domains. Almost by definition, problem solving in nonsymbolic domains involves the manipulation of real objects or egomotion with respect to a real environment. In borderline cases like spatial problem solving on the basis of imagery, it is clear that the constraints on mental activity must correspond to those on perceptual-enactive performance (e.g., Shepard, 1993).

On the present analysis, similar abstract structures are observed because the organization of activity, on the basis of cospecification and egolocative processing, is the same. Problem solving in both symbolic and nonsymbolic domains is based on procedural knowledge that embodies the causal texture of the domain, organized by consequences. The problem is not so much to see how the problem-space hypothesis (and related theories of problem solving) applies to real-world problem solving in nonsymbolic domains as to see how to understand symbolic problem solving in terms of the causal texture of the medium.

In summary, novice problem solving may be seen as a case of diagnostic causal reasoning in which possible actions are chosen to accomplish goals. Because many goals cannot be achieved in a single step, problem solving results in a decomposition of the task into subgoals. These subgoals correspond to causal knowledge of the problem-solving domain. Novice problem solvers therefore simultaneously generate goal structures and acquire knowledge of problem domains. This knowledge will reflect the affordances for action of domain objects. In most domains, acquiring skill will involve generating procedural subroutines for accomplishing recurring subgoals based on these affordances. The development and tuning of these subroutines, and the acquisition of organized knowledge about the affordances of objects in a domain, mark a shift from novice to skilled problem solving.

SKILLED PROBLEM SOLVING: RESTRUCTURING
SUBROUTINES AND LEARNING AFFORDANCES

Research on practice in problem-solving situations shows that practice allows individuals to discover coordinative modes or subgoal-level routines at multiple levels of description, and to strategically restructure those routines to meet various parameters of higher-order goals (e.g., Carlson et al., 1990). Case (1985) argued for similar picture of cognitive development generally. The gist of his neo-Piagetian argument is that when cognitive routines become sufficiently skilled (thus reliable and relatively automatic), they can serve as components of higher level routines. Although some of the factors driving development (e.g., neurological maturation; Case, 1985) may differ from the factors involved in adult skill acquisition, the formal parallel likely reflects the fundamental organization of cognitive skill.

Subroutines and Affordances

For the most part, problem-solving research has concentrated on individuals' first few encounters with a task. Problem-solving skill, on the other hand, reflects the result of many problem-solving episodes in a domain. It seems reasonable to assume that domain-specific problem-solving skills (as distinct from general problem-solving skills, for which there is little evidence) consist of learned routines for achieving common goals within the domain. For example, bisecting a line segment might be viewed as a routine in the domain of geometry exercises. Because routines may be assembled into more extended problem-solving episodes, such as generating a particular geometry proof, I refer to these units of procedural skill as *subroutines*. In a study of complex problem solving, my colleagues and I (Carlson et al., 1990) argued that with practice, problem-solving skill became organized at this subroutine level, in addition to the levels of operator knowledge and search identified by Newell and Simon (1972). We identified these subroutines with repeated subgoals involved in solving many problems in the domain.

Koedinger and J. R. Anderson (1990), in a study of geometry skill, found that expert knowledge appeared to be organized around objects rather than subgoals. An example of an object in this domain is a configuration such as a line segment with a perpendicular, whereas goals are stated in terms like, "Prove that line segment *AE* bisects line segment *BD*." Because problems that require the construction of geometry proofs are typically presented and solved with the use of diagrams, Koedinger and Anderson referred to these configurations as perceptual chunks. On the basis of this and other evidence, J. R. Anderson (1993) revised the learning process in his theory to suggest that "new productions can enter only by analogy to an example" (p. 88). He wrote:

> The unit of organization in the example is the object, whereas the unit of organization in the process is the goal. This distinction can be seen in geometry, where a diagram naturally decomposes into a set of geometric objects, whereas a proof decomposes into a set of subgoals. (p. 88)

The important point here is the apparent contrast between the acquisition of subroutines on the basis of repeated subgoals, as suggested by Carlson et al. (1989b) and by earlier versions of Anderson's theory (e.g., J. R. Anderson, 1987b), and the acquisition of skills organized around objects in a domain.

We can understand this apparent contrast by considering the relation between problem solving and the causal texture of the domain. More specifically, my hypothesis is this: *The subroutines constituting skill in a domain are organized around the affordances of objects in the domain for the exercise of component skills corresponding to operators.* In a symbolic domain (e.g., geometry, arithmetic, textbook physics), these affordances support drawing inferences or generating new symbolic objects. In nonsymbolic domains, affordances support locomotion with respect to the environment (e.g., solving the problem: How do I reach location *x*?) or manipulating physical objects. In either case, the corresponding knowledge is causal, reflecting how the problem solver's actions have consequences for the objects in the domain.

In many domains, goals and objects will map to one another because the basic actions intended by instantiated subgoals are supported by the affordances of the objects. When the same object affords a number of actions, however, it will serve as an organizing element in expert knowledge. The object will thus also serve as a causal locus in "working knowledge" of the domain. This organization of knowledge around the affordance of objects in a domain supports the "working forward" characteristic of expertise in conventional symbolic domains, as well as the phenomena known as "functional fixedness" (see Seifert, Meyer, Davidson, Patalano, & Yaniv, 1995). Both phenomena seem to be cases in which component skills are performed without prior deliberation, based on affordances of the problem domain.

In the problem domain studied by Carlson et al. (1990), participants acquired subroutines for making inferences about the components in computer-simulated digital electronic circuits. The conclusions of these inferences included the appropriate outputs of correctly operating components, the status (correct or incorrect) of actual outputs, and the fault status (good or bad) of particular components. Consider a problem solver facing the situation depicted in Fig. 10.1. He or she is currently focusing on the component marked *A*, a logic gate realizing the *AND* function (i.e., its output is 1 if and only if all its inputs are 1). At this point, the goal is to determine whether or not component *A* is faulty. The routine for achieving this goal might involve determining the input and output states of the component, evaluating their relation in light of knowledge that this component (when it is working correctly) realizes the *AND* function. Performing this routine requires moving a cursor to component *A* and to the components whose outputs serve as inputs to *A*, pressing a function key to request that the output state of each component be displayed. Assuming that the nature of a fault, if one is present, is that the faulted component produces an output opposite the one specified by its function (e.g., a faulty *AND* gate produces a *0* when all of its inputs are *1*), this information together with knowledge of the rule governing the component's operation suffices to determine its status (faulted or not). In fact, the problems confronted by our subjects were more complex than this example suggests—some faults involved "locking" a component's output

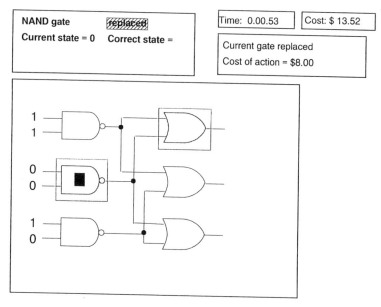

FIG. 10.1. Electronic troubleshooting screen display: This figure shows a sample screen display seen by subjects in the study by Carlson et al. (1990). The main display shows symbols for digital electronic components, linked by lines representing wires; information flows from left to right through the circuit. Subjects moved a cursor from component to component, requesting information, replacing components, or testing the status of the circuit.

in a particular state, so that not all patterns of input allowed this diagnostic inference.

This example illustrates several general points. First, individuals continued to improve in making such inferences, as shown by both analyses of problem-solving performance and by tests that abstracted particular inferences from the problem-solving context. Second, it shows that in this domain, as in many others, goals are themselves organized around objects in the domain. Third, the routine shows both decompositional and instrumental hierarchies (chapter 9); a series of actions (e.g., requesting information about particular components' output states) is accomplished by means of moving a cursor and pressing keys. The goal structure that constitutes a decomposition of the task thus also serves to organize the instrumental relations embodied in component skills, although these instrumental relations need not appear as contents of mental states.

Subroutines as Coordinative Modes

Subroutines constitute coordinative modes, mutually constraining arrangements of component skills that accomplish subgoals. We are now ready to consider this assertion in more detail. First, note that the results of individual problem-solving actions that achieve subgoals may be related in one of two ways to a higher level goal: They may constitute part of that higher level goal (e.g., cleaning the kitchen accomplishes part of the higher level goal of cleaning the house), or they may enable the performance of subsequent actions by producing conditions (including required operands) for those actions. At least in the second case, coordination is thus required because an action must precede any subsequent step for which it produces a condition. Second, note that (on any plausible theory of inference), operands must be available in close temporal contiguity to the instantiated goals that specify operations to be performed on them. In many instances of mental skills (e.g., mental arithmetic), this requirement must be met by using working memory strategies to keep operands available. Third, these working memory strategies may impose additional constraints on or provide different opportunities for coordination. For example, persisting memory activation is very short-lived, but more durable external strategies such as note-taking may require additional placekeeping effort. Alternative arrangements of component skills may satisfy these constraints in different ways—for example, individuals report using a variety of routines for calculating restaurant tips "in the head" (Wenger, 1994).

In the electronic troubleshooting task presented to our subjects, there are several possible ways to reach a conclusion about the status of a particular component. These possible routines differ in terms of their demands on working memory, their dependence on knowledge of the logic gate functions, and in their simulated costs. We arranged feedback such that simulated cost was negatively correlated with cognitive demands. For example, the simulated cost of requesting the correct output state of a component was set at six times the cost of requesting the actual current state. Redisplaying requested information (presumably to refresh working memory) also incurred a simulated cost.

One premise of the inference that a component is faulty is that its output state is incorrect. This could be established by (a) comparing requested information about actual and correct output states, or (b) using information about the component's current inputs and functions to infer the correct output state, and comparing that state to a requested actual state. Routine b could be accomplished at lower simulated cost, but has substantially greater cognitive demands. With practice, participants in our study appeared to shift from routine a to routine b. Presumably, this shift follows from increasing reliability and efficiency of procedural knowledge for collecting necessary information and applying knowledge of logic-gate functions. This knowledge is causal in two senses: knowing the causal function of logic gates, and knowing the causal relations between possible actions and their consequences. Both types of causal knowledge may, of course, be procedural rather than (or as well as) declarative; that is, possibly performed rather than consulted. Treating procedural knowledge as declarative by consulting it, as may be necessary for considering the consequences of possible actions, requires that the (possibly covert or imagined) performance itself be consulted. For example, we may "run" mental models of our own activity (Brewer, 1987) in order to solve problems. As discussed in chapter 13, skill acquisition may in some cases follow a sequence that transforms argument structures (which organize declarative knowledge of a domain) into deliberate goal structures (which organize procedural knowledge of the domain), and then into procedural routines that minimize the need for deliberate control.

The coordinative modes developed by participants in this study are similar to routines that most individuals have for mental arithmetic. Hitch (1978), for example, demonstrated that requiring participants to perform multiple-digit addition in unaccustomed sequences interfered with performance in a way that suggested loss of information from working memory. Similarly, Bruner, Goodnow, and Austin (1956) discussed ideal strategies of participants in their studies of hypothesis testing in terms of the need to coordinate information available on individual trials with information remembered from previous trials.

On this view, then, problem solving involves finding an assembly of component skills (operators) that achieves a goal (or subgoal). Not only must the resulting assembly "get you there" from starting point, it must be "doable" in terms of constraints on performance. Thus we can see the assembly of a cognitive routine as the discovery or creation of a coordinative mode. The coordinative structure in this case is not a set of mechanical components (as the muscles and joints may be viewed), but a set of processes that maintain and manipulate information. Current research suggests that we rarely create coordinative modes for cognitive tasks from scratch. Rather, we typically adapt routines from past performances, preserved in memory or in external notation based on conventional symbol systems (e.g., written equations or words). The current version of Anderson's ACT theory, ACT–R (J. R. Anderson, 1993) suggests that this process of analogical problem solving is the primary basis for acquiring new skills. In this theory, base problems are represented as declarative knowledge that is explicitly consulted in order to generate a new problem-solving performance.

Strategic Restructuring and Goal Parameters

The results presented by Carlson et al. (1990) indicate not just the discovery of coordinative modes, but restructuring that reflects a shift from one coordinative mode to another. Initially, a problem solver must find any routine that accomplishes a particular subgoal. However, alternative routines may be more effective in terms of some goal parameters. For example, an implicit goal in many situations is speed; a routine that depends on single-step retrieval will generally be faster than a routine that depends on multiple-step calculation (Logan, 1988). In the troubleshooting study, participants continued to restructure their subroutines to minimize cost after speed was essentially maximal. In the computerized problem-solving environment of this study, minimizing simulated cost conflicted with minimizing cognitive demand—the cheapest way to obtain a result involved substantially more inference than other alternatives. This result therefore suggests that restructuring was strategic rather than an automatic consequence of practice, consistent with a number of other results that suggest that restructuring is not an inevitable consequence of practice (e.g., Carlson, Sullivan, & Schneider, 1989a, 1989b; Elio, 1986; Lewis, 1981).

CAUSAL THINKING AND EXPERIENCED COGNITION

The experienced cognition framework thus suggests that our experience of ourselves as causal agents is critical in problem solving, and serves as the basis for acquiring both problem-solving skill and causal knowledge of domains. Reflecting on the cause-and-effect relations in which our mental states are embedded contributes to our intuitions about consciousness, and it is important to understand the implications of the experienced cognition analysis for interpreting those intuitions. A starting point is research concerned with causal thinking about persons.

Causal Attribution and the Experience of Agency

Social psychologists have devoted much attention to understanding how individuals make causal attributions for events socially significant to themselves and others (e.g., Kelley, 1973; Kelley & Michela, 1980). A central focus of this work has been discovering the conditions under which individuals attribute behavior to internal (person) versus external (situation) factors. Formulating the central issues for attribution theory in this way parallels the "poles of attention" to self and object found in perceptual cospecification.

Two frequently observed biases are among the central results of attribution research: The *fundamental attribution error* is the bias toward attributing the behavior of others to internal factors, and the *actor-observer bias* is the tendency to attribute one's own actions to external factors while attributing the actions of others to internal factors (Ross, 1977). These much-replicated observations about attribution may seem at odds with the experienced cognition framework, which suggests that experience of oneself as agent is the fundamental form of causal knowledge. Why are individuals not more likely to attribute their own actions to themselves as agents? Reconciling this apparent contradiction provides some insight into the links between causal thinking and problem solving.

The central consideration here is that, according to the experienced cognition framework, the self as specified in the intentional structure of mental states is not part of the content of nonreflective states. Causal self-reference, that an intention is satisfied only if the intention figures causally in the desired outcome, is a property of the state as a whole, considered from the theorist's point of view (or from the actor's reflective point of view). The action itself is generally the means or vehicle of awareness, rather than its content. In attribution studies, participants are asked to reflect on the causal precursors of events. To make attributions for their own actions, individuals presumably reflect on their prior mental states, and contents of those states are presumably more accessible than are noncontent variables or relations among states. Because the contents of nonreflective states are about objects, not about the self taken as an object of thought, participants are likely to make reports that refer to situations. Considering the information available to individuals asked to make causal attributions for their own actions is important in understanding claims about what is conscious and not in particular cognitive phenomena.

Causal Attribution as a Criterion of Consciousness?

Production of appropriate causal attributions, either spontaneously or when prompted by an experimenter, is often taken as a criterion of consciousness. Consider the much-cited instances of unconscious influence described by Nisbett and Wilson (1977). For example, they discussed a study in which participants evaluated the quality of items of clothing. Although individuals tended to choose the right-most of an identical set of items as having the highest quality, "no subject ever mentioned spontaneously the position of the article in array" (pp. 243–244) in explaining why they chose the item they did. Nisbett and Wilson also described a number of other cases in which experimental participants asked to describe the causes of their behavior mentioned plausible aspects of the available information rather than the factors identified as the true causes by experimental manipulation. That is, individuals failed to correctly identify the causes of their actions as seen by the researcher. Similarly, researchers describe instances of learning and memory as implicit or unconscious when individuals fail to attribute their answers to specific recollections or prior experiences. Subliminal (unconscious) perception is said to occur in cases in which experimental participants fail to identify displayed information shown to influence their responses. Summarizing the implications of such research, Jacoby et al. (1993) made the criterion explicit, "One of the most exciting developments in the last decade has been the discovery of effects on memory and perception that are not accompanied by *awareness of the source* of those effects" (p. 261, italics added). This relatively careful statement must be set in context of claims by Jacoby and others (see Greenwald, 1992, for a review) that such instances provide evidence for a range of powerful unconscious mental processes. Similarly, the failure to confidently identify appropriate mental processes as causes of current experience is taken as evidence of unconscious mental activity in domains such as problem solving and insight. Smith (1995) picturesquely captured the strong implication often drawn from such examples:

> The term sometimes used for the idea that insights are created unconsciously while the conscious mind is otherwise occupied is the *unconscious work hypothesis*. Like the little elves that would cobble beautiful shoes only while the cobbler was sleeping, unconscious mental forces are imagined to work away at insights only when the conscious mind temporarily retreats. (p. 242)

The analysis offered here helps us to understand why causal attribution might be considered as a criterion of consciousness: The experience of causality as agency, or in perception, is central to the intentional structure of mental states involved in goal-directed activity. However, a careful consideration of the contents of mental states suggests an alternative view of apparent failures of causal attribution—they are informational consequences of the structure of experienced cognition. One might point to those aspects of mental states that do not appear as contents, or appear as contents only in metacognitive states that need not accompany conscious experience of our goal-directed activity, and label them *unconscious*. However, this does not imply the existence of unconscious mental processes in any interesting sense (chapter 14).

PROBLEM SOLVING AND THE EXPERIENCE OF SKILLED ACTIVITY

I argued that problem solving can best be described as the generation or discovery of routines for skilled activity, based on the affordances and continuing informational support provided by domain-specific mediums. As we solve problems, we act to cause changes in a medium, experiencing the causal texture of the environment by intervening as causal agents. The informational support for problem solving is distributed between cognitive performance (including memory retrieval) and the problem-solving environment. Knowledge-rich problem solving is based on understanding a domain in terms of the affordances of its objects for skilled cognitive activity.

With increasing skill, the affordances of objects in a problem-solving medium change. In one sense, this is an obvious observation: Printed numerals afford addition for older children and adults, but not for very young infants, and words afford reading only for the literate. However, research on both problem solving and causal thinking often treats both the environment and the individual's capacities for action as fixed. Understanding problem solving and causal thinking as suggested in this chapter lets us see how we experience ourselves as causal agents and the environment as having causal texture. With increasing skill, the opportunities for experience change as our activity changes the ways in which self and object can be cospecified.

Levels of Awareness in Problem Solving

This discussion of problem solving also provides an opportunity to consider how we should think about metacognition in the experienced cognition framework. At several points, I have suggested that a metacognitive state is one whose content explicitly refers to the self. In the case of problem solving, we can identify three levels or degrees of metacognitive awareness. In highly skilled problem solving (such as simple mental calculation for most educated adults), much of experienced cognition is *routine*: Although goals are instantiated as intentions whose contents refer to both self and object (chapter 9), no further process makes use of the self–object distinction. We know what to do, and we just do it. The somewhat more novel cases in which we must decide what to do might be called *deliberate*: Possible intentions are objects of thought as we consider the likely consequences of various courses of action. Our experience in these cases involves more elaborate egolocative processing, because the currently problem-solving self must be distinguished from the potentially acting self. This definition of deliberate differs from that suggested by Newell (1990), in requiring that the selection of possible actions follow from actually considering alternatives (i.e., representing them as contents of mental states). Deliberate problem solving in this sense probably corresponds most closely to our everyday, intuitive definition. Finally, in the most difficult cases of problem solving, our experienced cognition may be *reflective*: Some of our mental states have contents whose objects include our own problem-solving activity. For example, while learning new computer software, I often have mental states whose contents could be paraphrased as, "I'm really stuck." Here, the reflecting self must be distinguished from the (in my example, unsuccessfully) problem-solving self.

Maintaining these distinctions is important for understanding experienced cognition, and the framework developed in Part 1 provides the theoretical resources for doing so. In practice, however, it is very difficult to establish these distinctions empirically. There are two reasons for this: First, different portions of even a single problem-solving episode will likely be experienced at different levels. For example, even in hard problems, some component skills will be performed at the routine level. Second, the acquisition of skill in problem solving situations is very rapid. J. R. Anderson (1987b), for example, discussed cases in which solution time for the second problem in a domain is less than half that for the first problem. The repeated observations needed for many of our empirical methods are simply not available in such cases.

Despite the practical difficulties, this analysis illustrates the value of the analysis of intentional structure presented in chapters 4 through 6. By systematically distinguishing content and mode (here, usually *intend*), we can understand how problem-solving activity produces experience of the self as causal agent and of the causal texture of the environment. In the next two chapters, we consider two ends of the continuum of metacognitive awareness: First, in chapter 11, experienced cognition in reasoning tasks that are prototypes of deliberate (and sometimes reflective) mental activity, and second, in chapter 12, experienced cognition in expert and everyday routine activity. This will lay the foundation for chapter 13, a theoretical sketch of conscious control and how it changes with increasing skill.

11

Belief and Reasoning

*It is, of course, no more possible to define inferential thinking than to define
life. Such matters can be elucidated only by a theory. It is useful, however,
to give a working definition that delimits the domain of study. An inference
is a process of thought that leads from one set of propositions to another.*
—Johnson-Laird, 1983, pp. 23–24

*Premises do not lead to conclusions in themselves, independent of reason-
ers—they lead to conclusions only insofar as their meaning is grasped, and
their implications are seen, by a human being situated in the world.*
—Johnson, 1987, p. 57

THINKING TASKS IN COGNITIVE RESEARCH

A variety of thinking tasks studied by cognitive scientists are of special
interest because they represent the direct translation of relatively straightforward normative models into laboratory paradigms. These tasks include
reasoning with propositional arguments or quantified syllogisms, simple
probability judgments, revision of beliefs construed as subjective probabilities, and decision making with clear alternatives. Perhaps because
the normative status of logic, probability theory, and utility theory has
seemed clear, these tasks have often been taken as prototypes of rational
thinking, presumably the highest of the higher mental processes.

Despite (or perhaps because of) this special status, research on these
thinking tasks occupies a peculiar position in cognitive psychology. The
literatures on these tasks are relatively insular, and they seem to have

217

had a disproportionately minor impact on general cognitive theory. For example, most textbooks in cognitive psychology devote only one or two chapters to these literatures, and it is not uncommon to find one or more of these topics missing altogether. Consider the status of research on deductive reasoning. A number of authors (e.g., Baron, 1994; Harman, 1989; Minsky, 1986) expressed doubt that deductive thinking even exists as such. Yet Johnson-Laird (1983) described syllogistic reasoning as a test case for cognitive science, pursuing a course of research that attempts to provide a computational account of both deductive competence (the possibility of thinking rationally) and empirical deviations from that competence. And Rips (1984) argued that deduction is a central intellective ability involved in many cognitive processes. Furthermore, research and discussion have very often focused on phenomena that are taken to represent systematic biases or departures from rationality (e.g., Kahneman, Slovic, & Tversky, 1982).

In contrast to the view that problem solving is the basic form of cognition, Rips (1994) argued that deduction underlies problem solving:

> What causes trouble for the idea of deduction as problem solving is the asymmetry of cognitive explanations: Although deduction may be helpful in accounting for how one solves such chess puzzles, no one would appeal to solving chess puzzles in accounting for deduction. (p. 28)

That is, we can see many of the individual steps or component skills for complex tasks as realizing deductive inference. Rips thus viewed deduction as a foundation for, rather than an instance of, problem solving conceived as search in a problem space. Similarly, the experienced cognition framework suggests that deductive inferences, described as relations among mental states, serve as components of a variety of more complex mental activities such as problem solving.

In this chapter, I discuss thinking tasks from the point of view of the experienced cognition framework. My major thesis is that these tasks can be analyzed in terms of relations among mental states, as described in Part II. I focus on tasks typically described as deductive reasoning, then generalize the analysis to other thinking tasks. Finally, I describe research on Dulany's (Carlson & Dulany, 1988; Dulany, 1979; Dulany & Carlson, 1983) Theory of Propositional Learning, the most fully developed example of an analysis of thinking compatible with the experienced cognition framework.

Thinking Research and Rationality

Tasks used in research on thinking represent a refinement of folk psychology views of thinking and rationality (Rips & Conrad, 1989). On standard analyses, these tasks require the construction of new mental representations from previously existing ones, or assume relations among contents, on the basis of a normative model such as logic or probability theory. Common examples of the relations among contents assumed in the domain of reasoning include *modus ponens* and the universally quantified categorical syllogism (Fig. 11.1). In psychological theory, these arguments may be conceived as reasoning schemas that generate conclusions on the basis of the syntactic form of premises. The mental processes associated with these logical relations are thus supposed to be concerned with the generation or evaluation of contents.

Judgment under uncertainty and revision of belief are usually conceived in terms of probability theory. These models differ from those invoked in accounting for reasoning in that they focus on degree of belief or commitment (as expressed by subjective probabilities) rather than on the relations among contents per se. In the domain of multiattribute decision making, researchers have generally focused on how individuals choose among well-defined alternatives, modeling rationality with some variety of utility theory (which describes how values or utilities of possible outcomes resulting from a choice should be weighted by the probabilities of those outcomes; see Baron, 1994, for an introduction to utility theory).

Modus ponens

If A is true, then B is true
A is true
Therefore, B is true

Modus tollens

If A is true, then B is true
B is false
Therefore, A is false

Universally quantified categorical syllogism

All A's are B's
All B's are C's
Therefore, All A's are C's

FIG. 11.1. Argument structures: The figure depicts three argument structures commonly used in research on reasoning. *A* and *B* stand for propositions in modus ponens and modus tollens arguments, and for categories in the categorical syllogism.

Especially in the domain of deductive reasoning, researchers have generally considered it desirable that cognitive theories of thinking allow for a competence that corresponds to some normative model (e.g., Johnson-Laird, 1983). Cognitive theorists seldom discuss the reasons for this desirability, although some philosophers concerned with cognitive science have done so (e.g., Cherniak, 1986; Fodor & Pylyshyn, 1988; Haugeland, 1985). I believe that the primary reason that many cognitive scientists assume that normative models are important for understanding cognition is that some degree of competence in thinking appears to be necessary if the information-processing or computational view of the mind is correct (Cherniak, 1986). That is because an important assumption of this framework is that mental representations can serve as surrogates for objects and relations in the represented domain, for example, the physical environment (Palmer & Kimchi, 1986; chapter 2, this volume). The symbol system in which mental representations are constructed therefore must be truth preserving in the sense that the result of manipulating mental representations must correspond to states of the represented domain. For example, integer addition is truth preserving in this sense because the sum of several separately enumerated sets (e.g., the students seated in several rows in a classroom) corresponds to the number in the superset (the students in the classroom as a whole). Adding can therefore be used to derive a true conclusion about a state of affairs in the world. Insofar as normative models typically prescribe operations and relations in symbolic domains, it is important to understand how symbolic thinking is grounded so that thinking can have this truth-preserving character, at least under ideal circumstances. I consider the possibility of a psychological approach to this issue later in this chapter.

This sometimes implicit focus on rationality may be one reason why research in the domains of deductive reasoning, judgment under uncertainty (including belief revision), and multiattribute choice has been somewhat self-contained. The normative models that provide the basis for experimental tasks in these research domains are difficult to apply to either realistic situations or more complex laboratory tasks, and their application is sometimes controversial even for simple laboratory tasks. For example, one unproductive debate in the reasoning literature concerns the possibility that experimental subjects add premises from their general knowledge to those provided by the experimenter (Henle, 1962; see Evans, 1982, for a review). Furthermore, there has been relatively little explicit cross-reference among the literatures on these topics. For example, with rare exceptions (e.g., Wyer, 1975) there has been little consideration of how deduction and judgment under uncertainty might be related. In my view, considering the mental processes involved in these tasks as sequences of mental states, described as outlined earlier in this book (chapter 5), has the potential of bringing some theoretical unity to research in these domains.

Reasoning as a Relation Among Mental States

The experienced cognition framework suggests that reasoning processes may be described as relations among mental states, each of which may be analyzed in terms of its intentional structure (i.e., mode and content). For most reasoning tasks studied by cognitive scientists, the most relevant cognitive mode is *belief*, and the contents of the relevant states are *propositional* (i.e., sentence-like). The process of reasoning could thus be described as the generation or derivation of new belief states based on prior belief states. This description contrasts with typical cognitive science accounts of reasoning framed only in terms of the generation of new mental representations, which correspond to only the contents of mental states.

Most laboratory research on reasoning involves "as-if" tasks, requiring subjects to generate conclusions (e.g., Johnson-Laird, 1983) or evaluate arguments (e.g., Rips, 1983) on the basis of sentences that the subjects cannot be expected to literally believe and that usually refer to imagined situations. At least one cognitive text (Reed, 1992) discusses research on deductive reasoning in a chapter on language, under the heading "relations among sentences." The focus is therefore almost entirely on relations among contents (whether or not these contents are taken literally to be sentences). In contrast, in the experienced cognition framework, reasoning, judgment, and decision are conceived as relations among mental states with intentional structure as described in chapters 4 through 6, requiring consideration of both content and mode. The analysis of thinking tasks should therefore address both relations among contents, traditionally the domain of research on reasoning, and relations among degrees of belief (more generally, degrees of commitment if we consider psychological modes other than belief), traditionally the domain of research on judgment or Bayesian inference. In addition, because cognition is generally goal-directed, the role of goals in reasoning should also be considered (Carlson et al., 1992; Cheng & Holyoak, 1985; Rips, 1984).

Experienced Cognition and Thinking

The experienced cognition framework thus emphasizes two neglected aspects of thinking: the role of goals in thinking, and the distinction between content and mode in the structure of mental states. Consider the case of deductive reasoning: In the laboratory, individuals performing deductive reasoning tasks are generally asked to do one of two things: (a) given a verbally expressed (usually written) argument consisting of premises and conclusions, judge whether the argument is valid; or (b) given premises (again, usually written), generate a valid conclusion. Johnson-Laird (1983) argued that the second type of task is more useful for studying reasoning because (he argued) it corresponds to a default goal for reasoning: Find an informative conclusion. However, others have argued that this is a poor model of the role of deduction in everyday life (Baron, 1994; Harman, 1989; Rips, 1994).

As a working hypothesis, I assume that the goal of reasoning is typically to answer a question or test a hypothesis on the basis of other available information (Carlson et al., 1992). Thus the content corresponding to a conclusion is considered at the beginning, not just as the final outcome, of a reasoning episode. This view of the phenomenon to be explained by reasoning theories corresponds more closely to that in Rips's (1983, 1994) mental logic approach than to Johnson-Laird's (1983) view that his mental models approach should explain how individuals answer the question "What follows?" from premises they are given. In Rips' theory, reasoning is modeled as a process of constructing proofs in working memory, taking conclusions as hypotheses to be tested. Some rules postulated in Rips' theory are thus characterized as backward, operating on the basis of goals to prove particular proposition. For example, Rips (1983) proposed that deduction involves a backward version of *modus ponens*: Given that a current subgoal is to establish the truth of q, and that the assertion *if p, then q* is in working memory, the rule establishes a subgoal to deduce p. Although it makes extensive use of goals in this sense, like Johnson-Laird's mental models theory, Rips' theory is primarily concerned with the construction of representations—that is, the contents of reasoning processes. Neither theory directly addresses transfer of belief.

In my view, the analysis of reasoning processes should instead begin with describing a mental state in which an individual holds some propositional content in the mode of belief, and has the goal of evaluating that belief state. Consideration of premises may or may not precede construction of the conclusion. Premises are then considered as evidence, with possible variations in relevance and degree of strength (Harman, 1989). In terms familiar from earlier chapters, we might describe reasoning as a performance in a (symbolic) medium. The series of mental state contents constitute a path through that medium to the goal of evaluating a proposition considered as a conclusion. The series of mental state modes reflect the egolocative processing involved in the performance. In order to develop this view, we must begin by considering the variety of concepts indicated by the term *inference*.

TYPES OF INFERENCE

The experienced cognition framework suggests a classification of inferential processes that differs in some respects from standard classifications. This classification is based on considering the distinction between the contents and modes of mental states.

Inductive Inferences

A wide variety of cognitive phenomena, ranging from very rapid perceptual processes (see chapter 2) to the development and testing of science-like theories (e.g., Klahr & Dunbar, 1988), have received accounts in terms of inference. Most of these phenomena are inductive in the sense that (a) no normative account guarantees certainty, and (b) the conclusions may be said to add to the information provided by the premises (unlike deductive inferences, which add no new information; Johnson-Laird, 1983). As Garnham and Oakhill (1994) noted, a wide variety of definitions of induction have been offered, including some that are essentially coextensive with cognition generally (Holland, Holyoak, Nisbett, & Thagard, 1986). Inductive or generalizing inferences may range from single-step processes that do not involve separate conscious representation of premises and conclusions (e.g., pattern recognition in which a new pattern is assimilated to previously observed patterns) to very complex processes that involve many component skills (e.g., scientific inference). It is therefore not at all clear that induction as such constitutes a fundamental category for cognitive theory.

Connectionist and related associative network models show us how some pattern recognition, classification, and generalizing inductions may be made without symbolic computation. For example, Gluck and Bower (1988) described a connectionist model of category learning. On the other hand, scientific inference (and its common-sense counterparts) is very complex, incorporating a great deal of declarative knowledge and procedural skill. Indeed, it is hard to see how science could be done at all without the use of symbol systems. Some instances of induction may therefore not require cognitive explanation at all, in the sense of stories about sequences of mental states with intentional structure. Other instances may require explanations in terms of problem solving, symbolic knowledge, and acquired skills.

Each of the kinds of inductive inference discussed here also lacks two criterial features of deductive reasoning: (a) separate representation of premises, and (b) combination of premises based on their formal (compositional) structure. As with induction, researchers concerned with deduction have sometimes included a variety of mental processes that differ in terms of the kinds of theoretical explanation required. The next sections address how these processes might be analyzed in the experienced cognition framework.

Deductive Construction

Inference processes that involve generating new mental representations from currently entertained contents on the basis of syntactic relations among those contents might be called *deductive constructions*. For example, deductive construction would be drawing the conclusion or generating the statement, "All the artists are chemists," on the basis of the syntactic form of the statements, "All the artists are beekeepers," and, "All the beekeepers are chemists" (example from Johnson-Laird, 1983, pp. 94–95). It seems unlikely, however, that deductive construction is part of our unschooled repertoire of mental processes. Instead, the generation of new contents seems to involve a variety of nonformal processes such as associative reminding and acquired problem-solving strategies. At most, it seems that deductive construction is one of many acquired skills for recruiting appropriate knowledge for particular purposes.

In attempting to study deductive construction, researchers have focused on simple conditional arguments and simple categorical syllogisms. The contents suggested by laboratory tasks based on these arguments include simple causal and set relations. One reason for interest in conditional arguments is their suitability for reasoning about causal relations, although conditional statements may of course represent other kinds of relations. A variety of research (reviewed by Evans, 1982, 1993) has established several general conclusions about performance with these tasks. First, typical college-student research participants perform quite poorly except with the simplest arguments (e.g., modus ponens or universally quantified categorical syllogisms). Second, a great deal of evidence points to *content effects* with these tasks; the conclusions that subjects draw or affirm depend on the meaning (content) of the premises and conclusions. These lines of evidence support the hypothesis that deduction in typical laboratory tasks is based on a variety of knowledge-recruiting processes and simplifying strategies in addition to mental processes that correspond to deduction as such.

Perhaps the most discussed laboratory task thought to involve deductive reasoning is the *selection task* introduced by Wason (1968). In the original version of this task, individuals are shown four cards, and told that each has a letter on one side and a number on the other. The exposed sides of the cards contain an even number, an odd number, a consonant, and a vowel; for example, { 4 7 R E }. Participants are asked which cards should be turned over (revealing the other side) in order to test a conditional rule like, "If a card has a vowel on one side, then it has an even number on the other side." For this example, the correct answer is that the cards showing E and 7 should be turned over, corresponding to the minor premises in *modus ponens* and *modus tollens* (Fig. 11.1). The other cards do not allow valid deductions given a conditional (rather than biconditional) interpretation of the rule. Individuals performing this task, at least in an abstract presentation similar to this example, rarely make both and only the correct choices. Data demonstrating this difficulty have sometimes been taken, along with results concerning biases in judgment under uncertainty, as evidence that human thinking is inherently irrational. The debate over this conclusion sometimes has been quite heated (e.g., Cohen, 1981, and commentaries).

It is important to note that correct performance in the selection task involves not just deduction, but *metadeduction* (Evans, 1982; Johnson-Laird & Byrne, 1991). That is, correctly performing the task requires that the valid reasoning schemes (*modus ponens* and *modus tollens*) themselves serve as objects of cognition and premises in a reasoning process. The argument structure of the reasoning process for modus tollens (apparently the most difficult portion of the selection task) must go something like this:

If I believe that *If A then B*, then *not B* implies *not A*;
Not B is present on one of the cards;
Therefore, the other side of that card should display *not A*;
If I turn over the card displaying *not B*, I might find that *A* is displayed;
A is not (*not A*);
Therefore, the card contradicts the rule *If A, then B*.
If I want to test the rule, I should look for cards that contradict it;
Therefore, I should turn over the card containing *not B*.

This roughly phrased argument is not meant as a process model, and there are of course other ways to present equivalent argument structures. My point is simply that the reasoning needed to successfully complete the selection task is much more elaborate than simply applying a reasoning schema corresponding to modus tollens. Deducing which premises are needed is a significantly more complex task than performing deduction given the premises.

Although it may not provide direct evidence concerning deductive thinking, the selection task does seem to capture one assumption involved in my hypothesis about the role of deductive reasoning in cognition. That is, the reasoning in which individuals engage is directed toward the goal of testing a hypothesis—at a global level, the hypothesis that the conditional premise correctly describes the set of cards as a whole. At a somewhat lower level, the reasoning could be described as testing hypotheses that the exposed side of each card is consistent with the conditional rule.

Thus the selection task is very likely approached with a hierarchical goal structure, at least by those participants who succeed in the task.

A striking finding, many times replicated, is that performance in the selection task depends on the content of the conditional rules. For example, Wason and Johnson-Laird (1972) demonstrated that presenting the selection task with a meaningful rule familiar to their subjects resulted in dramatically improved performance. On the basis of a number of similar results, Cheng and Holyoak (1985) argued that concrete versions of the selection task evoke pragmatic reasoning schemas that specify the selection of minor premises to test a rule. For example, one such schema is the permission schema, reflecting abstract knowledge of permission situations in which some condition must be met in order that an action be allowed. A case familiar to American college students is the requirement that an individual be 21 years old (or older) in order to legally consume alcohol: In conditional form, "If someone is drinking alcohol, then they must be 21." Pragmatic reasoning schemas may be identified for a variety of situations, at several levels of abstraction (Nisbett, 1993). In all cases, however, these reasoning schemas are relatively abstract; for example, the permission schema applies to a wide variety of specific situations. This degree of abstraction is such that it may support normatively appropriate reasoning in many cases.

This brief discussion of research in the selection task suggests two conclusions. First, it seems clear that individuals do have acquired skills that support at least some of their reasoning in at least some of the situations used to study the selection task. Therefore a discussion of reasoning should not be detached from a consideration of skill and knowledge acquisition (Nisbett, 1993). Second, note that the evidence from experiments with concrete versions of the selection task is directly relevant only to understanding how individuals generate or select premises, not to how they combine or integrate those premises to generate conclusions. Research on reasoning about spatial relations (e.g., Byrne & Johnson-Laird, 1989) also emphasizes the selection or construction of premises. In experiments on spatial reasoning, participants are typically asked questions that require them to construct an imagined point of view that serves as a premise for reasoning. As Rips (1984, 1986) pointed out, cognitive scientists have often just assumed that experimental participants have some basic deductive abilities that are reflected in their performance, thus focusing on the larger tasks in which deductions are embedded.

Together with evidence from research on problem solving (e.g., B. H. Ross, 1987) and judgment (Kahneman et al., 1982), the results of reasoning studies suggest that the generation of new mental representations rarely depends only on processes corresponding to deductive construction. Instead, individuals rely on memory (as in B. H. Ross' 1987 studies of reminding in problem solving), acquired problem-solving skills (as in Cheng & Holyoak's 1985 work on pragmatic reasoning schemas), and perhaps other knowledge-recruiting strategies to generate mental contents that may function as conclusions in deductive arguments. Although it is likely that each of these types of process is sometimes involved in laboratory tasks based on deductive arguments, another possible role for models of deduction is in describing the transfer of belief from premises to conclusions.

Deductive Transfer of Commitment

A relatively neglected aspect of reasoning (at least in research paradigms based on normative models drawn from logic) is what we might call *deductive transfer of commitment*. Certainly an important consequence of reasoning in real life is that we come to believe something that we formerly did not. However, it is not always—or even typically—the case that this event corresponds to the first time we have ever considered the content of the new belief. Very often, it seems that the conclusion or proposition we come to believe is first considered hypothetically, without firm commitment. In coming to believe a conclusion, we somehow move from propositions we already believe to a proposition we come to believe. This *transfer of belief* is an aspect of reasoning central to the experienced cognition framework.

My hypothesis concerning deductive transfer of commitment is straightforward: At least for the case of belief, deductive transfer occurs when premises we already believe support—in the sense of fitting a deductive argument structure—a conclusion entertained hypothetically. Deductive reasoning schemas or rules describe the structures—the relations among contents of conscious mental states—that allow for transfer of belief. Why should this be so? One answer would be that at least some deductive rules are innate (Rips, 1994). That answer of course calls for a deeper answer in evolutionary terms, and Cosmides (1989) suggested that something like the pragmatic reasoning schemas suggested by Cheng and Holyoak (1985) evolved under selection pressure from social situations.

An alternative that suggests a more abstract view of the mental counterparts of deductive rules is this: Deductive transfer of commitment (e.g., belief) follows formal rules because those rules capture the abstract constraints on action in a physical environment and thus describe the truth-preserving character of symbolic mediums. This view is similar to that developed by Piaget (Chapman, 1988), and the possibility that these rules are constructed in the course of development is considered in more detail next. Regardless of whether the constraints of action in a physical environment shape the mind in the course of development or have done so over the course of evolution (Shepard, 1984), the principle governing transfer of belief is the same: Deductive transfer of belief occurs when the knowledge structures representing an argument allows repeatable, reversible performance. That is, we can "follow" the argument without "losing our place," and can "return to" the premises. This corresponds to egomotion with respect to the spatial layout of an environment, or to manipulation of a physical object. This account captures M. K. Johnson's (1987) view of reasoning as (metaphorically) following a path. It is also compatible with the implicitly spatial description of mental models in Johnson-Laird's (1983) theory of deductive reasoning, although he is concerned with the generation of conclusion contents rather than with degrees of belief associated with those contents.

Some deductive inferences, notably *modus ponens* and the universally quantified categorical syllogism (All A are B, All B are C, Therefore all A are C), are phenomenally very immediate and compelling (Adams, 1984; Nickerson, 1986). At least in the case of modus ponens, the reason for this may be that (a) all of the objects referred to are mentioned in the major (conditional) premise, and (b) the form of the conditional can be construed as capturing the abstract structure of basic actions (i.e., if action, then consequence). In fact, when conditional arguments are presented to experimental subjects in a way that suggests they describe causal relations, reasoning performance may be substantially facilitated (e.g., Staudenmeyer, 1975), although that facilitation may depend on the context of the causal statement (Cummins, 1995). And as Rips (1994) noted, *modus ponens* also is embodied in the basic idea of a production, as in production system models like those proposed by J. R. Anderson (1983, 1993) and Newell (1990). The parallel to nested affordances in visually guided egomotion (E. J. Gibson, 1993) is that when individuals follow these intuitively compelling arguments, information specifying the next step is readily available. So, for example, when a categorical syllogism is presented in the figure { A-B, B-C }, the inference to A-C is much easier than it is for syllogisms presented in other figures such as { B-A, C-B } (Johnson-Laird, 1983). We might say that the adjacent occurrences of the middle term B provide a path for the transfer of belief.

The parallel between egomotion and reasoning may be extended to more complex cases. For example, researchers have asked participants in some mental imagery tasks to traverse mental images, generally finding that the time required to do so is proportional to the distance traveled (see Finke & Shepard, 1986, for a review), just as the time required for multiple-step reasoning depends on the number of steps required (e.g., Carlson et al., 1992). Furthermore, there is evidence that individuals pass through intermediate parts of mental images under some circumstances (Finke & Shepard, 1986). Similarly, *referential continuity*—analogous to the adjacent appearances of the middle term in a syllogism—facilitates understanding both of spatial descriptions and of event sequences in discourse (Garnham, Oakhill, & Johnson-Laird, 1982; Mani & Johnson-Laird, 1982; Oakhill & Johnson-Laird, 1984; Tversky, 1991). The movement along these symbolic paths is a form of transfer of commitment as viewed in the experienced cognition framework. The parallels between spatial and verbal tasks point out the egolocative nature of belief, considered in more detail here.

THE PSYCHOLOGICAL GROUNDING OF NORMATIVE THEORY

Normative theories such as a particular logic are hardly the established, unquestioned models of rationality one might infer from reading the psychological literature on reasoning. In fact, there is a long and active literature concerning how normative theories are to be grounded, and their ontological status (see Baron, 1994, for an introduction accessible to psychologists). The preceding discussion of structural parallels in visually guided locomotion, scanning or traversing mental images, and following arguments suggest an approach to understanding the cognitive basis of normative theories of thinking: From the perspective of cognitive science, normative theories should be conceived primarily as theoretical accounts of the formal structures of symbolic mediums in which skills may be exercised. Although philosophers and mathematicians generally reject psychologism in foundational discussions of logic or mathematics, the grounding problem is an issue for cognitive theory. The hypothesis considered here is that normative constraints on thinking are developmentally or evolutionarily grounded in the formal structure of ecological constraints on action.

Piaget and the Grounding of Logic

Piaget (e.g., 1972) was much concerned with the development of logical thinking, suggesting that mental or operatory logic is constructed through a series of stages in the course of development.[1] The basic idea is that

---

[1]Many researchers (e.g., Gelman & Baillargeon, 1983) have criticized Piaget's account of cognitive development, on a variety of empirical and theoretical grounds. My use of some of Piaget's ideas here is not meant as a defense of any particular aspect of his theory, although my reading of some of his work is apparently quite different from that of his critics. In thinking about and discussing Piaget's theory, I have relied very heavily on Chapman's (1988) excellent book. However, I have interpreted both Piaget and Chapman very freely in some cases to make my points.

activity is organized on the basis of physical constraints and that the formal structure of these constraints corresponds to the formal structure of logical thinking. For example, as discussed in chapter 4, the set of possible displacements of objects in space has constraints corresponding to *group structure*, which also characterizes the domain of integer arithmetic. Action involving displacement of objects (including the body) is thus organized according to this structure. In the course of development, action is interiorized, becoming truly mental as it operates on symbolic rather than physical objects. At the stage of formal operations, symbolic thought may proceed independently of concrete objects. Arithmetic is thus a truth-preserving symbol system because its mental realization is as a set of operations preserving the structure of action on concrete objects.

Piaget (e.g., 1972) offered much the same account of logic, at several points proposing his own systems of logic in terms corresponding with his psychological theorizing. He described the relation between logic and thought in this way, "Logic is the axiomatics of operatory structures, the real functioning of which is studied by the psychology and sociology of thought" (Piaget, 1972, quoted in translation by Chapman, 1988, p. 235). *Structures* here are sets of related operations that together make up systems in which thinking can occur.

Chapman (1988) argued convincingly that we should not identify Piaget's (e.g., 1972) genetic epistemology with psychological theory as it is usually understood. One of Piaget's major goals was to provide a psychological basis for normative theory, and thus for the possibility of knowledge. The principle of noncontradiction appears to be the basis of all efforts at normative theories of thinking, and much research on normative models per se consists of finding ways to demonstrate noncontradiction in the context of specific arguments or means for constructing arguments. Piaget (1954) derived this principle from the observation that it held in the world of physics, and that action in physical space was thus constrained to obey the principle. Because an object cannot occupy two locations at once, and two objects cannot occupy the same location at the same time (at least for objects identified at a constant, ecological grain size), the set of possible spatial displacements is constrained to avoid contradiction. Similarly, systems of mental operations must be constrained to avoid contradiction and allow rational thought.

Reversibility and Noncontradiction

An important aspect of operational thought, according to Piaget (e.g., 1972), is that mental operations are reversible. In the case of sensorimotor activity, this may be simple physical doing and undoing—an object moved from one location to another can be moved back to the starting location.

The actions for doing so are constrained, and related to one another, by the group structure of spatial displacements (see chapter 4). Although of course not all actions are empirically reversible (consider dropping an egg!), it is hypothetical reversibility—knowing what would restore the original situation—that is important. Beginning at the stage of concrete operations, reversibility is said to be simultaneous in the sense that performing a mental action includes understanding that the action implies its inverse. For example, gathering objects into a set implies the possibility of separately identifying them as individual members of the set. Such reversibility guarantees noncontradiction, allowing systems of symbolic action to be truth preserving. Operations on symbols can then serve as surrogates for manipulating environmental objects—for example, if we reason correctly about an imagined series of spatial transformations as we listen to directions for a series of left and right turns, we can infer the resulting point of view in the environment.

The possibility of truth-preserving symbol systems is a prerequisite for the symbol-processing approach to cognitive theory. The formula "take care of the syntax, and the semantics will take care of itself" (Haugeland, 1985, p. 106) reflects this assumption. Although many cognitive scientists have recently criticized the symbol-processing approach, the central issues are important for any version of the information-processing approach. Any theoretical framework (including the experienced cognition approach described in this book) that makes use of mental representations must consider how those representations are grounded (Harnad, 1982) so that operations on them (such as reasoning) can yield results that can be mapped back to the represented domain. The current trend toward solving problems in artificial intelligence by understanding cognition as embodied (e.g., Ballard et al., in press; Dennett, 1996; Kirsh & Maglio, 1994) reflects a recognition of this issue.

As previously noted, researchers studying thinking have relied on normative models such as logic as a basis for developing experimental tasks and as a standard of comparison for the performance of their experimental participants. The normative status of theories such as logic or probability theory is often (although not always; Baron, 1994) implicit or assumed in cognitive research. What is seldom noticed is that normative models of cognitive performance are ubiquitous in cognitive science, assumed in essentially all empirical research. For example, studies of memory generally adopt a simple normative model that prescribes accurate verbatim memory as a criterion of performance. Only rarely do memory researchers explicitly consider the question of what memory should accomplish (but see J. R. Anderson, 1990). And generally, researchers set themselves as judges of normatively appropriate performance. This approach leads to some limitations in cognitive theory. For example, Schank et al. (1986) noted that most theories of category learning presuppose an authoritative source of information concerning category membership. Often, the implicit assumption is that a language of thought embodies the constraints of physical activity (see also Shepard, 1984, 1993).

Belief and Egolocative Processing

What does all this have to do with reasoning and belief? The hypothesis derived from the experienced cognition approach is this: Degree of belief is based on the degree to which a knowledge structure affords resampling and exploration. This hypothesis is compatible with Johnson-Laird's (1983; Johnson-Laird & Byrne, 1991) mental models theory of reasoning, although it goes beyond the scope of that theory. He argued that individuals perform reasoning by constructing models that represent relations among objects specified by premises, and that the ability to construct and hold such models in working memory is the major determinant of success in reasoning. If an individual cannot construct an appropriate model because of contradictions among premises, or cannot hold the model in working memory due to its complexity, he or she will fail to draw an appropriate conclusion. Although not a part of Johnson-Laird's theory, it seems a reasonable extrapolation to predict that degree of belief in a conclusion will be in part a function of the stability of the model (which will be greater when premises are related in deductively simple ways).

This account is parallel to the stability of perceptual objects in the environment. Visual resampling and exploration of stable features of the environment allows for egolocation and thus for the control of egomotion. Similarly, resampling and exploration of a stable symbolic object of cognition allows repeatable egolocation. Object-specific invariants are informational descriptions that hold regardless of perspective; this is analogous to searching for counterexamples in verbal reasoning. If there is a contradiction among the contents involved in reasoning, this repeatability will be compromised; for example, if additional knowledge is brought to mind, the path back to the goal (conclusion) may not be reversible. This account can be generalized to degrees of commitment in other modes; for example, hope or desire.

What counts as rationality, given this analysis of reasoning? According to Baron (1994) and others (e.g., Harman, 1989), rationality in thinking cannot be identified simply with reasoning in accord with the rules of deductive logic. Instead, rationality must be defined more broadly in terms of the degree to which our thinking succeeds in meeting our goals. Baron summarized his view of rationality with the phrase "active open-mindedness" (p. 31), emphasizing that to be rational is to generate hypotheses and seek evidence broadly so as to increase the chances of meeting goals. J. R. Anderson (1990) argued for a rational approach to cognition, demonstrating that many features of laboratory cognitive phenomena can be predicted by assuming that cognition is optimal (in a specific probabilistic sense developed by Anderson). Either of these approaches can also be described in ecological terms: Rational activity is activity guided by the broadest possible set of affordances. However, my purpose is not to discuss the concept of rationality, but to point out that the present view, like other recent discussions in cognitive science, suggests that rationality be considered with respect to action in an environment rather than with respect to normative models of symbolic thinking.

MODE AND CONTENT IN THINKING TASKS

Perhaps the most important implications of the experienced cognition framework for the study of thinking follow from the distinction between mode and content. If we pursue the hypothesis that thinking should be described in terms of mental states with intentional structure, we can see that most researchers have investigated only limited aspects of the processes they have tried to study. For example, research on deductive reasoning has focused on relations among contents whereas research on likelihood judgment has focused on degrees of belief.

Applying the mode/content distinction to thinking tasks suggests separate analyses of the generation of conclusions and of the transfer of belief, pointing the way toward a reconciliation of reasoning, judgment, and decision tasks. In particular, understanding thinking in terms of mental states with this intentional structure, organized into goal-directed sequences, lets us see each of these literatures as exploring primarily one aspect of thinking—the relations among contents in reasoning research, the relations among degrees of belief in judgment research, and the relations between goals and other mental states in decision research.

Logic and Basic Action

To understand experienced cognition, it is important to consider the relations between thinking and action. One place to look for such relations is in the mapping between logical operations and actions. Consider modus ponens, perhaps the most basic reasoning schema (Fig. 11.1). This argument describes the logic of basic action, as that logic is represented in production-system models (J. R. Anderson, 1983; A. Newell, 1990). That is, given certain circumstances, a particular action will be performed. As always, of course, we must distinguish between consulting a rule and embodying a regularity. Both mental logic (e.g., Braine, 1978) and mental models (e.g., Johnson-Laird, 1983) theorists have suggested that modus ponens is in effect performed rather than consulted. For example, Braine (1978; Braine & Reiser, 1984) has suggested that the knowledge expressed in conditional statements captures what we might call procedural regularities in thinking. That is, to attribute belief in the statement "If A, then B" to an individual is simply to note that believing A causes that individual to believe B. Or, given that A is believed, one is to begin believing B. On this view, we might say that conditional statements just are units of procedural knowledge, or productions, regardless of whether they support so-called "practical inference" (*doing* B when A is true) or symbolic reasoning (*coming to believe* B when A is true).

Goals and Conclusions

Reasoning typically involves a goal, such as testing a hypothesis or answering a question; the process that sets the goal thus instantiates the content of the conclusion. Many authors (e.g., Minsky, 1986; Rips, 1994) have noted the need for goals to constrain the activity of inference systems. Johnson-Laird (1983) suggested that deriving informative conclusions is a general goal for deduction, based on considerations of comprehension and cognitive economy. More specific goals embedded in purposive activity seem characteristic of real-life reasoning, at least outside of intellectual contexts (e.g., Lave, 1988; Scribner, 1984).

Consider the possible role of deductive reasoning in problem solving, the domain in which cognitive scientists have most explicitly considered goals. Deliberate or reflective problem solving (see chapter 10) might be described as generating argument structures that relate possible intentional actions ("If I do A, then B will occur") as premises to desired outcomes (e.g., goal states in the problem-space sense). Commitment to these premises constitutes instantiating subgoals, converting argument structures to goal structures by changing the psychological mode associated with the contents from *believe* to *intend*. The deductive relations among the contents of these metacognitive state allow planning in the sense of foreseeing the outcomes of possible courses of action.

Inferences as Mental Functions

Propositional inferences—what we ordinarily think of as deductive reasoning—can be described as functions that take mental states as their arguments (see chapter 5). Contents may be related roughly as suggested by theories of deductive reasoning; this corresponds to constructing a stable path that obeys the principles of group structure and allows reversible mental operations. Note that it is contents that are related by syntactic rules and that have compositional structure. *Degrees of commitment* may be related roughly as suggested by probability or information-integration models of judgment; this corresponds to path traversal. In the next section, I consider one effort to develop a theoretical account of reasoning that makes use of the mode/content distinction.

DULANY'S THEORY OF PROPOSITIONAL LEARNING

In chapter 5, I discussed Dulany's (e.g., 1991) mentalist approach to cognitive theory as an important influence on my thinking about experienced cognition. Dulany (e.g., 1962) has long been concerned with the role of consciousness in learning, and has developed formal theories of the control of activity by propositional contents of consciousness (Dulany, 1968; Wilson & Dulany, 1983) and of how individuals learn such propositions in hypothesis-testing situations. In this section, I discuss Dulany's (1979) Theory of Propositional Learning (TPL), focusing on a specific model developed in TPL for diagnostic reasoning with circumstantial evidence (Carlson & Dulany, 1988). This model illustrates several aspects of the analysis of thinking suggested by the experienced cognition framework. In particular, TPL describes the component inferences embedded in diagnostic problem solving as relations among mental states characterized in terms of contents and degrees of belief. According to this theory, belief is transferred from state to state on the basis of relations among the contents of those states.

TPL and Diagnostic Reasoning

The theory of propositional learning is concerned with how individuals revise their degrees of belief in causal hypotheses. The theory assumes an analysis of conscious mental states similar to that discussed in chapter 5, describing each state involved in belief revision as a propositional content held with some degree of belief. The theory can be applied to a wide range of situations and was initially developed in the context of experiments that construed learning as the discovery of contingencies between actions and their consequences in the manner of classic research on hypothesis testing (e.g., Bruner et al., 1956; Levine, 1975). A *causal hypothesis* in this sense is a proposition that identifies some agent (perhaps the self) as causally responsible for some target outcome. Although there are complexities hidden in the phrase "causally responsible," it is enough for our purposes to note that such a proposition supports counterfactuals—had the agent not performed some action or actions, the target outcome would not have occurred.

The knowledge involved in understanding a causal hypothesis of this form can be construed as a hypothetical network or theory specifying enabling conditions and causal pathways. This network supports the use of *circumstantial evidence*, observations not of the covariation between cause and effect but of events plausibly linked to possible agents and to the target outcome. In the case of both fictional and real murder mysteries, these observations are the familiar "motive, means, and opportunity" that provide the framework for detective stories (Bennett, 1979). In the research reported in Carlson and Dulany (1988), we applied TPL to develop a formal model of participants' thinking as they solved fictional murder mysteries. This form of reasoning is diagnostic because it involves determining the (likely) cause of a given outcome. The causal hypotheses being evaluated thus had the form "Suspect *I* is (is not) the murderer." Participants read a brief story describing a murder mystery setting and naming four suspects.

After reading the story, participants worked through a series of clues, each associated with a subset of one to three of the four suspects. The clues described enabling conditions and side effects related positively or negatively to the crime. For example, having access to the murder weapon is a positive enabling condition, whereas having an alibi is a negative enabling (or disabling) condition. An example of a positive side effect would be fingerprints at the scene of the crime.

Carlson and Dulany (1988) summarized the hypothesized reasoning process like this:

> The central idea of this model is that revision of belief results from a reasoning process based on three premises: the *association* of a clue with a possible cause, the *forward implication* from the "true cause" or its denial to the clue, and the *backward implication* from the clue or its denial to the "true cause." A cascaded reasoning process combines beliefs in these premises to revise belief in proportion to the prior certainty of a hypothesis. (p. 465; italics in original)

Here, the "true cause" refers to the murderer, the agent of the effect (the murder) that begins the reasoning process. Clues are observations causally linked, for example as side effects or enabling conditions, to the true focal cause. Thus, fingerprints at the scene of the crime might be a side effect of the murderer's presence, and thus tend to be incriminating. The scales used to assess these beliefs, shown in Fig. 11.2, help to clarify the meaning in our experiments of these premises and conclusion.

Figure 11.3 depicts the hierarchical, cascaded process by which individuals are hypothesized to reason from beliefs about clues to a belief that a particular suspect is guilty or innocent. The process involves two intermediate conclusions, labeled here as *subjective evidence* and *subjective convincingness*. Note that the relations among propositional contents here depend on their formal structure, as in theories of reasoning based on deductive logic.

Association of clue and possible cause, β (A)

How certain are you that this clue is true of Sam?

— — — — — ___ — — — — __

| Certain | Completely | Certain |
| False | Uncertain | True |

Forward implication, β (F)

What is the relative likelihood that this clue would be true of the murderer or of an innocent suspect?

— — — — — ___ — — — — __

| Innocent | Equally | Murderer |
| Only | Likely | Only |

Backward implication, β (B)

What is the relative likelihood that the murderer would be someone of whom this clue is true, or someone of whom this clue is false?

— — — — — ___ — — — — __

| False | Equally | True |
| Only | Likely | Only |

Subjective evidence, β (E)

How strongly do you think the evidence provided by this clue suggests guilt or suggests innocence for Sam?

— — — — — ___ — — — — __

| Suggests | Completely | Suggests |
| Innocence | Uncertain | Guilt |

Subjective convincingness, β (V)

How convincing, that Sam is guilty or innocent, do you find the evidence provided by this clue?

— — — — — ___ — __ — — __

| Convincing | Completely | Convincing |
| Innocence | Uncertain | Guilty |

Belief in causal hypothesis, β (H)

How certain are you now that Sam is guilty or innocent?

— — — — — ___ — __ — — __

| Certain | Completely | Certain |
| Innocent | Uncertain | Guilty |

FIG. 11.2. Degree of belief scales: Subjects in the study by Carlson and Dulany (1988) reported their degrees of belief on these scales. Each report was scored on a numerical scale ranging from -1 to $+1$, with a midpoint of 0 (see text for details).

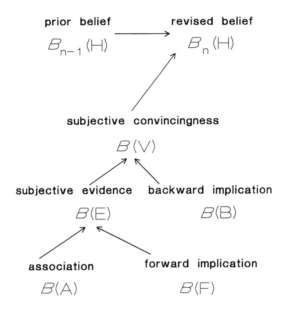

FIG. 11.3. Argument structure for belief revision: This figure depicts the hierarchical argument structure for revision of belief in causal hypotheses as described in Dulany's (1979) Theory of Propositional Learning.

However, these relations may be specific to the domain of causal thinking. For example, it is an open question whether this model would apply to reasoning about category membership (but see Dulany, 1979).

The TPL model is intended to capture the deductive transfer of commitment, in that degrees of belief in hypotheses depend on degrees of belief in premises formally related to those hypotheses. In knowledge-rich causal domains (e.g., human action as in the murder mystery task), the construction of premises likely results from a combination of knowledge-recruiting inferences (e.g., reminding) and acquired problem-solving skills (e.g., procedures for considering means, motives, and opportunity). In this sense, TPL could be seen as in part a theory about how deduction underlies a complex problem solving process that, as a whole, accomplishes induction (Rips, 1984, 1994).

A Formal Model and Experimental Test

The formal model specifies inferences as mathematical functions, as depicted in Fig. 11.4. The mathematical functions are quite simple, specifying multiplicative relations for each inference except the final revision of belief. These relations are based on scaling each specified belief on a scale of −1 to +1, with the scale midpoint of 0 indicating complete uncertainty.

INFERENCES IN THE THEORY OF
PROPOSITIONAL LEARNING

1. Subjective evidence

$$\beta (E_{ij}) = \beta (A_{ij}) \, \beta (F_j)$$

2. Subjective convincingness

$$\beta (V_{ij}) = |\beta (B_j)| \, \beta (E_{ij})$$

3. Revision of belief

$$\beta_n (H_i) = \beta_{n-1}(H_i) + \beta (V_{ij}) \, D$$

D = Distance to certainty in direction
indicated by sign of β (E)

FIG. 11.4.   Inferences in belief revision: This figure shows the mathematical formulation of the inferences shown in Fig. 11.2 (see text for details).

Figure 11.2 shows the actual scales on which participants reported their beliefs. Given assessments of degrees of belief for the premises, we can make mathematical predictions of the amount of belief revision for each of a set of hypotheses.

The main alternative to TPL is a descriptive model of belief revision based on Bayes theorem. Bayes theorem is a part of probability theory that specifies how belief in a hypothesis (construed as subjective probability) should change on the basis of evidence, relating the probability of a hypothesis prior to a piece of evidence to its probability after considering the evidence. Strength of evidence in this approach may be described as the ratio of conditional probabilities of the evidence when the hypothesis is assumed to be true or false. There has been a great deal of research concerned with Bayes theorem as a model of belief revision (e.g., Birnbaum & Mellers, 1983; Fischhoff & Beyth-Marom, 1983). Proponents of Bayesian models have generally focused on the relations among degrees of belief (construed as subjective probabilities), and have simply taken for granted the syntactic relations among propositions implied by a mapping of a belief revision task into probabilities and conditional probabilities. Although individuals are often roughly Bayesian in revising subjective probabilities, most research has found that in comparison to Bayes theorem, individuals are biased in a variety of ways depending on the specific situation (see Baron, 1994, for an accessible review of this literature).

Carlson and Dulany (1988) presented evidence supporting the TPL analysis of hypothesis testing, using the murder-mystery task previously described. The role of experimental manipulations in this type of research is to produce a range of degrees of belief, allowing assessment of mathematically specified functions representing the transfer of belief. The strength of this evidence is limited by the use of an "as if" thinking task, although one that was constructed to be psychologically involving. The TPL model presented in Figs. 11.2 through 11.4 provided excellent quantitative fits to participants' reported degrees of belief, and was much superior to a Bayesian model of this task. Our fundamental methodological assumption was that participants could report degrees of belief for the postulated states, and could do so without seriously changing the belief revision process. A control experiment (Carlson & Dulany, 1988) in fact showed that the belief revision process, and subjects' final conclusions, were very similar when we did not assess degrees of belief for premises. Note, however, that in the present analysis, reporting degrees of belief is a metacognitive task superimposed on the reasoning process. There is no implication that individuals must experience mental contents corresponding to degrees of belief in order to reason, much less that the multiplicative relations specified in Fig. 11.3 represent explicit rules consulted in order to carry out the postulated inferences. This research thus embodies the hypotheses discussed earlier (and in chapter 14) concerning the contents of mental states that make up experienced cognition.

CONCLUSION: UNIFYING THE THINKING LITERATURE

In this chapter, I have sketched an approach to analyzing thinking tasks based on the experienced cognition framework. Unfortunately, I have been able to only briefly consider the range of research on thinking. However, I have tried to convey how the analysis suggested by the experienced cognition approach might help to unify some of the very diverse approaches found in the literature. The basic idea is that we can view most research on thinking as directed primarily at deductive construction—often leading to skill-oriented theories such as the pragmatic inference theory (Cheng & Holyoak, 1985)—or at deductive transfer—often leading to abstract-formal theories (e.g., N. H. Anderson, 1981; Carlson & Dulany, 1988).

Much judgment research that takes probability theory as a normative model (see Kahneman et al., 1982) can be seen as approximating the account of thinking sketched here. The contents (assertions) to which probability equations are applied can be described in terms of conditional logic. Research aimed at developing formal models of belief formation and revision can then be seen as an effort to describe the transfer of commitment among these propositions. Several kinds of questions can be raised about the mapping of degree of belief into subjective probability statements, and alternative formulations have been proposed (e.g., Shafer & Tversky, 1985). Nevertheless, research in the probability-theory tradition (including the information-integration approach) implicitly acknowledges the mode–content distinction described here, assuming deductively appropriate relations among contents and focusing on what I would describe as intentional variables related to psychological modes (chapter 5).

Research on reasoning has generally focused on the generation or assessments of contents, rather than the transfer of belief. The analysis suggested in this chapter depicts the construction of contents as primarily based on acquired skills in symbolic domains. Theories of mental logic may, however, describe conditions for the deductive transfer of belief. Mental logic is grounded in (and thus gets its normative status and truth-preserving character from) constraints on physical activity; this grounding might be realized developmentally or evolutionarily.

Dulany's Theory of Propositional Learning illustrates the kind of detailed analysis that can follow from considering thinking as functional relations among mental states with intentional structure. The specific TPL model examined by Carlson and Dulany (1988) captured an impressive amount of regularity in these functional relations for the specific case of diagnostic reasoning, and Dulany (1979) suggested ways that TPL might be generalized to a variety of other thinking tasks, such as category learning. Like most theories in cognitive science, however, TPL captures only some aspects of the processes in its domain. In particular, it does not address traditional information-processing questions concerning the real-time dynamics of cognition, nor does it directly address how the reasoning it describes might figure in goal-directed action. However, Carlson and Dulany (1988) did consider some implications of their analysis for participants' memory, showing some regularity in the relations between reasoning and later memory for problems. Dulany (1968) also considered how beliefs with propositional contents might control instrumental actions.

Most important, I have tried to show in this chapter the value of the experienced cognition framework for understanding those mental processes most prototypical of thinking as we normally understand it. In the next chapter, I return to the topic of skill, reviewing current theories of cognitive skill. We will then be in a position to consider how the argument structures discussed here and the goal structures discussed in chapters 9 and 10 contribute to experienced cognition in everyday skilled activity and to understanding the changes in conscious experience and control that accompany increasing skill.

12

Expertise, Skill, and Everyday Action

People always seem to be doing something.
—Vallacher & Wegner, 1987, p. 3

The everyday world is just that: what people do in daily, weekly, monthly, ordinary cycles of activity.
—Lave, 1988, p. 15

The performances of experts, and our performance of routine everyday actions such as getting dressed or driving to work, pose a serious challenge for a consciousness-centered cognitive theory. These activities are clearly goal-directed, but seem to be performed with a kind of mindlessness often associated with automaticity (Langer, 1978, 1992). Mindlessness in this sense is sometimes evoked to explain how experts are apparently able to attend to high-level aspects of their tasks while performing lower-level components automatically, and how it is that we make such everyday errors as pouring coffee on our breakfast cereal. At the same time, expert and routine performance is closely tuned to environmental regularities, relying on informational support from the environment.

In this chapter, I discuss some of the research on expertise and on everyday action, considering its implications for understanding experienced cognition. The central theme of my argument is that understanding the role of consciousness in expertise and in everyday action depends on recognizing that action can be described at multiple levels and that high levels of skill are associated with informational constraints on cospecification and egolocative processing.

ROUTINE ACTIVITY AND EXPERIENCED COGNITION

Studies of expertise and everyday action provide similar insights into the nature of experienced cognition. It might seem strange to link these categories, given the common identification of expertise with outstanding or superior performance (e.g., Ericsson & Smith, 1991), apparently quite the opposite of routine everyday activity. I would argue, however, that in many everyday activities, each of us is an expert. This everyday expertise is less visible than is expertise in often-studied domains such as physics, computer programming, or medicine primarily because it is ubiquitous, and most individuals do not stand out from others by virtue of their expertise in dressing, getting to work, or navigating their homes. Although some authors have argued that the term *expert* should be restricted to individuals whose performance is exceptional relative to others (e.g., Salthouse, 1991), this restriction seems to preclude the possibility of finding common cognitive accounts of expertise in a range of domains (Sloboda, 1991). In this chapter, I am concerned with the expertise that can result from practice and skill acquisition, rather than giftedness or exceptional ability not based on practice (Posner, 1988).

Novice–Expert Differences

Following the early work of Simon and his colleagues (e.g., Chase & Simon, 1973; Larkin et al., 1980), cognitive scientists have generated a large literature concerned with expertise. Most of this research involves comparing the performance of experts and novices on laboratory tasks intended to capture theoretically significant aspects of expertise (see Proctor & Dutta, 1995, chapter 8; or Mayer, 1992, chapter 13 for brief reviews; volumes edited by Chi et al., 1988; and by Ericsson & Smith, 1991 provide broader overviews of this literature). The comparisons made in this research are thus usually cross-sectional, providing snapshot views of individuals with very different levels of skill. We might expect that the phenomena of expertise would be similar to those found in studies of practice and skill acquisition, but in fact researchers working in these literatures generally have focused on somewhat different aspects of performance.

Most theoretical accounts of expertise emphasize differences between experts and novices in the units and organization of knowledge. For example, Larkin (1983) argued that physics experts represent textbook problems in terms of underlying physical principles, whereas novices represent the same problems in terms of surface features. A variety of evidence supports this claim for a range of domains. Chase and Simon

(1973) demonstrated that expert chess players remembered meaningful board layouts (arrangements of chess pieces) much better than did novices. However, there was little difference between experts and novices in memory for random arrangements. Experts in other domains show similar memory skills; for example, Egan and Schwartz (1979) demonstrated a similar phenomenon in the domain of electronic circuits. Using more complex tasks requiring comprehension, recall, and generation of text, Voss and his colleagues (Chiesi, Spilich, & Voss, 1979; Spilich, Vesonder, Chiesi, & Voss, 1979; Voss, Vesonder, & Spilich, 1980) showed that expert–novice differences in knowledge organization had similar effects across a range of situations in which knowledge may be applied. Ericsson and his colleagues (Chase & Ericsson, 1982; Ericsson, 1985; Ericsson & Kintsch, 1995; Ericsson & Polson, 1988a, 1988b) have developed a theoretical account of expert memory that emphasizes the role of domain knowledge in supporting working memory performance.

Experts and novices also differ, of course, in the quality and speed with which they perform domain-specific tasks. For example, Larkin and her colleagues (Larkin et al., 1980) reported a four-to-one difference in the speed with which physics professors (presumably experts) and physics students (novices) solved textbook physics problems. A variety of strategic differences between experts and novices have also been reported. For example, expert computer programmers produce finer-grained analyses of problems and are more likely to consider alternatives than novices (Jeffries, Turner, Polson, & Atwood, 1981). In the domain of textbook physics problems, experts tend to work forward from given information, constructing a problem representation by calculations based on information in the problem description. Novices, in contrast, tend to work backward from the goal of obtaining the requested quantity, using means–ends analysis or other weak methods (Larkin et al., 1980). The specific differences between experts and novices of course depend on the problem-solving domain. For example, in computer programming, experts tend to work backward from overall goals (J. R. Anderson et al., 1984; Jeffries et al., 1981; see Holyoak, 1991, for discussion). A fair summary of research in a variety of domains is that experts consider more factors, and more appropriate factors, than do novices, representing situations in greater detail.

Glaser and Chi (1988) summarized the differences between novice and expert performance, as shown in Table 12.1. One implication of these differences is that experts experience events, including their own actions, in their domains of expertise differently than do novices. For example, Murphy and Wright (1984) presented evidence that experts' categories in their domains of expertise are richer than those of novices, including more characteristic features. At the same time, there was more featural overlap

TABLE 12.1
Characteristics of Expertise (from Glaser & Chi, 1988)

---

1. Experts excel mainly in their own domains.
2. Experts perceive large meaningful patterns in their domain.
3. Experts are fast; they are faster than novices at performing the skills of their domain, and they quickly solve problems with little error.
4. Experts have superior short-term and long-term memory [for material in their domains of expertise].
5. Experts see and represent a problem in their domain at a deeper (more principled) level than novices; novices tend to represent a problem at a superficial level.
6. Experts spend a great deal of time analyzing a problem qualitatively.
7. Experts have strong self-monitoring skills.

---

among experts' categories, suggesting that experts see more similarities or links among categories. Together with evidence on experts' perception of and memory for meaningful patterns in their domain (discussed earlier), such results suggest that the contents of mental states during task performance are quite different for experts and novices. Less obvious, but at least equally important, is that experts may be more able to rely on information available in the environment than are novices. For example, the chess studies previously discussed suggest that experts directly recognize meaningful patterns whereas novices must consult their declarative knowledge of the domain and laboriously construct such patterns.

Information-Processing Accounts of Expertise

Most cognitive scientists have interpreted these observations about expert–novice differences in information-processing terms, focusing on the representation and organization of knowledge. The information-processing approach to expertise has been characterized by representationalism (see chapter 2), the tendency to explain systematicity in behavior by positing representations with the corresponding properties. This might suggest that becoming an expert can be reduced to finding the right representation for a particular problem. However, as Patel and Groen (1991) and others have noted, there is more to expertise than appropriate problem representations. Despite efforts toward a general theory of expertise (e.g., Ericsson & Smith, 1991), it is not clear that current approaches will lead to such a theory.

A number of authors (e.g., Barsalou, 1993; Kolers & Roediger, 1984; Neisser, 1983, 1992) have argued for a more procedural approach to understanding expertise (and cognition generally; see chapter 7). In the domain of everyday action, Norman (1981; Norman & Shallice, 1986) argued for a procedural account of expert performance. Norman's account assumes a hierarchy of action schemas, which may be evoked by environmental circumstances with little deliberate control by the actor. This account points the way toward understanding routine activity in terms of the reciprocal interaction of agent and environment. In order to see this interaction in more concrete terms, I turn to research on everyday action.

Everyday Action

Everyday action reflects mundane skill and expertise. In contrast to many skills studied in the laboratory (chapter 3), the routines of everyday life are performed in ways that mix symbolic and nonsymbolic mediums. For example, the commonplace activity of navigating the environment typically involves integrating symbolic sources of information such as maps, street signs, and verbal directions with the nonsymbolic information available directly from the environment and body (e.g., Gauvain, 1993). These routines are therefore generally more reliant on familiar environmental affordances than are the skills acquired or demonstrated in laboratory experiments.

Research on everyday cognition, such as Scribner's (1984) study of dairy workers, demonstrates individuals' reliance on environmental support and adaptation of routines to that support. Scribner observed workers preparing orders for delivery, a task that requires arithmetic to calculate (for example) the number of cases needed to contain a certainty quantity of product (e.g., so many quarts of milk), as well as manipulation of the actual objects (cases and cartons). She found that these individuals had developed a number of very reliable routines specific to the conditions in which they worked. Of particular interest is that these routines are adapted to arithmetic units corresponding to objects in the work environment; for example, to the number of milk cartons in a case, or in a row in a case. In this and other studies of everyday mathematical reasoning (see Lave, 1988, for a review), a striking result is the contrast between very accurate performance situated in familiar environments and relatively poor performance by the same individuals on school-like tests of mathematical skill.

Perhaps more important, Lave's (1988) observations of mathematical reasoning by grocery shoppers demonstrate that the setting may structure the form of mathematical reasoning. For example, she reported that shoppers adopted a variety of strategies for determining which of several similar products to purchase. Only occasionally did shoppers actually calculate unit (e.g., per ounce) prices, instead performing rough calculations to assess marginal value (e.g., is the number of extra sheets in a larger roll of paper towels worth the extra cost) and invoking nonmathematical considerations such as storage space or convenience. In part, these varied strategies reflect the real-time construction or elaboration of goals on the basis of information available in the shopping environment. In addition, as particular activities become routine, direct reliance on environmental regularities comes to replace calculation. For example, in observing meal preparations by dieters, Lave (1988) reported that, "The more expert the Weight Watchers, the less they calculated" (p. 128). In this case, the symbol-based calculations initially required to determine portion-size, structure-resulting activity, which is supported by nonsymbolic features of the environment.

Recently, Cary (1996) demonstrated the role of external support in shaping the development of routines for mental arithmetic. In her study, participants performed a realistic arithmetic task, calculating incomes on the basis of wages and commissions. The information needed for this task was available piecemeal, but in sequences and for durations requested online by the participant. Participants allowed to use pencil and paper adopted routines based on the conceptual structure of the task, calculating first wages and then commissions. Other participants not allowed such external memory aids quickly developed routines that minimized the need to maintain intermediate results, which resulted in less obvious correspondence to the task's conceptual structure.

A number of authors have recently argued that everyday cognition is quite different from cognitive activity evoked in laboratory experiments (e.g., Lave, 1988). Although I have considerable sympathy for this point of view (e.g., chapter 10), I find much discussion of this issue to be very ideological in tone (e.g., chapter 1 in Lave, 1988), in a way that is unhelpful for the development of theory. Furthermore, much discussion of everyday cognition relies for evidence on the same handful of studies reviewed by Lave. And often the evidence is less rigorous than we might prefer. For example, Lave prefaced some of her discussion with this comment, "But in large part I am able to present only an impressionistic summary of diffuse conversations and observations of a more casual variety" (p. 125). Nevertheless, this small body of research does demonstrate that naturally occurring cognitive activity depends in critical ways on the reciprocal nature of agent–environment interactions, and on the continuing availability of information in the environment as well as from memory.

Research on human error (Norman, 1981; Reason, 1990) also illustrates the reliance on environmental support, demonstrating that the guidance of action may rely minimally on ongoing support by internal representation. For example, Norman (1981) described a number of capture errors, in which a familiar situation evokes an apparently unintended action. In his words, "A capture error occurs when a familiar habit substitutes itself for the intended action sequence. The basic notion is simple: Pass too near a well-formed habit and it will capture your behavior" (p. 8). Norman cited an example reported by James (1890, p. 115, cited in Norman, 1981) in which:

> very absent-minded persons in going to their bedroom to dress for dinner have been known to take off one garment after another and finally to get into bed, merely because that was the habitual issue of the first few movements when performed at a later hour. (p. 3)

The study of these and other errors has substantial practical importance, especially for situations in which individuals must control or monitor large and potentially dangerous mechanical systems such as airplanes or nuclear power plants (Reason, 1990). More important for my purpose, these cases demonstrate the extent to which information available in the environment supports everyday action. Although errors stand out as interesting cases, presumably much of our successful action is also supported in the same way—when we in fact intend to get ready for bed, we rely on skills adapted to and supported by the familiar environment of the bedroom. In particular, it appears that the specification of goals is supported by information in the environment; in a sense, what is around us tells us what we are doing. From the perspective of the experienced cognition framework, the puzzle is to understand the (apparently very limited) role of consciousness in such episodes.

Ballard, Hayhoe, and Pelz (1995) recently emphasized the dynamic role of environmental information in an account of the use of working memory in an object-manipulation task. Subjects in their experiment manipulated blocks displayed on a computer screen, with the goal of copying a displayed pattern of blocks. They argued that humans performing this task should be conceived as deictic systems that, "realize representational economies by using the momentary binding between the perceptual-motor system and the world. For example, with vision, this binding can be achieved by actively looking at, or fixating, an environmental point" (p. 66). In their experiments:

> The main result is that the information required for the task is acquired just prior to its use. The alternate strategy of memorizing the configuration to be copied in its entirety before moving blocks is never used. Subjects choose not to operate at the maximum capacity of short-term memory but instead seek to minimize its use. (p. 76)

Ballard and his colleagues go on to offer some speculations concerning the general implications of their results, emphasizing that this characterization of cognitive activity does not require the elaborate mental representations often postulated in information-processing theories. Their account might be characterized as a version of Neisser's (1976) perceptual-cycle framework for understanding cognition. Perhaps most important for my purpose, this study demonstrates not just the reliance on environmental affordances characteristic of everyday activity, but the role of self-specific (deictic) information in coordinating series of actions.

Limits on Introspection in Routine Activity

Because most everyday experience is mundane and routine, research on expertise may provide insights into the nature of experienced cognition, especially the so-called limits of introspection (e.g., Nisbett & Wilson, 1977). A commonplace observation is that much of experts' knowledge is not accessible to report, but must be performed. For example, in a chapter on representing expert knowledge, Olson and Biolsi (1991) wrote:

> It is not always the case that experts have access to their knowledge. In many cases, objects are "seen" as related but the expert is not able to access the fleeting perception. Often inferences are drawn without the expert's knowledge. (p. 249)

A paradox in this observation is that although expert performance is sometimes said to be unconscious, it also appears that experts are better able to concentrate on their performance to let it more fully dominate their experience.

By considering these features of expert performance, and of everyday cognition, we may get some insight into experienced cognition. In particular, I want to consider the hypothesis that the differences in the contents of mental states experienced by experts and novices, or by individuals performing relatively novel versus routine activities, reflect differences in the level at which activity is controlled rather than differences between conscious and unconscious control.

SKILL ACQUISITION BY RESTRUCTURING

Understanding the process of skill acquisition can provide some insight into the nature of expert performance. Current theories of skill acquisition suggest a variety of possible mechanisms for the effects of practice. These mechanisms can be broadly divided into two categories: *component speedup* and *restructuring*. Component speedup mechanisms allow individual steps in a process to be performed more quickly with practice, and theorists have focused on how assumptions about the mathematical form of this speedup can predict overall performance speed (e.g., J. R. Anderson, 1983). In general, component speedup mechanisms reflect the lowest level of information-processing decomposition, in that these mechanisms (for example, strengthening of associative links) do not themselves receive cognitive explanations (chapter 2). MacKay (1982, 1987) developed a theory that relies primarily on component speedup at several hierarchical levels to predict practice effects.

Most theorists agree that the increased fluency that accompanies increasing skill results at least in part from some form of restructuring. Current theories include a variety of proposed restructuring mechanisms. In some cases, it is component strengthening or speedup that allows restructuring to occur, for example by allowing more information to be held in working memory together (e.g., Case, 1985). From the perspective of the experienced cognition framework, restructuring mechanisms are important because they imply changes in the sequences and contents of mental states that constitute the performance of cognitive skills. Alternative proposed mechanisms make different predictions about these changes, so they must be considered in some detail.

More Efficient Goal Structures. One form of restructuring may result from deliberate problem solving. As we solve similar problems repeatedly, we often discover goal structures that are more efficient than those guiding early performance, in the sense of reducing the time or other costs of satisfying an overall goal. One example of this restructuring was documented by Carlson et al. (1990) and discussed in chapter 9. Another example from a study of simpler mental arithmetic routines (Lundy et al., 1994) illustrates how strategic restructuring can simplify the conscious control of skilled performance.

Subjects in the Lundy et al. (1994) study practiced generating answers to equations like

$$D = [(P + U) + (R - A)] + [(C + E) - (F - T)]$$

with values that varied from trial to trial. One way to approach this problem is by using the hierarchical goal structure suggested by the parentheses. An alternative approach is to restructure the task so that a flat goal structure can be used, recognizing the associative nature of addition and subtraction. Subjects' reports and step-by-step solution times converged on the conclusion that more successful subjects restructured their performance to take advantage of this simpler goal structure. This restructuring may simplify the task in several ways, but one obvious difference is that it minimizes the need to hold intermediate results in working memory for later integration.

Prominent production-system models such as ACT–R (J. R. Anderson, 1993) and Soar (Newell, 1990) include mechanisms for restructuring. In

ACT–R, restructuring occurs as individuals reflect on successful problem solutions, using them as examples to build new, more efficient goal structures through a process known as *knowledge compilation* (an analogy to compiling a computer program). According to this proposal, compilation might fail because the entire example cannot be held in working memory. In Soar, restructuring occurs when performing an already learned routine results in an impasse, which shifts problem solving to a higher level in which the learner metacognitively considers the performance that produced the impasse (also see VanLehn, 1988). Once a solution is found, Soar generates a knowledge unit known as a chunk to represent the solution as a single cognitive step.

Earlier versions of Anderson's ACT theory (J. R. Anderson, 1982, 1983, 1987b) included the hypothesis that practice automatically results in more efficient goal structures. In this version of the theory, compilation was said to result from two mechanisms: composition, which collapses sequences of steps into single steps, and proceduralization, which results in domain-specific productions (if–then rules) that realize individual steps. Experimental evidence suggests, however, that practice does not always produce composition (Carlson et al., 1989a, 1989b; Elio, 1986; Lewis, 1981), although it may occur under some circumstances (Blessing & J. R. Anderson, 1996; Carlson & Lundy, 1992).

Replacement by Retrieval. Another form of restructuring is the replacement of multiple-step problem-solving routines with the retrieval of answers from memory. The best-developed theory of this process is Logan's (1988, 1990) Instance Theory of automaticity. This theory suggests that the speedup and other changes in performance observed with practice result from the accumulation of a repertoire of remembered episodes. As a particular problem is practiced, according to this theory, individuals may derive answers from either their original multiple-step routines or by remembering the goal, problem display, and answer from an earlier episode. As more instances are accumulated in memory, performance speeds up because the distribution of possible retrieval times includes more fast retrievals. This theory is similar in many respects to instance- or exemplar-based theories of category learning (e.g., Medin & Schaffer, 1978) and other memory phenomena (e.g., Hintzman, 1986), which share the assumption that learning is based on the storage of particular episodes.

A number of studies support the view that the phenomena of automaticity can be attributed to such replacement (Klapp, Boches, Trabert, & Logan, 1991; Logan & Etherton, 1994; Logan & Klapp, 1991; Strayer & Kramer, 1990), with concomitant changes in how the processes are controlled. A study by Logan and Klapp (1991), who trained their subjects to perform alphabet arithmetic, illustrates this point. In this task, letters are substituted for numbers; for example, A + 2 = C (because C is the 3rd letter). Subjects initially perform this task by counting, as evidenced by reports and patterns of response times (i.e., corresponding to the number of counting steps required). With practice, evidence of counting disappears, indicating that individuals perform the task by memory retrieval. Similarly, Lundy and I (Carlson & Lundy, 1992) demonstrated that with more complex arithmetic routines, practice with consistent data eliminated the step-by-step solution time patterns characteristic of the original algorithm used to perform the task. Evidence from search tasks often used to study automaticity similarly suggests that the step-by-step cognitive processes originally used to perform the tasks are replaced with simpler processes as a consequence of consistent practice (Schneider & Detweiler, 1987; Schneider & Shiffrin, 1977).

The storage of particular episodes or instances is of course not an essential assumption of theories that describe replacement by retrieval. Consider a common example of replacement by retrieval, mental arithmetic performed on the basis of remembered arithmetic facts. Most theories concerned with mental arithmetic assume some kind of network representation, in which arithmetic facts are theoretically represented as generic knowledge rather than as particular episodes. In either case, however, the central point is that with practice, memory retrieval comes to substitute for more complex, multiple-step procedures.

Distributive Strategies. A third kind of restructuring involves the development of what I call *distributive strategies*, strategies for distributing the informational burden of cognitive performance over internal and external resources. A simple example of a distributive strategy is the use of paper and pencil to perform mental arithmetic. The conventional representation of multiple-digit addition in columns, with column sums and carries written down as they are obtained, provides a means of distributing the maintenance of intermediate results and of placekeeping between mental and environmental media. In more idiosyncratic situations, of course, such conventional strategies are not available, but individuals invent their own distributive strategies. The examples of everyday cognition discussed earlier reflect these strategies.

It seems likely that all of these forms of restructuring are involved in the development of expertise. In fact, they seem to be interdependent. For example, the availability of reliable retrieval of arithmetic facts together with distributive strategies for particular problem types affords some options in terms of efficient goal structures. Furthermore, each form of restructuring depends on regularities in performance and in the environment supporting the performance.

EXPERTISE AS RELIANCE ON REGULARITIES

Expert activity, then, reflects the restructuring of algorithmic performance to rely on regularities in cognition and in the environment. In this sense, expertise is continuous with narrower skills: As discussed in chapter 3, perhaps the most powerful variable in determining the effects of practice in laboratory tasks is consistency (e.g., Carlson & Lundy, 1992; Wenger & Carlson, 1996). For example, the development of automatic processes in visual search tasks depends on a consistent mapping of items (e.g., specific letters) to response categories (e.g., target). Although consistency usually is operationally defined in terms of simple stimulus–response (or stimulus–interpretation; Logan, 1988) relations, establishing consistency in this way also generates a network of consistencies or regularities among goals, activities, and environmental events that include both stimulus and feedback displays. These networks of regularity include relations naturally seen as causal, and provide the basis for the development of skilled routines that constitute expertise.

Argument Structures, Goal Structures, and Routines

As skills come to be performed rather than knowledge consulted, argument structures tend to be converted first to deliberate goal structures, then to routines that involve minimal deliberate intervention. Initially, individuals figure out what must be done, then organize the corresponding goals in ways that accomplish particular tasks. With practice, these goal structures shape routines that can be performed with minimal deliberate control, so that little egolocative processing is involved—as we sometimes say, we become absorbed in our activities. That is, to the extent that both goals and the environments in which they are achieved remain stable, there is little need to functionally distinguish the acting self and the environment that affords the action.

This is seen in comparisons of expert and novice protocols, or in the transition from novice to expert. For example, Anzai and Simon (1979) studied a single individual learning to solve the Tower of Hanoi problem (see Fig. 9.1). They report this subject's verbal protocol as she made four attempts to solve the puzzle, first failing, then succeeding by the application of three somewhat different strategies. Most of the statements in this protocol announce intentions to make particular moves; for example, "I'll take 1 from B and place it on A" (statement 15, p. 138; A and B refer to particular pegs on the puzzle apparatus, and "1" refers to a particular disk). However, a number of statements also explicitly mention inferences; for example, "Therefore, since 1 is the only disk I can move, and last I moved it to B, I'll put it on C this time ... from A to C" (statement 26,

p. 138); "But, if you think of it as two disks, this will certainly go as 1 from A to B and 2 from A to C, then 1 from B to C" (statement 77, p. 139). Here, we can see the problem solver constructing arguments on the basis of declarative rules specifying problem constraints ("the only disk I can move"), possible configurations of problem elements ("if you think of it as two disks"), and her own prior actions ("last I moved it to B"). The conclusions of these arguments are subgoals to be achieved, particular intended moves that can be easily translated into actions. Later in each problem-solving episode, the protocol consists largely of telegraphic announcements of moves (e.g., "2 from C to A," statement 133, p. 140), mostly uninterrupted by explicit inferences (e.g., statements 131–162, p. 140). This shift reflects the transition from argument structures whose conclusions are intended moves to goal structures in which one intended move follows another.

With more extended practice, experts often report very little in the way of intermediate steps or deliberate goals as they solve problems. The restructuring that occurs with practice results in characterizing objects in the domain in terms of affordances rather than verbally labeled features. In many domains, expertise is characterized by special vocabulary for these affordances. However, the routines performed by experts often seem impervious to introspection. Scardamalia and Bereiter (1991) noted that this contrast between the routine character of commonly studied expert performance and experts' greater knowledge can be resolved by considering what experts really do in their domains of expertise. In their words:

> The point we want to make is that studies of reading and writing bring out an aspect of expertise that is typical of expertise as it is practiced in the real world and that tends to be hidden in most expert-novice research. Expert physicists do not spend their days solving textbook problems. They spend their days, or at least the high points of their days, working on problems that are hard for them. That is how they make advances in their fields, and it is also how they advance their own competence. Experts acquire their vast knowledge resources not by doing what falls comfortably within their competence but by working on real problems that force them to extend their knowledge and competence. That is not only how they become experts, we suggest, but also how they remain experts and avoid falling into the ruts worn by repeated execution of familiar routines. (pp. 173–174)

Thus, experts have repertoires of skilled routines but employ these routines in service of new goals to solve difficult problems. This observation might in fact serve as a means for distinguishing skill from the broader concept of expertise.

Metacognition, Autobiographical Memory, and Expertise

Expertise is thus characterized by a puzzling mix of enhanced and limited metacognition. This mix can be explained in part by considering how the self is cospecified in expert performance. Consider the case of fluent reading. Expert readers appear to have greater skill than do novices at *comprehension monitoring*, the real-time evaluation of reading success. Yet expert reading is also characterized by fluency and smoothness, without many obvious pauses for reflection or verification (at least for material of moderate difficulty). For example, Forlizzi (1988, 1992) provided evidence that monitoring may be implicit in skilled reading, in the sense that readers are much more likely to detect comprehension problems that disrupt the smooth flow of reading than those that do not. Experts may be better self-monitors in some cases because their performance is fluent and closely coordinated with features of the environment, and thus more sensitive to disruptions. As in the case of emotional awareness (chapter 6), disruption of ongoing activity serves to prompt egolocative processing, facilitating the distinction between self- and object-specific aspects of currently available information. This account suggests a resolution of the paradox just noted, in that experts may be more sensitive to disruption but less likely to encounter it.

This resolution has implications for autobiographical memory, memory for the self engaged in past activity. On a reasonable theory of memory, autobiographical recollection will be possible only when egolocative processing has occurred in the episode to be recollected. If self and object are not explicitly distinguished in the original experience, distinguishing them in recollection must be inferential. Expert performance is tied very closely to the features of the domain, and coordination among component skills and the environment is very fluent, providing neither the conditions nor motivation for egolocative processing. In expert performance, the self is likely specified over larger units of time and perhaps spatial scale than is the case for novice performance. The literature on everyday action includes some theoretical resources for elaborating this point, and in the next section I consider these proposals.

LEVELS OF DESCRIPTION AND CONTROL
IN EVERYDAY ACTION

The experience of everyday action reflects the availability of multiple descriptions of most activities. Furthermore, the metacognitive use of egolocative information to control activity varies with fluency of performance. A variety of evidence indicates that individuals tend to agree on the level of description, units, and organization of everyday actions they observe (e.g., Abelson, 1981; Lichtenstein & Brewer, 1980; Reed,

Montgomery, Palmer, & Pittenger, 1995; Reed, Montgomery, Schwartz, Palmer, & Pittenger, 1992). However, there is relatively less evidence concerning how individuals experience and control their own actions. In the domain of motor skills acquired in the laboratory, researchers have known for a long time that practice may change the information used to control performance. For example, Fuchs (1962) showed that individuals practicing a tracking task shifted from relying on the position of a stimulus to relying on its acceleration to guide their tracking movements (see Pew, 1966, and Proctor & Dutta, 1995, for additional discussion). Acceleration is a higher level of description because it characterizes a set of positions, thus describing the event over a larger time scale. More generally, the level of description at which everyday activity appears in the contents of mental states may vary with practice and with other circumstances. Higher-level descriptions may be said to characterize activity at a larger temporal scale that is also more abstract in the sense of encompassing a range of lower-level descriptions. The relation of these observations to cognitive control is addressed by Action Identification Theory.

Action Identification Theory

In their Action Identification Theory, Vallacher and Wegner (1987) suggested that activity is always under conscious control under some description or identity. The idea is that any activity can be described at multiple levels of abstraction, and that at any one moment the actor experiences one description as the identity of his or her action. For example, the same activity might variously be described as "checking to see if someone is home," "ringing the doorbell," or "pressing a button" (Vallacher & Wegner, 1987, p. 4). Here, "checking to see if someone is home" is the highest-level of these descriptions, because it identifies the action at a scale that links it with a broad goal structure. This level is also more abstract, in that the action as identified at this level could be realized (in appropriate circumstances) by different low-level actions such as "knocking at the door." In this particular example, the hierarchy of descriptions corresponds both to a possible decompositional hierarchy of subgoals (for example, pressing a button is done in order to ring the doorbell) and to an instrumental hierarchy (for example, ringing the doorbell is done by means of pressing a button). It is the instrumental relation among levels (see chapter 9) that is critical for Action Identification Theory.

Action Identification Theory is concerned with which of these simultaneously available descriptions serves to constitute experience and to support control of activity. The theory is based on three principles:

> Principle 1 holds that people maintain action in accord with their prepotent identity for the action . . .

Principle 2 holds that people embrace higher level identities when these become available, . . .

Principle 3 holds that failure to maintain action under one identity will move people to a lower level of identification. (Vallacher & Wegner, 1987, pp. 12–13)

These principles are presented by Vallacher and Wegner with relatively little theoretical rationale, but we can understand them in terms of co-specification and egolocative processing.

Vallacher and Wegner offered many examples of evidence for these principles. For instance, in one study (Wegner, Vallacher, Macomber, Wood, & Arps, 1984) they asked subjects to drink coffee from either a normal cup or an exceptionally heavy cup that was awkard to use. When performing the (presumably skilled) action of drinking from a normal cup, participants identified their actions using such high-level phrases as "promoting my caffeine habit." When the use of an unusual cup made it difficult for subjects to perform this skilled action with their normal fluency, they tended instead to identify their actions with relatively lower level phrases such as "drinking a liquid."

Higher level action identities usually correspond to longer term or larger scale goals. Maintaining these higher level identities as contents of experienced mental states thus helps to maintain goal-directed activity over extended episodes. Furthermore, higher level identities reflect egolocative processing that identifies the self at a broader scale. In order to maintain action with respect to a goal, information specifying the individual's goals must be functionally distinguished from information specifying objects present in the environment. Actions identified at a low level are ambiguous with respect to egolocation, because they can participate in alternative goal structures. For example, in James' (1890) anecdote discussed earlier, unbuttoning a shirt can be a subgoal for the goal of changing for dinner, or for the goal of getting ready for bed.

According to Vallacher and Wegner (1987) (although they of course do not use this terminology), egolocative processes that identify the self as engaging in a higher level activity are the source of flexibility in skilled activity:

High-level identification, meanwhile, lends itself to action stability because it effectively shields the person against the emergence of alternative identities that could substantially change the nature of subsequent action. (p. 8)

With increments in identification level, there is a corresponding increase in the range of interchangeable means available for maintaining the action, and this imparts a noteworthy degree of flexibility to action. (p. 9)

> If consistency exists at all for an action identified at a low level, it is because of stable environmental cues that keep the person mindful of the task at hand. Flexibility, meanwhile, reflects impulsive emergence to new courses of action when the environmental cues change. (p. 9)

According to Vallacher and Wegner, then, increasing expertise changes the action descriptions that are relevant to understanding conscious control and that contribute to autobiographical memory of performance. An important aspect of their theory is that the multiple identities of an action can be simultaneously available, picking out different aspects of the current informational manifold. However, only one of the available identities is experienced as the content of a mental state at a given moment. If correct, this observation accounts for some cases of so-called unconscious mental processes: If we assess subjects' experience of their activity using (e.g., as a recall cue or recognition item) an identity that does not correspond to the level at which they experienced that activity, we are likely to find evidence that they were not conscious of a description that is both true and useful for some theoretical purposes. In fact, we may get individuals to agree that a description of their activity is true but does not correspond to their experience. This might be one reasonable sense of the term *unconscious*, but does not support the common claim that there are separate systems for conscious and unconscious cognition (see chapter 14).

Expertise is generally considered a broader concept than *skill*, in the sense that expertise spans a relatively broad domain and includes a number of more specific skills (Ericsson & Smith, 1991). Considering the availability of multiple action identities allows us to make this point more specifically: Expertise is constituted in part by the availability of multiple levels of action description. These multiple action identities allow for flexible control of action, and for reconstruction or reinstantiation of appropriate subgoals when activity is disrupted (cf. Gillie & Broadbent, 1989). This flexibility also allows for adjustment to temporal constraints, allowing experts to maintain temporal coordination of their activity with demands of the task environment. For example, one mark of expertise in winter driving is careful and appropriately timed use of the brake pedal, which may require identifying an action as "pumping the brake" rather than the higher level "stopping at a traffic signal." The ability to move among levels is one aspect of the ability of experts to apply routines in the service of difficult or novel goals, as noted by Scardamalia and Bereiter (1991, discussed previously).

CAPTURE AND PLACEKEEPING ERRORS

Capture and placekeeping errors reflect our normal reliance on environmental support for the guidance of our activities. As already noted, capture errors are action slips in which an ongoing activity is diverted by an alternative routine that depends on the same environmental support as the intended routine. Placekeeping errors are action slips in which a step in an intended routine is omitted or repeated. Both kinds of errors point to a normally effective aspect of experienced cognition, the role of available information in specifying the acting self and thus maintaining ongoing activity.

Capture Errors and Cospecification

Capture errors demonstrate the specification of the acting self on the basis of information available in the environment. As we engage in routine activity, information specifying the conditions for executing actions and information specifying that those intended actions are satisfied are intermingled. For example, the visual information available when pouring a cup of coffee specifies both enabling conditions such as the relative positions of cup and carafe and conditions of satisfaction such as the arrival of coffee in the cup. This information can also specify the self in action (as pouring coffee in this case). Unless something goes wrong, there is little need for cognitive processes to distinguish among these aspects of the available information. Although self and object are cospecified, egolocative processing plays little role because goals can be maintained by information available in the environment. However, the current purpose of the routine may be less familiar than some alternative purpose defined at a higher level—for example, pouring coffee for a guest rather than for oneself. Such circumstances can lead to capture errors such as drinking the coffee oneself rather than delivering it to a guest.

There are two points to be drawn from considering capture errors in terms of cospecification. First, the specification of self by externally available information is likely to be ambiguous, requiring additional support from memory or other sources to maintain goal-directed action. Egolocative processing that is not needed for momentary control may be necessary if the current action is to fit appropriately into a larger-scale plan. This is presumably Norman's (1981) point in arguing that the performance of action sequences may be largely autonomous, "without further need for intervention except at critical choice points" (p. 4). At these "critical choice points," however, what will be critical is that appropriate self-specific information be available, supported by memory or perhaps by the "endlessly repeated biological state" discussed by Damasio (1994, p. 238; also see chapter 6).

Second, this discussion points to a general principle of cognitive control elaborated in the next chapter. That is, cognitive control is achieved at least in part by temporal synchrony of considered information rather than by explicitly tagging information with its role in mental processes. Given that an activity is underway, the availability of corresponding information at the right point in time is sufficient to sustain the activity. In some cases, certain activities may be more or less continually underway. For example, routines for reading (or language processing generally) might be continually active for literate adults. That is, if text is available, we will read it, resulting in phenomena such as Stroop interference (MacLeod, 1991).

Placekeeping Errors and Real-Time Control

Placekeeping errors are a special (and experimentally tractable) case of action slips that show the real-time basis of conscious control. Norman (1981) identified two kinds of placekeeping errors in everyday routines, omissions (skipping steps) and repetitions (repeating already performed steps). For example, in making coffee, one might fail to grind the beans, placing whole beans in the filter basket (an omission). Or, one might fill the basket twice, using twice as much coffee as needed (a repetition). Norman described these errors as resulting when schemas "lose activation as a result of the normal decay and interference properties of primary memory" (p. 9). This account may be correct at the implementation level, but an explanation at the level of experienced cognition is more informative for my purpose. Placekeeping errors like these can be demonstrated in tasks as simple as counting (e.g., Healy & Nairne, 1985). These errors appear to result from confusing intended and completed actions—that is, "Did I already say it, or just plan to say it?" Although on a smaller time scale, this phenomenon parallels failures of *reality monitoring*, in which individuals confuse imagined or intended events with those actually experienced or performed (Johnson, 1988; Johnson & Raye, 1981). This account is supported by Healy and Nairne's finding that counting errors are most likely at steps involving repeated digits (e.g., 66). Presumably these steps provide the greatest opportunity for confusion because of the greater similarity to prior and following steps.

These errors can also be described in terms of cospecification in the arrays of available information. For simple counting (simply producing numbers in order, as opposed to enumerating objects present in the environment), the available information is supported by memory and by perceptual feedback (listening to oneself count). If, as argued in previous chapters, memory representation is performatory, there will be little to distinguish an intended counting step from a repeated one. The acting (here, counting) self can therefore not be reliably distinguished from the environmental consequences of counting, and it will be difficult for egolocative processing to provide a stable reference point for placekeeping.

Alternative Accounts of Action Slips

Norman's approach to action slips can usefully be compared to the account offered by MacKay's (1982, 1987) node structure theory. Norman's (1981) approach emphasizes the environmental support for ongoing activity, and the organization of skill into subroutines. MacKay's approach emphasizes instead the top-down control of activity, providing a rather Freudian account of some action slips. Thinking about a topic is represented in MacKay's theory by the activation of high-level conceptual nodes that prime associated nodes, some of which are directly responsible for the generation of action. When a node not required for an action has nevertheless been primed, it can be inappropriately activated, resulting in an action slip. This allows for so-called "Freudian slips," in which a thought that is suppressed as inappropriate is nevertheless revealed in action. At one level of description, these theories differ largely in emphasis, sharing the central hypothesis that action slips result from complex interactions of information available from various sources.

These differences can be reconciled by considering the role of the self as agent in controlling skilled activity. According to the cospecification hypothesis, the self is specified in the dynamically evolving manifold of available arrays of information. The self can be specified as engaging in some current activity by information from a variety of sources including memory and the environment. Because skilled performance reflects the adaptation of routines to environmental affordances, even "top-down" control depends on specification of self by information available in the environment. Considered in light of the reciprocal cycle of interaction with the environment, the differing emphases of Norman's and MacKay's theories can be seen as reflecting different analytic starting points rather than as fundamental differences in how to account for cognitive control.

THE MINDLESSNESS OF ROUTINE ACTIVITY

I began this chapter by noting the commonplace observation that routine activity may be mindless, apparently performed without conscious control and sometimes without autobiographical memory. One interpretation of such phenomena is that consciousness is no longer involved, and that the mindlessness of such activities should be interpreted literally as indicating that no agency is involved, that we are not present at such performances. Our consideration of highly skilled performance, together with the observation that expert performers must maintain their concentration to perform fluently, suggests a hypothesis about mindlessness that both offers an explanation for these phenomena and is compatible with the experienced cognition framework.

Briefly, the hypothesis is this: *Syntropic* (literally, "turning together") evolution of self- and object-specific aspects of the informational manifold minimizes egolocative processing in the course of highly fluent performance. As discussed in earlier chapters, differences in the relative rates of change of self-specific and object-specific information typically provide a basis for egolocative processes. At very high levels of skill, the dynamics of action are closely tuned to the dynamics of information availability; as a consequence, the dynamic discrepancies on which egolocative processes operate are not available. In the remainder of this section, I elaborate these statements.

Conditions for Egolocative Processing

Consider the conditions for egolocative processing that distinguishes self- and object-specific information. As noted in chapter 4, egolocation in the case of visually guided motion is based on motion parallax; that is, on discrepancies between changes in various aspects of the ambient optical array. Egomotion, a ubiquitous feature of visual experience and of goal-directed activity, guarantees that these discrepancies are present in the evolving optic array. The stability of certain features of the environment is of course a condition for such discrepancies—the environment normally holds still while we move about.

In highly skilled performance, selection of informational aspects of the environment is finely tuned to the time course of performance. Perhaps the clearest examples of this can be found in artistic and athletic performance. Expert musicians, figure skaters, and gymnasts all perform complex series of actions with very precise timing closely coordinated with environmental information. Even in perceptual-motor skills for which timing is not a criterion of success—for example, typing—fluent performance depends on temporal coordination, and experts adopt rhythmic routines that presumably support such coordination (e.g., Gentner, 1988). And with practice, control appears to be streamlined in the sense that individuals sample information more sparsely (Pew, 1966), an observation considered at greater length in the next chapter. This sparser sampling of information likely serves to maintain activity with higher-level action identities because fewer alternative activities are compatible with the sampled information.

Syntropic Evolution of the Informational Manifold

Highly skilled performance, then, minimizes the differences in rates of change of the self-specific and object-specific aspects of informational arrays guiding activity. We can therefore describe the evolution of informational arrays as syntropic: Self- and object-specific information change together because action is finely tuned to the temporal characteristics of environmental affordances. As outstanding performers attest, truly syntropic performance over extended episodes—"being as one" with the medium—is a rare and valuable experience. Achieving the level of temporal coordination required for such experiences likely also requires finely tuned shifts among levels of action identities. However, on smaller time scales and for more mundane tasks, I believe such experiences are commonplace, constituting the mindlessness of both expert performance and everyday activity.

13

Practice and Conscious Control of Cognitive Activity

Sometimes it feels as though we can control our minds.
—Wegner & Schneider, 1989, p. 287

Mental processes are often studied in isolation, with little attention paid to how they might work together in complex tasks. The underlying idea is that separate theories of individual processes can be fit together like the pieces of a jigsaw puzzle to describe the working of the entire cognitive system, as if the whole were no more than the sum of its parts. However, significant problems of control and coordination may emerge when the separate processes must work together, and it may not be possible to anticipate these problems by studying the processes in isolation. The whole may be more than the sum of its parts.
—Logan, 1985, pp. 193–194

In short, two things happen with practice: skill becomes better attuned to the affordances of the medium and hence more economical, better coordinated and hence more graceful.
—Neisser, 1992, p. 5

As individuals engaged in our daily activities, we experience ourselves as agents, in control of at least some of our own activity. As cognitive scientists, however, we are often concerned to find causes of behavior that do not involve the self as a conscious agent, because doing so would invoke a mysterious "homunculus" and beg the theoretical questions we set out to answer. This tension between our first-person experience and the third-person point of view adopted for scientific purposes is at the

264

heart of the most difficult question in cognitive theory: How can there be conscious agents who control their own activities?

The experienced cognition framework suggests an answer to this question: A conscious agent is the self informationally specified in the series of mental states that constitute an individual's experienced cognition. Cognitive control is the guidance of action with respect to goals and in coordination with the availability of information from the environment and from memory. The intentional structure of mental states in which goals are instantiated, together with appropriate temporal juxtapositions of mental contents and available information, realizes this control. In these states, the self is cospecified with the objects of experience, inevitably and necessarily embedded in reciprocal interaction with the environment. It is when we reify the self as a thing, detaching it from its informational basis and thinking of it as an original uncaused cause, that the idea of conscious agency becomes mysterious.

In this chapter, I consider the problem of conscious control of skilled activity. A number of authors (e.g., Baars, 1988; Carr, 1979) have suggested that a function of consciousness is the control of activity. Cognitive scientists, and psychologists generally, have of course been concerned with understanding the control of cognitive activity. There is a large literature on the concepts of motivation and self-regulation (e.g., Bandura, 1986; Halisch & Kuhl, 1987; Sorrentino & Higgins, 1986). Reviewing this literature is beyond the scope of my purpose here, in part because researchers working on these concepts have generally not focused on the moment-to-moment control of activity (although some authors have recently tried to bridge this gap; e.g., Kuhl, 1987). My focus here is instead on control at the level of individual mental steps, corresponding to conscious mental states, and how the information-processing structure of those steps allows them to be woven together to make up larger routines. I begin by discussing the issues involved in cognitive control to develop principles for conscious control, then present a model that realizes those principles by describing the temporal dynamics of mental states in which goals are instantiated.

CONTROLLING SKILLED ACTIVITY

The starting point for understanding conscious control of purposive action is not, "What is the ultimate source of our goals?" but, "Given relatively high-level goals, how is activity guided and maintained?" The only kind of scientific answer possible for the first question is evolutionary in character and beyond the scope of this book. The second question, however, can be approached in terms of the experienced cognition framework and existing theoretical resources in cognitive science. Several aspects of cognitive control provide a basis for deriving principles that must be embodied in a theory of conscious control.

Three Aspects of Control

The problem of cognitive control of established routines can be analyzed into three aspects: what to do, when to do it (coordination), and how to monitor performance for placekeeping, accuracy, and other parameters of performance. In addressing each of these aspects, I assume a general view of complex cognitive routines as assemblies of component skills organized by goal structures, as discussed in previous chapters.

Selection of Means. At one level, our previous discussions of goal structures and instantiated goals address the question "what to do?" At a finer grain, it seems clear that even for many established routines, there is a problem of selecting means for realizing component skills. For example, schooled adults can typically apply addition facts (e.g., 5 + 3 = 8) either by memory retrieval or by counting. When presented with running arithmetic problems requiring multiple addition steps, adults often appear to add by retrieval on some steps and by counting on others (Cary & Carlson, 1995). Furthermore, when individuals switch between procedures for realizing the skill of adding, they do so with little apparent loss of fluency and appear to have no experience of deliberately choosing one procedure rather than another.

Several authors have noted this lack of deliberation when individuals choose a means for accomplishing tasks in discrete-trial experiments that require a single response to a display on each trial. In these studies, alternative means for accomplishing the experimental task are often referred to as *strategies*, although that term connotes deliberate choice that need not occur. For example, Siegler (1989) examined children's strategy selection in a simple arithmetic task that required an answer to an arithmetic-fact problem on each trial. The results indicated that children responded appropriately to instructions to emphasize speed or accuracy, but that these instructions did not change the proportion of trials on which they used alternative procedures. Siegler (1988, 1989) developed a model based on the assumption that individual arithmetic problems are associated to varying degrees with alternative strategies, allowing for "mindless" choices among these strategies. Similarly, Reder (1987; Reder & Ritter, 1992; Reder & Schunn, 1995) argued that strategy selection in answering both general knowledge and arithmetic questions is implicit in the sense that subjects do not deliberately consider alternative approaches before choosing one.

These empirical results indicate that the selection of means to achieve instantiated goals must be based on recognition of circumstances rather than more elaborate processes comparing the costs and benefits of various alternatives. However, researchers have often assumed the existence of such elaborate decision processes; as Siegler (1989) noted, "Underlying most research on how children choose strategies is the plausible belief that they consider task demands and available strategies and then rationally choose which strategy to use" (p. 6). In fact, of course, this belief is not plausible if we take experienced cognition seriously: Individuals very often seem to have no experience of such deliberation in fluent performances. This is true both for mental activities such as arithmetic and for perceptual–motor activities such as typing—for example, consider the various ways of reaching for a particular key on a keyboard (Gentner, 1988).

Intuition and laboratory results thus agree in suggesting that selection of means for achieving subgoals in routine performance cannot be deliberate, in the sense that options are consciously considered. There is also a metatheoretical basis for this conclusion: The information-processing framework requires that at some level of analysis, there is no consideration of alternatives at all, but rather a mechanical process that results in a particular procedure being executed. The GOER model discussed later suggests that conscious control of a particular step in a cognitive activity comprises instantiating a goal that provides a procedural frame for considering operands, allowing a procedure to be evoked.

Coordination. Coordinating basic actions or component skills with one another and with the availability of information from the environment and from memory has received little attention from cognitive psychologists (Logan, 1985). It seems beyond doubt, however, that such coordination must be accomplished somehow if our activity is to be adaptive. Bringing mental contents and available information together temporally appears to be critical for cognitive performance, and a wide variety of research can be interpreted as support for this principle. On a large time scale, it seems obvious that temporal juxtaposition is necessary for cognitive activity. For example, if the intention to deliver a (spoken) message to someone is to be effective, both the intention and the message must come to mind when the individual is present. On a smaller time scale—on the order of tenths of a second—something similar is true. For example, Carlson, Shin, and Wenger (1994) demonstrated that in a running arithmetic task, subjects adjusted the pace of their performance to 800-millisecond differences in the delay between a keypress request for an operand and its brief display. They also showed that learning in a serial reaction time task (Nissen & Bullemer, 1987) was expressed in the fluency of performance when the response-to-stimulus interval was constant but not when it varied randomly, a finding that has since been replicated (Marks & Cermak, 1995; Willingham, Greenberg, & Thomas, 1995). These findings in cognitive tasks echo long-standing results in motor learning demonstrating the tuning of movements to temporal features of the environment (see Rosenbaum, 1991, for a review). Temporal juxtaposition of mental contents at a relatively fine-grained time scale is thus also essential in supporting fluent cognitive activity. Neisser (1992), in fact, suggested that finer coordination may be largely responsible for the effects of practice on symbolic skills, "Improvements will appear in all symbolic skills. Shall we explain them only as a result of better timing? The possibility cannot be ignored; coordination is important for symbolic skill" (p. 9).

The literature on motor learning contains a number of theoretical suggestions concerning the temporal control of action (Rosenbaum, 1991). It seems likely that similar mechanisms are involved in controlling the timing of mental activity, especially given the performatory character of cognition, as described in earlier chapters. Some evidence for the hypothesis of common timing mechanisms for symbolic and perceptual-motor skills is available. Burgess and Hitch (1992; Hitch, Burgess, Shapiro, Culpin, & Malloch, 1995) have presented evidence that timing is critical in working memory performance (also see Jones, 1993). In general, the available hypotheses about timing are concerned with possible sources of timing information (e.g., internal clocks or emergent properties of dynamic systems), and with how this information is propagated through a system. For example, in his Node Structure Theory, MacKay (1982) assumed a set of autonomous timing nodes that provide signals at regular intervals. The effects of these signals then propagate through the activation of primed nodes, yielding activity. In contrast, Rumelhart and Norman (1982) developed a simulation model of skilled typing in which timing emerges from patterns of activation and inhibition of schemas that generate keystrokes. Activity is again generated by activation, but control of timing is implicit in the organization of schemas. These accounts thus address the sources of timing information and constraints on coordination; however, they do not address the roles that conscious control might play in such coordination. According to the analysis next developed, goal instantiation may directly establish a temporal reference point, or skilled performance of a temporally organized activity may serve to control the timing of a second activity.

Monitoring. Individuals are able to monitor their performances according to a number of criteria. A wide variety of evidence demonstrates that for many mental and perceptual-motor tasks, individuals can deliberately choose tradeoffs between speed and accuracy. We know from research in a number of domains that individuals can and do monitor the accuracy or effectiveness of their performances. Norman (1981) noted that many action errors are detected very quickly, often while the action is still underway. In speech production, some errors are detected within 100 milliseconds (MacKay, 1987) or less (Blackmer & Mitton, 1991). Skilled readers monitor their comprehension of text as they read, sometimes engaging in repair strategies such as rereading (Baker, 1989). In the domain of complex problem solving, Carlson et al. (1990) demonstrated that learners adjusted their performance to a goal stated in terms of simulated cost. Subjects' reports in this study indicated that they deliberately adjusted their choice of actions on the basis of monitoring this cost.

These studies and a large number of others indicate that skilled performance involves both generating activity and monitoring its consequences on a variety of bases. A review of this literature is beyond the scope of this chapter, but two points are especially important for my purpose here. First, with increasing skill, performance monitoring may become implicit in the sense discussed in chapter 12—expert performers may have skills for responding to disruptions of fluent ongoing activity without constantly employing deliberate checking or verification strategies (e.g., Forlizzi, 1988). Monitoring in this sense corresponds to a definition of control in terms of maintaining an activity in the face of disturbance (Marken, 1986). As discussed in chapter 12, experts have repertoires of actions specified at multiple levels of description, allowing them to cope with such disturbances. For example, lower levels of description may provide mental contents that allow finer-grained control of the pace of an activity, such as reading word-by-word when comprehension fails. Second, monitoring may be based on the consequences or performatory characteristics of an activity, which may be imperfectly correlated with goal parameters. For example, Cary and Carlson (1995) studied the private speech involved in performing a running arithmetic task. In this multiple-step task, subjects add a series of digits to obtain an overall sum. In our study, participants responded to instructions to emphasize speed rather than accuracy with small declines in solution time but large increases in the rate of private speech. This result suggests that individuals monitored the rate of overt activity rather than solution time as such.

Another aspect of monitoring illustrated by the Cary and Carlson study is *placekeeping*. Placekeeping refers to monitoring the completion of actions in multiple-step routines—for example, which objects have been counted, which numbers have been added, or which forms have been processed. Placekeeping depends on working memory and requires distinguishing between intentions-in-action and symbolic contents of instantiated goals that have not yet produced overt actions. As anyone who has been interrupted while counting objects can testify, placekeeping can be demanding and error-prone.

Monitoring fluent cognitive activity thus depends on the informational consequences of our actions, both environmental effects and performatory characteristics of those actions. However, fluency entails minimizing the explicit consideration of these consequences, at least while our activity is proceeding smoothly.

Principles of Cognitive Control

Four principles of cognitive control can be derived from these observations and theoretical considerations discussed in earlier chapters. These principles are:

1. The *goal instantiation* principle: Cognitive control depends on current, instantiated goals whose contents specify outcomes to be achieved by one's own action (chapter 9); and

2. The *juxtaposition* principle: Cognitive activity results from the juxtaposition (or synchronous activation) of mental state contents and available information (chapter 7).

These principles follow from the basic picture of cognitive activity presented in Parts I and II of this book, and are essentially consistent with the picture presented by the ACT family of theories (J. R. Anderson, 1983, 1993). As in the ACT production system approach, these principles suggest that each step in a cognitive activity involves performing a basic action on the basis of a current goal and the match between mental contents and available information. The reciprocal interaction of agent and environment is thus reflected at each step in a goal-directed episode.

Two additional principles follow from considerations of how cognitive activity changes with practice (chapter 3) and how we experience our activity in everyday and expert performance (chapter 12):

3. The *minimal deliberation* principle: Cognitive control by instantiated goals involves minimal deliberation or planning, at least for routine activities; and

4. The *minimal control* principle: Fluency is achieved by minimizing the amount of explicit information involved in the cognitive control of activity.

In both cases, *minimal* refers to the representation of information as contents of conscious mental states. And by *explicit*, I mean information that directly specifies parameters to be controlled. These principles should be reflected in the information-processing structure of individual steps, and their realization will depend on noncontent properties of the mental states realizing those steps. These four principles are of course interrelated. For example, Minsky (1986) argued that temporal synchrony is important to allow processes to interact without specific command messages. The juxtaposition principle is thus connected with the minimal control principle.

The distinction between content and noncontent properties of mental states is important for understanding these principles. The contents of a series of mental states that make up an episode of activity reflect the argument and goal structures involved in organizing the activity, and the objects toward which actions are directed. However, other aspects of control depend on noncontent properties of those states. For example, the duration of a particular state may be critical for coordination, and the reliability with which one content evokes another may be critical in supporting fluent performance.

One way to understand the realization of these principles in conscious control is to consider the temporal dynamics of the conscious mental states that realize instantiated goals. These states serve two functions that can be described in temporal terms: providing here-and-now referents for the organization of activity, and juxtaposing mental contents to provide the informational links that allow mechanisms of control to operate. Understanding these functions requires that we consider the time scale of experienced cognition.

THE TEMPORAL SCALE OF EXPERIENCED COGNITION

"Quite different things happen at different time scales" (Newell, 1990, p. 153).

One of the major advantages of the information-processing perspective on cognition is its focus on the real-time character of mental activity. Considerations of temporal structure have important implications for cognitive theory. For example, Newell (1990) developed an analysis of constraints on human cognitive architecture on the basis of temporal considerations, such as the approximately 10 milliseconds required for the activation of neural circuits and the observation that genuinely cognitive behavior occurs at least within one second. Considering the time frame of conscious mental states provides a basis for understanding their role in the control of cognitive activity.

The Serial Nature of Experienced Cognition

A starting point for considering the temporal structure of experienced cognition is the observation that conscious experience is serial—one conscious mental state follows another, and our experience can be characterized as a "stream of consciousness" (James, 1890). It is difficult, if not impossible, to imagine an individual whose experience was not serial (although some science fiction authors have tried). As James also noted, conscious experience seems to be unitary, in the sense that a stream of consciousness constitutes the experience of a single individual.

The experienced cognition framework suggests a kind of explanation for this serial and unitary character of conscious experience: Conscious experience is grounded in perceptually guided activity in an environment. As an individual moves about and acts in an environment, information available to the perceptual systems specifies a point of view sequentially occupying a series of locations. This perceptual grounding, together with continuously available information specifying the state of the body (Damasio, 1994), supports the experienced unity of consciousness (see chapters 4 and 6). According to this view, the serial and unitary nature of conscious experience is a fundamental consequence of the embodied and situated character of the mind. This account contrasts sharply with Dennett's (1991) view that, "Human consciousness . . . can best be understood as the operation of a *'von Neumannesque'* virtual machine *implemented* in the *parallel architecture* of a brain that was not designed for any such activities" (p. 210). In Dennett's view, then, the serial character of conscious experience results from the operation of culturally transmitted *memes* (roughly speaking, "ideas"). Presumably, this implies that nonhuman species generally do not have serial streams of experience. In contrast, the experienced cognition framework implies that in many respects, any organism that moves around its environment on the basis of distal senses such as vision will have a stream of perceptual-enactive experience much as humans do.

The serial character of experienced cognition should not be taken as implying that the here-and-now defined by individual conscious states is either spatially or temporally punctate. Dennett and Kinsbourne (1992; Dennett, 1991) argued convincingly that at a sufficiently fine temporal grain (not explicitly specified, but at approximately the scale of tens of milliseconds), questions about the sequencing of experienced contents may not be well-formed. The conscious mental states that make up experienced cognition constitute a series of mental moments of relatively brief duration, and there is some basis for speculating on just how brief.

The Time Scale of Conscious States

A variety of evidence suggests that the duration of conscious mental states—or, conversely, the time scale of events with respect to which the experiencing self can be specified—ranges from roughly 30 milliseconds to 3 seconds. For those not used to thinking about time at this scale, 200 milliseconds (one fifth of a second) is about the time required to utter a single syllable (hence the familiar one thousand and one count to measure a second). Pöppel (1988) drew together a variety of evidence supporting this estimated range of mental-state durations. At the lower end of this range, the estimate is based on the shortest intervals at which individuals can identify two environmental events as separate, ordered occurrences. At the upper end, 2.5 to 3 seconds is approximately the limit over which we can impose subjective structure on a steady auditory beat, or the longest typical phrase in speech or music (atypical longer units sometimes occur, but generally for special effect). Pöppel also cited behavioral and neurophysiological evidence suggesting that mental states of longer duration are composed of quanta of approximately 30 to 40 milliseconds.

The central point here is that experienced mental states, like other events, are not instantaneous. The experienced now is not a knife-edge separating past and future; as Pöppel (1988) noted:

> To regard the present only as a boundary between past and future is a theory that fails to correspond to our experience. A person uncontaminated by theory would never hit upon the idea of denying the reality of the present. Our experiences happen *now*, not in some theoretical hodgepodge of past and future. (p. 52)

He went on to note that:

> The *now*, the subjective present, is nothing independently; rather, it is an attribute of the content of consciousness. Every object of consciousness is necessarily always *now*—hence, the feeling of *nowness*. But *now* is not itself the content of consciousness: it must be that we make it such in retrospect. (p. 63)

And that, "The temporal machinery of our brain is not primarily in place to make time available to us, but to assure the orderly functioning of our experience and behavior" (p. 63). As Pöppel argued, the experience of time as such is secondary to the role of consciousness in defining a *now* referent for organizing activity (also see Michon, 1990). As discussed in chapters 4 through 7, duration is a noncontent, nonintentional property of mental states. To consider how consciousness relates to the time course of other events in the brain and in the environment, we return briefly to the Cartesian Theater.

The Cartesian Theater Revisited

As cognitive scientists, we generally adopt an external, "third-person" view of our subjects, a view that some have argued cannot be reconciled with the first-person perspective of consciousness (Velmans, 1991; Watson, 1930). One aspect of this external point of view is the availability of devices for controlling and measuring the timing of environmental events and subjects' actions. For example, many if not most experiments in cognitive psychology now rely on computers to precisely control the onset of displays (containing stimuli) that constitute the environmental information of interest. Often the time that elapses between the onset of a display and a subject's response (such as a keypress), measured to the nearest millisecond, is an important dependent variable, the outcome of the experiment. The differences in response time between experimental conditions that serve as the basis for theoretical conclusions are sometimes as small as 10 milliseconds or less, much shorter than the estimated minimum times for conscious mental states. Given this generalized experimental paradigm, the goal of information-processing theories is to provide a story that accounts for this time, and the differences in time produced by experimental manipulations. As Massaro and Cowan (1993) put it, "The basic notion of IP is that one must trace the progression of information through the system from stimuli to responses" (p. 386), and "Each of the hypothesized underlying mechanisms of psychological processing can be associated with a separate segment of time between a stimulus and the response to that stimulus" (p. 386).

As Dennett (1991; Dennett & Kinsbourne, 1992; also see chapter 2) pointed out, this approach suggests that if consciousness is involved at all, it must happen somewhere in between stimulus and response. This temporal center is often theoretically associated with a spatial center, which Dennett disparagingly called the Cartesian Theater. But the time scale of conscious mental states relative to many experimentally identified phenomena seems not to allow for this. For example, Dennett and Kinsbourne (1992) discussed the color phi phenomenon: When two nearby lights are alternately illuminated at the appropriate pace, observers have the perceptual experience of a single light moving back and forth. If the lights are of different colors, the perceived moving light appears to change color midstream as it moves back and forth. This implies that the light is "seen" to change color before the information specifying the color change is available, indicating that conscious experience must, at minimum, span several cycles of alternation. In general, it seems that many information processes in the brain occur in parallel, with a variety of time courses, leaving no theoretical room for consciousness to operate online in the course of many cognitive phenomena. A similar line of reasoning underlies a number of arguments that consciousness is epiphenomenal (e.g., Harnad, 1982).

Dennett (1991) argued convincingly that the time course of cognitive processes rules out Cartesian Theater models of consciousness, which are typical of information-processing habits of thought. His analysis did establish that the intuition that consciousness happens at some particular time and place between stimulus and response is misleading with respect to the role of consciousness in cognitive theory. However, his argument is framed largely within the linear-flow, stimulus-to-response conception of cognition criticized in chapter 2, and it is not clear exactly how it would generalize to a more ecological, reciprocal view of individuals acting in environments. More important, conscious mental states exist at an intermediate time scale, larger in scope than the neural band and smaller than the social band identified by Newell (1990). Conscious control therefore occurs at the scale of individual steps defined by mental state contents, and the coordination of those steps with one another.

The durations of conscious mental states constrain the possibilities for juxtaposing contents, a constraint sometimes discussed in terms of working memory and chunk size (e.g., J. R. Anderson, 1983, 1993). Less often discussed is the structure of control within mental states, the information-processing dynamics of individual mental steps (but see J. R. Anderson, 1993). The experienced cognition framework suggests that this information-processing structure be understood in terms of the intentional structure discussed in earlier chapters. We therefore turn next to considering the dynamics of the skills that constitute these steps, asking how their structure allows them to serve as components of larger-scale episodes of cognitive activity.

THE DYNAMICS OF COMPONENT SKILLS: THE GOER MODEL

I argued (in chapters 3, 9, and 10) that mental activities can be characterized in terms of hierarchical goal structures that constitute coordinative modes for organizing component skills. An important feature of many such activities is that the steps realized by component skills are cascaded, in the sense that the result of one step may serve as an input or operand for a subsequent step. Because the representation of results is performatory (e.g., by private speech) and thus both temporally located and limited in duration, fluent performance of multiple-step routines requires temporal coordination of component skills. This coordination in turn depends on the dynamic structure of component skills, how individual mental steps are temporally organized.

Behaviorist theory emphasized stimulus–response relations as the basis for understanding the control of activity (Hilgard & Bower, 1966). For example, Razran (1971) developed a very elaborate account of the control of behavior and cognition, based on the Soviet view of the (Pavlovian) conditioned reflex as the unit of both mental and perceptual-motor activity. Accounts of automatic processes in cognition (Shiffrin & Dumais, 1981) often have reflected a similar view of control by stimuli. For example, after some kinds of consistent practice, particular stimuli are said to automatically attract attention (e.g., Schneider & Shiffrin, 1977). In Stroop interference, subjects are unable to avoid reading words centrally located in the visual field, despite instructions to ignore the words and instead name the colors in which they are printed (MacLeod, 1991). Reading, like some other mental processes, is therefore sometimes said to be autonomous: beginning without intention, and continuing to completion without conscious control (Logan, 1985; Zbrodoff & Logan, 1986). Similarly, memory retrieval sometimes appears to be an automatic, nonconscious and unintended consequence of exposure to retrieval cues (e.g., Jacoby & Witherspoon, 1982).

More recently, a number of authors have argued that automaticity is conditional (Bargh, 1989), in the sense that automatic processes are evoked in the context of intended, goal-directed activity (Jacoby, Ste-Marie, & Toth, 1993; Logan, 1989). Most psychologists would now accept, as Shiffrin and Schneider (1977) noted, that cognitive activities generally involve a mixture of automatic and controlled components. With the exception of Schneider and Detweiler's (1987, 1988) connectionist/control model, most theories of automaticity have not explicitly addressed issues of how automatic processes are coordinated.

As Bargh (1994) noted, researchers at one time seemed to agree that automatic processes are characterized by a conjunction of properties including unintended initiation, lack of awareness, and uncontrollability. But we can clearly distinguish among these hypothesized properties. Of particular importance for my purposes is the distinction between the hypothesis that component skills are autonomous and the hypothesis that they may be completed ballistically. As defined by Logan (1985), an autonomous process is defined by the combination of two characteristics: It is initiated without intention and proceeds to completion without control (e.g., without the possibility of inhibition). A ballistic activity, however, is one that is initiated by intention, but can then continue to completion without guidance. The research reviewed later this chapter suggests that in order to be effectively used as components of higher level tasks, skills must be structured so that they can be initiated intentionally (by goal instantiation), but can be completed ballistically in this sense. Note, however, this does not imply that the activity cannot be guided, only that it need not be.

One characteristic of novice performance of many tasks is that it is very deliberate, depending on establishing explicit correspondences between symbolic, declarative information and information available in the task environment (chapters 2, 10). The instantiation of goals initially depends on mental processes characterized by an argument structure: The intention to act is a conclusion that follows from beliefs about action-consequence contingencies and desires concerning the values of those consequences (Dulany, 1968). With practice, the instantiation of goals becomes procedural rather than deliberate in this sense.

To serve as components of multiple-step routines, component skills for individual steps must be realized as procedural frames. The notion of a procedural frame provides a way of addressing the information-processing implications of mental states with intentional structure (chapters 4 and 5). In research on perception and spatial cognition, adopting a visual perspective or point of view is often said to provide a reference frame for considering spatial relations (e.g., Feldman, 1985; Pick & Lockman, 1981). The procedural frame idea is the same: An instantiated goal or intention provides a point of view from which physical or symbolic objects are considered as operands to be manipulated by an operator corresponding to the instantiated goal (cf. Newell, 1990, discussed in chapter 9). Arithmetic provides a prototype example of this structure: The intention to add (for example) specifies a procedural frame in which particular numbers are considered as operands. The content of the mental state thus juxtaposes these operands, represented under their aspects as numbers to be added. The cospecification hypothesis developed in previous chapters suggests that a similar account can be given for other kinds of procedures, such as those involved in egomotion or the manipulation of mental images. For example, adopting a point of view or orientation— paralleling the instantiation of a goal—is a prerequisite for both egomotion (Lee, 1976; Owen, 1990) and laboratory imagery tasks (Finke & Shepard, 1986).

Several lines of evidence from my laboratory support the procedural frame hypothesis in the domain of arithmetic routines. The benefit of a consistent sequence of operators even when operands vary from trial to trial (Carlson & Lundy, 1992; Lundy et al., 1994) suggests that individuals can instantiate goals to apply those operators in advance of information specifying the operands. Carlson and Shin (1996) demonstrated that the opportunity to preview symbols specifying upcoming operators was critical to obtaining the random-practice benefit previously discussed, again suggesting that individuals instantiate goals in anticipation of the avail-ability of operands. The ability to adapt to fairly fine-grained temporal constraints on the availability of operands in cascaded tasks (Carlson, Shin, & Wenger, 1994, discussed earlier) suggests that procedural knowl-edge and temporal coordination are adapted to the time course of arith-metic component skills. This study demonstrated that individuals can apparently time the initiation of arithmetic operations in anticipation of the availability of results, requesting (by keypress) a next operand in anticipation of completing a current step.

In a series of studies, Sohn and I (Carlson & Sohn, 1995; Sohn & Carlson, 1996) addressed the question of internal structure directly, for both Boolean rules learned in the laboratory and previously learned skills for applying arithmetic facts. In these experiments, subjects answered simple problems involving a single operator on each trial, similar to many studies of simple arithmetic (Ashcraft, 1992). The important manipulation was the order in which information was presented: operator symbol first, operands first, or both simultaneously. In the serial-presentation condi-tions, we used several values of SOA (stimulus onset asynchrony, the time between the appearance of one display element and the next), most often 300 milliseconds. The central result was that across experiments, operation types, and other variations in conditions, presenting the opera-tor symbols first provided a greater head start than did presenting oper-ands first. This result supports the procedural frame hypothesis, demon-strating that the opportunity to instantiate the goal first allows the most fluent performance. It allows us to reject several alternative hypotheses, such as a configural cue view that suggests that the problem as a whole (operator plus operand symbols) serves to initiate retrieval of a result from memory. More important, the results support a specific model of the mental states that realize these component skills of arithmetic.

The GOER Model

The GOER—Goal instantiation, Operand processing, Execution, and Re-sult availability—model, introduced briefly in chapter 9, summarizes an information-processing analysis of the dynamics of a class of mental intentions-in-action (chapter 4). We developed this model to illustrate the procedural frame hypothesis for the case of calculation skills, in which each step realizes the application of an arithmetic fact. The model, de-picted schematically in Fig. 13.1, represents the procedural frame hypothe-sis discussed previously, indicating that the performance of a component skill begins with goal instantiation that provides a framework for proc-essing an operand or operands. Considering operands in the context of the instantiated goal initiates an execution process, presumably retrieval

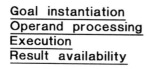

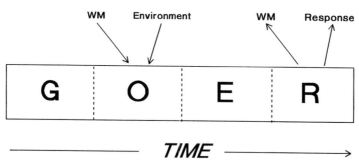

FIG. 13.1. The GOER model: The figure depicts the basic assumptions of the GOER model of calculation steps. Goal instantiation provides a perspective from which operands are considered. The relation of this model to the intentional structure of mental states is discussed in the text.

from memory in the case of arithmetic facts. This execution process culminates in the availability of a result, given performatory representation, for example by private or overt speech. The result may serve to guide an instructed response (e.g., giving the answer to a problem), or as an operand for a subsequent step. The dashed lines between stages are meant to indicate that the temporal boundaries between stages need not be sharp. The stages might be cascaded in the sense suggested by McClelland (1979), for example with execution beginning as operands are still being considered.

The GOER model represents several related hypotheses concerning the conscious mental states involved in skilled performance. First, the model is meant to represent the dynamics of an intention in action, as described in chapters 4 and 5. Goal instantiation is how the self is specified, as discussed in chapter 9, reflecting the psychological mode *intend*. The operands considered from the point of view specified by the instantiated goal constitute the objects the state is about. Using Piagetian terminology, one might also say that operands are assimilated to a scheme for realizing the goal. The mode of the mental state is of course *intend*, and the content is (for example) *that I obtain the sum of these operands by adding*. Note that in this example, the specification of operands is deictic ("*these* operands"), and the conditions of satisfaction include the result of performing the specified operation.

Second, the model is meant to represent a hypothesis about the relation between conscious and nonconscious aspects of skilled performance. Goal instantiation and operand processing represent the conscious mental state realizing component skill performance, whereas execution represents activity of nonconscious information systems and need contribute no experienced (phenomenal) content. This component of the mental step might thus be regarded as ballistic, in the sense previously discussed. Furthermore, the model suggests that the selection of means is a process of performatory retrieval, realized by nonconscious information processes that operate on dispositional representations cued by the combination of goal and operands (Sohn & Carlson, 1996).

Third, the consequence or outcome of the component skill is a performatory representation of a result, perhaps an item placed in working memory by private speech. This result contributes to the informational array available to subsequent mental states in the temporal limits of whatever processes support working memory for the result.

The GOER model embodies few if any unique theoretical claims in an information-processing sense. For example, the claim that component skills that constitute individual steps of mental activity have a goal-operand structure and an execution phase realized by nonconscious processes is consistent with J. R. Anderson's (1983, 1993; chapter 12) ACT theories. In the most recent version of ACT (ACT-R), J. R. Anderson (1993) described a scheme for sequential matching of chunks in the condition of a production that suggests a dynamic structure similar to that represented by the GOER model. Similarly, Logan (1988, 1990) described the remembered instances that support skilled performance as including goals, stimulus interpretations with respect to those goals, and answers. The goal-operand structure of component skills suggested by these theories and by the GOER model seems necessary to tie component skills into extended hierarchical goal structures, and this is of course the motivation for J. R. Anderson's (1983) use of goals in his production-system theory. However, to my knowledge neither theory has been developed to account for individuals' apparent ability to overlap and temporally tune the execution of steps within fluent cognitive sequences, as discussed in the next section.

CONTROL OF EXTENDED EPISODES

Control of extended episodes involves hierarchical goal structures, as discussed in chapter 9. Controlling established routines on the basis of these goal structures involves initiating component skills and coordinating their execution with one another and with information available from the environment. In this section, the GOER model is applied to understanding how this is accomplished.

Goal Structures and Routines

A variety of evidence points to the need for a schema-like concept to account for the control of at least some cognitive activities. In my own lab, for example, we have shown that subjects can learn consistent sequences of mathematical operators (Carlson & Lundy, 1992; Lundy et al., 1994), consistent goal structures even when operator sequences vary (Wenger & Carlson, 1996), and consistent patterns for coordinating the production of two lists of digits (Wenger & Carlson, 1995). Each of these demonstrations suggests that individuals acquire abstract procedural knowledge of a sequence of mental steps—abstract, because the steps themselves vary in several ways. As a general account of control, however, schema approaches have several limitations. They de-emphasize environmental support and the self-organization provided by coordinative structures (Newell, 1991). Furthermore, such approaches do not provide an account of conscious control in the sense of showing how the self can function as an agent. Instead, there is often an implicit or explicit assumption of an agent outside the theory. However, we can understand schemas as dispositional representations (chapter 7) whose cognitive reality is as patterns in the series of mental states constituting episodes of skilled performance. In each of these states, an acting self is cospecified with environmental and memorial objects. At each step, it is the egolocative processes involved in goal instantiation that constitute conscious control (chapter 9).

As already discussed, a variety of evidence from my laboratory suggests that individuals can—with practice—achieve fluency in mental activities such as arithmetic routines by overlapping steps. The basic idea is that instantiating multiple goals (or subgoals) is necessarily serial, just as visual specification of the self in motion is constrained to a serially traversed viewpath. This hypothesis follows from the cospecification hypothesis developed in earlier chapters, together with the assertion that the structure of perceptual-enactive awareness grounds the structure of other (e.g., symbolic) forms of awareness. However, because the execution phase of component skill performance does not itself involve cospecification, the goal for a next step can be instantiated during the execution phase of the current step. This idea is depicted in Fig. 13.2. We can understand this idea by considering in more detail the experiments reported in Carlson et al. (1994). Subjects in these experiments performed running arithmetic tasks presented in a computer display like that shown in Fig. 13.3. At each of 12 steps per trial, a number appears in a box labeled with an operation. *Add* and *Subtract* are self-explanatory; *min* indicates that subjects should retain the smaller of the current total or the displayed number, and *max* indicates the converse. The assignment of

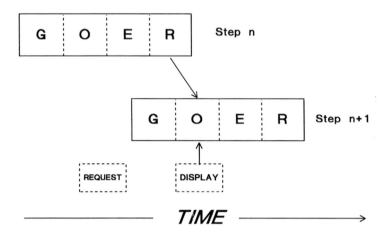

FIG. 13.2. Temporal coordination of GOER steps: According to the GOER model, individuals achieve fluent performance by overlapping calculation steps. Goal instantiation for step $n + 1$ can begin during the ballistic execution phase of step n. The most fluent performance is achieved when the result of step n is available just as the goal for step $n + 1$ is instantiated and a new operand is picked up from the display.

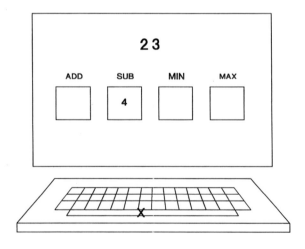

FIG. 13.3. Running arithmetic task: This figure illustrates the running arithmetic task performed by subjects in the study by Carlson, Shin, and Wenger (1994). At each step, subjects modified a running total on the basis of the screen display. For example, given the display shown in the figure, the subject would subtract 4 from the starting value of 23, for a new running total of 19 (see text for details).

operations to screen locations was fixed. The task was self-paced, and subjects moved through the trials by pressing the space bar to request the next number. At each step, an asterisk precedes the number display by 300 milliseconds to ensure that subjects shift attention to the appropriate location. The number itself is displayed for 300 milliseconds, then erased. At the end of 12 steps, the subject is prompted to enter the final result using the computer's numeric keypad.

For present purpose, the important manipulation is the delay between each keypress request and the appearance of the next asterisk–number sequence. For some subjects, this delay was 200 milliseconds, whereas for others it was 1 second. At the beginning of practice, the average latency for requests (measured from the appearance of a number to the keypress requesting the next number) was the same for both groups. This unsurprising result suggests that individuals performed the calculation for each step, verified that they had obtained a result, then requested the next operand. With practice, however, this pattern changed—individuals practicing with the long delays began to respond sooner than those practicing with short delays. This result suggests that subjects learned to anticipate when they would be ready for the next operand, including the time required for instantiating the appropriate goal based on which displayed box was indicated. Presumably, according to the juxtaposition principle and standard assumptions concerning activation, this would be in close temporal proximity to the availability of the result from the previous step.

I have previously discussed other evidence for the GOER model. Although more theoretical development and empirical work is required to test and extend the model, the points I want to make here are fairly straightforward. As presented here, the GOER model illustrates two theoretical points: (a) the mapping of the goal-operand structure of component skills assumed in other theories to the intentional structure of mental states described by the experienced cognition framework; and (b) one kind of change in control (and thus experience) as skill is acquired—temporal coordination and tuning of multiple steps of mental activity. Put another way, the model suggests how the goal instantiation, juxtaposition, and minimal deliberation principles outlined at the beginning of the chapter might be realized.

The Here-and-Now: Egolocation and Synchronal Control Strategies

The observations and theoretical considerations discussed to this point indicate the importance of temporal coordination in skilled performance and suggest that improvements in this coordination are partly responsible for increased fluency with practice. The GOER model tells us something about how temporal coordination is possible, but little about how it is actually achieved. There are a number of implementation-level theories of timing phenomena in cognitive and action skills, some depending on explicit (i.e., clock-like) timing mechanisms and some suggesting that temporal coordination is an emergent characteristic of the organization of information processes (Elman, 1990; Jones & Boltz, 1989; Keele, 1987; MacKay, 1987; Michon, 1990). Analogously, the experienced cognition framework suggests two ways in which consciousness figures in temporal coordination.

First, goal instantiation may serve as a temporal reference point: The content of an intention-in-action implicitly includes that the action is being performed now, and each conscious mental state of course defines an experienced present. As discussed earlier, this present has a duration of tens or hundreds of milliseconds, providing a window of temporal opportunity for the juxtaposition of mental contents. In reflective problem solving (chapter 10), this temporal reference may be explicit in the content of a metacognitive state: Perhaps if I do x now, y will happen. And the cospecification hypothesis reminds us that we must consider the specification of both self and object, suggesting that "now" can always be construed as "while" or "during" some event that is an object of the mental state. The deliberate problem solving involved in finding coordinative modes that achieve the temporal coordination necessary for particular activities must operate on the basis of such information. For example, participants in the Carlson et al. (1994) study just discussed may have adjusted the timing of their keypresses by reflecting on the time course of events as they performed the arithmetic task.

Often, however, the conscious control of timing seems to be less direct, in that noncontent properties of established skills (and thus of the mental states that realize them) are used to control other performances. These *synchronal control strategies* may be learned by example, by weak-method problem solving, or by direct instruction. In these strategies, the ability to reliably perform one sequence of actions provides a basis for controlling aspects of a second sequence. For example, the use of private speech as a synchronal control strategy was discussed in chapter 8—as when counting to oneself controls the rhythm of a performance such as dancing. In these cases, one might say that the conscious control of timing is emergent from the noncontent properties of the activities in question.

Developing a detailed theory of the various aspects of control discussed here is beyond the scope of this chapter. My point, however, has been to use the GOER model to illustrate how the analysis of intentional structure can contribute to an understanding of conscious agency in cognitive control. In the final section, we turn to understanding some intuitions about conscious control and its limits.

PRACTICE AND THE EXPERIENCE OF CONSCIOUS CONTROL

In the last several chapters, we considered a number of implications of the experienced cognition framework for understanding our experience as conscious agents. In this chapter, we examined conscious control at the level of individual steps of cognitive activity, in order to link the analysis of conscious mental states to the information-processing dynamics involved in control. Cospecification of self and object has been a running theme of these analyses, and we have discussed a number of ways in which experienced cognition changes with increasing skill. In this final section, I consider how the streamlining of control associated with increasing skill affects our experience of conscious agency, and how that experience supports some common intuitions about conscious control.

Streamlining of Control

The minimal control principle I introduced suggests that fluency is achieved in part by minimizing the explicit representation of parameters to be controlled. One way to understand this streamlining is by considering the role of feedback, the informational consequences of our actions. For example, Pew's (1966) study of the use of feedback in tracking tasks provides one demonstration of the streamlining of control. In difficult visual-manual tracking tasks, novices continuously monitor the available visual feedback. With practice, skilled trackers monitor feedback less frequently. Furthermore, they appear to shift to prospective modes of control, anticipating what movements will be necessary to achieve acceptable performance. This shift with practice to sparser sampling of available information, and to selecting prospective (i.e., future-specific) information, may be a general characteristic of skill development (Flach et al., 1990; E. J. Gibson, 1993; Lee, 1976, 1992; von Hofsten, 1993).

Part of what makes streamlining possible is the greater reliability of skilled actions. A novice driver is likely to be uncertain about the result of pressing the accelerator with a particular pressure, and a novice calculator is likely unsure whether the answer delivered by memory is correct. Underwood (1982) summarized the streamlining of conscious control in this way:

> When we use feedback about the current state of the environment and of ourselves, in order to select between alternative courses of future action, then we have an awareness of performance. As actions become highly skilled, however, we lose awareness of the components of actions, and they appear to become automatized. Feedback is then no longer used to assess

the current state of the environment, probably because we can rely upon output commands without having to check their effects. When we do not need to check on the consequences of our actions or select the next sequence of actions from amongst a set of alternatives, then behaviour is automatized, and we can perform without self-awareness. (p. 111)

In this passage, Underwood captured some of the central ideas I have developed in this chapter: As we acquire skills, we learn to rely on regularities in the environment and the activities of our own nonconscious information systems (e.g., memory) to perform with minimal deliberation and minimal explicit control.

Intuition and the Experience of Skilled Cognition

As syntropic performance is approached with increasing skill, the opportunities for resampling and exploration that support metacognition are changed and reduced (chapter 12). Our experience of skilled cognitive activity often differs from our intuitive explanations of how that activity is controlled because our intuitions derive from relatively unskilled performance. The observation that "thinking too much" interferes with skilled performance is trite but true; adding reflective, metacognitive processes to finely tuned performances disrupts the temporal coordination developed through strategic restructuring, synchronal control strategies, and streamlining of control.

The argument presented in this chapter can be summarized in terms of the four principles previously suggested: An individual controls his or her own skilled activity through instantiating goals to perform basic actions with critical timing that achieves appropriate juxtapositions of mental contents and environmental information, thus allowing action with minimal deliberation and minimal explicit control. To say "an individual controls," however, misleadingly emphasizes one pole of cospecification—it would be equally apt to say that an acting self is specified in the course of goal-directed action toward objects in a medium, characterized as shown. Egolocative processing that distinguishes self from object, in the form of goal instantiation (chapter 9), is the essence of conscious cognitive control. Instantiating a goal both specifies the acting self and initiates critically timed action directed at a (physical or symbolic) object. This is an informational sense of conscious control and agency, quite unlike the Cartesian view that the self is an independent cause of activity. Not only is there no Cartesian theater where phenomenal experience is projected, there is no Cartesian cockpit from which our activities are piloted.

IV

IMPLICATIONS

The experienced cognition framework presented in earlier chapters provides a basis for consciousness-centered cognitive theory that is compatible with the central commitments of current cognitive science. Analyzing the intentional structure of conscious mental states and their relations to the nonconscious processes that support them shows how cognition can be understood as the experience of a conscious agent in reciprocal interaction with the environment. Applying this analysis to skilled cognitive activity provides an approach to a cognitive theory of conscious agency.

In this final section, I consider some implications of the experienced cognition framework. Chapter 14 is concerned with a very compelling idea, the *cognitive unconscious* said to be revealed by much contemporary research and theory. The experienced cognition framework provides a means for understanding the phenomena supporting this idea, clarifying the relations between such phenomena and intuitions about consciousness. In chapter 15, I conclude by discussing the prospects for person-centered cognitive theory that avoids the euphemisms for agency and subjectivity common in cognitive science.

14

*Implicit Cognition and Automaticity:
A Perspective on the Cognitive
Unconscious*

> *Postulating unconscious activity in direct analogy with human conscious processing is by no means specific to this area of research. This view is standard in domains such as cognitive ethology, linguistics, psychoanalysis, formal models in artificial intelligence, and the information-processing approach in cognitive psychology.*
>
> —Perruchet, 1994, p. 829

> *Freud thinks that our unconscious mental states exist both as unconscious and as occurrent intrinsic intentional states even when unconscious.*
>
> —Searle, 1992, p. 168

> *In fact, just about every author who has written about consciousness has made what we might call the* first-person plural presumption: *Whatever mysteries consciousness may hold, we (you, gentle reader, and I) may speak comfortably together about our mutual acquaintances, the things we both find in our streams of consciousness.*
>
> —Dennett, 1991, p. 67

The current surge of interest in the topic of consciousness is, oddly enough, often reflected in empirical and theoretical efforts to establish the existence and theoretical respectability of unconscious mental processes. In my view, much of this work is characterized by vague hypotheses about consciousness and extravagant hypotheses about the cognitive unconscious that stand in the way of theoretical progress on the topic of consciousness.

As recently as 1985, Erdelyi (in a book largely concerned with adducing support from information-processing psychology for a psychodynamic view of the unconscious) wrote, "The modern literature is replete with synonyms such as *automatic, inaccessible,* and *preattentive,* but only rarely does the unconscious itself make an appearance" (p. 59). One might now add the term *implicit* to this list. Research on so-called implicit learning and implicit memory is increasingly popular (e.g., Berry & Dienes, 1993; Reber, 1993; Schachter, 1987), and generally taken as evidence for unconscious cognition. But it is no longer rare for the term *unconscious* to appear, perhaps more often in talks than in formal written contributions. Researchers have published many empirical studies said to demonstrate various unconscious mental processes, and some have proclaimed the so-called cognitive unconscious as a major discovery (e.g., Greenwald, 1992; Kihlstrom, Barnhardt, & Tataryn, 1992; Reber, 1993). In many ways, this research and the surrounding debate recapitulate earlier literatures on subliminal perception and learning (conditioning) without awareness (e.g., Brewer, 1974; Eriksen, 1962).

In my view, many if not most of the empirical demonstrations of supposedly unconscious phenomena are methodologically or theoretically flawed. Few stand up to serious attempts to replicate or to more carefully assess the contents of subjects' awareness and their relation to observed performance (e.g., Carlson & Dulany, 1985; Dulany, Carlson, & Dewey, 1984, 1985; Perruchet, 1994). Although I believe that some real and interesting phenomena are present in recent research on supposedly unconscious phenomena (Carlson, 1994), I also think that this research has generally failed to establish its authors' claims. I discuss the methodological issues in more detail soon.

More important, however, is that the literature contains no clear theory of consciousness that could serve to sharpen hypotheses about what it might mean for something to be unconscious. Instead, authors generally rely on what Dennett (1991) called the first-person plural presumption—that the author and reader share an understanding of what it means to say that something is conscious or unconscious. As a result, demonstrations of rather narrow phenomena are often inappropriately combined and generalized to draw broad conclusions about the scope of unconscious cognition (e.g., Velmans, 1991). The problem, in my view, is that vague or unsupported claims about what is conscious and not—although often based on genuine empirical phenomena and compelling intuitions—interfere with understanding the nature of conscious, experienced cognition and its place in cognitive theory. My major goal in this chapter is to apply the experienced cognition framework to understanding the phenomena and theoretical views underlying claims about the cognitive unconscious.

THE COGNITIVE UNCONSCIOUS

Contemporary claims for the existence of a *cognitive unconscious* (Rozin, 1976) depend on arguments that individuals' activities are influenced or controlled by mental contents that are unconscious in one of several senses. Ordered from most to least radical, these senses include the control or influence of activity by:

1. mental contents that never enter individuals' conscious experience;
2. mental contents that individuals cannot report under particular circumstances;
3. mental contents to which individuals cannot (or do not) attribute causal roles in shaping their activities; and
4. mental contents with unintended consequences for experience or activity.

Each of these senses of unconscious implies a corresponding criterion of consciousness, although these criteria are often left implicit rather than developed in theoretical detail. Identifying these senses of unconscious in terms of mental contents is important because it is that aspect of the claims that makes them both controversial and noteworthy: Restating each claim with *information* substituted for *mental content* results in a statement that I would take to be noncontroversial. For example, neither ecological nor computational accounts of visual perception (chapter 4) suggests that the information specifying objects in the environment itself constitutes the contents of mental states.

A second dimension of variation in claims for the cognitive unconscious is the complexity or sophistication attributed to the unconscious contents, or to processes defined over these contents. For example, researchers have devoted much attention to demonstrations that words displayed briefly, dimly, or outside the spatial focus of attention nevertheless receive semantic analysis—that is, are processed in a manner that evokes knowledge of their meaning. Such processing is often described as sophisticated and complex (Greenwald, 1992). However, other claims for unconscious processes involve (at least arguably) more complex mental contents, such as procedural knowledge of extended sequences (Nissen & Bullemer, 1987) or abstract knowledge of complex rule systems (Lewicki, Czyzewska, & Hoffman, 1987; Reber, 1989).

These experimentally derived senses of unconscious often evoke discussion of more elaborate and less scientific ideas about unconscious mental activity, ranging from the Freudian unconscious (Greenwald, 1992) to popular fears of the power of so-called subliminal advertising or of subliminal messages hidden in popular music. In discussing the status of the cognitive unconscious, it is therefore important to consider the intuitions underlying both experimentally based and popular notions of the unconscious. The experienced cognition framework provides theoretical resources for doing so.

Experimental Evidence for the Cognitive Unconscious

Evidence for the cognitive unconscious is based primarily on three categories of empirical phenomena: *unconscious perception*, *implicit learning*, and *implicit memory*. In each of these categories, a family of experimental paradigms has served as the basis for demonstrating influences on behavior of information that, it is argued, lies outside subjects' awareness.

Claims for unconscious perception are based on evidence that environmental events (e.g., stimulus displays in experiments) that are not consciously experienced nevertheless influence cognitive processes. The environmental events said to be unconscious may be subliminal in the traditional sense that the energy involved (e.g., the brightness of light) is below a threshold for detection, or in an extended sense in which a display would be above this threshold but is masked by other displays (Greenwald, 1992; Holender, 1986). Alternatively, unconscious perception may be said to occur when part of a display that would be sufficient for conscious perception is unattended, usually because it is outside the spatial focus of attention needed for a task that subjects are instructed to perform (e.g., MacKay, 1973). The effects attributed to unconsciously perceived material include priming, disambiguation, and biasing responses to consciously perceived material.

A recent example of research said to demonstrate unconscious perception is an extensive series of studies reported by Greenwald, Klinger, and Schuh (1995). In these studies, subjects saw displays designed to produce *dichoptic masking* by binocular fusion. In this procedure, a word is presented to one eye and a mask (a pattern of lines and shapes) to the other. When the images presented to the two eyes are fused, the word is masked and cannot be identified. The central finding (developed with an elaborate statistical analysis) was that masked words that were informationally related to the instructed task, but that were not consciously experienced, biased subjects' responses to the instructed tasks. For example, the masked word *left* biased subjects to answer "left" for a position-discrimination judgment concerning to which eye a word had been presented. The effects reported were very small but statistically reliable. Greenwald and his colleagues described this result as evidence for subliminal semantic activation, or unconscious cognition.

Claims for implicit learning are usually based on evidence that individuals can learn complex rule-governed materials such as artificial grammars or movement sequences, but cannot report or otherwise explicitly identify the structure of the learned material (Berry & Dienes, 1993; Reber, 1993). For example, Reber and his colleagues (see Reber, 1989, 1993 for reviews) reported a large number of experiments in which subjects learned artificial finite-state grammars that generate letter strings. These experiments typically contrast explicit learning on the basis of deliberate hypothesis testing with implicit learning on the basis of simple exposure or memorization. Learning is demonstrated by the ability to classify new letter strings as grammatical or not. The major results are that subjects in implicit-learning conditions sometimes perform better than those in explicit-learning conditions, and that subjects said to learn implicitly cannot report the rules constituting the grammar. Subjects are thus argued to acquire knowledge of the grammar that is unconscious and abstract (Reber, Allen, & Regan, 1985). More recently, researchers have focused on implicit learning in serial reaction time (SRT) tasks that may require less abstract knowledge. In these tasks, subjects simply respond to a series of characters displayed on a computer screen by pressing keys corresponding to the locations of those characters. Willingham, Nissen, and Bullemer (1989), among others, demonstrated that when a sequence of locations is repeated, subjects respond faster than when nonrepeating random sequences are used. This result demonstrates learning, but subjects find it difficult to report the sequences they have seen and performed. These claims for implicit learning are similar in some respects to earlier arguments based on conditioning views of learning, that classical or instrumental conditioning could occur without subjects' awareness of the contingencies being learned (see Brewer, 1974, for a review). In both literatures, subjects are generally thought to be conscious of the materials to be learned, but not of relational information such as contingencies or rules.

Claims for implicit memory are based on demonstrations that prior experience influences current performance, in the absence of a goal to remember or an experience of recollection (Schachter, 1987). For example, the results of a number of studies show that exposure to words can improve performance on *word fragment completion* (identifying a word on the basis of a few displayed letters), even when standard recall or recognition measures show no memory for the words (Roediger, 1990). Implicit memory is sometimes defined as evidence for an influence of prior experience when the individual cannot make an appropriate attribution to memory as the cause of that influence: "One of the most exciting developments in the last decade has been the discovery of effects on memory and perception that are not accompanied by *awareness of the source of those effects*" (Jacoby et al., 1993, p. 261; italics added). However, the ability to make an appropriate causal attribution is usually assumed to be an index of recollective experience, and it is the absence of recollective experience that is usually taken to define the implicit nature of memory phenomena. Memory is implicit in performances that are not experienced as instances or consequences of remembering.

The Experienced Cognition Perspective

Each of these categories of claims for the cognitive unconscious is at least somewhat controversial. Each has generated a large literature, including challenges to the empirical methodology and theoretical arguments supporting the claims (e.g., Carlson, 1991, 1994; Carlson & Dulany, 1985; Dulany et al., 1984, 1985; Holender, 1986; Perruchet, Gallego, & Savy, 1990; Perruchet & Pacteau, 1990; Shanks & St. John, 1994). However, it seems to me that we are making little progress in resolving these disputes. As I (Carlson, 1994) recently wrote (commenting on Shanks & St. John, 1994):

> I believe the problem is that very compelling intuitions, supported by commonsense observations, lend credence to the notion of implicit learning. In teaching and discussing this literature, I find that sufficiently detailed experimentation and argumentation may silence—but rarely if ever *convince*—students who begin with a belief in unconscious or implicit learning. (p. 400)

And I would extend this comment to literatures on unconscious perception and implicit memory. The prescientific intuitions underlying beliefs about unconscious cognition are very powerful, and I discuss some of the possible bases for these beliefs below.

More fundamentally, I think our lack of progress on this issue reflects the lack of a detailed theory of consciousness: When we say some mental process or mental event is unconscious, just what hypothesis is being rejected? That the process or event can be verbalized? Remembered the next minute or the next day? That awareness is unitary? That the process can be volitionally controlled? And so on.

The experienced cognition framework provides a perspective from which to evaluate claims about the cognitive unconscious. In particular, the cospecification hypothesis suggests that for any phenomenon said to demonstrate unconscious mental processes, we begin by asking (a) how the self is specified during the performance said to indicate implicit cognition (and at both learning and test, in the cases of implicit learning and memory); and (b) what egolocative processing might be likely or necessary, in the circumstances that generate the phenomenon. In contrast, the theories of consciousness implied by most claims for unconscious cognition are less specific and focus on reflective access to particular mental contents.

Implicit Theories of Consciousness

Claims about the unconscious imply particular views of what it means for a process, state, or content to be conscious, but these views are often implicit or vague. The most common operational definition of awareness is reportability outside the context of performance. For example, Reber (e.g., 1989) argued that individuals have unconscious, implicit knowledge of finite state grammars when they can classify symbol strings as grammatical better than chance but cannot verbally describe the rules of the grammar. Although verbal report is the most common criterion of consciousness, other proposed measures also fit this characterization as a report outside the context of performance. For example, Nissen and her colleagues (Nissen & Bullemer, 1987; Willingham, Nissen, & Bullemer, 1989) examined learning of a perceptual-motor sequence. Although subjects demonstrated learning in the sense of faster responding with practice, they performed poorly on a test requiring instructed generation of the next item in a partial sequence.

As discussed in chapter 10, appropriate causal attribution is often taken as criterial for consciousness. With exceptions like the quote from Jacoby et al. (1993) cited earlier, this criterion is seldom made explicit. The idea is that a mental process or state is conscious when we can make a correct causal attribution to its source. For example, the common experience of having a song stuck in the head but being unable to identify its immediate source (perhaps the music piped into the supermarket) is an example of an unconscious mental process in this sense, as are the supposed effects of subliminal advertising.

The implicit theory of consciousness that seems to underlie much of the research discussed in this section is something like this (also see Dulany, 1991, 1996, for careful analyses of the theories implied by these literatures):

> Conscious mental contents are available to guide verbal report, and to serve a variety of other goal-directed functions such as reasoning or the deliberate or instructed transfer of learning. One of these functions is causal attribution concerning the influence of prior mental states on current decisions or judgments. This availability is relatively unlimited by context. Given that a mental content is consciously available, there is no problem in applying it to guide goal-directed activity (i.e., no elaborate theory linking mental contents and performance is needed). Conscious and unconscious processes are supported by separate systems; however, states of the systems may have identical mental contents. Finally, consciousness is usually seen as all-or-none: a given mental content is either conscious or unconscious.

From the perspective of the experienced cognition framework, none of these is an essential characteristic of consciousness.

METATHEORETICAL AND METHODOLOGICAL CONSIDERATIONS

Evaluating claims for unconscious processing requires careful analysis of empirical methods as well as theoretical and metatheoretical assumptions. The central issue is often taken to be the sensitivity with which conscious contents are measured. However, what is measured and how it is measured depends on (often implicit) theories about consciousness and about the relation of particular contents to observed performance. Also, the nature of metatheoretical assumptions and the preferred style of theorizing influence the kind of evidence taken as relevant to questions about conscious and unconscious cognition.

Metatheoretical Motivations

Claims about unconscious processing often seem motivated by metatheoretical concerns rather than by any clear view of what it would mean for a process to be conscious. As discussed in chapter 2, some of the habits of thought of IP psychology imply that there logically must be unconscious processes. This is related to Dennett's critique of the Cartesian Theater view of consciousness, previously discussed. Two points should be noted here: First, the information-processing framework is sometimes interpreted in a way that renders empirical evidence concerning the conscious or unconscious status of particular functions essentially moot because some processes are seen as necessarily unconscious. Second, the nature of presumed unconscious processes—for example, what mental contents are said to be unconscious—depends in this interpretation of IP theory on what is seen as theoretically necessary to explain observed behavior (Jackendoff, 1987).

Some metatheoretical motivations for assuming the existence of unconscious mental processes seem to follow from more general concerns about the status of psychological theories. I previously (Carlson, 1992) discussed several possible motivations for postulating unconscious processes, based on concerns for theoretical realism, methodological rigor, and the contrast of scientific with commonsense understanding. For example, statements that experimental participants were unaware that a particular independent variable was manipulated often primarily support claims for methodological rigor and only secondarily support claims about the unconscious status of some hypothesized process. Dulany (1968) noted that the most powerful factor affecting behavior in most psychological experiments is the instruction to report to the laboratory at a particular time, clearly an effect in some sense of subjects' consciousness of that instruction. However, as good experimentalists we want to attribute the effects observed in our studies to our experimental manipulations rather than to subjects' beliefs. Furthermore, many cognitive scientists have wanted to argue for the psychological reality of mental contents that are not plausibly experienced as contents of conscious mental states (chapter 2).

Black-Box Theorizing

Many cognitive scientists have commented on the black box problem in developing cognitive theory. The idea is that we can publicly observe only inputs or stimuli, and outputs or responses, leaving the mental processes between as theoretical inferences. One consequence of this view (discussed in more detail in chapter 7) is that many cognitive scientists regard the mental representations and processes postulated in cognitive theory as just notation. For example, J. R. Anderson (1990) argued that, "There is no convincing evidence or argument that there is any real level between the biological and the algorithm level" (p. 18). The algorithm level, for J. R. Anderson (1987a) is the level of contents of working memory, that I argued in chapter 12 corresponds at least roughly to the contents of conscious mental states.

The central point about this issue for my purpose here is this: If we do not attribute any ontological status, any real existence, to some descriptions or representations in our theories, it makes little sense to argue whether or not they are unconscious. As Bandura (1986; see chapter 2 and my next argument) noted, theoretical constructs cannot be taken as an authoritative standard for evaluating consciousness. We can, however, ask how the contents of conscious mental states are related to the phenomena we want to explain.

The Content Criterion of Consciousness

Given theoretical realism about the mental contents presumed to be involved in particular cognitive activities, and a theoretical account in which the conscious status of those contents may be an empirical question (rather than a metatheoretical commitment), the assessment of conscious contents becomes a central scientific task. Ericsson and Simon (1983; also see Ericsson & Oliver, 1988) addressed many of the issues involved in obtaining accurate and sensitive measures of experimental subjects' conscious contents. The validity of such measures is often controversial. An even more central, and widely neglected, issue is the relation of particular conscious contents to the performance (e.g., on a test of learning) to be explained.

Carlson and Dulany (1985) proposed a *content criterion* of consciousness for studies of learning without awareness. The idea is quite simple, but rarely applied in research said to demonstrate unconscious learning—we should ask what the content is of subjects' conscious mental states, and how is that content related to the observed performance.

Consider the unconscious abstraction said to result from implicit learning of artificial grammars (e.g., Reber, 1976, 1989, 1993). In these experiments, individuals study letter strings generated by rule sets constituting finite-state grammars. When instructed to simply memorize or observe the strings (as opposed to being instructed to learn the rules of the grammar), subjects can classify new strings as grammatical or ungrammatical with above-chance accuracy (usually 60 to 70% correct, where chance is 50%). However, they can usually not report rules resembling the grammar used to generate the strings. Reber argued that such findings demonstrate implicit learning of the grammars, resulting in unconscious, abstract representations of the grammatical rules. However, the modest level of performance achieved by subjects in these experimental conditions need not require knowledge of the grammars as such. For example, Dulany, Carlson, and Dewey (1984) showed that subjects in this paradigm could identify partial strings serving as rules of the form, "If this feature is present, the string is grammatical." The aggregate validity of these rules (the probability of a correct classification given that the rule is followed) predicted proportion-correct classifications without significant residual. The content of subjects' reported awareness thus predicted the observed behavior, given reasonable assumptions about the process linking awareness and action.

This study is one of many pointing to the importance of experimental subjects' correlated hypotheses—descriptions of task environments and contingencies that do not correspond to, but are correlated with, the descriptions to which researchers compare their subjects' behavior. Remembered instances and fragments may be sufficient to account for subjects' performance in the artificial grammar task, a point discussed at length by Shanks and St. John (1994). No mental representation of the grammar as such is needed to account for the results of many artificial grammar experiments. One might say, as Berry and Dienes (1993) suggested, "that only explicit knowledge is represented at all and that implicit knowledge consists only of a sign or relevant set of signs" (pp. 157–158). The explicit but fragmentary—and conscious—knowledge that subjects acquire in artificial-grammar experiments (Dulany et al., 1984, 1985) implies the regularities embodied in the grammar and imposed on the experimental situation by the researcher's use of the grammar to construct items to be learned or judged.

These methodological and metatheoretical concerns are important, but it is also important not to become mired in debate over whether particular empirical phenomena are conscious or unconscious. A more productive way to read some authors' (e.g., Greenwald, 1992; Reber, 1989, 1993) insistence on the scientific respectability of the unconscious is to see them as arguing for the reality and importance of particular classes of phenomena, however labeled. I therefore turn to considering how some of these phenomena might be viewed from the perspective of experienced cognition.

ALTERNATIVE SENSES OF UNCONSCIOUS

The experienced cognition framework provides specific hypotheses about what it means for mental contents, states, and processes to be conscious. These ideas allow us to classify several alternative senses of unconscious and to say something about the source of the intuitions underlying each sense. The categories suggested here do not correspond exactly to those derived from the experimental literature discussed earlier. Instead, they reflect categories of phenomena that might underlie common intuitions and beliefs about unconscious mental processes.

The cospecification hypothesis suggests that consciousness just is that feature of mental states, that self and object are cospecified in a current informational array. Beyond this primary awareness sense of consciousness, the experienced cognition framework suggests additional levels of consciousness discussed in more detail in the previous chapter. For example, *egolocative processes* are mental processes that somehow distinguish, or operate on the distinction between, self-specific and object-specific information. For example, instantiated goals are egolocative because their contents explicitly distinguish self, action, and object. *Metacognitive states* are mental states whose objects (the referents of their contents) are other mental states; that is, states of reflective awareness or self-consciousness. As such, metacognitive states necessarily involve egolocative processes, although the converse is not true. I do not mean to suggest that there are sharp lines between these levels of awareness. Instead, they are meant to capture some common notions about consciousness in a way that allows us to apply the experienced cognition framework to understanding the intuitions and phenomena underlying claims that some mental process or other is unconscious. Much more fundamental, in my view, is the description of mental states in terms of the variables of intentional structure discussed in chapters 4 through 7.

The most radical sense of unconscious refers to states that are fundamentally like conscious states, but somehow outside the field of awareness and thus in principle inaccessible. Being like a conscious state presumably at least involves mode and content; that is, on this view it makes sense to talk about unconscious beliefs and desires as in psychodynamic theory (e.g., Erdelyi, 1985). This conception corresponds to what is sometimes called the deep unconscious (see Searle, 1990, 1992). According to this view, many (or all) of the mental processes that can occur as sequences of conscious mental states could also occur unconsciously. The unconscious is thus a separate realm of mental activity, as powerful (or more powerful) than consciousness. Although some cognitive scientists may believe that the unconscious in this sense exists (e.g., Reber, 1989, 1993), I think that this view is quite uncommon. Instead, I think most cognitive scientists believe that conscious and unconscious processes are qualitatively different (e.g., Marcel, 1983) and typically linked in their roles in mental activity (e.g., Farthing, 1992). I therefore have little more to say about this conception.

A second sense of unconscious is captured by Greenwald et al.'s (1995) notion that some events are marginally perceptible. The idea is that some environmental events cannot be consciously perceived because they are subliminal (below the energy threshold for perception) or very brief and masked by concurrent or subsequent events (see Holender, 1986, for a review). Nevertheless, such events are said to be semantically processed, unconsciously identified and interpreted, and hence affect behavior. A closely related sense of unconscious refers to similar effects of environmental events that could be consciously perceived, but do not receive focal attention. For example, MacKay (1973) and others presented evidence for effects of audible but ignored speech in dichotic listening tasks.

The experienced cognition framework offers a straightforward account of these phenomena. It seems quite reasonable in this framework, as in the general information-processing metatheory (chapter 2), that some activity in nonconscious information systems fails to appear directly in the contents of conscious mental states. When this activity can be experimentally detected, it is natural to describe it in the same terms used for contents of mental states—to take an intentional stance toward this activity. In interpreting such demonstrations, however, it is important to note the task relevance of the supposedly unconscious events. That is, these effects can be demonstrated only when the information provided by nonconscious events can guide ongoing, goal-directed activity (Greenwald, 1992).

Furthermore, in a variety of circumstances, arranged by experimenters or occurring in everyday activity, the activity of nonconscious information systems can contribute to the course of experienced cognition without supporting egolocative processing or the metacognitive reflection required for causal attribution. For example, brief environmental events may not support mental contents that "hold still" for reports or other activities. The partial-report paradigm developed by Sperling (1960) illustrates such phenomena. In this paradigm, a field of 12 letters is very briefly (e.g., 50 milliseconds) displayed. Subjects can report only 4 or 5 letters, but if cued quickly enough after the display, they can report any row of 4 letters, demonstrating persistence of the information in the nervous system. One interpretation is that performatory representation (naming the letters to oneself) is necessary to support longer-term memory for display elements. There is also some evidence that such extended representation is necessary for learning, in that individuals seem not to learn contingencies involving nonreported items in the partial-report procedure (Carlson & Dulany, 1985).

A third sense of unconscious is something like, "Doesn't contribute to autobiographical memory." This is essentially the converse of Dennett's (1991) criterion for consciousness discussed earlier. The intuition underlying this sense of unconscious is, I think, something like this: I have evidence that I have done something that would seem to require complex mental activity, such as driving home from the office or finding the solution to a problem. However, I cannot recollect the intermediate stages of this presumed process; therefore, it must have occurred unconsciously. In fact, this sense of unconscious is hardly profound, and really ought not to be controversial. We know from many years of laboratory research on memory, as well as from everyday experience, that consciously experienced events can be quickly forgotten under some circumstances. Furthermore, the experienced cognition framework suggests that skilled activity need not involve much egolocative processing, providing few "hooks" for autobiographical retrieval cues.

A fourth sense of unconscious is based on the utility of some description of behavior that does not match the description under which activity is experienced. This includes description in terms of the unforeseen or unnoticed consequences of some activity. The most challenging example of this category is probably the Freudian slip. Other examples arise from lack of perfect control or the unwitting production of certain consequences. In my view, there are two kinds of accounts appropriate for various instances of this category of phenomena. One kind of account relies on the considerations discussed in chapter 12, to the effect that most activities can be described at multiple levels, as in Vallacher and Wegner's (1987) Action Identification Theory. We may experience some activity at a particular level of description, noticing only later that an alternative description is equally apt (or perhaps more apt, given hindsight knowledge of our actions' consequences). Second, some instances—including, I believe, many so-called Freudian slips—simply reflect cases in which we accept an incorrect theory of our activities.

A fifth sense of unconscious is based on the observation that the execution of many activities is nonconscious; this may refer to the ballistic execution of component skills, or to comparing experience of a restructured skill to an account based on the novice algorithm for that skill. For example, an arithmetic fact now applied by memory retrieval may suggest to some that the novice counting algorithm is now performed unconsciously. An alternative that I prefer is to consider how we come with practice to rely on regularities in the environment and in the operation of nonconscious systems such as memory. However, the only intuitive explanations available to us may be based on memory of novice performance.

Finally, a sixth sense of unconscious points to the description of processes as relations among mental states; these relations themselves enter experience only as the objects of metacognitive states. Thus, lack of some metacognition presumed to be necessary or inevitable is taken as evidence of unconscious processing. Many of Nisbett and Wilson's (1977) examples of failures of introspection in decision making and judgment are instances in which individuals fail to identify how two conscious experiences are related. For example, subjects may fail to correctly report how a particular feature they consciously considered is related to a (consciously made) choice (White, 1980).

Except for the first, "deep unconscious" or "separate realm," sense, I believe that each of these senses of the term *unconscious* picks out a real and interesting class of cognitive phenomena. However, I believe none of them requires the assumption of a separate system or hidden realm of unconscious mental representations and processes. Instead, I believe that each can be seen as a region in the theoretical space defined by the variables of intentional structure that describe conscious mental states, and the noncontent variables that describe the nonconscious processes that support conscious mental states. I turn next to some points about those nonconscious processes.

FAST NONCONSCIOUS PROCESSES

The relation to consciousness of fast nonconscious processes such as preattentive processes and automatic processes acquired through practice can be understood by thinking about how those processes contribute to cospecification and the opportunity for various types of egolocative processing.

Preattentive Processing

Theorists have sometimes argued that *preattentive* (Broadbent, 1977) or *postattentive* (Bargh, 1994) processes are unconscious. These arguments depend on two assumptions: (1) that consciousness should be conceived as a processing stage between stimulus and response (see chapter 2), and (2) that a privileged description of stimuli or responses is available for characterizing the input to or output from a computational process. For example, describing the input to vision in terms of a sequence of static, two-dimensional images requires us to postulate elaborate computational (inferential) processes to reconstruct a three-dimensional experience (e.g., Marr, 1982). Gibson's argument for direct perception reflects a concern with this issue; it is neatly summarized by Medin and Thau (1992), "By our reading, Gibson argued that inadequate analyses of the information available to the perceptual system may lead one to posit all sorts of complex computations to derive information that is actually already available" (p. 167). The problem is that the utility of a particular description to a theorist does not in itself imply that the description is or could be a mental content for the subject of the theory. To return to comments by Bandura (1986) cited in chapter 2, "The notion that thought processes are inaccessible presupposes that valid methods exist for certifying what the nonconscious processes are"; "The issue of who is unaware of what is not that easily resolvable"; "The investigators' conjectures can hardly be regarded as the authentic process against which to judge whether or not others are unaware of the thoughts governing their actions" (all quotes, pp. 122–123). These observations are brought into sharp relief by recent theoretical work inspired by connectionism. As discussed in chapter 7, a characteristic of connectionist theory is that the units of computation are not themselves contents allowing for semantic interpretation. Even proponents of the cognitive unconscious (e.g., Greenwald, 1992) have suggested that connectionist models might point toward accounts of the empirical phenomena discussed earlier in this chapter. However, they have not developed in any detail how such accounts might be related to conscious, experienced cognition.

Automatized Processes

Pre- and post-attentive processes are often considered automatic and relatively "hard-wired." For example, Fodor's (1983) notion of modularity of domain-specific input and output processes emphasizes the uncontrollability by intention or knowledge of these processes. With respect to consciousness, similar comments might be made about processes that become automatic as a result of practice (chapter 3).

Claims about the unconscious status of automatized processes depend on an account of how the relevant tasks are accomplished. For example, as I have already noted in several places, restructuring changes the opportunities for experienced cognition. We cannot expect experimental subjects to report awareness of processes they no longer need to perform in order to accomplish particular tasks.

Some of the cognitively tuned information processing that supports perception, memory, and action must occur very rapidly. As discussed in chapter 13, when we focus theoretical attention on processes at this time scale, it is not plausible that series of conscious mental states account for the phenomena observed in information-processing experiments. The appropriate question to ask about such processes is: What goal-directed activities can they support? A similar question can be asked about blindsight (e.g., Weiskrantz, 1986) and related phenomena associated with brain damage. For example, Farah (e.g., 1994) suggested that many of these phenomena can be understood in terms of diminished quality or persistence of information normally preserved by damaged parts of the brain. A plausible generalization about these classes of phenomena is that informational persistence that is too brief or unstable to support resampling and exploration can nevertheless guide activity, if that activity is independently chosen and initiated. For example, blindsight subjects can make use of visual information in the "blind" areas of their visual fields only when encouraged by experimenters to engage in tasks that the subjects reflectively believe to be impossible.

THE ATTRIBUTION OF CONSCIOUSNESS

The attribution of consciousness should be driven by a theoretical analysis of experienced cognition. This analysis includes identifying variables of intentional structure that describe conscious mental states, and noncontent variables that describe other aspects of cognitive activity. Furthermore, this analysis must take account of the intentional or design stance we can take toward nonconscious systems.

Variables of Intentional Structure: Consciousness as a Matter of Degree

The experienced cognition framework suggests a number of ways in which consciousness might be seen as a matter of degree, as variation in the values of variables of intentional structure. For example, I discussed in chapter 5 how symbolic vehicles of content such as private speech can result in greater intentional distance between content and object than is present in direct perception. This variation is one plausible sense in which consciousness might be seen as a matter of degree: To the extent that we can reflectively distinguish between content and object, we might consider a state more conscious.

The contrasts between *content* and *noncontent* variables of intentional structure, and between variables of intentional structure and other information-processing variables, are also critical for understanding many phenomena of implicit cognition. For example, most implicit memory and unconscious perception phenomena can be described in terms of variations in the activation and thus availability or fluency of existing knowledge. These are not variables of intentional structure, although they may have consequences for the conscious contents that will be experienced in particular circumstances.

The Intentional Stance

The ways in which we talk about information processes may reflect either *intrinsic* (ontologically genuine) or *extrinsic* (as if) intentionality (Searle, 1990, 1992). Conscious mental states have intrinsic intentionality, in that they are necessarily characterized by intentional structure. However, when we consider machines such as computers, plants and animals, and even inanimate objects, we sometimes understand them in intentional terms. For example, it may seem that my car "wants" to be warmed up on a cold morning or that my houseplant "believes" it is spring. Adopting this intentional stance (Dennett, 1987) can provide a heuristic theory for organizing our observations and predicting the behavior of objects, although the objects have only extrinsic intentionality. Put another way, we often treat objects as if they had mental states with intentional structure. Dennett (1987, 1991) argued that we should see this approach as a heuristic (rather than a theory with ontological implications) even when talking about our fellow human beings. However, we need not accept the details of Dennett's view in order to see that we often take an intentional stance toward the activities of our own brains, as discussed in chapter 7.

The intentional stance that we take toward artifacts and toward the brain is appropriate for the control of cognition, but not for theorizing about it. In fact, there appears to be a growing consensus among cognitive theorists that nonconscious (or unconscious) processes serve to support conscious mental activities, as suggested by the experienced cognition framework. Mandler (1994) summarized this consensus:

> One of the hallmarks of contemporary cognitive psychology has been the exploration of the effects of unconscious mental events on conscious (intentional) perceptions and memories. Apart from the fact that cognitive theories usually invoke "unconscious" representations as the underlying mental contents for observable thought and action, the main thrust of these recent investigations has been twofold: to show the operation of networks— mental, neural, semantic, distributed, schematic—in perception and memory and to demonstrate that representations can be activated, primed, or otherwise energized by operations of which the subject is generally unaware ... However, the demonstration of either sub- or suprathreshold priming always involves an intentional (conscious) effort. (p. 9)

There is a great deal of confusion caused by the mentalist or cognitivist interpretation of theories of these networks, which are properly viewed as an implementation level of theory. Consider, for example, "semantic analysis (activation) outside awareness." What sense can be made of this phrase? The obvious answer is that information processing has resulted in a mental content that is like the content of some conscious mental state, but without the consciousness. The contrast is to some presumed conscious version of the process. This contrast really makes sense only in the context of a sense data theory of perception and meaning: The sense data are first captured by a conscious mental content, then analyzed in that they serve as premises (together with some knowledge from long-term memory) in an inference process that has as its conclusion the meaning of the input. This implicit theory, however, is a strawman not seriously held by any current theorist of perception.

Greenwald (1992) summarized the evidence concerning unconscious perception this way: "The preceding review establishes that attentionless unconscious cognition is generally quite limited in the sophistication of analyses it can perform" (p. 773). Except for terminology, I have little problem with this statement. I would put it this way: Information relevant to a current activity (and the goals that direct that activity) may influence the course of that activity without concurrently supporting identification of that information as either (a) the source or cause of that influence, or (b) a distinguishable event (object) available for assimilation to a different goal-directed activity (such as verbal or other instructed report). However, as noted, we need to consider what hypothesis about consciousness is being rejected in claiming that a particular phenomenon is unconscious.

Attention

Many psychologists seem to think that attention is the information-processing concept most closely related to consciousness (e.g., Umiltà & Moscovitch, 1994). In fact, I am skeptical about whether the term *attention* really picks out anything other than a set of empirical phenomena related more by family resemblance than by a core set of defining features. However, it is worth briefly considering how the concept of attention might fit the experienced cognition framework.

There are two common ways of defining attention. One is in terms of effort or concentration—the sense in which we "pay careful attention" to an event or task. This sense leads to theoretical formulations in terms of limited attentional resources (Kahneman, 1973; cf. Navon, 1984). Perhaps more common in psychological research is a definition in terms of selection of information (e.g., Broadbent, 1958). The central idea here is the observation that only a small portion of the information available in the environment actually enters experience or influences activity.

In the experienced cognition framework, the effort sense of attention is captured by the idea of stable self-specification during some episode of activity. This might be discussed in terms of emotionality (chapter 6), goal maintenance (chapter 9), or action identification (chapter 12). In understanding this sense of attention, it is important to keep in mind the reciprocal, recursive nature of interaction with the environment. With respect to the selection sense of attention, the experienced cognition framework suggests what Johnston and Dark (1986) called an effect theory of attention. That is, the selection of information is a consequence of activity, not a mental function to be evoked as an explanation. From this point of view, the contrast between early and late selection theories of attention is not a contrast between theoretical alternatives, but between tasks that must be maintained in terms of lower or higher identities, corresponding to different levels of description of the available information.

Openness of Access

Perhaps the most important implication of the experienced cognition framework for understanding claims for unconscious mental processes is this: Many of these claims seem to be based on the implausible view that the conscious status of a mental content implies complete openness of access to that content by other processes. Openness of access here means availability for report, for inference, to guide goal-directed activity, and so on. It is as if consciousness were not just the "tip of the iceberg" (Farthing, 1992) but the top of the mountain of cognition, a place from which all is visible and which is visible from all places. But we often seem to forget that from any point of view, some things are visible while others are hidden. No conscious mental state, no matter how uncontroversially conscious, is open to all kinds of access at all times. We forget, we are distracted, we represent information in ways suitable for some purposes but not others.

One implication of these considerations is that introspection, or access to one's own mental activity, must be defined more broadly than simply by verbal report. A better definition might be in terms of deliberate or instructed communication. For example, in experiments on perception we typically take keypresses as indicating the occurrence of particular mental contents, although we may ask for converging evidence from other sources if we have reason to suspect these reports (something similar is true of verbal reports, of course). As discussed previously, some events that participate in conscious experience are too fleeting to allow introspection even in this broader sense.

Conclusion

My primary argument in this chapter has been that the experienced cognition framework allows us to understand the phenomena and intuitions underlying claims for the cognitive unconscious, without supposing that there are separate systems or separate realms for conscious and unconscious cognition. In particular, I believe that it is a theoretical and methodological mistake to assume—explicitly or implicitly—that there are unconscious, hidden mental states on the model of conscious cognitive activity. Doing so deprives us of an important source of evidence on cognition, shielding some of our hypotheses from disconfirmation. For example, some researchers talk about the "cult of the unconscious," the almost-religious belief in a powerful but hidden realm of the mind. More important, the standard interpretation of information-processing metatheory that provides the basis for contemporary arguments for a cognitive unconscious stands in the way of developing a cognitive psychology that is really about persons. In the final chapter, I suggest how we can develop such a psychology.

15

Toward a Cognitive
Psychology of Persons

Our own awareness of what, who, and where we are, and what we experience, is a fact of nature more certain than any observations we can make, or any measures we can take, of other existences, relations, and happenings beyond the reach of our immediate experience.

—Tulving, 1994, p. x

But a psychologist can no more evade consciousness than a physicist can side-step gravity.

—Baars, 1988, p. xvi

We will know what science can tell us only after it has done so.

—Akins, 1993, p. 272

Cognition is experienced by individual persons engaged in purposeful activity in their environments, and it is this personal experience that is consciousness, the "constitutive problem of psychology" (Miller, 1985, p. 40). Yet cognitive scientists often have developed their theories in ways that explicitly (e.g., Dennett, 1987) or implicitly (see chapter 2) disregard person-level concepts. As a consequence, the literature of cognitive science is filled with euphemisms: "the *system* understands," "the *central executive* decides," "the *brain* plans action," and so on. Because our explicit theory is often officially subpersonal, it is easily seen as dehumanizing. And critics of cognitive science, both in our universities and our popular press, are using this subpersonal character of cognitive theory in support of alternative approaches to understanding human activity that can only be called antiscientific.

One of my central goals in developing the experienced cognition framework has been to argue that an appropriate theory of consciousness and its relation to nonconscious information processes points the way toward a person-level cognitive psychology. Given a theory at the person level, a theory that tells us what it is to be a conscious agent, we can avoid the need for euphemism and understand the subjects of our research as subjects in the sense of individuals with points of view and subjective experience. A theoretical approach that accommodates subjectivity would both answer critics of cognitive science and improve our science by including consciousness in the range of phenomena explained by cognitive theory. My purpose in this final chapter is to offer some comments about the prospects for such theory from the perspective of the experienced cognition framework.

THE ACTIVITY OF CONSCIOUS AGENTS

The experienced cognition framework provides a vision of cognition as the activity of a conscious agent—a person—in an environment described in ecological terms. By identifying sets of variables that describe the intentional structure of conscious mental states, and distinguishing between those variables and others that describe nonintentional features of cognitive processes, the framework points toward the possibility of a science of conscious agents. Such a science would include a theoretical approach to traditional questions about consciousness and the relation of those questions to theoretical treatments of individuals considered as physical organisms.

The Subjectivity of Consciousness

Subjectivity, the "first-person" nature of experience, has been a sticking point for many psychological and philosophical attempts to understand consciousness. Essentially behaviorist criteria of consciousness—such as the possibility of verbal reports treated as behavior—can fit comfortably into theories that treat the individual as a "black box" whose inner workings are not observable. The subjective aspect of consciousness—the sense in which the black box somehow contains a point of view and experiences from that point of view—is less easily accommodated. This is what Chalmers (1995) called the "hard problem" of consciousness, and some authors have argued that first-person and third-person views of cognition cannot be reconciled (Velmans, 1991). There are two aspects to the problem of subjectivity: First, how can there be first-person points of view at all, given that the subjects of psychological research are seen (scientifically) as objects in the physical world? And second, how can cognitive theory—or any scientific theory—account for the private, ineffable character of conscious experience?

I believe that the cospecification hypothesis answers the first of these questions. Understanding consciousness on the model of a point of view specified by information available to visual perception gives an unproblematically informational, and thus potentially computational, account of subjectivity in the first sense. And, by the standard arguments discussed in chapter 2, computational accounts are metaphysically unproblematic; we can point to many physical systems that realize computational processes in ways that are scientifically well understood. Throughout this book, and especially in chapters 4 through 7, I have discussed how the cospecification hypothesis and the associated framework for understanding the intentional structure of conscious mental states account for our experience as selves, conscious agents engaged in purposeful activity.

The second question—about the intangible qualities of conscious experience—is, I believe, not well formed. The problem is that phenomenal experience can be difficult to communicate and can seem mysterious because it is difficult to reconcile with the language of either scientific or common-sense theories of physical events. This has been the source of a great deal of confusion. The so-called *qualia* of subjective experience are supposed to be ineffable properties that make up how it feels to have phenomenal experiences. However, I think the problem is not the nature of phenomenal experience but a failure to recognize that descriptions of experience abstracted for one purpose (describing physical events, abstracted from any particular point of view) may not be appropriate for another (describing what it is like to have a particular point of view, or to experience something from that point of view).

Dennett (1991) correctly identified the supposedly ineffable properties of experience as properties of the world to which our perceptual systems are tuned—in other words (which Dennett did not use), affordances. The contents of our mental states depend on our actions and on the informational support for those actions. As Dennett wrote:

> When we marvel, in those moments of heightened self-consciousness, at the glorious richness of our conscious experience, the richness we marvel at is actually the richness of the world outside, in all its ravishing detail. It does not "enter" our conscious minds, but is simply available. (p. 408)

The philosophical puzzles about qualia can thus be construed as parallel to the puzzles about first-person points of view: How can descriptions of mental content be reconciled with the scientific description of the world? The answer is that the physical description of the environment appropriate for developing cognitive theory is "ecological" in Gibson's sense: in terms of the affordances for action specified by available information. As Dennett (1991) pointed out, these properties seem especially subjective exactly because the appropriate descriptions are necessarily relative to individuals' dispositions and skills, rather than "objective" in the sense of descriptions in third-person physical theories. Choosing an appropriate level or style of description is thus critical for understanding experienced cognition.

A Privileged Level of Description

The experienced cognition framework offers support for the traditional but somewhat battered view that there is a privileged level of description for developing psychological theory. By *privileged*, I mean a level of description that is essential in that it must be evoked to identify central phenomena and critical theoretical notions that constitute the scientific domain of psychology (Natsoulas, 1992). The level that I see as privileged is, of course, the level of conscious mental states. The contents of these states correspond to an ecological level of description in the sense that they reflect the level at which we experience and interact with the environment. When those contents have environmental objects, it is the affordances for action of those objects that are important.

Psychology has often struggled to find appropriate levels for theory and to relate the various levels of description actually used in empirical research. This struggle is often apparent in the empirical and theoretical literature of cognitive science. For example, the literature contains a number of controversies concerning how to interpret the relation between symbol-processing and connectionist theories (Broadbent, 1985; Fodor & Pylyshyn, 1988; Rumelhart & McClelland, 1985; Smolensky, 1988). One way to understand this relation is to see symbol-processing descriptions of information processes like perception and memory as approximations to a true subsymbolic level (e.g., Smolensky, 1988). This view is probably correct in the sense that the units of computation in connectionist theory do not support semantic interpretation (Chalmers, 1992), and symbolic descriptions of these systems reflect the intentional stance we adopt toward them (chapter 7). As J. R. Anderson (1987a, 1990) noted, much of cognitive theory is formulated at this implementation level. I would argue, however, that it is the contents of conscious mental states that are sometimes truly symbolic, and a theory that describes them as such will be no more approximate than any scientific theory. I believe that exploring these issues from the perspective of experienced cognition will help us to understand the implications of the computational view of mind.

The Computational Mind and Its Critics

Experienced cognition provides a means of reconciling the core ideas of computational cognitive science with critical movements such as situated cognition. A number of authors have criticized aspects of the information-processing or computational approach to understanding the mind (e.g., Dreyfus, 1992; Greeno & Moore, 1993; Harré & Gillett, 1994; Lave, 1988; Searle, 1980, 1992). The gist of these critiques is generally that the computational approach to understanding the mind leaves out important person-level concepts. This critical view of cognitive science is based, I believe, on an accurate if somewhat narrow reading of much of the literature. Consider, for example, Tulving's (1994) comment:

> Although the information-processing paradigm was already well on its way in 1965, it had not brought much relief from behaviorism's stranglehold on consciousness, the historical, true subject matter of psychology. The mental processes with which the newly emerging cognitive scientists began filling the "black box" were the observer's abstractions rather than the individual's conscious experiences. It was the study of the mind from the point of view of the "third" person, and in that sense did not differ greatly from the basic orienting attitudes of behaviorists. (p. viii)

Although there are signs that things are beginning to change, this characterization still fits much of the literature in cognitive science.

In my view, however, many of the contemporary critiques of cognitive science miss the mark because they point to habits of thought that are not essential to the computational view of mind (chapter 2; Vera & Simon, 1993). Perhaps the most important of these habits concerns the way in which we think about the concept of mental representation.

REPRESENTATIONALISM RECONSIDERED

The habit of representationalism (chapter 2) is the major bad habit of IP theory that prevents the development of a cognitive psychology of persons. The problem is that theorists' representations of regularities in their subjects' behavior are often taken as descriptions of those subject's mental contents. Although this is sometimes so—for those aspects of a theory that in fact paraphrase the contents of conscious mental states—for the most part it is a pernicious mistake that gets in the way of understanding cognition as it is experienced. Yet the computational view of mind requires theories framed in terms of representation in the sense of computational tokens that carry information. As Mandler (1985) wrote:

The concept of representation is intimately tied to, and possibly identical with, the issue of useful theory. Representational systems are theoretical constructs that are postulated as responsible for (that cause or generate) the observable thoughts, actions, etc. of the organism . . . The representation of knowledge, in other words, is the theoretical system that is constructed in order to understand, explain, and predict the behavior of organisms. (p. 11)

However, the stance we adopt toward these theoretical representations is critical; Mandler went on to note that:

There is an unnecessary tendency to reify the computational model, to imply that the human mind does in fact work like a computer. Reification is a danger that has bedeviled psychology throughout its history, and we must guard against the theoretical excesses that it spawns. (p. 21)

The experienced cognition framework suggests that one of these theoretical excesses is the postulation of a cognitive unconscious discussed in the previous chapter. The power of representational theory is often reified and thus confused with the powers of the agents described by the theory.

AGAINST SUPERCOGNITIVE THEORY

Representationalism also leads to what I call supercognitive views of cognition and the self that support dehumanizing denials of personal agency in cognitive theory. By supercognitive, I mean accounts that invoke more intelligence or cognition than is necessary to explain the phenomena. By supposing that cognitive phenomena require accounts in terms of intelligent agency, when that hypothesized agency does not plausibly correspond to conscious experience, we are led to theories in which actual conscious experience is seen as epiphenomenal and thus irrelevant.

There are two senses in which the accounts of phenomena provided by cognitive theory, or the pretheoretical commitments of cognitive theorists, are often supercognitive. The first sense is reflected in the myth of the all-powerful consciousness—the idea that if some content is conscious, it must be available for use in any kind of process we can imagine. Thus authors sometimes argue that if a mental process were conscious, there would be no need for effortful construction of theories of that process (see Dulany, 1968, for a careful consideration and rebuttal of this view). However, the conscious status of a mental content implies only that some information is embodied in a mental state with intentional structure, in which an experiencing self and an experienced object are cospecified. How that state is related to other mental states and to activity in an environment is a matter for theoretical and empirical investigation. As discussed in the previous chapter, consciousness is often mistakenly taken to imply completely open access to any and all kinds of inferences, causal attributions, or links to other mental processes. And because the mental contents that guide many activities are apparently not accompanied by this kind of open access, consciousness is seen as irrelevant to understanding those activities. Dennett's (1991) argument that mental processes need only satisfy epistemic hungers is also relevant here. The idea is that although we have the illusion that the conscious contents we actually experience reflect a selection from a huge number of possible contents, it is a mistake to think of these possible contents as present but not experienced. A particular conscious state is what it is, not the tip of an iceberg of simultaneously present but only potentially conscious states.

The second sense in which accounts in cognitive theory are often supercognitive is that we adopt an intentional stance toward—anthropomorphize, in Searle's (1990) terms—nonconscious processes that support conscious mental states. We thus tend to see these nonconscious processes as if they were the activities of unconscious but intelligent agents (as in Minsky, 1986). Perhaps the most pernicious symptom of this stance is the attribution of wide ranges of function to an executive system or similar construct. As discussed in chapters 7 and 14, there are a variety of reasons for rejecting this stance as a basis for theory. Although the implementation level of cognitive theory is important, we must look to the person level to understand experienced cognition.

PERSON-CENTERED COGNITIVE RESEARCH

The experienced cognition framework suggests a novel approach to reconciling third-person and first-person views, pointing the way toward person-centered rather than systems-centered cognitive research. My own empirical research is laboratory-based and generally in the tradition of information-processing approaches to cognition. Although other research approaches such as observation of everyday activities (e.g., Lave, 1988) may make important contributions to our understanding of cognition, I believe that experimental laboratory studies that rely on converging evidence from self-report and behavioral measures, in the context of carefully controlled environments, will continue to provide the foundation for the development of cognitive theory. Laboratory studies conceived in the information-processing framework have the important advantage of a focus on the moment-to-moment dynamics of cognition. Such research also provides the paradigms and documents the person-level phenomena that guide neuroscience approaches to understanding cognition in terms of brain function.

The experienced cognition framework provides a different perspective on much of the laboratory research that makes up the literature of cognitive psychology. However, unlike many critics of the information-processing approach to cognition (e.g., Lave, 1988), I do not advocate abandoning the general research paradigms and methods currently in use. The most striking characteristic of laboratory research on cognition is careful control of the nature and timing of information available to subjects as they perform goal-directed tasks, and I believe that this feature is essential for detailed understanding of experienced cognition.

One implication of the experienced cognition framework is that questions about learning are central to understanding cognitive phenomena generally. Learning changes our possibilities for interaction with environments, and thus our experience of those environments and of our own activity. Some of these changes can be observed in the course of brief laboratory studies whereas others span months, years, or decades. I believe that studies of learning, skill acquisition, and development will become increasingly central to cognitive theory generally. In the next section, I sketch a few specific empirical issues that I currently think are particularly important for understanding experienced cognition.

Empirical Issues

Theoretical frameworks or paradigms, like the information-processing framework or the experienced cognition framework, are not hypotheses subject to single, critical, empirical tests. Instead, frameworks must be judged on the coherence they bring to broad research domains, and their heuristic value in generating research that increases our understanding of a range of phenomena. Nevertheless, a number of empirical issues or topics seem to me especially important at this point in time, and relevant to evaluating the experienced cognition framework. These include:

1. understanding in greater detail how the self is specified in a range of cognitive activities, including especially temporal orientation in remembering and in skilled performance;
2. exploring the formal parallels between spatially organized, physically constrained activities such as egomotion and object manipulation, and mental activities such as reasoning and problem solving;
3. examining the roles in controlling activity of emotion and other factors that affect the salience of self-specific information and the opportunities for egolocative and metacognitive processes;
4. understanding the development of spatial and temporal awareness, and how the embodied nature of this awareness contributes to the

development of mental skills for generating and manipulating symbolic representations;

5. examining the idiosyncratic and conventional strategies that individuals use for distributing working memory demands over internal resources and the environment; and

6. understanding how skilled mental activity comes to be temporally tuned, so that the principles of control discussed in chapter 13 can be realized.

Not surprisingly, this list bears considerable resemblance to the goals of my own current empirical research. My purpose in presenting this brief list is not to argue that these issues are more important than a number of others. In particular, I have not mentioned either work on the socially situated character of cognition or research exploring the neural substrates of cognition. Rather, the list reflects my belief that experienced cognition is best understood by directing research efforts at the moment-to-moment organization of skilled activity, how that activity is controlled and informationally supported, and how it changes with practice. These research questions speak to how cognitive activity can be understood as series of mental steps, considered as sequences of conscious mental states that make up the experience of conscious agents.

Methodological Issues

Several methodological issues are important for pursuing research on these topics and others relevant to understanding experienced cognition. One issue is the development of converging techniques for assessing the variables describing conscious mental states. In some circumstances, verbal protocols can provide data on the contents of subjects' mental states as they perform laboratory tasks (Ericsson & Simon, 1983). However, the field does not yet possess a repertoire of established procedures appropriate for studying the stream of conscious experience. A second, related issue concerns the need to capture more of the intentional structure of mental states. For example, as discussed in chapter 11, much research on reasoning treats the topic as concerned merely with relations among contents—in laboratory tasks, realized as relations among sentences—rather than addressing issues concerned with the transfer of belief or the place of inferential steps in goal structures that lead to action. A third issue is the need to track the time course of mental steps in extended, multiple-step cognitive tasks. As I argued in chapter 13, understanding how component skills are coordinated to meet temporal constraints and achieve fluent performance is central to understanding cognitive skill.

A fourth issue is the development of ecological-level descriptions of laboratory tasks and the informational support for performance of these tasks. As noted previously, such descriptions are often adopted implicitly and tested in the course of pilot research in which investigators act as participants in tasks later to be performed by experimental subjects. However, research based on the ecological approach to visual perception and action makes it clear that developing systematically ecological descriptions of the information available from the environment is a major scientific undertaking that calls for programmatic experimentation.

All of these methodological issues of course turn on the development of theories that provide accounts of cognitive activity in terms of mental states. I believe that the development of such accounts will lead us to different mixes of experimental manipulations than are now typical in laboratory cognitive research. For example, manipulating the opportunity or environmental support for egolocation in the course of cognitive tasks is likely to provide new information on how those tasks are performed.

FINAL COMMENTS

The cospecification hypothesis provides a unifying principle allowing us to recognize the theoretical and experiential continuity of consciousness in all kinds of experience. Thinking about experienced cognition in the activity of conscious agents is important for developing a cognitive psychology of persons. And a scientific psychology that can do justice to the concept of a person is important for a variety of reasons. Understanding our selves and others as persons is central to human experience, and an account of this understanding is thus essential to any cognitive theory that aspires to completeness. It also seems impossible to deny that scientific psychology contributes to our culture's general view of human nature. What we value in life depends on the concept of personhood, and I believe that this concept can and will be deepened and enriched by cognitive science.

Understanding our selves is the most central goal of psychology and cognitive science. My hope is that I have contributed something toward that goal.

References

Abelson, R. P. (1981). Psychological status of the script concept. *American Psychologist, 36,* 715–729.

Adams, M. J. (1984). Aristotle's logic. In G. H. Bower (Ed.), *The psychology of learning and motivation* (Vol. 18, pp. 255–311). New York: Academic Press.

Adelson, B. (1981). Problem solving and the development of abstract categories in programming languages. *Memory & Cognition, 9,* 422–433.

Ahlum–Heath, M. E., & DiVesta, F. J. (1986). The effect of conscious controlled verbalization of a cognitive strategy on transfer in problem solving. *Memory & Cognition, 14,* 281–285.

Akins, K. A. (1993). A bat without qualities? In M. Davies & G. W. Humphreys (Eds.), *Consciousness: Psychological and philosophical essays* (pp. 258–273). Oxford, England: Blackwell.

Albrecht, J. E., O'Brien, E. J., Mason, R. A., & Myers, J. L. (1995). The role of perspective in the accessibility of goals during reading. *Journal of Experimental Psychology: Learning, Memory, and Cognition, 21,* 364–372.

Allport, D. A., Antonis, B., & Reynolds, P. (1972). On the division of attention: A disproof of the single-channel hypothesis. *Quarterly Journal of Experimental Psychology, 24,* 225–235.

Anderson, J. R. (1982). Acquisition of cognitive skill. *Psychological Review, 89,* 369–406.

Anderson, J. R. (1983). *The architecture of cognition.* Cambridge, MA: Harvard University Press.

Anderson, J. R. (1985). *Cognitive psychology and its implications* (2nd ed.). New York: Freeman.

Anderson, J. R. (1987a). Methodologies for studying human knowledge. *Behavioral and Brain Sciences, 10,* 467–505.

Anderson, J. R. (1987b). Skill acquisition: Compilation of weak-method problem solutions. *Psychological Review, 94,* 192–210.

Anderson, J. R. (1990). *The adaptive character of thought.* Hillsdale, NJ: Lawrence Erlbaum Associates.

Anderson, J. R. (1992). Automaticity and the ACT* theory. *American Journal of Psychology, 105,* 165–180.

Anderson, J. R. (1993). *Rules of the mind.* Hillsdale, NJ: Lawrence Erlbaum Associates.

Anderson, J. R., Farrell, R., & Sauers, R. (1984). Learning to program in LISP. *Cognitive Science, 8,* 87–129.

319

Anderson, N. H. (1981). *Foundations of information integration theory.* New York: Academic Press.

Anderson, R. C., & Pichert, J. W. (1978). Recall of previously unrecallable information following a shift in perspective. *Journal of Verbal Learning and Verbal Behavior, 17,* 1–12.

Anzai, Y., & Simon, H. A. (1979). The theory of learning by doing. *Psychological Review, 86,* 124–140.

Ashcraft, M. H. (1992). Cognitive arithmetic: A review of data and theory. *Cognition, 44,* 75–106.

Atkinson, R. C., & Shiffrin, R. M. (1968). Human memory: A proposed system and its control processes. In K. W. Spence & J. T. Spence (Eds.), *The psychology of learning and motivation* (Vol. 2, pp. 89–195). New York: Academic Press.

Austin, J. L. (1962). *How to do things with words.* Oxford, England: Clarendon Press.

Austin, J. T., & Vancouver, J. B. (1996). Goal constructs in psychology: Structure, process, and content. *Psychological Bulletin, 120*(3), 338–375.

Baars, B. J. (1988). *A cognitive theory of consciousness.* New York: Cambridge University Press.

Baddeley, A. D. (1986). *Working memory.* Oxford, England: Clarendon Press.

Baddeley, A. D. (1993). Working memory and conscious awareness. In A. F. Collins, S. E. Gathercole, M. A. Conway, & P. E. Morris (Eds.), *Theories of memory* (pp. 11–28). Hillsdale, NJ: Lawrence Erlbaum Associates.

Baddeley, A. D., & Hitch, G. J. (1974). Working memory. In G. H. Bower (Ed.), *The psychology of learning and motivation* (Vol. 8, pp. 47–89). New York: Academic Press.

Baillargeon, R., Kotovsky, L., & Needham, A. (1995). The acquisition of physical knowledge in infancy. In D. Sperber, D. Premack, & A. J. Premack (Eds.), *Causal cognition* (pp. 79–116). Oxford, England: Clarendon Press.

Baker, L. (1989). Metacognition, comprehension monitoring, and the adult reader. *Educational Psychology Review, 1,* 3–38.

Ballard, D. H. (1996). On the function of visual representation. In K. Akins (Ed.), *Perception* (pp. 111–131). Oxford, England: Oxford University Press.

Ballard, D. H., Hayhoe, M. M., & Pelz, J. B. (1995). Memory representations in natural tasks. *Journal of Cognitive Neuroscience, 7,* 66–80.

Ballard, D. H., Hayhoe, M. M., Pook, P. K., & Rao, R. P. N. (in press). Deictic codes for the embodiment of cognition. *Behavioral and Brain Sciences.*

Bandura, A. (1986). *Social foundations of thought and action.* Englewood Cliffs, NJ: Prentice-Hall.

Bandura, A. (1989). Human agency in social cognitive theory. *American Psychologist, 44,* 1175–1184.

Bargh, J. A. (1989). Conditional automaticity: Varieties of automatic influence in social perception and cognition. In J. S. Uleman & J. A. Bargh (Eds.), *Unintended thought* (pp. 3–51). New York: Guilford.

Bargh, J. A. (1992). The ecology of automaticity: Toward establishing the conditions needed to produce automatic processing effects. *American Journal of Psychology, 105,* 181–199.

Bargh, J. A. (1994). The four horsemen of automaticity: Awareness, intention, efficiency, and control in social cognition. In R. S. Wyer, Jr. & T. K. Srull (Eds.), *Handbook of social cognition* (Vol. 1, pp. 1–40). Hillsdale, NJ: Lawrence Erlbaum Associates.

Baron, J. (1994). *Thinking and deciding* (2nd ed.). Cambridge, England: Cambridge University Press.

Barrow, H. G., & Tenenbaum, J. M. (1986). Computational approaches to vision. In K. R. Boff, L. Kaufman, & J. P. Thomas (Eds.), *Handbook of perception and human performance* (Vol. II, pp. 38:1–38:70). New York: Wiley.

Barsalou, L. W. (1993). Flexibility, structure, and linguistic vagary in concepts: Manifestations of a compositional system of perceptual symbols. In A. F. Collins, S. E. Gathercole,

M. A. Conway, & P. E. Morris (Eds.), *Theories of memory* (pp. 29–101). Hillsdale, NJ: Lawrence Erlbaum Associates.

Bennett, D. (1979). The detective story: Towards a definition of the genre. *PTL: A journal for descriptive poetics and theory of literature, 4*, 233–266.

Berk, L. E. (1992). Children's private speech: An overview of theory and the status of research. In R. M. Diaz & L. E. Berk (Eds.), *Private speech: From social interaction to self-regulation* (pp. 17–53). Hillsdale, NJ: Lawrence Erlbaum Associates.

Berry, D. C., & Broadbent, D. E. (1987). The combination of explicit and implicit learning processes in task control. *Psychological Research, 49*, 7–15.

Berry, D. C., & Dienes, Z. (1993). *Implicit learning: Theoretical and empirical issues.* Hillsdale, NJ: Lawrence Erlbaum Associates.

Biederman, I., & Shiffrar, M. M. (1987). Sexing day-old chicks: A case study and expert systems analysis of a difficult perceptual-learning task. *Journal of Experimental Psychology: Learning, Memory, and Cognition* (Vol. 13, pp. 640–645).

Birnbaum, M. H., & Mellers, B. A. (1983). Bayesian inference: Combining base rates with opinions of sources who vary in credibility. *Journal of Social and Personality Psychology, 45*, 792–804.

Blackmer, E. R., & Mitton, J. L. (1991). Theories of monitoring and the timing of repairs in spontaneous speech. *Cognition, 39*, 173–194.

Blessing, S. B., & Anderson, J. R. (1996). How people learn to skip steps. *Journal of Experimental Psychology: Learning, Memory, and Cognition, 22*(3), 576–598.

Block, N. (1995). On a confusion about a function of consciousness. *Behavioral and Brain Sciences, 18*, 227–287.

Bogdan, R. J. (1994). *Grounds for cognition.* Hillsdale, NJ: Lawrence Erlbaum Associates.

Bovair, S., Kieras, D. E., & Polson, P. G. (1990). The acquisition and performance of text-editing skill: A cognitive complexity analysis. *Human Computer Interaction, 5*, 1–48.

Bower, G. H. (1981). Mood and memory. *American Psychologist, 36*, 129–148.

Braine, M. D. S. (1978). On the relation between the natural logic of reasoning and standard logic. *Psychological Review, 85*, 1–21.

Braine, M. D. S., & Reiser, B. J. (1984). Some empirical justification for a theory of natural propositional logic. In G. H. Bower (Ed.), *The psychology of learning and motivation* (Vol. 18, pp. 313–371). New York: Academic Press.

Brentano, F. (1973). The distinction between mental and physical phenomena. In A. C. Rancurello, D. B. Terrell, & L. L. McAlister (Trans.), *Psychology from an empirical standpoint* (pp. 39–61). London: Routledge and Kegan Paul. (Original work published 1874)

Brewer, W. F. (1974). There is no convincing evidence for operant or classical conditioning in adult humans. In W. B. Weimer & D. S. Palermo (Eds.), *Cognition and the symbolic processes* (pp. 1–42). Hillsdale, NJ: Lawrence Erlbaum Associates.

Brewer, W. F. (1987). Schemas versus mental models in human memory. In P. Morris (Ed.), *Modelling cognition* (pp. 187–197). Chichester, England: Wiley.

Broadbent, D. E. (1957). A mechanical model for human attention and immediate memory. *Psychological Review, 64*, 205–215.

Broadbent, D. E. (1958). *Perception and communication.* London: Pergamon.

Broadbent, D. E. (1975). The magic number seven after fifteen years. In R. A. Kennedy & A. Wilkes (Eds.), *Studies in long-term memory* (pp. 3–18). London: Wiley.

Broadbent, D. E. (1977). The hidden preattentive processes. *American Psychologist, 32*, 109–118.

Broadbent, D. E. (1982). Task combination and selective intake of information. *Acta Psychologica, 50*, 253–290.

Broadbent, D. (1985). A question of levels: Comment on McClelland and Rumelhart. *Journal of Experimental Psychology: General, 114*, 189–192.

Brooke, J. B., & Duncan, K. D. (1983). Effects of prolonged practice on performance in a fault-location task. *Ergonomics, 26*, 379–393.

Brown, J. S., Collins, A., & Duguid, P. (1989). Situated cognition and the culture of learning. *Educational researcher, 18*, 32–42.

Bruner, J. S., Goodnow, J. J., & Austin, G. A. (1956). *A study of thinking.* New York: Wiley.

Burgess, N., & Hitch, G. J. (1992). Toward a network model of the articulatory loop. *Journal of Memory and Language, 31*, 429–460.

Byrne, R. M., & Johnson–Laird, P. N. (1989). Spatial reasoning. *Journal of Memory and Language, 28*, 564–575.

Card, S. K., Moran, T. P., & Newell, A. (1980). Computer text editing: An information processing analysis of a routine cognitive skill. *Cognitive Psychology, 12*, 32–74.

Carey, S. (1995). On the origin of causal understanding. In D. Sperber, D. Premack, & A. J. Premack (Eds.), *Causal cognition* (pp. 268–302). Oxford, England: Clarendon.

Carlson, R. A. (1991). Consciousness and content in learning: Missing or misconceived? *Behavioral and Brain Sciences, 14*, 673–674.

Carlson, R. A. (1992). Starting with consciousness. *American Journal of Psychology, 105*, 598–604.

Carlson, R. A. (1994). Is implicit learning about consciousness? *Behavioral and Brain Sciences, 17*, 400.

Carlson, R. A., & Cary, M. (1993, November). *Working memory and calculation strategies in running addition.* Paper presented at the 34th annual meeting of the Psychonomic Society, Washington, DC.

Carlson, R. A., & Dulany, D. E. (1985). Conscious attention and abstraction in concept learning. *Journal of Experimental Psychology: Learning, Memory, and Cognition, 11*, 45–58.

Carlson, R. A., & Dulany, D. E. (1988). Diagnostic reasoning with circumstantial evidence. *Cognitive Psychology, 20*, 463–492.

Carlson, R. A., Khoo, B. H., Yaure, R. G., & Schneider, W. (1990). Acquisition of a problem solving skill: Levels of organization and use of working memory. *Journal of Experimental Psychology: General, 119*, 193–214.

Carlson, R. A., & Lundy, D. H. (1992). Consistency and restructuring in learning cognitive procedural sequences. *Journal of Experimental Psychology: Learning, Memory, and Cognition, 18*, 127–141.

Carlson, R. A., Lundy, D. H., & Yaure, R. G. (1992). Syllogistic inference chains in meaningful text. *American Journal of Psychology, 105*, 75–99.

Carlson, R. A., & Schneider, W. (1989a). Acquisition context and the use of causal rules. *Memory & Cognition, 17*, 240–248.

Carlson, R. A., & Schneider, W. (1989b). Practice effects and composition: A reply to Anderson. *Journal of Experimental Psychology: Learning, Memory, and Cognition, 15*, 531–533.

Carlson, R. A., & Shin, J. C. (1996). Practice schedules and subgoal instantiation in cascaded problem solving. *Journal of Experimental Psychology: Learning, Memory, and Cognition, 22*, 157–168.

Carlson, R. A., Shin, J. C., & Wenger, J. L. (1994, November). *Timing and the control of fluent cognitive sequences.* Paper presented at the 35th annual meeting of the Psychonomic Society, Saint Louis, MO.

Carlson, R. A., & Sohn, M. H. (1995, November). *Rule-application skills have internal structure.* Paper presented at the 36th annual meeting of the Psychonomic Society, Los Angeles.

Carlson, R. A., Sullivan, M. A., & Schneider, W. (1989a). Component fluency in a problem solving context. *Human Factors, 31*, 489–502.

Carlson, R. A., Sullivan, M. A., & Schneider, W. (1989b). Practice and working memory effects in building procedural skill. *Journal of Experimental Psychology: Learning, Memory, and Cognition, 15*, 517–526.

Carlson, R. A., Wenger, J. L., & Sullivan, M. A. (1993). Coordinating information from perception and working memory. *Journal of Experimental Psychology: Human Perception and Performance, 19*, 531–548.

Carlson, R. A., & Yaure, R. G. (1990). Practice schedules and the use of component skills in problem solving. *Journal of Experimental Psychology: Learning, Memory, and Cognition, 16,* 484–496.

Carr, T. H. (1979). Consciousness in models of human information processing: Primary memory, executive control, and input regulation. In G. Underwood & R. Stevens (Eds.), *Aspects of consciousness* (Vol. 1, pp. 123–153). New York: Academic Press.

Carr, T. H. (1986). Perceiving visual language. In K. R. Boff, L. Kaufman, & J. P. Thomas (Eds.), *Handbook of perception and human performance* (Vol. II, pp. 29:1–29:92). New York: Wiley.

Carver, C. S., & Scheier, M. F. (1981). *Attention and self-regulation, a control theory approach to human behavior.* New York: Springer-Verlag.

Carver, C. S., & Scheier, M. F. (1982). Self-awareness and the self-regulation of behavior. In G. Underwood (Ed.), *Aspects of consciousness: Awareness and self-awareness* (Vol. 3, pp. 235–266). London: Academic Press.

Carver, C. S., & Scheier, M. F. (1990). Origins and functions of positive and negative affect: A control-process view. *Psychological Review, 97,* 19–35.

Cary, M. (1996). *External support and the development of problem-solving strategies.* Unpublished doctoral dissertation, The Pennsylvania State University.

Cary, M., & Carlson, R. A. (1995). *Control of a fluent cognitive routine: Running arithmetic.* Unpublished manuscript.

Case, R. (1985). *Intellectual development: Birth to adulthood.* Orlando, FL: Academic Press.

Catrambone, R. (1994). Improving examples to improve transfer to novel problems. *Memory & Cognition, 22,* 606–615.

Catrambone, R. (1995). Aiding subgoal learning: Effects on transfer. *Journal of Educational Psychology, 87,* 5–17.

Catrambone, R., & Holyoak, K. J. (1990). Learning subgoals and methods for solving probability problems. *Memory & Cognition, 18,* 593–603.

Chalmers, D. J. (1992). Subsymbolic computation and the Chinese room. In J. Dinsmore (Ed.), *The symbolic and connectionist paradigms* (pp. 25–48). Hillsdale, NJ: Lawrence Erlbaum Associates.

Chalmers, D. J. (1995). The puzzle of conscious experience. *Scientific American, 273,* 80–86.

Chapman, M. (1988). *Constructive evolution: Origins and development of Piaget's thought.* Cambridge, England: Cambridge University Press.

Charness, N. (1979). Components of skill in bridge. *Canadian Journal of Psychology, 33,* 1–16.

Charness, N., & Campbell, J. I. D. (1988). Acquiring skill at mental calculation in adulthood: A task decomposition. *Journal of Experimental Psychology: General, 117,* 115–129.

Chase, W. G., & Ericsson, K. A. (1982). Skill and working memory. In G. H. Bower (Ed.), *The psychology of learning and motivation* (Vol. 16, pp. 1–58). New York: Academic Press.

Chase, W. G., & Simon, H. A. (1973). The mind's eye in chess. In W. G. Chase (Ed.), *Visual information processing* (pp. 215–281). New York: Academic Press.

Cheng, P. W. (1985). Restructuring versus automaticity: Alternative accounts of skill acquisition. *Psychological Review, 92,* 414–423.

Cheng, P. W., & Holyoak, K. J. (1985). Pragmatic reasoning schemas. *Cognitive Psychology, 17,* 391–416.

Cheng, P. W., & Novick, L. R. (1991). Causes versus enabling conditions. *Cognition, 40,* 83–120.

Cherniak, C. (1986). *Minimal rationality.* Cambridge, MA: MIT Press.

Chi, M. T. H., Feltovich, P. J., & Glaser, R. (1981). Categorization and representation of physics problems by experts and novices. *Cognitive Science, 5,* 121–152.

Chi, M. T. H., Glaser, R., & Farr, M. J. (Eds.). (1988). *The nature of expertise.* Hillsdale, NJ: Lawrence Erlbaum Associates.

Chiesi, H. L., Spilich, G. J., & Voss, J. F. (1979). Acquisition of domain-related information in relation to high and low domain knowledge. *Journal of Verbal Learning and Verbal Behavior, 18*, 257–274.

Chomsky, N. (1959). A review of Skinner's Verbal Behavior. *Language, 35*, 26–58.

Chomsky, N., & Katz, J. J. (1974). What the linguist is talking about. *The Journal of Philosophy, LXXI*, 347–367.

Christianson, S. A. (1992). Emotional stress and eyewitness testimony: A critical review. *Psychological Bulletin, 112*, 284–309.

Cleeremans, A., & McClelland, J. L. (1991). Learning the structure of event sequences. *Journal of Experimental Psychology: General, 120*, 235–253.

Cohen, J. (1981). Can human irrationality be experimentally demonstrated? *The Behavioral and Brain Sciences, 4*, 317–370.

Cohen, J. D., & Huston, T. A. (1994). Progress in the use of interactive models for understanding attention and performance. In C. Umilta & M. Moscovitch (Eds.), *Attention and performance* (Vol. XV, pp. 453–476). Cambridge, MA: MIT Press.

Collins, A. M., & Loftus, E. F. (1975). A spreading-activation theory of semantic processing. *Psychological Review, 82*, 407–428.

Collins, A. M., & Quillian, M. R. (1969). Retrieval time from semantic memory. *Journal of Verbal Learning and Verbal Behavior, 8*, 240–247.

Cosmides, L. (1989). The logic of social exchange: Has natural selection shaped how humans reason? *Cognition, 31*, 187–276.

Cowan, N. (1988). Evolving conceptions of memory storage, selective attention, and their mutual constraints within the human information-processing system. *Psychological Bulletin, 104*, 163–191.

Cowan, N. (1993). Activation, attention, and short-term memory. *Memory & Cognition, 21*, 162–167.

Crowder, R. G. (1982). The demise of short-term memory. *Acta Psychologica, 50*, 291–323.

Crowder, R. G. (1989). Modularity and dissociations in memory systems. In H. L. I. Roediger & F. I. M. Craik (Eds.), *Varieties of memory and consciousness* (pp. 217–294). Hillsdale, NJ: Lawrence Erlbaum Associates.

Crowder, R. G. (1993a). Short-term memory: Where do we stand? *Memory & Cognition, 21*, 142–145.

Crowder, R. G. (1993b). Systems and principles in memory theory: Another critique of pure memory. In A. F. Collins, S. E. Gathercole, M. A. Conway, & P. E. Morris (Eds.), *Theories of memory* (pp. 139–161). Mahwah, NJ: Lawrence Erlbaum Associates.

Cummins, D. D. (1995). Naive theories and causal induction. *Memory & Cognition, 23*, 646–658.

Cutting, J. E., Springer, K., Braren, P. A., & Johnson, S. H. (1992). Wayfinding on foot from information in retinal, not optical, flow. *Journal of Experimental Psychology: General, 121*, 41–72.

Damasio, A. R. (1994). *Descartes' error: Emotion, reason, and the human brain*. New York: Putnam.

Dark, V. J. (1990). Switching between memory and perception: Moving attention or memory retrieval? *Memory & Cognition, 18*, 119–127.

Davies, M., & Humphreys, G. W. (1993). Introduction. In M. Davies & G. W. Humphreys (Eds.), *Consciousness: Psychological and philosophical essays* (pp. 1–39). Oxford, England: Blackwell.

DeGroot, A. (1965). *Thought and choice in chess*. The Hague, Netherlands: Mouton.

Dennett, D. C. (1978). *Brainstorms*. Montgomery, VT: Bradford.

Dennett, D. C. (1987). *The intentional stance*. Cambridge, MA: MIT Press.

Dennett, D. C. (1991). *Consciousness explained*. Boston: Little, Brown.

Dennett, D. C. (1996). *Kinds of minds*. New York: Basic Books.

Dennett, D. C., & Kinsbourne, M. (1992). Time and the observer: The where and when of consciousness in the brain. *Behavioral and Brain Sciences, 15,* 183–247.

Dickinson, A., & Shanks, D. (1995). Instrumental action and causal representation. In D. Sperber, D. Premack, & A. J. Premack (Eds.), *Causal cognition* (pp. 5–25). Oxford, England: Clarendon.

Dixon, P., & Gabrys, G. (1991). Learning to operate complex devices: Effects of conceptual and operational similarity. *Human Factors, 33,* 103–120.

Donald, M. (1993). Precis of Origins of the modern mind: Three stages in the evolution of culture and cognition. *Behavioral and Brain Sciences, 16,* 737–791.

Dretske, F. I. (1981). *Knowledge and the flow of information.* Cambridge, MA: MIT Press.

Dreyfus, H. L. (1992). *What computers still can't do.* Cambridge, MA: MIT Press.

Dulany, D. E. (1957). Avoidance learning of perceptual defense and vigilance. *Journal of Abnormal and Social Psychology, 55,* 333–338.

Dulany, D. E. (1962). The place of hypotheses and intentions: An analysis of verbal control in verbal conditioning. In C. W. Eriksen (Ed.), *Behavior and awareness* (pp. 102–129). Durham, NC: Duke University Press.

Dulany, D. E. (1968). Awareness, rules, and propositional control: A confrontation with S-R behavior theory. In T. Dixon & D. Horton (Eds.), *Verbal behavior and general behavior theory* (pp. 340–387). Englewood Cliffs, NJ: Prentice-Hall.

Dulany, D. E. (1979). *Outline of a theory of propositional learning.* Unpublished manuscript, University of Illinois.

Dulany, D. E. (1991). Conscious representation and thought systems. In R. S. Wyer, Jr. & T. K. Srull (Eds.), *Advances in social cognition* (Vol. 4, pp. 97–117). Hillsdale, NJ: Lawrence Erlbaum Associates.

Dulany, D. E. (1996). Consciousness in the explicit (deliberative) and implicit (evocative). In J. Cohen & J. Schooler (Eds.), *Scientific approaches to the study of consciousness* (pp. 179–212). Mahwah, NJ: Lawrence Erlbaum Associates.

Dulany, D. E., & Carlson, R. A. (1983, November). *Consciousness in the structure of causal reasoning.* Paper presented at the 24th annual meeting of the Psychonomic Society, Minneapolis.

Dulany, D. E., Carlson, R. A., & Dewey, G. I. (1984). A case of syntactical learning and judgment: How conscious and how abstract? *Journal of Experimental Psychology: General, 113,* 541–555.

Dulany, D. E., Carlson, R. A., & Dewey, G. I. (1985). On consciousness in syntactic learning and judgment: A reply to Reber, Allen, and Regan. *Journal of Experimental Psychology: General, 114,* 25–32.

Dunbar, K. (1995). How scientists really reason: Scientific reasoning in real-world laboratories. In R. J. Sternberg & J. Davidson (Eds.), *The nature of insight* (pp. 365–395). Cambridge, MA: MIT Press.

Duval, S., & Hensley, V. (1976). Extensions of objective self-awareness theory: The focus of attention-causal attribution hypothesis. In J. H. Harvey, W. J. Ickes, & R. F. Kidd (Eds.), *New directions in attribution research* (Vol. 1, pp. 165–198). Hillsdale, NJ: Lawrence Erlbaum Associates.

Duval, S., & Wicklund, R. A. (1972). *A theory of objective self awareness.* New York: Academic Press.

Easterbrook, J. A. (1959). The effect of emotion on cue utilization and the organization of behavior. *Psychological Review, 66,* 183–201.

Easton, R. D., & Sholl, M. J. (1995). Object-array structure, frames of reference, and retrieval of spatial knowledge. *Journal of Experimental Psychology: Learning, Memory, and Cognition, 21*(2), 483–500.

Easton, T. A. (1972). On the normal use of reflexes. *American Scientist, 60,* 591–599.

Edelman, G. M. (1989). *The remembered present.* New York: Basic Books.

Egan, D. E., & Schwartz, B. J. (1979). Chunking in recall of symbolic drawings. *Memory & Cognition, 7,* 149–158.

Eich, J. M. (1985). Levels of processing, encoding specificity, elaboration, and CHARM. *Psychological Review, 92,* 1–38.

Einhorn, H. J. (1980). Learning from experience and suboptimal rules in decision making. In T. S. Wallsten (Ed.), *Cognitive processes in choice and decision behavior* (pp. 1–20). Hillsdale, NJ: Lawrence Erlbaum Associates.

Einhorn, H. J., & Hogarth, R. M. (1985). Ambiguity and uncertainty in probabilistic inference. *Psychological Review, 92,* 433–461.

Einhorn, H. J., & Hogarth, R. M. (1986). Judging probable cause. *Psychological Bulletin, 99,* 3–19.

Einstein, G. O., & McDaniel, M. A. (1990). Normal aging and prospective memory. *Journal of Experimental Psychology: Learning, Memory, and Cognition, 16,* 717–726.

Elio, R. (1986). Representation of similar well-learned cognitive procedures. *Cognitive Science, 10,* 41–73.

Elman, J. L. (1990). Finding structure in time. *Cognitive Science, 14,* 179–211.

Engelkamp, J., & Cohen, R. L. (1991). Current issues in memory of action events. *Psychological Research, 53,* 175–182.

Engelkamp, J., Zimmer, H. D., Mohr, G., & Sellen, O. (1994). Memory of self-performed tasks: Self-performing during recognition. *Memory & Cognition, 22,* 34–39.

Erdelyi, M. H. (1985). *Psychoanalysis: Freud's cognitive psychology.* New York: Freeman.

Ericsson, K. A. (1985). Memory skill. *Canadian Journal of Psychology, 39,* 188–231.

Ericsson, K. A., & Kintsch, W. (1995). Long-term working memory. *Psychological Review, 102,* 211–245.

Ericsson, K. A., & Oliver, W. L. (1988). Methodology for laboratory research on thinking: Task selection, collection of observations, and data analysis. In R. J. Sternberg, & E. E. Smith (Eds.), *The psychology of human thought* (pp. 392–428). New York: Cambridge University Press.

Ericsson, K. A., & Polson, P. G. (1988a). A cognitive analysis of exceptional memory for restaraunt orders. In M. T. H. Chi, R. Glaser, & M. J. Farr (Eds.), *The nature of expertise* (pp. 23–70). Hillsdale, NJ: Lawrence Erlbaum Associates.

Ericsson, K. A., & Polson, P. G. (1988b). An experimental analysis of the mechanisms of a memory skill. *Journal of Experimental Psychology: Learning, Memory, and Cognition, 14,* 305–316.

Ericsson, K. A., & Simon, H. A. (1980). Verbal reports as data. *Psychological Review, 87,* 215–247.

Ericsson, K. A., & Simon, H. A. (1983). *Protocol analysis: Verbal reports as data.* Cambridge, MA: MIT Press.

Ericsson, K. A., & Smith, J. (1991). Prospects and limits of the empirical study of expertise: An introduction. In K. A. Ericsson & J. Smith (Eds.), *Toward a general theory of expertise* (pp. 1–38). Cambridge, England: Cambridge University Press.

Eriksen, C. W. (1962). Figments, fantasies, and follies: A search for the subconscious mind. In C. W. Eriksen (Ed.), *Behavior and awareness* (pp. 3–26). Durham, NC: Duke University Press.

Estes, W. K. (1980). Is human memory obsolete? *American Scientist, 68,* 62–69.

Evans, J. S. B. T. (1982). *The psychology of deductive reasoning.* London: Routledge & Kegan Paul.

Evans, J. S. B. T. (1993). *Human reasoning: The psychology of deduction.* Hillsdale, NJ: Lawrence Erlbaum Associates.

Fabiani, M., Buckley, J., Gratton, G., Coles, M. G. H., Donchin, E., & Logie, R. (1989). The training of complex task performance. *Acta Psychologica, 71,* 259–299.

Farah, M. J. (1988). Is visual imagery really visual? Overlooked evidence from neuropsychology. *Psychological Review, 95,* 307–317.

Farah, M. (1994). Visual perception and visual awareness after brain damage: A tutorial overview. In C. Umilta & M. Moscovitch (Eds.), *Attention and performance* (Vol. XV, pp. 37–76). Cambridge, MA: MIT Press.

Farthing, G. W. (1992). *The psychology of consciousness.* Englewood Cliffs, NJ: Prentice-Hall.

Feldman, J. A. (1985). Four frames suffice: A provisional model of vision and space. *Behavioral and Brain Sciences, 8,* 265–313.

Finke, R. A., & Shepard, R. N. (1986). Visual functions of mental imagery. In K. R. Boff, L. Kaufman, & J. P. Thomas (Eds.), *Handbook of perception and human performance* (Vol. II, pp. 37:1–37:55). New York: Wiley.

Fischer, K. W., Bullock, D. H., Rotenberg, E. J., & Raya, P. (1993). The dynamics of competence: How context contributes directly to skill. In R. H. Wozniak & K. W. Fischer (Eds.), *Development in context: Acting and thinking in specific environments* (pp. 93–117). Hillsdale, NJ: Lawrence Erlbaum Associates.

Fischhoff, B., & Beyth–Marom, R. (1983). Hypothesis evaluation from a Bayesian perspective. *Psychological Review, 90,* 239–260.

Fischhoff, B., Slovic, P., & Lichtenstein, S. (1980). Knowing what you want: Measuring labile values. In T. S. Wallsten (Ed.), *Cognitive processes in choice and decision behavior* (pp. 117–141). Hillsdale, NJ: Lawrence Erlbaum Associates.

Fisk, A. D., Derrick, W. L., & Schneider, W. (1986–1987). A methodological assessment and evaluation of dual-task paradigms. *Current Psychological Research & Reviews, 5,* 315–327.

Fisk, A. D., Oransky, N. A., & Skedsvold, P. R. (1988). Examination of the role of "higher-order" consistency in skill development. *Human Factors, 30,* 567–581.

Flach, J. M., Lintern, G., & Larish, J. F. (1990). Perceptual motor skill: A theoretical framework. In R. Warren & A. H. Wertheim (Eds.), *Perception and control of self-motion* (pp. 327–355). Hillsdale, NJ: Lawrence Erlbaum Associates.

Fodor, J. A. (1975). *The language of thought.* New York: Crowell.

Fodor, J. A. (1980a). Methodological solipsism considered as a research strategy in cognitive psychology. *Behavioral and Brain Sciences, 3,* 63–109.

Fodor, J. A. (1980b). Searle on what only brains can do. *Behavioral and Brain Sciences, 3,* 431–432.

Fodor, J. A. (1983). *The modularity of mind.* Cambridge, MA: MIT Press.

Fodor, J. A., & Pylyshyn, Z. W. (1981). How direct is visual perception?: Some reflections on Gibson's "Ecological Approach." *Cognition, 9,* 139–196.

Fodor, J. A., & Pylyshyn, Z. W. (1988). Connectionism and cognitive architecture: A critical analysis. *Cognition, 28,* 3–71.

Forlizzi, L. (1988). *Relationships among use, predicted use, and awareness of use of comprehension-repair strategies: Converging evidence from different methodologies.* Unpublished doctoral dissertation, The Pennsylvania State University.

Forlizzi, L. A. (1992). *Exploring the comprehension skills and strategies of ABE students.* University Park, PA: Institute for the Study of Adult Literacy, The Pennsylvania State University.

Fowler, C. A., & Turvey, M. T. (1982). Observational perspective and descriptive level in perceiving and acting. In W. B. Weimer & D. S. Palermo (Eds.), *Cognition and the symbolic processes* (Vol. 2, pp. 1–19). Hillsdale, NJ: Lawrence Erlbaum Associates.

Frijda, N. H. (1986). *The emotions.* Cambridge, England: Cambridge University Press.

Frijda, N. H., Ortony, A., Sonnemans, J., & Clore, G. L. (1992). The complexity of intensity: Issues concerning the structure of emotional intensity. In M. S. Clark (Ed.), *Emotion* (pp. 60–89). Newbury Park, CA: Sage.

Fuchs, A. H. (1962). The progression-regression hypothesis in perceptual-motor skill learning. *Journal of Experimental Psychology, 63,* 177–192.

Gallistel, C. R., & Gelman, R. (1992). Preverbal and verbal counting and computation. *Cognition, 44,* 43–74.

Garnham, A., & Oakhill, J. (1994). *Thinking and reasoning.* Oxford, England: Blackwell.

Garnham, A., Oakhill, J., & Johnson–Laird, P. N. (1982). Referential continuity and the coherence of discourse. *Cognition, 11,* 29–46.

Gauvain, M. (1993). The development of spatial thinking in everyday activity. *Developmental Review, 13,* 92–121.

Gelman, R. (1990). First principles organize attention to and learning about relevant data: Number and the animate–inanimate distinction as examples. *Cognitive Science, 14,* 79–106.

Gelman, R., & Baillargeon, R. (1983). A review of some Piagetian concepts. In P. H. Mussen (Ed.), *Handbook of child psychology* (4th ed.). (Vol. 3, pp. 167–230). New York: Wiley.

Gentner, D. R. (1988). Expertise in typewriting. In M. T. H. Chi, R. Glaser, & M. J. Farr (Eds.), *The nature of expertise* (pp. 1–21). Hillsdale, NJ: Lawrence Erlbaum Associates.

Gibson, E. J. (1987). Introductory essay: What does infant perception tell us about theories of perception. *Journal of experimental psychology: Human perception and performance, 13,* 515–523.

Gibson, E. J. (1993). Ontogenesis of the perceived self. In U. Neisser (Ed.), *The perceived self: Ecological and interpersonal sources of self-knowledge* (pp. 25–42). Cambridge, England: Cambridge University Press.

Gibson, E. J., & Adolph, K. E. (1992). The perceived self in infancy. *Psychological Inquiry, 3,* 119–121.

Gibson, J. J. (1960). The concept of the stimulus in psychology. *American Psychologist, 15,* 694–703.

Gibson, J. J. (1961). Ecological optics. *Vision Research, 1,* 253–262.

Gibson, J. J. (1966). *The senses considered as perceptual systems.* Boston: Houghton-Mifflin.

Gibson, J. J. (1979). *The ecological approach to visual perception.* Boston: Houghton-Mifflin.

Gillie, T., & Broadbent, D. (1989). What makes interruptions disruptive? A study of length, similarity, and complexity. *Psychological Research, 50,* 243–250.

Gillund, G., & Shiffrin, R. M. (1984). A retrieval model for both recognition and recall. *Psychological Review, 91,* 1–67.

Glaser, R., & Chi, M. T. H. (1988). Overview. In M. T. H. Chi, R. Glaser, & M. J. Farr (Eds.), *The nature of expertise* (pp. xv–xxvii). Hillsdale, NJ: Lawrence Erlbaum Associates.

Gluck, M. A., & Bower, G. H. (1988). From conditioning to category learning: An adaptive network model. *Journal of Experimental Psychology: General, 117,* 227–247.

Gopher, D. (in press). Attention control: Explorations of the work of an executive controller. In *Brain and mind: The Ninth Toyota Conference.* Amsterdam: Elsevier.

Gopher, D., Weil, M., & Siegel, D. (1989). Practice under changing priorities: An approach to the training of complex skills. *Acta Psychologica, 71,* 147–177.

Goschke, T., & Kuhl, J. (1993). Representation of intentions: Persisting activation in memory. *Journal of Experimental Psychology: Learning, Memory, and Cognition, 19,* 1211–1226.

Greeno, J. G. (1989). Situations, mental models, and generative knowledge. In D. Klahr & K. Kotovsky (Eds.), *Complex information processing: The impact of Herbert A. Simon* (pp. 285–318). Hillsdale, NJ: Lawrence Erlbaum Associates.

Greeno, J. G., & Moore, J. L. (1993). Situativity and symbols: Response to Vera and Simon. *Cognitive Science, 17,* 49–59.

Greenwald, A. G. (1992). New Look 3: Unconscious cognition reclaimed. *American Psychologist, 47,* 766–779.

Greenwald, A. G., Klinger, M. R., & Schuh, E. S. (1995). Activation by marginally perceptible ("subliminal") stimuli: Dissociation of unconscious from conscious cognition. *Journal of Experimental Psychology: General, 124,* 22–42.

Grice, H. P. (1975). Logic and conversation. In P. Cole & J. L. Morgan (Eds.), *Syntax and semantics 3: Speech acts* (pp. 41–58). London: Academic Press.

Groen, G. J., & Parkman, J. M. (1972). A chronometric analysis of simple addition. *Psychological Review, 79,* 329–343.

Groen, G., & Resnick, L. B. (1977). Can preschool children invent addition algorithms? *Journal of Educational Psychology, 69,* 645–652.

Grossberg, S., & Stone, G. (1986). Neural dynamics of attention switching and temporal-order information in short-term memory. *Memory & Cognition, 14,* 451–468.

Haberlandt, K. (1994). *Cognitive psychology.* Boston: Allyn & Bacon.

Halisch, F., & Kuhl, J. (Eds.). (1987). *Motivation, intention, and volition.* Berlin: Springer-Verlag.

Harman, G. (1989). *Change in view: Principles of reasoning.* Cambridge, MA: MIT Press.

Harnad, S. (1982). Consciousness: An afterthought. *Cognition and Brain Theory, 5,* 29–47.

Harnad, S. (1990). The symbol grounding problem. *Physica D, 42,* 335–346.

Harré, R., & Gillett, G. (1994). *The discursive mind.* Thousand Oaks, CA: Sage.

Haugeland, J. (1985). *Artificial intelligence: The very idea.* Cambridge, MA: MIT Press.

Hayes–Roth, B., & Hayes–Roth, F. (1979). A cognitive model of planning. *Cognitive Science, 3,* 275–310.

Healy, A. F. (1982). Short-term memory for order information. In G. H. Bower (Ed.), *The psychology of learning and motivation* (Vol. 16, pp. 191–238). New York: Academic Press.

Healy, A. F., & Nairne, J. S. (1985). Short-term memory processes in counting. *Cognitive Psychology, 17,* 417–444.

Henle, M. (1962). On the relation between logic and thinking. *Psychological Review, 69,* 366–378.

Hertel, P. T. (1993). Implications of external memory for investigations of mind. *Applied Cognitive Psychology, 7,* 665–674.

Hilgard, E. R., & Bower, G. H. (1966). *Theories of learning* (3rd ed.). New York: Appleton-Century-Crofts.

Hilton, D. J., & Slugoski, B. R. (1986). Knowledge-based causal attribution: The abnormal conditions focus model. *Psychological Review, 93,* 75–88.

Hintzman, D. L. (1986). "Schema abstraction" in a multiple-trace memory model. *Psychological Review, 93,* 411–428.

Hitch, G. J. (1978). The role of short-term working memory in mental arithmetic. *Cognitive Psychology, 10,* 302–323.

Hitch, G. J., & Baddeley, A. D. (1976). Verbal reasoning and working memory. *Quarterly Journal of Experimental Psychology, 28,* 603–621.

Hitch, G. J., Burgess, N., Shapiro, J., Culpin, V., & Malloch, M. (1995, November). *Evidence for a timing signal in verbal short-term memory.* Paper presented at the 36th annual meeting of the Psychonomic Society, Los Angeles.

Holender, D. (1986). Semantic activation without conscious identification in dichotic listening, parafoveal vision, and visual masking: A survey and appraisal. *Behavioral and Brain Sciences, 9,* 1–66.

Holland, J. H., Holyoak, K. J., Nisbett, R. E., & Thagard, P. R. (1986). *Induction: Processes of inference, learning, and discovery.* Cambridge, MA: MIT Press.

Holyoak, K. J. (1991). Symbolic connectionism: Toward third-generation theories of expertise. In K. A. Ericsson & J. Smith (Eds.), *Toward a general theory of expertise* (pp. 301–335). Cambridge, England: Cambridge University Press.

Humphreys, M. S., Bain, J. D., & Pike, R. (1989). Different ways to cue a coherent memory system: A theory for episodic, semantic, and procedural tasks. *Psychological Review, 96,* 208–233.

Humphreys, M. S., Wiles, J., & Dennis, S. (1994). Toward a theory of human memory: Data structures and access processes. *Behavioral and Brain Sciences, 17,* 655–692.

Hunt, E., & Agnoli, F. (1991). The Whorfian hypothesis: A cognitive psychology perspective. *Psychological Review, 98*(3), 377–389.

Intons–Peterson, M. J., & Fournier, J. (1986). External and internal memory aids: When and how do we use them? *Journal of Experimental Psychology: General, 115,* 276–280.

Isaacs, E. A., & Clark, H. H. (1987). References in conversation between experts and novices. *Journal of Experimental Psychology: General, 116,* 26–37.

Isen, A. M. (1984). Toward understanding the role of affect in cognition. In R. S. J. Wyer & T. K. Srull (Eds.), *Handbook of social cognition* (Vol. 3, pp. 179–236). Hillsdale, NJ: Lawrence Erlbaum Associates.

Jackendoff, R. (1987). *Consciousness and the computational mind.* Cambridge, MA: MIT Press.

Jacoby, L. L., Ste–Marie, D., & Toth, J. P. (1993). Redefining automaticity: Unconscious influences, awareness, and control. In A. Baddeley & L. Weiskrantz (Eds.), *Attention: Selection, awareness, and control* (pp. 261–282). Oxford, England: Clarendon.

Jacoby, L. L., & Witherspoon, D. (1982). Remembering without awareness. *Canadian Journal of Psychology, 36,* 300–324.

James, W. (1890). *Principles of psychology.* New York: Henry Holt.

Jeffries, R., Turner, A. A., Polson, P. G., & Atwood, M. E. (1981). The processes involved in designing software. In J. R. Anderson (Ed.), *Cognitive skills and their acquisition* (pp. 255–283). Hillsdale, NJ: Lawrence Erlbaum Associates.

Jenkins, J. J. (1992). The organization and reorganization of categories: The case of speech perception. In H. L. Pick, Jr., P. van den Broek, & D. C. Knill (Eds.), *Cognition: Conceptual and methodological issues* (pp. 11–31). Washington, DC: American Psychological Association.

Johansson, G. (1975). Visual motion perception. *Scientific American, 232,* 76–87.

Johnson, E. J. (1988). Expertise and decision under uncertainty: Performance and process. In M. T. H. Chi, R. Glaser, & M. J. Farr (Eds.), *The nature of expertise* (pp. 209–228). Hillsdale, NJ: Lawrence Erlbaum Associates.

Johnson, M. (1987). *The body in the mind.* Chicago: University of Chicago Press.

Johnson, M. K. (1988). Reality monitoring: An experimental phenomenological approach. *Journal of Experimental Psychology: General, 117,* 390–394.

Johnson, M. K., & Raye, C. L. (1981). Reality monitoring. *Psychological Review, 88,* 67–85.

Johnson-Laird, P. N. (1983). *Mental models.* Cambridge, MA: Harvard University Press.

Johnson-Laird, P. N., & Byrne, R. M. J. (1991). *Deduction.* Hillsdale, NJ: Lawrence Erlbaum Associates.

Johnson-Laird, P. N., Hermann, D. J., & Chaffin, R. (1984). Only connections: A critique of semantic networks. *Psychological Bulletin, 96,* 292–315.

Johnston, W. A., & Dark, V. J. (1986). Selective attention. *Annual Review of Psychology, 37,* 43–75.

Jones, D. (1993). Objects, streams, and threads of auditory attention. In A. Baddeley & L. Weiskrantz (Eds.), *Attention: Selection, awareness, and control* (pp. 87–104). Oxford, England: Clarendon Press.

Jones, M. R., & Boltz, M. (1989). Dynamic attending and responses to time. *Psychological Review, 96,* 459–491

Just, M. A., & Carpenter, P. A. (1976). Eye fixations and cognitive processes. *Cognitive Psychology, 8,* 441–480.

Just, M. A., Carpenter, P. A., & Woolley, J. D. (1982). Paradigms and processes in reading comprehension. *Journal of Experimental Psychology: General, 111,* 228–238.

Kahneman, D. (1973). *Attention and effort.* Englewood Cliffs, NJ: Prentice-Hall.

Kahneman, D., Slovic, P., & Tversky, A. (1982). *Judgment under uncertainty: Heuristics and biases.* Cambridge, England: Cambridge University Press.

Kahneman, D., & Tversky, A. (1982a). On the study of statistical intuitions. *Cognition, 11,* 123–141.

Kahneman, D., & Tversky, A. (1982b). The simulation heuristic. In D. Kahneman, P. Slovic, & A. Tversky (Eds.), *Judgment under uncertainty: Heuristics and biases* (pp. 201–208). Cambridge, England: Cambridge University Press.

Kail, R. (1986). The impact of extended practice on rate of mental rotation. *Journal of Experimental Child Psychology, 42,* 378–391.

Karmiloff–Smith, A. (1994). Precis of Beyond Modularity: A developmental perspective on cognitive science. *Behavioral and Brain Sciences, 17,* 693–745.

Keele, S. W. (1987). Sequence and timing in skilled perception and action: An overview. In A. Allport, D. G. MacKay, W. Prinz, & E. Scheerer (Eds.), *Language perception and production: Relationships between listening, speaking, reading, and writing.* London: Academic Press.

Kelley, H. H. (1973). The processes of causal attribution. *American Psychologist, 28,* 107–128.

Kelley, H. H., & Michela, J. L. (1980). Attribution theory and research. *Annual Review of Psychology, 31,* 457–501.

Kempton, W. (1986). Two theories of home heat control. *Cognition, 10,* 75–90.

Kihlstrom, J. F., Barnhardt, T. M., & Tataryn, D. J. (1992). The psychological unconscious: Found, lost, and regained. *American Psychologist, 47,* 788–791.

Kintsch, W. (1992). A cognitive architecture for comprehension. In H. L. Pick, Jr., P. van den Broek, & D. C. Knill (Eds.), *Cognition: Conceptual and methodological issues* (pp. 143–163). Washington, DC: American Psychological Association.

Kirby, K. N., & Kosslyn, S. M. (1992). Thinking visually. In G. W. Humphreys (Ed.), *Understanding vision* (pp. 71–86). Oxford, England: Blackwell.

Kirsh, D. (1995). Complementary strategies: Why we use our hands when we think. In *Proceedings of the Seventeenth Annual Conference of the Cognitive Science Society.* Mahwah, NJ: Lawrence Erlbaum Associates.

Kirsh, D., & Maglio, P. (1994). On distinguishing epistemic from pragmatic action. *Cognitive Science, 18*(4), 513–549.

Klahr, D., & Dunbar, K. (1988). Dual space search during scientific reasoning. *Cognitive Science, 12,* 1–48.

Klapp, S. T., Boches, C. A., Trabert, M. L., & Logan, G. D. (1991). Automatizing alphabet arithmetic: II. Are there practice effects after automaticity is achieved? *Journal of Experimental Psychology: Learning, Memory, and Cognition, 17,* 196–209.

Klapp, S. T., Marshburn, E. A., & Lester, P. T. (1983). Short-term memory does not involve the working memory of information processing: The demise of a common assumption. *Journal of Experimental Psychology: General, 112,* 240–264.

Klayman, J., & Ha, Y. W. (1987). Confirmation, disconfirmation, and information in hypothesis testing. *Psychological Review, 94,* 211–228.

Klinger, E., & Cox, W. M. (1987–1988). Dimensions of thought flow in everyday life. *Imagination, Cognition, and Personality, 7,* 105–128.

Koedinger, K. R., & Anderson, J. R. (1990). Abstract planning and perceptual chunks: Elements of expertise in geometry. *Cognitive Science, 14,* 511–550.

Kolers, P. A., & Roediger, H. L. I. (1984). Procedures of mind. *Journal of Verbal Learning and Verbal Behavior, 23,* 425–449.

Kosslyn, S. M. (1981). The medium and the message in mental imagery: A theory. *Psychological Review, 88,* 46–66.

Kosslyn, S. M. (1994). *Image and brain.* Cambridge, MA: MIT Press.

Kosslyn, S. M., & Hatfield, G. (1984). Representation without symbol systems. *Social Research, 51,* 1019–1045.

Kotovsky, K., Hayes, J. R., & Simon, H. A. (1985). Why are some problems hard? Evidence from Tower of Hanoi. *Cognitive Psychology, 17,* 284–294.

Kramer, A. F., Strayer, D. L., & Buckley, J. (1990). Development and transfer of automatic processing. *Journal of Experimental Psychology: Human Perception and Performance, 16,* 505–522.

Kuhl, J. (1987). Action control: The maintenance of motivational states. In F. Halisch & J. Kuhl (Eds.), *Motivation, intention, and volition* (pp. 279–291). Berlin: Springer-Verlag.

Kummer, H. (1995). Causal knowledge in animals. In D. Sperber, D. Premack, & A. J. Premack (Eds.), *Causal cognition* (pp. 26–36). Oxford, England: Clarendon.

Kvavilashvili, L. (1987). Remembering: Intention as a distinct form of memory. *British Journal of Psychology, 78,* 507–518.

Lachman, R., Lachman, J. L., & Butterfield, E. C. (1979). *Cognitive psychology and information processing: An introduction.* Hillsdale, NJ: Lawrence Erlbaum Associates.

Laird, J. D., & Bresler, C. (1992). The process of emotional experience: A self-perception theory. In M. S. Clark (Ed.), *Emotion* (pp. 213–234). Newbury Park, CA: Sage.

Lang, P. J. (1995). The emotion probe: Studies of motivation and attention. *American Psychologist, 50,* 372–385.

Lang, P. J., Bradley, M. M., & Cuthbert, B. N. (1992). A motivational analysis of emotion: Reflex-cortex connections. *Psychological Science, 3,* 44–49.

Langer, E. (1978). Rethinking the role of thought in social interaction. In J. H. Harvey, W. J. Ickes, & R. F. Kidd (Eds.), *New directions in attribution research* (Vol. 2, pp. 35–58). Hillsdale, NJ: Lawrence Erlbaum Associates.

Langer, E. J. (1992). Matters of mind: Mindfulness/mindlessness in perspective. *Consciousness & Cognition, 1,* 289–305.

Langley, P., & Simon, H. A. (1981). The central role of learning in cognition. In J. R. Anderson (Ed.), *Cognitive skills and their acquisition* (pp. 361–380). Hillsdale, NJ: Lawrence Erlbaum Associates.

Larkin, J. H. (1983). The role of problem representation in physics. In D. Gentner & A. L. Stevens (Eds.), *Mental models* (pp. 75–98). Hillsdale, NJ: Lawrence Erlbaum Associates.

Larkin, J. H. (1989). Display-based problem solving. In D. Klahr & K. Kotovsky (Eds.), *Complex information processing: The impact of Herbert A. Simon* (pp. 319–341). Hillsdale, NJ: Lawrence Erlbaum Associates.

Larkin, J. H., McDermott, J., Simon, D. P., & Simon, H. A. (1980). Expert and novice performance in solving physics problems. *Science, 208,* 1335–1342.

Latham, G. P., & Locke, E. A. (1991). Self-regulation through goal setting. *Organizational Behavior and Human Decision Processes, 50,* 212–247.

Lave, J. (1988). *Cognition in practice.* New York: Cambridge University Press.

Lee, D. N. (1976). A theory of visual control of braking based on information about time-to-collision. *Perception, 5,* 437–459.

Lee, D. N. (1993). Body–environment coupling. In U. Neisser (Ed.), *The perceived self: Ecological and interpersonal sources of self-knowledge* (pp. 43–67). Cambridge, England: Cambridge University Press.

Lesgold, A., & LaJoie, S. (1991). Complex problem solving in electronics. In R. J. Sternberg & P. A. Frensch (Eds.), *Complex problem solving: Principles and mechanisms* (pp. 287–316). Hillsdale, NJ: Lawrence Erlbaum Associates.

Lesgold, A., Rubinson, H., Feltovich, P., Glaser, R., Klopfer, D., & Wang, Y. (1988). Expertise in a complex skill: Diagnosing x-ray pictures. In M. T. H. Chi, R. Glaser, & M. J. Farr (Eds.), *The nature of expertise* (pp. 311–342). Hillsdale, NJ: Lawrence Erlbaum Associates.

Levenson, R. W. (1992). Autonomic nervous system differences among emotions. *Psychological Science, 3,* 23–27.

Levine, M. (1975). *A cognitive theory of learning: Research on hypothesis testing.* Hillsdale, NJ: Lawrence Erlbaum Associates.

Lewicki, P., Czyzewska, M., & Hoffman, H. (1987). Unconscious acquisition of complex procedural knowledge. *Journal of Experimental Psychology: Learning, Memory, and Cognition, 13,* 523–530.

Lewis, C. (1981). Skill in algebra. In J. R. Anderson (Ed.), *Cognitive skills and their acquisition* (pp. 85–110). Hillsdale, NJ: Lawrence Erlbaum Associates.

Lichtenstein, E. H., & Brewer, W. F. (1980). Memory for goal-directed events. *Cognitive Psychology, 12,* 412–445.

Logan, G. D. (1985). Executive control of thought and action. *Acta Psychologica, 60,* 193–210.

Logan, G. D. (1988). Toward an instance theory of automatization. *Psychological Review, 95,* 492–527.

Logan, G. D. (1989). Automaticity and cognitive control. In J. S. Uleman & J. A. Bargh (Eds.), *Unintended thought* (pp. 52–74). New York: Guilford.

Logan, G. D. (1990). Repetition priming and automaticity: Common underlying mechanisms? *Cognitive Psychology, 22,* 1–35.

Logan, G. D. (1992). Attention and preattention in theories of automaticity. *American Journal of Psychology, 105,* 317–339.

Logan, G. D. (1995). Linguistic and conceptual control of visual spatial attention. *Cognitive Psychology, 28,* 103–174.

Logan, G. D., & Cowan, W. B. (1984). On the ability to inhibit thought and action: A theory of an act of control. *Psychological Review, 91,* 295–327.

Logan, G. D., & Etherton, J. L. (1994). What is learned during automatization? The role of attention in constructing an instance. *Journal of Experimental Psychology: Learning, Memory, and Cognition, 20,* 1022–1050.

Logan, G. D., & Klapp, S. T. (1991). Automatizing alphabet arithmetic: I. Is extended practice necessary for automaticity? *Journal of Experimental Psychology: Learning, Memory, and Cognition, 17,* 179–195.

Lundy, D. H., Wenger, J. L., Schmidt, R. J., & Carlson, R. A. (1994). Serial step learning of cognitive sequences. *Journal of Experimental Psychology: Learning, Memory, and Cognition, 20,* 1183–1195.

Lunn, J. H. (1948). Chick sexing. *American Scientist, 36,* 280–287.

Mace, W. M. (1974). Ecologically stimulating cognitive psychology: Gibsonian perspectives. In W. B. Weimer & D. S. Palermo (Eds.), *Cognition and the symbolic processes* (pp. 137–164). Hillsdale, NJ: Lawrence Erlbaum Associates.

MacKay, D. G. (1973). Aspects of the theory of comprehension, memory and attention. *Quarterly Journal of Experimental Psychology, 25,* 22–40.

MacKay, D. G. (1982). The problems of flexibility, fluency, and speed-accuracy trade-off in skilled behavior. *Psychological Review, 89,* 483–506.

MacKay, D. G. (1987). *The organization of perception and action.* New York: Springer-Verlag.

MacKay, D. G. (1990). Perception, action, and awareness: A three-body problem. In O. Neumann & W. Prinz (Eds.), *Relationships between perception and action* (pp. 269–303). Berlin: Springer-Verlag.

Mackie, J. L. (1974). *The cement of the universe.* Oxford, England: Clarendon Press.

MacLeod, C. M. (1991). Half a century of research on the Stroop effect: An integrative review. *Psychological Bulletin, 109,* 163–203.

Mandler, G. (1984). Consciousness, imagery, and emotion—with special reference to autonomic imagery. *Journal of Mental Imagery, 8,* 87–94.

Mandler, G. (1985). *Mind and body.* New York: Norton.

Mandler, G. (1992). Toward a theory of consciousness. In H. G. Geissler, S. W. Link, & J. T. Townsend (Eds.), *Cognition, information processing, and psychophysics: Basic issues* (pp. 43–65). Hillsdale, NJ: Lawrence Erlbaum Associates.

Mandler, G. (1994). Hypermnesia, incubation, and mind popping: On remembering without really trying. In C. Umilta & M. Moscovitch (Eds.), *Attention and performance* (Vol. XV, pp. 3–33). Cambridge, MA: MIT Press.

Mani, K., & Johnson–Laird, P. N. (1982). The mental representation of spatial descriptions. *Memory & Cognition, 10,* 181–187.

Marcel, A. J. (1983). Conscious and unconscious perception: An approach to the relations between phenomenal experience and perceptual processes. *Cognitive Psychology, 15,* 238–300.

Marken, R. S. (1986). Perceptual organization of behavior: A hierarchical control model of coordinated action. *Journal of Experimental Psychology: Human Perception and Performance, 12,* 267–276.

Marks, A. R., & Cermack, L. S. (1995, November). *The response-to-stimulus interval (RSI) in the serial reaction time task.* Poster presented at the 36th annual meeting of the Psychonomic Society, Los Angeles.

Marr, D. (1982). *Vision.* San Francisco: Freeman.

Massaro, D. W. (1992). Broadening the domain of the fuzzy logical model of perception. In H. L. Pick, Jr., P. van den Broek, & D. C. Knill (Eds.), *Cognition: Conceptual and methodological issues* (pp. 51–84). Washington, DC: American Psychological Association.

Massaro, D. W., & Cowan, N. (1993). Information processing models: Microscopes of the mind. *Annual Review of Psychology, 44,* 383–425.

Mauro, R. (1992). Affective dynamics: Opponent processes and excitation transfer. In M. S. Clark (Ed.), *Emotion* (pp. 150–174). Newbury Park, CA: Sage.

Mayer, R. E. (1992). *Thinking, problem solving, cognition* (2nd ed.). New York: Freeman.

Mayer, R. E., Lewis, A. B., & Hegarty, M. (1992). Mathematical misunderstandings: Qualitative reasoning about quantitative problems. In J. I. D. Campbell (Ed.), *The nature and origin of mathematical skills* (pp. 137–153). Amsterdam: North-Holland.

McClelland, J. L. (1979). On the time relations of mental processes: An examination of systems of processes in cascade. *Psychological Review, 86,* 287–330.

McClelland, J. L., & Rumelhart, D. E. (1986). *Parallel distributed processing.* Cambridge, MA: MIT Press.

McDaniel, M. A., & Einstein, G. O. (1993). The importance of cue familiarity and cue distinctiveness in prospective memory. *Memory, 1,* 23–41.

McGinn, C. (1991). *The problem of consciousness, essays toward a solution.* Oxford, England: Blackwell.

McKeithen, K. B., Reitman, J. S., Rueter, H. H., & Hirtle, S. C. (1981). Knowledge organization and skill differences in computer programmers. *Cognitive Psychology, 13,* 307–325.

McKendree, J., & Anderson, J. R. (1987). Effect of practice on knowledge and use of basic LISP. In J. M. Carroll (Ed.), *Interfacing thought: Cognitive aspects of human computer interaction* (pp. 236–259). Cambridge, MA: Bradford.

Medin, D. L., & Schaffer, M. M. (1978). A context theory of classification learning. *Psychological Review, 85,* 207–238.

Medin, D. L., & Thau, D. M. (1992). Theories, constraints, and cognition. In H. L. Pick, Jr., P. van den Broek, & D. C. Knill (Eds.), *Cognition: Conceptual and methodological issues* (pp. 165–187). Washington, DC: American Psychological Association.

Michon, J. A. (1990). Implicit and explicit representations of time. In R. A. Block (Ed.), *Cognitive models of psychological time* (pp. 37–58). Hillsdale, NJ: Lawrence Erlbaum Associates.

Michotte, A. (1963). *The perception of causality.* New York: Basic Books.

Miller, G. (1956). The magical number seven plus or minus two: Some limits on our capacity for processing information. *Psychological Review, 63,* 81–97.

Miller, G. A. (1985). The consitutive problem of psychology. In S. Koch & D. E. Leary (Eds.), *A century of psychology as a science* (pp. 40–45). New York: McGraw-Hill.

Minsky, M. A. (1986). *The society of mind.* New York: Simon & Schuster.

Mitchell, T. R., & Beach, L. R. (1990). "... Do I love thee? Let me count ..." Toward an understanding of intuitive and automatic decision making. *Organizational Behavior and Human Decision Processes, 47,* 1–20.

Monsell, S. (1984). Components of working memory underlying verbal skills: A distributed capacities view. In H. Bouma & D. G. Bouwhis (Eds.), *Attention and performance* (Vol. X, pp. 327–350). Hillsdale, NJ: Lawrence Erlbaum Associates.

Moray, N. (1986). Monitoring behavior and supervisory control. In K. R. Boff, L. Kaufman, & J. P. Thomas (Eds.), *Handbook of perception and human performance* (Vol. II, pp. 40:1–40:51). New York: Wiley.

Murdock, B. B., Jr. (1982). A theory for the storage and retrieval of items and associative information. *Psychological Review, 89,* 609–626.

Murphy, G. L., & Wright, J. C. (1984). Changes in conceptual structure with expertise: Differences between real-world experts and novices. *Journal of Experimental Psychology: Learning, Memory, and Cognition, 10,* 144–155.

Natsoulas, T. (1983). Concepts of consciousness. *The Journal of Mind and Behavior, 4,* 13–59.

Natsoulas, T. (1992). Is consciousness what psychologists actually examine? *American Journal of Psychology, 105,* 363–384.

Navon, D. (1984). Resources—A theoretical soup stone? *Psychological Review, 91,* 216–234.

Neisser, U. (1967). *Cognitive psychology.* New York: Appleton-Century-Crofts.

Neisser, U. (1976). *Cognition and reality.* San Francisco: Freeman.

Neisser, U. (1982). *Memory observed.* San Francisco: W.H. Freeman.

Neisser, U. (1983). Toward a skillful pychology. In D. R. Rogers & J. A. Sloboda (Eds.), *Acquisition of symbolic skill* (pp. 1–17). New York: Plenum.

Neisser, U. (1988). Five kinds of self-knowledge. *Philosophical Psychology, 1,* 35–59.

Neisser, U. (1991). Two perceptually given aspects of the self and their development. *Developmental Review, 11,* 197–209.

Neisser, U. (1992). The development of consciousness and the acquisition of skill. In F. S. Kessel, P. M. Cole, & D. L. Johnson (Eds.), *Self and consciousness: Multiple perspectives* (pp. 1–18). Hillsdale, NJ: Lawrence Erlbaum Associates.

Neisser, U. (1993). The self perceived. In U. Neisser (Ed.), *The perceived self: Ecological and interpersonal sources of self-knowledge* (pp. 3–21). Cambridge, England: Cambridge University Press.

Newell, A. (1980). Reasoning, problem solving, and decision processes: The problem space as a fundamental category. In R. S. Nickerson (Ed.), *Attention and performance* (Vol. VIII, pp. 693–718). Hillsdale, NJ: Lawrence Erlbaum Associates.

Newell, A. (1981). Physical symbol systems. In D. A. Norman (Ed.), *Perspectives on cognitive science* (pp. 37–85). Hillsdale, NJ: Lawrence Erlbaum Associates.

Newell, A. (1989). Putting it all together. In D. Klahr & K. Kotovsky (Eds.), *Complex information processing: The impact of Herbert A. Simon* (pp. 399–440). Hillsdale, NJ: Lawrence Erlbaum Associates.

Newell, A. (1990). *Unified theories of cognition.* Cambridge, MA: Harvard University Press.

Newell, A., & Rosenbloom, P. S. (1981). Mechanisms of skill acquisition and the law of practice. In J. R. Anderson (Ed.), *Cognitive skills and their acquisition* (pp. 1–55). Hillsdale, NJ: Lawrence Erlbaum Associates.

Newell, A., & Simon, H. A. (1972). *Human problem solving.* Englewood Cliffs, NJ: Prentice-Hall.

Newell, K. M. (1991). Motor skill acquisition. *Annual Review of Psychology, 42,* 213–237.

Nickerson, R. S. (1986). *Reflections on reasoning.* Hillsdale, NJ: Lawrence Erlbaum Associates.

Nisbett, R. E. (1993). *Rules for reasoning.* Hillsdale, NJ: Lawrence Erlbaum Associates.

Nisbett, R. E., & Wilson, T. D. (1977). Telling more than we can know: Verbal reports on mental processes. *Psychological Review, 84,* 231–259.

Nissen, M. J., & Bullemer, P. (1987). Attentional requirements of learning: Evidence from performance measures. *Cognitive Psychology, 19,* 1–32.

Norman, D. A. (1981). Categorization of action slips. *Psychological Review, 88,* 1–15.

Norman, D. A., & Shallice, T. (1986). Attention to action: Willed and automatic control of behavior. In R. J. Davidson, G. E. Schwartz, & D. Shapiro (Eds.), *Consciousness and self-regulation: Advances in research and theory* (Vol. 4, pp. 1–18). New York: Plenum.

Oakhill, J. V., & Johnson-Laird, P. N. (1984). Representation of spatial descriptions in working memory. *Current Psychological Research and Reviews, 3,* 52–62.

Olson, J. R., & Biolsi, K. J. (1991). Techniques for representing expert knowledge. In K. A. Ericsson & J. Smith (Eds.), *Toward a general theory of expertise* (pp. 240–285). Cambridge, England: Cambridge University Press.

Ortony, A., & Turner, T. J. (1990). What's basic about basic emotions? *Psychological Review, 97,* 315–331.

Owen, D. H. (1990). Perception and control of changes in self-motion: A functional approach to the study of information and skill. In R. Warren & A. H. Wertheim (Eds.), *Perception and control of self-motion* (pp. 289–326). Hillsdale, NJ: Lawrence Erlbaum Associates.

Palmer, S. E., & Kimchi, R. (1986). The information processing approach to cognition. In T. J. Knapp & L. C. Robertson (Eds.), *Approaches to cognition: Contrasts and controversies* (pp. 37–157). Hillsdale, NJ: Lawrence Erlbaum Associates.

Pashler, H. (1990). Do response modality effects support multiprocessor models of divided attention? *Journal of Experimental Psychology: Human Perception and Performance, 16,* 826–842.

Pashler, H. (1994). Dual-task interference in simple tasks: Data and theory. *Psychological Bulletin, 116,* 220–244.

Patel, V. L., & Groen, G. J. (1986). Knowledge based solution strategies in medical reasoning. *Cognitive Science, 10,* 91–116.

Patel, V. L., & Groen, G. J. (1991). The general and specific nature of medical expertise: A critical look. In K. A. Ericsson & J. Smith (Eds.), *Toward a general theory of expertise* (pp. 93–125). Cambridge, England: Cambridge University Press.

Pennington, N. (1987). Stimulus structures and mental representations in expert comprehension of computer programs. *Cognitive Psychology, 19,* 295–341.

Penrose, R. (1989). *The emperor's new mind.* Oxford, England: Oxford University Press.

Perner, J. (1991). *Understanding the representational mind.* Cambridge, MA: MIT Press.

Perruchet, P. (1994). Learning from complex rule-governed environments: On the proper functions of nonconscious and conscious processes. In C. Umilta & M. Moscovitch (Eds.), *Attention and performance* (Vol. XV, pp. 811–835). Cambridge, MA: MIT Press.

Perruchet, P., Gallego, J., & Savy, I. (1990). A critical reappraisal of the evidence for unconscious abstraction of deterministic rules in complex experimental situations. *Cognitive Psychology, 22,* 493–516.

Perruchet, P., & Pacteau, C. (1990). Synthetic grammar learning: Implicit rule abstraction or explicit fragmentary knowledge? *Journal of Experimental Psychology: General, 119,* 264–275.

Pew, R. W. (1966). Acquisition of hierarchical control over the temporal organization of a skill. *Journal of Experimental Psychology, 71,* 764–771.

Piaget, J. (1954). *The construction of reality in the child.* New York: Basic Books.

Piaget, J. (1970). *Genetic epistemology.* New York: Norton.

Piaget, J. (1972). *Principles of genetic epistemology* (W. Mays, Trans.). London: Routledge & Kegan Paul.

Pick, H. L., & Lockman, J. J. (1981). From frames of reference to spatial representations. In L. S. Liben, A. H. Patterson, & N. Newcombe (Eds.), *Spatial representation and behavior across the life span: Theory and application* (pp. 39–61). New York: Academic Press.

Pinker, S. (1984). Visual cognition: An introduction. *Cognition, 18,* 1–63.

Poincaré, H. (1914). *La valeur de la science.* Paris: Flammarian.

Polanyi, M. (1958). *Personal knowledge.* Chicago: University of Chicago Press.

Polk, T. A., & Newell, A. (1995). Deduction as verbal reasoning. *Psychological Review, 102,* 533–566.

Pomerantz, J. R., & Kubovy, M. (1986). Theoretical approaches to perceptual organization. In K. R. Boff, L. Kaufman, & J. P. Thomas (Eds.), *Handbook of perception and human performance* (Vol. II, pp. 36:1–36:46). New York: Wiley.

Pöppel, E. (1988). *Mindworks: Time and conscious experience.* Boston: Harcourt Brace.

Posner, M. I. (1978). *Chronometric explorations of mind.* Hillsdale, NJ: Lawrence Erlbaum Associates.

Posner, M. I. (1988). Introduction: What is it to be an expert? In M. T. H. Chi, R. Glaser, & M. J. Farr (Eds.), *The nature of expertise* (pp. xxix–xxxvi). Hillsdale, NJ: Lawrence Erlbaum Associates.

Premack, D. N. (1992). On the origins of domain-specific primitives. In H. L. Pick, Jr., P. van den Broek, & D. C. Knill (Eds.), *Cognition: Conceptual and methodological issues* (pp. 189–212). Washington, DC: American Psychological Association.

Premack, D., & Premack, A. J. (1995). Intention as psychological cause. In D. Sperber, D. Premack, & A. J. Premack (Eds.), *Causal cognition* (pp. 185–199). Oxford, England: Clarendon Press.

Pribram, K. H. (1986). The cognitive revolution and mind/brain issues. *American Psychologist, 41,* 507–520.

Proctor, R. W., & Dutta, A. (1995). *Skill acquisition and human performance.* Thousand Oaks, CA: Sage.

Putnam, H. (1975). The meaning of meaning. In K. Gundersen (Ed.), *Minnesota studies in the philosophy of science: 7. Language, mind, and knowledge.* Minneapolis: University of Minnesota Press.

Pylyshyn, Z. W. (1980). Computation and cognition: Issues in the foundations of cognitive science. *Behavioral and Brain Sciences, 3,* 111–169.

Quastler, H. E. (Ed.). (1955). *Information Theory in Psychology: Problems and methods.* Glencoe, IL: The Free Press.

Rabbitt, P. M. A. (1981). Sequential reactions. In D. Holding (Ed.), *Human skills* (pp. 153–175). New York: Wiley.

Razran, G. H. S. (1971). *Mind in evolution.* Boston: Houghton Mifflin.

Reason, J. T. (1990). *Human error.* Cambridge, England: Cambridge University Press.

Reber, A. S. (1976). Implicit learning of synthetic languages: The role of instructional set. *Journal of Experimental Psychology: Human Learning and Memory, 2,* 88–94.

Reber, A. S. (1989). Implicit learning and tacit knowledge. *Journal of Experimental Psychology: General, 118,* 219–235.

Reber, A. S. (1993). *Implicit learning and tacit knowledge: An essay on the cognitive unconscious.* Oxford, England: Oxford University Press/Clarendon Press.

Reber, A. S., Allen, R., & Regan, S. (1985). Syntactical learning and judgment, still unconscious and still abstract: Comment on Dulany, Carlson, and Dewey. *Journal of Experimental Psychology: General, 114,* 17–24.

Reder, L. M. (1987). Strategy selection in question answering. *Cognitive Psychology, 19,* 90–138.

Reder, L. M., & Ritter, F. E. (1992). What determines the initial feeling of knowing? Familiarity with question terms, not with the answer. *Journal of Experimental Psychology: Learning, Memory, and Cognition, 18,* 435–451.

Reder, L. M., & Schunn, C. (1995, November). *Metacognition does not imply awareness: Implicit processes govern choice.* Paper presented at the 36th annual meeting of the Psychonomic Society, Los Angeles.

Reed, E. S. (1988). *James J. Gibson and the psychology of perception.* New Haven, CT: Yale University Press.

Reed, E. S., Montgomery, M., Palmer, C., & Pittenger, J. (1995). Method for studying the invariant knowledge structure of action: Conceptual organization of an everyday action. *American Journal of Psychology, 108,* 37–65.

Reed, E. S., Montgomery, M., Schwartz, M., Palmer, C., & Pittenger, J. (1992). Visually based descriptions of an everyday action. *Ecological Psychology, 4*, 129–152.

Reed, S. K. (1992). *Cognition: Theory and practice.* Pacific Grove, CA: Brooks/Cole.

Reisberg, D., Rappaport, I., & O'Shaughnessy, M. (1984). Limits of working memory: The digit-digit span. *Journal of Experimental Psychology: Learning, Memory, and Cognition, 10,* 203–221.

Reiser, B. J., Black, J. B., & Abelson, R. P. (1985). Knowledge structures in the organization and retrieval of autobiographical memories. *Cognitive Psychology, 17,* 89–137.

Reitman, J. S. (1976). Skilled perception in GO: Deducing memory structures from inter-response times. *Cognitive Psychology, 8,* 336–356.

Resnick, L. B. (1989). Developing mathematical knowledge. *American Psychologist, 44,* 162–169.

Rinck, M., Glowalla, U., & Schneider, K. (1992). Mood-congruent and mood-incongruent learning. *Memory & Cognition, 20,* 29–39.

Rips, L. J. (1983). Cognitive processes in propositional reasoning. *Psychological Review, 90,* 38–71.

Rips, L. J. (1984). Reasoning as a central intellective ability. In R. J. Sternberg (Ed.), *Advances in the psychology of human intelligence* (Vol. 2, pp. 105–147). Hillsdale, NJ: Lawrence Erlbaum Associates.

Rips, L. J. (1986). Mental muddles. In M. Brand & R. M. Harnish (Eds.), *The representation of knowledge and belief* (pp. 258–286). Tucson: University of Arizona Press.

Rips, L. J. (1994). *The psychology of proof.* Cambridge, MA: MIT Press.

Rips, L. J., & Conrad, F. G. (1989). Folk psychology of mental activities. *Psychological Review, 96,* 187–207.

Rock, I. (1983). *The logic of perception.* Cambridge, MA: MIT Press.

Roediger, H. L. I. (1980). Memory metaphors in cognitive psychology. *Memory & Cognition, 8,* 231–246.

Roediger, H. L. I. (1990). Implicit memory: Retention without remembering. *American Psychologist, 45,* 1043–1056.

Rosenbaum, D. A. (1987). Successive approximations to a model of human motor programming. In G. H. Bower (Ed.), *The psychology of learning and motivation* (Vol. 21, pp. 153–182). San Diego: Academic Press.

Rosenbaum, D. A. (1991). *Human motor control.* San Diego: Academic Press.

Rosenbaum, D. A., Hindorff, V., & Munro, E. M. (1987). Scheduling and programming of rapid finger sequences: Tests and elaborations of the hierarchical editor model. *Journal of Experimental Psychology: Human Perception and Performance, 13,* 193–203.

Rosenbloom, P., & Newell, A. (1987). Learning by chunking: A production system model of practice. In D. Klahr, P. Langley, & R. Neches (Eds.), *Production system models of learning and development* (pp. 221–286). Cambridge, MA: MIT Press.

Ross, B. H. (1987). This is like that: The use of earlier problems and the separation of similarity effects. *Journal of Experimental Psychology: Learning, Memory, and Cognition, 13,* 629–639.

Ross, L. (1977). The intuitive psychologist and his shortcomings: Distortions in the attribution process. In L. Berkowitz (Ed.), *Advances in experimental social psychology* (Vol. 10, pp. 173–220). New York: Academic Press.

Rozin, P. (1976). The evolution of intelligence and access to the cognitive unconscious. In J. M. Sprague & A. N. Epstein (Eds.), *Progress in physiological psychology* (Vol. 6, pp. 245–280). New York: Academic Press.

Rumelhart, D. E., & McClelland, J. L. (1985). Levels indeed! A response to Broadbent. *Journal of Experimental Psychology: General, 114,* 193–197.

Rumelhart, D. E., & Norman, D. A. (1982). Simulating a skilled typist: A study of skilled cognitive-motor performance. *Cognitive Science, 6,* 1–36.

Ryle, G. (1949). *The concept of mind*. London: Hutchinson.

Salthouse, T. A. (1991). Expertise as the circumvention of human processing limitations. In K. A. Ericsson & J. Smith (Eds.), *Toward a general theory of expertise* (pp. 286–300). Cambridge, England: Cambridge University Press.

Scardamalia, M., & Bereiter, C. (1991). Literate expertise. In K. A. Ericsson & J. Smith (Eds.), *Toward a general theory of expertise* (pp. 172–194). Cambridge, England: Cambridge University Press.

Schachter, D. L. (1987). Implicit memory: History and current status. *Journal of Experimental Psychology: Learning, Memory, and Cognition, 13*, 501–518.

Schacter, D. L. (1989). On the relation between memory and consciousness: Dissociable interactions and conscious experience. In H. L. I. Roediger & F. I. M. Craik (Eds.), *Varieties of memory and consciousness* (pp. 355–389). Hillsdale, NJ: Lawrence Erlbaum Associates.

Schachter, S., & Singer, J. E. (1962). Cognitive, social, and psychological determinants of emotional state. *Psychological Review, 69*, 379–399.

Schank, R. C., Collins, G. C., & Hunter, L. E. (1986). Transcending inductive category formation in learning. *Behavioral and Brain Sciences, 9*, 639–686.

Schneider, W., & Detweiler, M. (1987). A connectionist/control architecture for working memory. In G. H. Bower (Ed.), *The psychology of learning and motivation* (Vol. 21, pp. 53–119). New York: Academic Press.

Schneider, W., & Detweiler, M. (1988). The role of practice in dual-task performance: Toward workload modeling in a connectionist/control architecture. *Human Factors, 30*, 539–566.

Schneider, W., & Shiffrin, R. M. (1977). Controlled and automatic human information processing: I. Detection, search, and attention. *Psychological Review, 84*, 1–66.

Schoenfeld, A. H., & Hermann, D. J. (1982). Problem perception and knowledge structure in expert and novice mathematical problem solvers. *Journal of Experimental Psychology: Learning, Memory, and Cognition, 8*, 484–494.

Scholnick, E. K., & Hall, W. S. (1991). The language of thinking: Metacognitive and conditional words. In S. A. Gelman & J. P. Byrnes (Eds.), *Perspectives on language and thought: Interrelations in development* (pp. 387–439). Cambridge, England: Cambridge University Press.

Schooler, J. W., Ohlsson, S., & Brooks, K. (1993). Thoughts beyond words: When language overshadows insight. *Journal of Experimental Psychology: General, 122*, 166–183.

Schum, D. A. (1977). The behavioral richness of cascaded inference models: Examples in jurisprudence. In N. J. Castellan, D. B. Pisoni, & G. R. Potts (Eds.), *Cognitive theory* (Vol. 2, pp. 149–173). Hillsdale, NJ: Lawrence Erlbaum Associates.

Schum, D. A. (1980). Current developments in research on cascaded inference processes. In T. S. Wallsten (Ed.), *Cognitive processes in choice and decision* (pp. 179–210). Hillsdale, NJ: Lawrence Erlbaum Associates.

Scribner, S. (1984). Studying working intelligence. In B. Rogoff & J. Lave (Eds.), *Everyday cognition: Its development in social context* (pp. 9–40). Cambridge, MA: Harvard University Press.

Searle, J. R. (1969). *Speech acts*. London: Cambridge University Press.

Searle, J. R. (1980). Minds, brains, and programs. *Behavioral and Brain Sciences, 3*, 417–457.

Searle, J. R. (1983). *Intentionality: An essay in the philosophy of mind*. Cambridge, England: Cambridge University Press.

Searle, J. R. (1990). Consciousness, explanatory inversion, and cognitive science. *Behavioral and Brain Sciences, 13*, 585–642.

Searle, J. R. (1992). *The rediscovery of the mind*. Cambridge, MA: MIT Press.

Seifert, C. M., Meyer, D. E., Davidson, N., Patalano, A. L., & Yaniv, I. (1995). Demystification of cognitive insight: Opportunistic assimilation and the prepared-mind perspective. In R. J. Sternberg & J. Davidson (Eds.), *The nature of insight* (pp. 65–124). Cambridge, MA: MIT Press.

Shafer, C., & Tversky, A. (1985). Languages and designs for probability judgments. *Cognitive Science, 9*, 309–339.

Shallice, T. (1978). The dominant action system: An information-processing approach to consciousness. In K. S. Pope & J. L. Singer (Eds.), *The stream of consciousness* (pp. 117–157). New York: Plenum.

Shallice, T. (1988). *From neuropsychology to mental structure*. Cambridge, England: Cambridge University Press.

Shallice, T. (1991). The revival of consciousness in cognitive science. In W. Kessen, A. Ortony, & F. Craik (Eds.), *Memories, thoughts, and emotions* (pp. 213–226). Hillsdale, NJ: Lawrence Erlbaum Associates.

Shallice, T. (1994). Multiple levels of control processes. In C. Umilta & M. Moscovitch (Eds.), *Attention and performance* (Vol. XV, pp. 395–420). Cambridge, MA: MIT Press.

Shanks, D. R. (1993). Human instrumental learning: A critical review of data and theory. *British Journal of Psychology, 84*, 319–354.

Shanks, D. R., & St. John, M. F. (1994). Characteristics of dissociable human learning systems. *Behavioral and Brain Sciences, 17*, 367–447.

Shaver, P. R., Wu, S., & Schwartz, J. C. (1992). Cross-cultural similarities and differences in emotion and its representation: A prototype approach. In M. S. Clark (Ed.), *Emotion* (pp. 175–212). Newbury Park, CA: Sage.

Shepard, R. N. (1984). Ecological constraints on internal representation: Resonant kinematics of perceiving, imagining, thinking, and dreaming. *Psychological Review, 91*, 417–447.

Shepard, R. N. (1993). On the physical basis, linguistic representation, and conscious experience of colors. In G. Harman (Ed.), *Conceptions of the human mind: Essays in honor of George A. Miller* (pp. 217–245). Hillsdale, NJ: Lawrence Erlbaum Associates.

Shiffrin, R. M., & Dumais, S. T. (1981). The development of automatism. In J. R. Anderson (Ed.), *Cognitive skills and their acquisition* (pp. 111–140). Hillsdale, NJ: Lawrence Erlbaum Associates.

Shiffrin, R. M., & Schneider, W. (1977). Controlled and automatic human information processing: II. Perceptual learning, automatic attending, and a general theory. *Psychological Review, 84*, 127–190.

Sholl, M. J. (1995). The representation and retrieval of map and environment knowledge. *Geographical Systems, 2*, 177–195.

Siegler, R. S. (1988). Strategy choice procedures and the development of multiplication skill. *Journal of Experimental Psychology: General, 117*, 258–275.

Siegler, R. S. (1989). How domain-general and domain-specific knowledge interact to produce strategy choices. *Merrill-Palmer Quarterly, 35*, 1–26.

Siegler, R. S. (1991). In young children's counting, procedures precede principles. *Educational Psychology Review, 3*, 127–135.

Simon, D. P., & Simon, H. A. (1978). Individual differences in solving physics problems. In R. S. Siegler (Ed.), *Children's thinking: What develops?* (pp. 325–348). Hillsdale, NJ: Lawrence Erlbaum Associates.

Simon, H. A. (1992). What is an "explanation" of behavior? *Psychological Science, 3*, 150–161.

Singley, K., & Anderson, J. R. (1989). *The transfer of cognitive skill*. Cambridge, MA: Harvard University Press.

Skinner, B. F. (1971). *Beyond freedom and dignity*. New York: Knopf.

Skinner, B. F. (1957). *Verbal behavior*. New York: Appleton-Century-Crofts.

Sloboda, J. (1991). Musical expertise. In K. A. Ericsson & J. Smith (Eds.), *Toward a general theory of expertise* (pp. 153–171). Cambridge, England: Cambridge University Press.

Slovic, P. (1995). The construction of preference. *American Psychologist, 50*, 364–371.

Smith, S. M. (1995). Getting into and out of mental ruts: A theory of fixation, incubation, and insight. In R. J. Sternberg & J. Davidson (Eds.), *The nature of insight* (pp. 229–251). Cambridge, MA: MIT Press.

Smith, S. M., Brown, H. O., Toman, J. E. P., & Goodman, L. S. (1947). The lack of cerebral effects of d-Tubercurarine. *Anesthesiology, 8,* 1–14.

Smolensky, P. (1988). On the proper treatment of connectionism. *Behavioral and Brain Sciences, 11,* 1–74.

Smyth, M. N., & Scholey, K. A. (1994). Interference in immediate spatial memory. *Memory & Cognition, 22,* 1–13.

Sohn, M.-H., & Carlson, R. A. (1996). *Procedural frameworks for simple arithmetic skills.* Unpublished manuscript.

Sorrentino, R. M., & Higgins, E. T. (Eds.). (1986). *Handbook of motivation and cognition: Foundations of social behavior.* New York: Guilford Press.

Sperber, D., Premack, D., & Premack, A. J. (Eds.). (1995). *Causal cognition.* Oxford, England: Clarendon Press.

Sperling, G. (1960). The information available in brief visual presentations. *Psychological Monographs, 74,* 1–29.

Spilich, G. J., Vesonder, G. T., Chiesi, H. L., & Voss, J. F. (1979). Text processing of domain-related information for individuals with high and low domain knowledge. *Journal of Verbal Learning and Verbal Behavior, 18,* 275–290.

Staudenmeyer, H. (1975). Understanding conditional reasoning with meaningful propositions. In R. J. Falmagne (Ed.), *Reasoning: Representation and process in children and adults* (pp. 55–79). Hillsdale, NJ: Lawrence Erlbaum Associates.

Stigler, J. W., Lee, S. Y., & Stevenson, H. W. (1986). Digit memory in Chinese and English: Evidence for a temporally limited store. *Cognition, 23,* 1–20.

Strayer, D. L., & Kramer, A. F. (1990). An analysis of memory-based models of automaticity. *Journal of Experimental Psychology: Learning, Memory, and Cognition, 16,* 291–304.

Strongman, K. T. (1978). *The psychology of emotion.* New York: Wiley.

Thagard, P. (1986). Parallel computation and the mind-body problem. *Cognitive Science, 10,* 301–318.

Thelen, E. (1995). Motor development: A new synthesis. *American Psychologist, 50,* 79–95.

Thompson, E., Palacios, A., & Varela, F. J. (1992). Ways of coloring: Comparative color vision as a case study for cognitive science. *Behavioral and Brain Sciences, 15,* 1–74.

Tolman, E. C. (1932). *Purposive behavior in animals and men.* New York: Appleton-Century-Crofts.

Trabasso, T., Secco, T., & van den Broek, P. (1984). Causal cohesion and story coherence. In H. Mandl, N. L. Stein, & T. Trabasso (Eds.), *Learning and comprehension of text* (pp. 83–111). Hillsdale, NJ: Lawrence Erlbaum Associates.

Trabasso, T., & Sperry, L. L. (1985). Causal relatedness and importance of story events. *Journal of Memory and Language, 24,* 596–611.

Trabasso, T., & van den Broek, P. (1985). Causal thinking and the representation of narrative events. *Journal of Memory and Language, 24,* 612–630.

Tulving, E. (1983). *Elements of episodic memory.* Oxford, England: Clarendon Press.

Tulving, E. (1985). Memory and consciousness. *Canadian Psychology, 26,* 1–12.

Tulving, E. (1994). Foreword. In J. Metcalfe & A. P. Shimamura (Eds.), *Metacognition: Knowing about knowing* (pp. vii–x). Cambridge, MA: MIT Press.

Tulving, E., & Thomson, D. N. (1973). Encoding specificity and retrieval processes in episodic memory. *Psychological Review, 80,* 352–373.

Turvey, M. T. (1990). Coordination. *American Psychologist, 45,* 938–953.

Turvey, M. T. (1992). Affordances and prospective control: An outline of the ontology. *Ecological Psychology, 4,* 173–187.

Turvey, M. T., Shaw, R. E., Reed, E. S., & Mace, W. M. (1981). Ecological laws of perceiving and acting: In reply to Fodor and Pylyshyn (1981). *Cognition, 9,* 237–304.

Tversky, A., & Kahneman, D. (1981). The framing of decisions and the psychology of choice. *Science, 211,* 453–458.

Tversky, B. (1991). Spatial mental models. In G. H. Bower (Ed.), *The psychology of learning and motivation* (Vol. 27, pp. 109–145). New York: Academic Press.

Umilta, C., & Moscovitch, M. (1994). *Attention and performance* (Vol. XV). Cambridge, MA: MIT Press.

Underwood, G. (1982). Attention and awareness in cognitive and motor skills. In G. Underwood (Ed.), *Aspects of consciousness: Awareness and self-awareness* (Vol. 3, pp. 111–145). London: Academic Press.

Vallacher, R. R., & Wegner, D. M. (1987). What do people think they're doing: Action identification and human behavior. *Psychological Review, 94*, 3–15.

VanLehn, K. (1988). Toward a theory of impasse-driven learning. In H. Mandl & A. Lesgold (Eds.), *Learning issues for intelligent tutoring systems* (pp. 19–41). New York: Springer-Verlag.

Velmans, M. (1991). Is human information processing conscious? *Behavioral and Brain Sciences, 14*, 651–726.

Vera, A. H., & Simon, H. A. (1993). Situated action: Reply to reviewers. *Cognitive Science, 17*, 77–86.

von Hofsten, C. (1993). Prospective control: A basic aspect of action development. *Human Development, 36*, 253–270.

Voss, J. F., Greene, T. R., Post, T. A., & Penner, B. C. (1983). Problem solving skill in the social sciences. In G. H. Bower (Ed.), *The psychology of learning and motivation* (Vol. 17, pp. 165–213). New York: Academic Press.

Voss, J. F., Vesonder, G. T., & Spilich, G. J. (1980). Generation and recall by high-knowledge and low-knowledge individuals. *Journal of Verbal Learning and Verbal Behavior, 19*, 651–667.

Vygotsky, L. S. (1986). *Thought and language* (A. Kozulin, Trans.). Cambridge, MA: MIT Press. (Original work published 1934)

Wason, P. C. (1968). Reasoning about a rule. *Quarterly Journal of Experimental Psychology, 20*, 273–281.

Wason, P. C., & Johnson–Laird, P. N. (1972). *Psychology of reasoning: Structure and content.* Cambridge, MA: Harvard University Press.

Watson, J. (1930). *Behaviorism.* New York: Norton.

Waugh, N. C., & Norman, D. A. (1965). Primary memory. *Psychological Review, 72*, 89–104.

Weber, R. J., Burt, D. B., & Noll, N. C. (1986). Attention switching between perception and memory. *Memory & Cognition, 14*, 238–245.

Wegner, D. M., & Schneider, D. J. (1989). Mental control: The war of the ghosts in the machine. In J. S. Uleman & J. A. Bargh (Eds.), *Unintended thought* (pp. 287–325). New York: Guilford.

Wegner, D. M., Vallacher, R. R., Macomber, G., Wood, R., & Arps, K. (1984). The emergence of action. *Journal of Social and Personality Psychology, 46*, 269–279.

Weimer, W. B. (1977). A conceptual framework for cognitive psychology: Motor theories of the mind. In R. Shaw & J. Bransford (Eds.), *Perceiving, acting, and knowing: Toward an ecological psychology* (pp. 267–311). Hillsdale, NJ: Lawrence Erlbaum Associates.

Weiner, B. (1987). The role of emotions in a theory of motivation. In F. Halisch & J. Kuhl (Eds.), *Motivation, intention, and volition* (pp. 21–30). Berlin: Springer-Verlag.

Weiskrantz, L. (1980). Varieties of residual experience. *Quarterly Journal of Experimental Psychology, 32*, 365–386.

Weiskrantz, L. (1986). *Blindsight: A case study and implications.* New York: Oxford University Press.

Weiskrantz, L. (1993). Search for the unseen. In A. Baddeley & L. Weiskrantz (Eds.), *Attention: Selection, awareness, and control* (pp. 235–245). Oxford, England: Clarendon Press.

Wenger, J. L. (1994). *Cognitive sequence knowledge: What is learned?* Unpublished doctoral dissertation, The Pennsylvania State University.

Wenger, J. L., & Carlson, R. A. (1995). Learning and the coordination of sequential information. *Journal of Experimental Psychology: Human Perception and Performance, 21,* 170–182.

Wenger, J. L., & Carlson, R. A. (1996). Cognitive sequence knowledge: What is learned? *Journal of Experimental Psychology: Learning, Memory, and Cognition, 22,* 599–619.

White, P. (1980). Limitations on verbal reports of internal events: A refutation of Nisbett and Wilson and of Bem. *Psychological Review, 87,* 105–112.

Whorf, B. L. (1956). *Language, thought, and reality.* Cambridge, MA: MIT Press.

Wickens, C. D. (1984). Processing resources in attention. In R. Parasuraman & D. R. Davies (Eds.), *Varieties of attention* (pp. 63–102). Orlando, FL: Academic Press.

Willingham, D. B., Greenberg, A., & Thomas, R. C. (1995, November). *Response-to-stimulus interval affects performance, not implicit learning.* Poster presented at the 36th annual meeting of the Psychonomic Society, Los Angeles.

Willingham, D. B., Nissen, M. J., & Bullemer, P. (1989). On the development of procedural knowledge. *Journal of Experimental Psychology: Learning, Memory, and Cognition, 15,* 1047–1060.

Wilson, M. N., & Dulany, D. E. (1983). An analysis of cognitive control of self-disclosure in a clinical analogue. *Cognitive Therapy and Research, 7,* 297–314.

Wyer, R. S. J. (1975). The role of probabilistic and syllogistic reasoning in cognitive organization and social inference. In M. Kaplan & S. Schwartz (Eds.), *Human judgment and decision processes* (pp. 229–269). New York: Academic Press.

Zbrodoff, N. J., & Logan, G. D. (1986). On the autonomy of mental processes: A case study of arithmetic. *Journal of Experimental Psychology: General, 115,* 118–130.

Zechmeister, E. B., & Johnson, J. E. (1992). *Critical thinking: A functional approach.* Pacific Grove, CA: Brooks/Cole.

Zhang, G., & Simon, H. A. (1985). STM capacity for Chinese words and idioms: Chunking and the acoustical loop hypothesis. *Memory & Cognition, 13,* 193–201.

Zhang, J., & Norman, D. A. (1994). Representations in distributed cognitive tasks. *Cognitive Science, 18*(1), 87–122.

Zhang, J., & Norman, D. A. (1995). A representational analysis of numeration systems. *Cognition, 57*(3), 271–295.

Author Index

Subject Index